The International Politics of Sex

Oxford Studies in Gender and International Relations

Series editors: Rahul Rao, University of St Andrews, and Laura Sjoberg, University of Oxford

Windows of Opportunity: How Women Seize Peace Negotiations for Political Change
Miriam J. Anderson

Women as Foreign Policy Leaders: National Security and Gender Politics in Superpower America
Sylvia Bashevkin

Gendered Citizenship: Understanding Gendered Violence in Democratic India
Natasha Behl

Queering Governance and International Law: The Case of the International Criminal Tribunal for the Former Yugoslavia
Caitlin Biddolph

Gender, Religion, Extremism: Finding Women in Anti-Radicalization
Katherine E. Brown

Enlisting Masculinity: The Construction of Gender in U.S. Military Recruiting Advertising during the All-Volunteer Force
Melissa T. Brown

The Politics of Gender Justice at the International Criminal Court: Legacies and Legitimacy
Louise Chappell

The Other #MeToos
Iqra Shagufta Cheema

Cosmopolitan Sex Workers: Women and Migration in a Global City
Christine B. N. Chin

Intelligent Compassion: Feminist Critical Methodology in the Women's International League for Peace and Freedom
Catia Cecilia Confortini

The International Politics of Sex: Bodies, Images, and Russian State Homophobia
Dean Cooper-Cunningham

Hidden Wars: Gendered Political Violence in Asia's Civil Conflicts
Sara E. Davies and Jacqui True

Complicit Sisters: Gender and Women's Issues across North-South Divides
Sara de Jong

Gender and Private Security in Global Politics
Maya Eichler

This American Moment: A Feminist Christian Realist Intervention
Caron E. Gentry

The International Politics of Sex

Bodies, Images, and Russian State Homophobia

DEAN COOPER-CUNNINGHAM

OXFORD
UNIVERSITY PRESS

OXFORD

UNIVERSITY PRESS

Oxford University Press is a department of the University of Oxford.
It furthers the University's objective of excellence in research, scholarship,
and education by publishing worldwide. Oxford is a registered trade mark of
Oxford University Press in the UK and in certain other countries.

Published in the United States of America by Oxford University Press
198 Madison Avenue, New York, NY 10016, United States of America.

CIP data is on file at the Library of Congress

ISBN 9780197792513

ISBN 9780197792506 (hbk.)

DOI: 10.1093/9780197792544.001.0001

Paperback printed by Marquis Book Printing, Canada

The manufacturer's authorized representative in the EU for product safety is
Oxford University Press España S.A. of Parque Empresarial San Fernando de Henares,
Avenida de Castilla, 2 – 28830 Madrid (www.oup.es/en or product.safety@oup.com).
OUP España S.A. also acts as importer into Spain of products made by the manufacturer.

For Helen Cunningham.

You taught me it was okay to want more,
to dream of a better, less violent world,
and how to fearlessly lead a feminist life.

This book includes revised text, analysis, and data that have been published in the following articles:

Cooper-Cunningham, Dean. 2019. 'Seeing (In)Security, Gender and Silencing: Posters in and about the British Women's Suffrage Movement.' *International Feminist Journal of Politics* 21(3): 383–408.

Cooper-Cunningham, Dean. 2020. 'Drawing Fear of Difference: Race, Gender, and National Identity in Ms. Marvel Comics.' *Millennium: Journal of International Studies* 48(2):165–97.

Cooper-Cunningham, Dean. 2020. 'Visual Methods and International Security Studies.' *E-International Relations*.

Cooper-Cunningham, Dean. 2022. 'Security, Sexuality, and the Gay Clown Putin Meme: The Queer Politics of Play in International Responses to Russian State-Directed Homophobia.' *Security Dialogue* 53(4): 302–323.

All inclusion of previously published material in this book is used as per the terms set out in the respective publication agreements with Taylor & Francis, SAGE, and E-IR.

Contents

List of Figures

Acknowledgements

While the words on these pages are mine, a book is not an individual endeavour. The process would not have been possible nor would it have been bearable without a lot of wonderful people who have enriched my life incredibly over the years I spent doing this research. Some of you contributed by giving comments, helping me develop ideas, and demanding more of my writing. Some of you helped by joining me for a run, swim, beer, concert, or some overly competitive board game. All of you made writing this infinitely more enjoyable. I owe you all many thank yous, but also just a written signal of my appreciation for your companionship, your guidance, and the joy you bring me.

Thank you to:

The wonderful people in the New York Public Library Archives and Manuscripts Division, who were so welcoming and enthusiastic about the work I was doing for the visual genealogy. Tal Nadan, Meredith Mann, Cara Delatte, Kyle Triplett from the Reference Desk, and John Cordovez, Ted Teodoro, and Nasima Hasnat from the Circulation Desk. Thanks especially to Cara, Kyle, and Tal for your inspiring conversations and for pointing me in the direction of material I'd otherwise have missed. Your knowledge and assistance were amazing.

The many hosts I've had on my research trips. Especially, Steve and Jimmy the cat in Melbourne with whom I ended up spending the first weeks of the Covid-19 pandemic before returning to Scotland. Also, Aram, Giorgio, and their cat Bear in New York City, who directed me to all the fun queer places in NYC.

Christoffer Boll, for giving me the space to be myself and for gently (actually, more often than not, firmly) bringing me back down to earth when my tinted glasses became a little too rosy and idealistic. Thank you for asking tough questions, for being genuinely interested in what this project was about, for convincing me to have Sunday beers after *styrke*, and for showing me how even the most horrible curveballs life throws at you can be overcome. I am so grateful for your friendship. I am even more grateful for how you have embraced Scottish slang in your daily vocabulary. You have been a sounding board for some of my craziest ideas. Trust that there are many more to come, lassie.

Jakob Vase, for being one of the kindest, most joyful, and most loyal people I have ever met. I am so grateful that you shouted 'fuck, det er hårdt' at me while we were running around a muddy field in Odense during one of the less intense periods of the Covid-19 pandemic. That race remains the only time I have ever truly enjoyed running cross country. Life moves in unexpected ways, but I am forever grateful that one of the many unexpected things was meeting you. Thank you for unapologetically being yourself and for giving me a nudge to rediscover joy when things weren't quite going right. I am really looking forward to going on more adventures together, to continuing to have debates about what 'real' science is, and to keep on buying you wine and coffee that you hate.

Koen Slootmaeckers, for being a wonderful and astute friend. My parents are incredible judges of character and they weren't wrong when they said you are one of the most generous and caring people they have ever met. The metaphor of a 'journey' makes me dry-heave, but you have taught me the importance of being compassionate to oneself and taking breaks. Thank you for all you do and for nourishing our friendship at every possible opportunity. Thank you for forcing me to think about my theorisation of queer and for calling me out when that thinking got too abstract. I appreciate your advice and the time you have given to mentor me. More than that, I truly appreciate your friendship. We've been on some rollercoasters. We've seen some wonderful places together. I look forward to our collaborations.

Jess Gifkins, for being a supremely generous mentor and collaborator. Having met only once, we started a journey to queer atrocity prevention frameworks in the middle of the Covid-19 pandemic. We hadn't worked together before, but something clicked. Our collaboration is one of the most enriching and intellectually nourishing things I've done to date. I hope that I have given you as much as you have given me. Beyond writing and research, you've become a close friend. You welcomed me to Sheffield, coached me through career decisions, cooked for me, helped me through some tough mental health moments, and you've introduced me to your life with open arms. I am so grateful to you and Iz for making my year in Sheffield so joyful and full of love. I can't wait to come see you both in Sydney and to finally play 'birds' together!

Livia Rohrbach, for being the true life and soul of the party. You are such an inspiration and live life with such voracity that I've never seen in anyone else. I have never met anyone who opens their arms, their apartment, and their network to people who are new to a city and need to find their feet quite like you do. You not only take care of everyone around you but you also take everyone for who they are. You create intimate spaces of joy, creativity, and debauchery. Thank you for keeping me sane, for sending a lot of memes, and for being my partner in crime during your Copenhagen days. I miss you so much and I long for the days when we live on the same continent again. I cannot wait for another Schwarzwald reunion.

Christoffer Cappelen, for letting me join your smoke breaks, listening to me think, and for signing up to collaborate on one of my more adventurous projects. You've been a steady source of companionship and joy over the years. I'm not sure the Ph.D. programme would have been anywhere near as fun without you. I'll never meet someone as well-versed in music as you, and it brings me so much joy to spend evenings deep-diving into music and drinking beers with you.

Hannah Petrie, for being an angry feminist with me. We've come a long way since we were sitting on the ugly carpets in Wardlaw and reading each other's essays before submission. You're a light in my life and I wish that we could have thirty-second dance parties every single day again. Thank you for being my biggest fan and for all of your random FaceTimes. I can't wait to keep building RI memories with you.

Detmer Kremer, who turned from a co-author into a co-conspirator. We don't talk every day, but you teach me so much with your activism and vision for a better, fairer, more equal world. Your brain fires off in so many directions, you make links across topics and themes that seem oceans apart, and you work ferociously to defend those who have been marginalised. You do all of this with such care and compassion for nature and people that you leave me in awe. You are queer joy embodied and I cannot thank you enough for sparring with me and sharing your ideas with me. I look forward to more radical queer collaborations.

Asbjørn Eller Skaarup, Esben Krogh Rasmussen, Emil Jønsson Kristiansen, Marie Groth, Camilla Balle Bech, Stine Muldbak Andersen, and Signe Knigge Hylleberg, for all the runs, laughs, dinners, post-race parties, games nights, and trips across the world these past years. You made Denmark feel more like home and I will be endlessly grateful for that.

Matilde Willer-Jørgensen, Sif Marie Byrialsen Hansen, and Simon Platz Schmidt for brightening my mornings and always asking the uncomfortable question: 'How is writing going?' You might not have been there for the start of this project, but you have been sources of so much joy, laughter, and fun over the course of its last eighteen months. We came into each other's lives in a somewhat bizarre way, but I'll be forever grateful for it. I'm looking forward to much more silliness in the future.

John Wood, for our weekly coaching check-ins that are ostensibly about training but are more often than not about politics and society. I am so grateful for your guidance, support, and perseverance through multiple injuries, but also for helping me rediscover a love for running. You've seen me through my career highlights, and for that, I cannot ever repay you. I have learned more about coaching, teaching, and advising than any pedagogy course could ever teach me.

Karin von Schantz and Christian Franklin Svensson, for creating a home away from home in Copenhagen within the very first day of my arrival. When you live with random people, you can never quite be sure you'll all get on. Living on Østerbro with you both was such a joy and I am so glad that we have continued to spend many nights chatting the hours away with tea and beautiful food. You both have such energy and passion, such a care-free attitude, that inspires me every time we are together. Less like fresh air, you are both like a warm embrace that makes everyone around you feel loved.

Megan MacKenzie, for having the most positive outlook on life, possibly the most inspiring and realistic relationship with academia, for giving great advice, and for incredible comments that made this book infinitely better. You are an inspiration and I value your opinions and advice immensely.

The IR group at Copenhagen, who have been so intellectually generous with me. The opportunity to work with some of the brightest and friendliest scholars has been a source of incredible joy. Our seminars have taught me so much and it would be remiss of me not to say how indebted to you I am for my personal and academic growth. A particular thanks to Anders Wivel, Rebecca Adler-Nissen, Peter Marcus Kristensen, Kristin Eggeling, Olaf Corry (now in Leeds), Ole Wæver, and Maja Zehfuss for their support, advice, and detailed reading of my work over the years. Many of my PhD contemporaries in Copenhagen were second-to-none in helping me think this project through in its earliest stages: Anne Bach Nielsen, Niels

Byrjalsen, Wiebke Junk, Jeppe Vierø, Frederik Klaaborg Kjøller, Larissa Versloot, Benjamin Egerod, Tobias Liebetrau, Øyvind Svendsen, Minda Holm, Anine Hagemann, Mads Ejsing, and Jens van der Ploeg.

The wonderful team at Oxford University Press. In particular, Angela Chnapko who was so conscious of my inexperience in the book publication process, and Andrea Smith for being so on top of image permissions and the editorial process—you both helped me immensely and I look forward to future collaborations. Thank you also to Laura Sjoberg and Rahul Rao, the series editors.

Lene Hansen, who started as my Ph.D. supervisor and quickly became a close friend over the course of our collaboration. I struggle to put into words quite how many thank yous I want to say and how much I appreciate your friendship. I remember being incredibly nervous walking to Small Batch, the coffee shop at Seven Dials in Brighton, to meet you for the first time in 2017. We'd exchanged some emails and agreed to meet up to talk about working together. I'd done a rather shoddy Google Image search for you and was looking for a Norwegian bodybuilder also called Lene Hansen. I don't really remember much else about our meeting, but I do remember feeling in absolute awe of your knowledge, sharpness, and generosity. I remain so. You have been the kindest, most generous mentor I could ever have dreamed of; not just for me, but for so many others across the world. You truly live your feminist politics. I would not be the academic I am without your support and your friendship. I have never met anyone else who shows up to seminars so well prepared, so well read, and with a sharp eye for every single detail. I have learnt so much from watching you practice your art. Beyond mentorship, I am just really glad to call you my friend. I am so glad to be back in Copenhagen after my small stint in Sheffield because it means that I get to spar over big ideas with you, talk about everything culture over lunch, have Friday knock offs in one of our usual spots, and celebrate all things big and small to come.

Keegan Cooper-Cunningham, who, for as long as I can remember, has reminded me of every birthday, anniversary, big family event imaginable. Thank you for keeping me grounded and for remaining my most passionate supporter all these years. I don't say it often enough, at least not publicly, but I am so proud of you and the life you are building. You show me every day what it means to be determined, what it means to dream, what it means to never settle for the lot you've been dealt. You are the kindest person I have ever known and you are a real ray of sunshine that anyone would be privileged to have in their life. Thank you for being my dancing partner, for telling me to get off my high horse, and for refusing to be anyone but yourself.

Mum and dad, for every single sacrifice you made for me and for Keegan. We never wanted for anything, you gave us so much love, and you both built a family on foundations made of care, joy, respect, and ambition. I want you both to know that I see all of the sacrifices you made for us growing up and all of the things you continue to do. You both taught me the importance of working hard, the importance of following your dreams, and the importance of never giving up. You have been the best role models I could ever have asked for. Thank you for trusting me and supporting me when I said I wanted to go to university. Thank you for telling me to take a chance on Copenhagen. Thank you for showing me that you can be a grown up but still have a lot of fun. Thank you for showing me what a beautiful partnership of equals looks like. Thank you for showing me love. Thank you, most importantly, for being you. Not every child grows up to say they've become friends with their parents. I am so grateful for the adventures we have been on, for the deep discussions we have had and will have, for the lust for life you both show, and for your silliness. I have never met two people so up for fun, so ready for adventure, so loving and compassionate. Thank you for supporting all my crazy ideas and for putting up with all my silly decisions. Even although we're only a short flight apart, I miss you both every single day and hearing your voices on FaceTime always makes me smile—even when I sound grumpy . . . I promise! Words to live by: be good and always be happy.

Dean Cooper-Cunningham
Copenhagen, January 2025

1

Introduction

In this book, I argue that sex, the visual, and the body are important and central to how we understand and analyse international politics. In the years it has taken to research and write this, many people have asked me why I bring the visual, the body, and sex together.[1] More still have asked how they could possibly all connect to international politics. The answer is found in the pages that follow, but it is useful to start with a story about how I first encountered the Russian state homophobia that sparked my intellectual curiosity about the state's management of sex. Over a decade ago now, I encountered Russia's infamous 'gay propaganda law' in a news article while scrolling through Twitter on my then-cutting-edge iPhone 4. That news article was accompanied by a photograph of three bloodied individuals huddling together and surrounded by Russia's military police force, *OMOH*. That image, like the many others circulating at the time, is very similar to Mads Nissen's photograph in Figure 1.1. Seeing those photographs was my first encounter with state homophobia, not just Russian. It was the first time I realised the extent to which I could be persecuted for my sexual behaviour and desires. It was the first time I recognised my relative privilege. It was the first time I saw how politicised our 'private' lives are, how blurry the public/private, personal/political divide is. It prompted a question about how something so commonly constituted as 'personal' (i.e., sex) could have become a matter of international concern. It was also the first time I realised how affective photographs are; how images and emotions are political things

---

[1] In this book, 'sex' does not simply refer to consensual sexual activity and behaviour but also to the *idea* of people's sexual activity and the political work done to control and constrain the types of sex and pleasure sought out by certain (groups of) people. In this sense, while I do mean sex-as-sexual-activity (e.g., intercourse, non-penetrative sex, oral sex, etc.), the politics of sex is also about the *possibility* of sex, particularly sex that falls outside of societal norms or expectations (i.e., non-normative sex). When I say the *possibility* of sex, I mean simply that no sex need actually happen for it to be controversial. It is merely the possibility, no matter how small, that some form of supposedly deviant, immoral, abnormal sex might be happening, the possibility that people are pleasuring their bodies in ways that challenge the status quo, the possibility that some people actively opt out of sex entirely that has been constituted as a threat to the fabric of society and to the very foundations of the 'civilised' world in some cases (Chen 2020; Edelman 2004; McIntosh 1968; Rubin 2011; Warner 2000).

The International Politics of Sex. Dean Cooper-Cunningham, Oxford University Press.
© Oxford University Press (2025). DOI: 10.1093/9780197792544.003.0001

that organise, shape, and constitute the social and political. Images are frames of reference through which we understand political events. Seeing that photograph, I was confronted with a government's attempted management of sex and at that moment I was forced to grapple with how sex and images fitted together in terms of thinking about international politics.

Since then, I have been thinking about two main questions. First, what does sex have to do with international politics and how does it intersect with ideas about security? Second, what do images have to do with international politics and security? Both of these questions are situated in long-drawn-out debates in the international security studies literature about what 'security' is, whose security matters, who gets to speak security, and how security is constituted, articulated, and contested. There was, as will become clear later, a discrepancy between the national security discourses of the Russian government and the insecurity of (suspected) queer people. As I started to answer these questions in the process of researching and writing this book, the body became an additional empirical-theoretical focus. It is, after all, through the body that we practice sex and feel desire—the very things the Russian government was trying to manage through the propaganda law and other homophobic policies. The body was also very clearly the end point of violence in those photographs. The body is, however, not just a site of disciplining or a passive surface upon which politics plays out. It can also be a vehicle for political resistance by, for example, challenging established norms or engaging in protests.

I start with this story not out of self-indulgence, but to try to articulate how those images from 2013 did something. They did something to me personally, but also more broadly in terms of the discourse about Russia, the West, and sexuality. Those images provoked me to think about the politics of the visual, the politics of the body, the politics of sex, and how an IR analysis could help us better understand what was going on in Russia when the gay propaganda law was passed. More so than the words accompanying the news articles about Russia's new propaganda law, *seeing* homophobic violence was uncomfortably provoking. Seeing those images brought home how incredibly powerful the images used to represent international political issues are. Encountering that photograph, then, sparked a queer and a visual curiosity (Weber 2015a). What kind of politics underpins state policies that attempt to regulate people's sexual practices by granting legitimacy and respectability to some kinds of consensual sex but not others? What do images do politically? Encountering that photograph of homophobic violence forced me to see Russian state homophobia, but also how people in Russia and internationally were calling into question and attempting to challenge policies like the gay propaganda law. They used images and put their bodies into public spaces to contest and draw attention to state homophobia. They were engaged in visual and bodily activism that disturbed the way I had thought about sex, images, bodies, and international relations until that point.

Weaving all of this together, the central aim and purpose of this book is to demonstrate how we can understand and study the visual and the body as matters of international politics. Particularly, as they relate to an emergent post-liberal international order, part of which involves a moral panic about the regulation of sex, sexuality, gender, and bodily autonomy. In what follows, I provide a theoretical framework for understanding sexual shame and stigma in international politics as well as a framework for understanding what bodies and the visual do in international politics. In terms of sexual shame and stigma, I outline a framework that captures how moralising politics, particularly those that define 'normal' and 'appropriate' sex and sexualities, have come to influence states' foreign policies. I specifically build this framework using the case of Russian state homophobia, where sexual shame and stigma have been mobilised domestically but also as part of a broader geopolitical strategy that has discursively divided the world into decadent, uncivilised queer spaces and traditional, moral, and civilised spaces over the last two decades. In terms of the visual and the body, I outline a tripartite words-images-bodies approach that emphasises how words, images, and bodies are deeply intertwined and should be studied simultaneously as sites where international politics takes place. In the case of this book, they are sites where power is represented, contested, and resisted; where political struggles happen. This tripartite words-images-bodies approach offers a new way of thinking about and studying international politics that does not reify narratives of distinct individual/domestic/international levels of analysis and does not prioritise words as the primary (discursive) vehicle through which politics is done. In order to demonstrate the utility of the tripartite approach, as well as the international politics of sexual shame and stigma, the bulk of the empirical material in this book focuses on Western actors' contestation of Russian state homophobia and resistance to its moralistic geopolitical project.

I am under no illusion that the visual, the body, and sex are not the intuitive things, the intuitive matter or substance of the international, that

Figure 1.1 Photograph featured in Mads Nissen's series 'LGBT in Russia' (2013). Image courtesy of Panos Pictures. Image ID: MNN01267RUS.

come to mind when thinking about the study of Political Science and IR. However, as I will show, sex, the visual, and the body have a deep and intimate connection to international politics. Particularly when it comes to some of IR scholarship's central foci: *security*, *power*, and the way that *identities* are constituted. In terms of sex, moralising and normative discourses inform ideas about national identity, culture, and security. This can be around ideas about a nation's ability to reproduce itself, its cultural heritage, or about a state's position as a 'global leader' in protecting LGBT+ rights. In the case of Russian politics, the government has been particularly prolific and brilliant at connecting heterosexuality with national security, cultural sovereignty, and national identity. It also deploys normative discourses about sexuality as part of a moralising foreign policy, which I later conceptualise as *heteronormative internationalism*. In terms of bodies, discourses about appropriate/normal consensual sex shape how people use their bodies and start to limit the waywardness of bodily pleasure and desire by marking certain practices and desires as unspeakable or not pursuable. In terms of the visual, images shape how we meet and understand events of international political concern and are important in the constitution of national boundaries, imaginaries, and perceptions of the Self and the Other. The photograph I mentioned above is one example of how we meet international politics visually. Beyond being a medium through which we meet international events, the visual can also be a mode of resistance to power mobilised by marginalised subjects; a tool for contesting the identity one has been marked with. Especially when one is actively sought invisible by political figures and wider society.

Russian State Homophobia: A Theoretical-Empirical Starting Point

It seems a contradiction that something constituted as so ostensibly 'private' as sex and desire could be even remotely related to the machinations of the international. And yet, as others have already shown, they so very clearly are.[2] As outlined above, my first encounter with state homophobia was through Russia. In order to demonstrate how sex comes into international politics, I use the Russian case first as an empirical entry point, but later, by also engaging with Western reactions, for theorising the international politics of sexual shame and stigma.

For over two decades, Russia's political elite—supported by religious figures and political philosophers such as Patriarch Kirill and Aleksandr Dugin—have anchored national security policy in ideas about defending Russian culture, traditions, and gender/sexual norms from foreign influence (Gaufman 2017; Healey 2018; Wilkinson 2018). Throughout this period, there have been several key legislative steps: passing the so-called gay propaganda law in 2013 into federal law, prohibiting the 'positive' depiction of non-heteronormative relations to minors; passing the foreign agents act in 2012, which requires all NGOs engaged in political activity and receiving funding from outside Russia to register as foreign agents; amending the constitution to prohibit same-sex marriage in 2020; expanding the gay propaganda law in 2022 to prohibit positive (or even neutral) depiction of non-heteronormative lives in all public information to everyone

[2] Across the breadth of queer and feminist international relations scholarship, several scholars have been important to my thinking about gender and sexuality in international politics. In particular, though not exclusively, the following scholars' work was a jumping off point for exploring sex and the international: V. Spike Peterson (1999, 2014a, 2014b), Cynthia Weber (2014, 2016), Caron Gentry (2015 [with Sjoberg]; 2020), Laura Sjoberg (2012, 2014), Darcy Leigh (2017), Rahul Rao (2014a, 2014b), Michael Bosia (2014; 2013b), Cai Wilkinson (2017a, 2018), and Lene Hansen (2000a, 2000b).

regardless of age, effectively creating a blanket ban; and the Supreme Court's designation of an ill-defined 'international LGBT movement' as 'extremist' in 2023.

Clearly, a lot has happened since 2013, but even when I first encountered Russian state homophobia it was certainly nothing new. While the persecution of (suspected) queer individuals only really came to international attention in 2013 when news outlets reported the passing of the gay propaganda law and the increase of violence towards (suspected) queer individuals that followed, hostility towards those (suspected of) engaging in non-heterosexual behaviours and with non-cisgender[3] expressions/identifications was a well-established practice (Essig 1999; Healey 2018; Sperling 2014). This was mostly, though not exclusively, directed towards gay men. The arrest and controversial trial of Pussy Riot as well as two upcoming sports mega-events—the Sochi Winter Olympics and FIFA Men's World Cup—shone a bright spotlight on Russian politics, bringing state homophobia to the world's attention. Since then, the oppression of queer people has become a key battleground between Russia and the West.[4]

Despite increasing violence against queer people in Russia and the government's increasing predilection for targeting queer populations at home and abroad, it is important to look to June 2013 when, after years of growing anti-Western sentiment and a discourse that linked 'deviant' non-heteronormative sexualities with 'immoral' European values at odds with Russian culture, the Duma passed a new law prohibiting the promotion of so-called 'non-traditional' sexualities and gender. The gay propaganda law was a major political and legislative win for Putin in terms of domestic and foreign policy, shifting both in a moralistic—some might say activist—direction that included the strategic and political mobilisation of homophobia to support a specific formulation of Russian national identity rooted in a set of heteronormative[5] values labelled 'traditional'. Those 'traditional

---

[3] Cisgender is a term used to refer to those who identify with their gender assigned at birth.

[4] What 'the West' is and how the term is used are complicated. Here, I mean those states, actors, institutions, and geographies *discursively constituted* as 'Western' (Hellman and Herborth 2017). Here, the West is a set of actors and spaces constituted as opposed to and decidedly not Russian—its constitutive Other. Drawing on performative approaches to language, 'the West' is brought into being by that which it is said (not) to be: 'the West' is not a natural phenomena that exists a priori but is instead discursively constituted. In Russian, 'the West' (*zapad*) is a slippery term that can refer to 'Europe only, or to Europe and its former settler colonies' including the US (Neumann 2017, 4). Recently, 'Gayropa' emerged as a term conflating the West with sexual depravity (Foxall 2019; Riabov and Riabova 2014).

[5] Heteronormativity is: 'the institutions, structures of understanding, and practical orientations that make heterosexuality seem not only coherent—that is, organized as a sexuality—but also privileged' (Berlant and Warner 1998, 548 fn. 2).

values' have taken on more concrete, tangible forms in Russia's 2015 and 2021 National Security Strategies, including references to a 'strong' and 'traditional' family, marriage, religion, and morality, which are all constituted as sacrosanct and fundamental to Russian cultural sovereignty and socio-cultural security (Składanowski 2023, 40–1; Trenin 2021). This prioritisation of moral values in Russia's national security strategies and an emphasis on consolidating 'international efforts to ensure respect for and protection of universal and traditional spiritual and moral values (including ethical norms common to all world religions)' in its 2023 foreign policy priorities document (Ministry of Foreign Affairs of the Russian Federation 2023) is indicative of the key role that 'traditional values' play in Russian foreign policy, the co-constitution of national identity through said policy priorities, and Russia's geopolitical imaginary (Cooper 2021).

In official discourse, the West's increasing tolerance of non-normative[6] sexuality and gender has been constituted as an indicator of the West's descent into immorality, barbarity, and decadence.[7] Constituting a 'Western gay menace' has become a useful tool in Russian statecraft (on how this works as a tool of statecraft, see Bosia 2014; 2015, 40; Currier 2019; Edenborg 2017; Wilkinson 2018). As a result of the West's apparently increasing tolerance of queerness—something that can be and is disputed by many academics and activists—the West has been branded 'Gayropa' in official discourse. In particular, government- and Russian Orthodox Church-allied actors constitute European queer friendliness as infecting and corrupting the moral foundations of Europe and therefore threatening not just so-called 'true European' values but also Russian society and the nation (Fierstein 2013; Gaufman 2017; Neumann 2017, 177–8). Children, as the beacons of

---

[6] Throughout this book, I will use the terms non-normative and antinormative. The former is a descriptive term to capture that which falls outside of societal norms and expectations. This may be intentional or not. In this case, non-normative will usually refer to sexual identities, expressions, or behaviours that fall outside of normative scripts. Antinormative refers to intentional and deliberate actions to actively challenge and disrupt established norms. The main point of difference here is that anti-normative approaches involve a conscious decision to challenge, subvert, and reconstruct norms, while non-normative simply describes a state of being different.

[7] The Russian discourse about the moral decadence of non-hetero sexualities and non-cisgenders is noted by the European Court of Human Rights as early as 2011 in the case of *Alekseyev v. Russia* where the court declared that Russia's prohibition on Pride parades—and the invisibilising/silencing of a minority—contravened international law (2011a, §77–78). This is articulated in §82 where the court notes that it was 'the very fact that they [LGBT people] wished to openly identify themselves as gay men or lesbians, individually and as a group' in a *public* Pride parade that the Russian Government 'found objectionable'. In §16 the Mayor of Moscow is quoted saying that: 'That's the way morals work. If somebody deviates from the normal principles [in accordance with which] sexual and gender life is organised, this should not be demonstrated in public' and in §61 where queer sexual relations are equated with bestiality.

Russia's national future, have been constituted as especially vulnerable to the threat of gay propaganda.[8]

While the international dimension of Russian state homophobia is not new, this has become more explicit and forceful since Putin ramped up his invasion of Ukraine in February 2022. Since then, Putin has devoted a proportionally large space to sexuality and gender in almost every speech. Constituting Russia as diametrically opposite the decadent West, he has positioned Russia as 'a cultural, axiological, and even civilisational antithesis of the West' where gender and sexual disorder threaten to undermine the fundamental fabric of European civilisation (Składanowski 2023: 35). For example, when announcing the annexation of four Ukrainian territories in September 2022, he focused on morality and tradition, reiterating long-established arguments about the West's moral decay:

> They [Western countries] have already moved on to the radical denial of moral, religious, and family values. ... [D]o we want to have here, in our country, in Russia, "parent number one, parent number two and parent number three" (they have completely lost it!) instead of mother and father? Do we want our schools to impose on our children, from their earliest days in school, perversions that lead to degradation and extinction? Do we want to drum into their heads the ideas that certain other genders exist along with women and men and to offer them gender reassignment surgery? Is that what we want for our country and our children? This is all unacceptable to us. We have a different future of our own. Let me repeat that the dictatorship of the Western elites targets all societies, including the citizens of Western countries themselves. This is a challenge to all. This complete renunciation of what it means to be human, the overthrow of faith and traditional values, and the suppression of freedom are coming to resemble a "religion in reverse" – pure Satanism ... Today, we are fighting for a just and free path, first of all for ourselves, for Russia, in order to leave dictate and despotism in the past ... We must protect them against enslavement and monstrous experiments that are designed to cripple their minds and souls.
>
> (Putin 2022)

Shrouded in the veil of defending 'traditional values' at home and abroad, this speech follows the script of the well-established image of the 'Gayropean'

---

[8] See Lee Edelman (2004) for a queer troubling of the figure of the child.

Other in Russian foreign policy (on 'Gayropa' see: Foxall 2019; Riabov and Riabova 2014).[9] Gayropa, the supposed apex of moral decadence and a symbol of the threat posed by the liberal internationalist project, is now a part of the discursive legitimation for the war in Ukraine. Since at least 2014, Putin has discursively constituted Ukraine as a part of Russia. As part of what Maria Mälksoo calls a 'memory war', Putin has also constituted Ukrainians and Russians as one people (Düben 2020; Mälksoo 2023, 476–77). With these discursive moves, equating Russia and Ukraine as one people, Western sexual decadence has been constituted not just as a threat to Russia's cultural sovereignty and societal security, but also as a threat to Ukraine, which according to Putin's logic is Russia.

Moralising discourses about appropriate sexuality and gender do not just play a justificatory role in this imperial war in the sense that Russian national security is constituted as being entangled with sexuality and gender order, but US intelligence suggests that the Russian government also had a plan to target 'journalists and anti-corruption activists, and vulnerable populations such as religious and ethnic minorities and LGBTQI+ persons' upon successful takeover of Ukraine (Crocker 2022). This is part of 'a widespread trend ... [of] utiliz[ing] homophobia and gender-normativity in nationalist, militarist narratives to berate, humiliate and dehumanize the enemy as "other"—whether at the individual, collective or national level' (United Nations Independent Expert SOGI 2022, 10–11).

The mission to save Europe from itself, to protect 'true European' values, to bolster Russian national security, and to position Russia as a leader (not just militarily, but ideologically, morally, culturally) in the region is well underway. Sexuality is an odd but prominent part of Russia's vision for an illiberal international order within which Russia presents itself as the 'custodian of "traditional values"' (Holm 2020; Holm and Tjalve 2018). This moralising over appropriate, acceptable, and normal sexual behaviour and gender very clearly plays a not insignificant role in Russian geopolitics. Principally, it offers a different vision of world order than the liberal version enshrined in international institutions and law. The contours of this ideological project now seem to be appealing to European and North American actors (Abrahamsen et al. 2020; Abrahamsen et al. 2024; Ayoub and Stoeckl 2024). So much so that the United Nations Independent Expert on

---

[9] The values constituted as needing protection are interchangeably styled as 'traditional', 'Christian', and/or 'family' values.

protection against violence and discrimination based on sexual orientation and gender identity (UNIE-SOGI), Graeme Reid, argued in his report to the UN Human Rights Council that Russian state homophobia and its propaganda law in particular 'has become a template for other States in Central and Eastern Europe and Central Asia' and that '[t]he designation of LGBT groups as extremist or a threat to national security is another discernible trend' (2024, 6).

By now, I've spent a lot of words on Russia, which was the empirical-theoretical starting point for this project, but the book is not so strongly focused on Russian domestic politics. Rather, I am focused on the politics generated around a Russia-West conflict around sexuality and gender. So, now I will introduce Western responses to Russian state homophobia. In contrast to a Russian discourse of Western decadence and immorality, Western discourses constitute Russian homophobia as a problem of international concern and the abuse of basic human rights as an indicator of civilisational backwardness and barbarity. Actors from the West and institutions constituted by Russia as Western-dominated have responded to Russian politicised homophobia in numerous ways. The European Court of Human Rights condemned the Russian government in various legal cases, for example: Alekseyev v. Russia (2011b), Alekseyev and Others v. Russia (2018), Romanov and Others v. Russia (2023b), and Lapunov v. Russia (2023a). The UN Office of the High Commissioner for Human Rights issued press releases calling out Russia's homophobic politics (2012, 2013, 2017, 2019, 2023). The UN Children's Fund (UNICEF), in 2014, argued that eliminating discriminatory legislation that purports to 'protect' children ignores that children have diverse sexual orientations and gender identities, and that laws such as the propaganda law are harmful not just to queer adults but the very children who are the referent objects of such securitizing narratives (UNICEF 2014).

In the wake of the gay propaganda law, the UN Committee on the Rights of the Child also emphasised the points made by UNICEF, noting additionally that LGBTI youth are often the targets of abuse because of their sexual orientation or gender identity (United Nations Committee on the Rights of the Child 2014). The Council of Europe responded to the original gay propaganda law, calling it 'problematic', contravening 'international standards', and reiterating that Russia's punishment of non-normative sexuality infringes International Human Rights Law (Reuters 2013; Venice Convention 2013). Further emphasising the significance of Russian homophobia, the Council of Europe's Commissioner for Human Rights noted that 'exploiting anti-LGBTI prejudice to attract votes is a long-standing practice' and that on the European continent more broadly 'persisting homo/transphobia in our societies have now provided fertile ground for exploitation by opportunistic and anti-human rights political movements' (2021). The UN Human Rights Committee (2012) has repeatedly slammed Russia for infringing freedom of expression and several UNIE-SOGI reports condemn Russia's strategic politicisation of homophobia (2022, 2024).

Although the politics around queer issues has changed significantly since 2013 and we are witnessing a global backlash, in 2013, various foreign governments criticised Russia's treatment and invisibilisation of queer people as unacceptable. US President Barack Obama stated that 'Nobody's more offended than me about some of the anti-gay and lesbian legislation … in Russia' (Nakamura 2013b), British Prime Minister David Cameron urged people to 'challenge [Russia's] prejudice' against LGBT people (Hughes 2013), Danish Foreign Minister Villy Søvndal called the law 'objectionable' and announced Denmark would hold Russia to its international obligations (Carter 2013a), and German Foreign Minister Guido Westerwelle similarly criticised the law (Carter 2013b).

Later, in response to the 'gay purge' in the Chechen Republic of the Russian Federation, which has been ongoing since 2017, the OSCE published a report urging member states to take seriously 'the special security needs of refugees from Chechnya, in particular LGBTI persons' and to support 'civil society, NGOs and Human Rights Defenders and journalists' in their mission to expose and resist anti-queer politics and human rights violations (2018, 4–5 §C). This report singled out Russia as unsafe for queer people, urging OSCE states to: 'Use special caution in cases of extradition of persons from the Chechen Republic, in particular LGBTI persons, taking into account that they are usually not safe in other parts of the Russian Federation' (2018, 5 §C4). A 32-country joint statement was also issued at the 40th Session of the UN Human Rights Council calling for action against the 'persecution of LGBTI persons in Chechnya, Russian Federation' and the immediate release of 'all persons who remain in detention based on their actual or perceived sexual orientation or gender identity' (Human Rights Council 2019). In 2024, the UN Special Rapporteur on extrajudicial, summary, or arbitrary executions called attention to the continuing unlawful targeting, detention, and torture of queer people across the Russian Federation (2024), citing the 2023

Supreme Court decision as further cultivating already fertile ground for queer persecution.

The above list of responses to Russian state homophobia is absolutely not exhaustive, but they are indicative of sex being politicised internationally. As I pick up later, the international resonance of Russian state homophobia did not stop at international organisations' or states' responses but extended to civil society internationally. NGOs like Human Rights Watch (2018a, 2018b, 2014), Amnesty International (2013a, 2013b), and ILGA (2013, 2016, 2017, 2019) have issued multiple reports calling on the international community to take action against Russia and support queer people seeking asylum. Beyond these reports and looking further afield than the 'big-hitter' LGBT+ rights NGOs, civil society responses have tended to take more creative visual and bodily forms than written/spoken condemnations, reporting, and commentary. These interventions are the empirical material I work with in the second half of this book.

The Strategic Mobilisation of Sexuality

All of the above are examples of the strategic use of repression or extension of rights to sexual and gender minorities in international political struggles and how they serve states in their foreign policy agendas. These are practices of *politicised homophobia* and *politicised homophilia* (see Bosia 2015; Duggan 2002).[10] Increasingly, states are stigmatising Other states for their treatment of queer people when it is starkly against its own moral position on non-normative sex. In this sense, we can begin to talk about an *international politics of sex* replete with shaming and stigmatisation that is characterised by a conflict on the appropriate way to deal with those individuals/groups who fall outside of the 'normal' as it pertains to sex and gender, a conflict over how people use and display their bodies in ways that challenge particular visions of normalcy. This is ultimately about power, (moral) hierarchies, and jostling for influence in the current international order.

My answer to the question whether sex has an international politics is pretty clear: it does. It is more apt to ask how sex becomes politicised in

---

[10] As I outline with Detmer Kremer, 'Politicised homophilia is the strategic mobilisation of support for the rights and protections of some [queer] people and certain divergences from cis-heteronormativity. Homophilia is when a positive position on [queer] issues is used to justify or obfuscate identity-based violence. Focusing on homophilia exposes how people, institutions, and states instrumentalise gender and sexuality for other causes' (2024, 10).

international relations. This is a question that many in Queer IR have been thinking through for some time (on queer questions in IR, see Rao 2014b). The fight over who people can be romantically and sexually attracted to, what types of sex people can have, and what types of pleasure they can seek out—even just in the abstract realm of what is imaginable, possible, thinkable as ethical and moral—is foundational to the production of national identities, transnational ideologies, geopolitical games, and world orders (Berlant and Freeman 1992; Nagel 2003; Peterson 1999, 2014b). Broad international condemnation of and activism against the oppression of queer people also signals its importance in international politics.[11] How Russian homophobia becomes part of a geopolitical vision carving the world into decadent queer versus traditional and ordered spaces, and how it is responded to internationally is important for understanding how and under what auspices queer issues—broadly speaking, related to sex/uality—and individuals come into international politics, the type of international order emerging around politicised homophobia and queer-supporting activism, and how state-directed homophobia is contested and resisted by actors across the world.

The Visual and the Body

While it took a little longer to percolate than the first question about the role of sex in international politics, the second question emerging from my encounter with Russian state homophobia was about the visual and the body. What do they have to do with international politics and security?

I have already outlined a plethora of institutional and state responses to Russian homophobia. These have predominantly come in textual or oral form. In keeping with this, analyses of the response to Russian state-directed homophobia have primarily been empirically focused on textual/spoken material. A particular focus has been on official discourse from states and institutions such as the EU or UN (Edenborg 2017; Gaufman 2017; Healey 2018; Riabov and Riabova 2014; Sperling 2014; Tsaturyan 2024). There is, however, a distinctly visual component to all politicised homophobia, not just Russian. Phillip Ayoub (2016) and Emil Edenborg (2017) have argued

---

[11] Drawing on Deborah Gould's (2009, 51) work, I use a loose understanding of political activism, which can take many forms from service provision and lobbying to direct action and into-the-streets protesting.

that anti-queer politics is often about the in/visibility of queerness in society. While hugely important works for the study of (anti-) queer politics neither pay theoretical nor empirical attention to the visual in terms of images or ways of seeing—despite images being used to call attention to, condemn, and resist state-directed homophobia internationally. Nor do they pay any attention to bodies as a site of resistance. So, what would be the benefits of turning to bodies and the visual?

Let me address the visual first. Paying attention to the visual is crucial for answering questions about nationalism, identity, security, state-building, and international order (Bleiker 2018; Brown 1995; Hansen 2000b, Forthcoming; Nagel 2003; Peterson 2014b; Weber 1998, 2016). People increasingly draw on images to understand and make sense of the world. It is incredibly rare that we don't have some imagery about major social and political events both today and historically. This makes the visual a critical medium that structures how we encounter and negotiate major international political issues, including those related to security. Images produce, sustain, and potentially call into question the identities of certain political actors and they also produce, sustain, and potentially call into question the terms and frames of reference around social and political events. In epistemic terms, images also have a distinctly affective dimension, immediacy, and authority that differ from words, uniquely placing the visual as a powerful medium through which challenges to (international) power structures can be made.

This visual power has been harnessed by activists from the suffragettes who fought for women's enfranchisement to AIDS activists who campaigned against government inaction during the initial years of the AIDS crisis to racial justice movements such as Black Lives Matter and ecological movements such as Extinction Rebellion. The visual, which goes beyond images to include questions of in/visibility, is a repeatedly utilised force for oppressed individuals/groups to contest repressive power structures. It is a central part of thinking about and theorising international politics. Taking the visual as a crucial epistemic terrain through which knowledge is created, contested, and circulated, we cannot think about, understand, or analyse important issues such as nationalism, identity, security, state-building, and international order without bringing the visual into our analyses.

In terms of the body, beyond the regulatory norms that work upon the body that feminists and philosophers have studied at length (Butler 1993a; Foucault 1977), human bodies are quite literally the endpoints of every single piece of policy, foreign or domestic. All policies have effects on human bodies. In the case this book's focus, those policies are predominantly heteronormative but also homophilic with effects not just on queer but also straight people. Whether one is focusing on heteronormative or homophilic foreign policies, any policy has an impact on the conditions in which a person lives and inevitably constrains what those bodies are able to legitimately do. More generally, laws, systems, and social structures affect people's lives, whether it is in the form of access to food, healthcare, environmental resources, education, security, and so on. All policies shape the conditions in which bodies live, thrive, or suffer. This has a clear link to Foucault's (1984, 257) concept of biopolitics, which captures how the modern state exercises power not just through laws and institutions, but also through the regulation of human life itself. He talks about this in terms of disciplining bodies through monitoring and regulation in social institutions (or transmitters of culture in Steven Seidman's [1998] terms) such as schools, healthcare, the military, prison systems, and so on. It also has clear resonance with Achille Mbembe's (2003) concept of necropolitics, which captures not just how political power controls life, but how it determines who is allowed to die, or which populations are deemed expendable. In the former, the body is a site of management, optimisation, control, and disciplining. In the latter, the body is a target of violence, neglect, abandonment, and death.

Opening this chapter, I talked about the way I came into contact with Russian state homophobia: through a photograph. In that photograph were three individuals who had been protesting the state's oppression and were celebrating Pride. On one level, their bodies were marked by gender, by ethnicity, and by all manner of other things that make them intelligible in particular ways. In another, and recalling Foucault's argument that the presence of power always signals resistance, those individuals in that photograph were resisting the state's homophobia *using their bodies*, both by making their bodies visible in public space (and contravening the propaganda law) and by subjecting their bodies to violence by the state and other civil society actors. This maps onto several questions that have been raised both in and outside IR about the politics of visibility, the visuality of the body as a physical thing, and the politics of using the body as resistance (e.g., Butler 1993a; Cooper-Cunningham 2019; Dauphinee 2007; Fierke 2013; Purnell 2021; Scarry 1985; Shepherd and Sjoberg 2012; Wilcox 2015). The visual element of Russian homophobia enshrined in the propaganda law and the international response to Russian homophobia that works through images and bodies make an exploration of the international politics of sex, visuality, and the body possible in this book. My thinking on the international politics part of sex, visuality, and the body is both funnelled through and constituted by the Russian case as a centripetal force.

While institutional responses to Russian politicised homophobia have primarily been words-based, those by non-state, civil society actors have had a distinctly visual and body component. A major part of politicised homophobia in the case of Russia is about the invisibility/visibility of queerness in society. However, this is not the only way Russian state homophobia and the visual intersect. The visual has been used to represent, bring attention to, and contest politicised homophobia by activist actors across the world. In this case, the visual is important not just in terms of the images accompanying international news coverage, as discussed in Chapter 5, but the images and other forms of (bodily) visuality mobilised to contest and undermine Russian homophobia such as Mads Nissen's photoessays, the Hidden Flag Project, and the Gay Clown Putin meme discussed in Chapters 6 to 8.

The centrality of the visual and the body in activist projects that contest Russian state homophobia is not especially new and has a historicity and connection with earlier forms of queer political protest and resistance. Visuals and the body have been used repeatedly throughout history to call attention to, condemn, and resist social and politicised homophobia globally—as highlighted in Chapter 4, which is a visual genealogy of queer and AIDS activist projects in the US. However, despite a general acknowledgement in queer and LGBT studies that politicised homophobia is often about the invisibility/visibility of non-normative sexualities and genders in society, few studies pay significant theoretical or empirical attention to the visual and body politics of sex and queer activism.[12] This project fills that void by demonstrating how the visual and the body shape international politics and are central parts of the way people—especially marginalised actors and queer activists—engage politically.

In the case of Russian state homophobia, the visual and the body are politically important in at least three ways. First, the visual is constitutive of Russian politicised homophobia: invisibility is central to Russia's homophobic oppression, and images are used to represent Russian politicised homophobia internationally, thereby shaping how we understand the phenomenon as an international political issue. It is not just queerness but queer

---

[12] Some studies give credit to the visual (e.g., Gould 2009; France 2016) but few theorise its politics.

bodies that are sought invisible. Second, images are used in international activism, contestation, and condemnation: the visual is frequently deployed to challenge state homophobia, particularly by making queerness visible and showing moments of queer rapture even in all its abject associations. Third, the visual is used to rearrange regimes of queer in/visibility: actors use different forms of visuality from the body to images and the visibility of queerness to (re)claim public space, (re)articulate queer insecurity, and (re)constitute queer subjectivities.

In each of the chapters of this book, I engage with different visual genres to theorise the different political work they do in resisting Russian state-directed politicised homophobia and co-constituting an international politics of sex. In so doing, I put forth a theorisation of the international politics of sex that focuses on sexual shame and stigma, and I outline a tripartite word-image-body theorisation of the visual that situates words, images, and bodies in a flat, non-hierarchical epistemological-ontological configuration. My theorisation of the visual is grounded in an understanding of images—and by extension bodies as visual things (see Åhäll 2018)—as polysemous and I therefore show how the visual invokes different politics depending on how they are read and co-constituted by the words, bodies, and other images that surrounded them, and the context of their circulation. There is much to be gained by bringing the visual into the study of anti-queer politics. It is a novel way of approaching sexuality and gender-based security issues (Cooper-Cunningham 2019; Hansen 2000b, 2018) as well as questions about how moralistic foreign policies are enacted and contested—particularly in terms of in/visibility. Most importantly, non-state actors across the world are using the visual as a way of intervening in international politics (Cooper-Cunningham 2022; McGarry et al. 2020). From photojournalism and photoessays to meme-making and rainbow flag waving, they are using the visual in activist practices that bring attention to and contest Russia's politicisation of sex. All of these visual interventions can be considered activist in that they confront Russian homophobic practices and invite spectators to pay attention, perhaps even to act.

To fully understand the complexity of the international politics of sex, it is important to turn away from solely looking at practices of 'high level' political actors and an analysis of words. By broadening out the sites of analysis to include the visual and the body, this book addresses the politics of the images and the bodies that have become central to the international activism contesting Russian state homophobia and heteronormative internationalism.

If we are to fully exhume the (geo)political stakes of state homophobia—and also politicised homophilia—a turn to the visual is crucial because this is how Russia's heteronormative internationalist project is being contested. Looking at the visual and the body allows for the complexities of political participation and subjectivity to emerge and for marginalised voices to be included in the discursive environment studied. The various bodily and visual engagements studied in this book, in this regard, can be considered transversal[13] phenomena that reconfigure dominant spatialisations of international politics, the actors we consider as engaging in 'the international', and the narrow conceptualisation of IR's sites and methods of analysis.

Civil society actors—usually marginalised—are using the body and the visual as ways of intervening in international politics in playful and innovative ways that reconfigure the spaces of international relations/International Relations. We have been grossly inattentive to these actors and their practices. As civil society activists (often in an individual capacity as meme-makers or photojournalists) engage in the international and push back against the Russian government's heteronormative foreign policy agenda they (re)configure how we understand what international politics is and what it means to contest foreign policy through international activism. Through the various visual and bodily responses studied here, activists from photojournalists to internet meme-makers contest and undermine the political power of Russia's heteronormative projects. In the empirical analysis, I point to this as taking place by embracing antinormativity, showing the joy of being queer, and revelling in the stigmatic abjections attached to non-normative sexuality and gender.

Queer

Picking up this point on antinormativity, I now turn to how I theorise queer in this book. I use the concept 'queer' as a way of capturing those whose sexual behaviours/desires and those whose gender falls outside of what is constituted as normal and appropriate. In doing so, I fully acknowledge that queer is not just a catch all or umbrella term (Wilcox 2014) and that many of the people I am writing about will likely use other terms to identify

---

[13] A transversal phenomenon is 'a political practice that not only transgresses national boundaries, but also questions the spatial logic through which these boundaries have come to constitute and frame the conduct of international relations' (Bleiker 2000, 2).

themselves (Riemer and Brown 2019). I do not think about queer as an identity to be occupied. Rather, it is a political, theoretical, and empirical phenomenon. Political in that it resists stable identity categories and the disciplinary, restrictive gravitational pull that 'normal' has. Theoretical in that it focuses on the power and disciplinary structures that flow from discourses about normative sex and gender. Empirical in that it focuses on those who are constituted as queer because of their non-normative sexual behaviours/desires.

Any act of translating sexualities is political and 'entangled in power politics, imperialism and foreign intervention' because 'translation happens usually from dominant to dominated languages' (Cottet and Picq 2019, 3). This means that translating sexualities or using the English word 'queer' to talk about non-Western or non-Anglosphere sexualities is a political act. No term will ever perfectly capture the waywardness of desire and sexuality. Nor will it adequately capture the multiple ways that people describe their sexual orientations or gender. When I talk about queer people, I am using queer as a descriptive but also political category for those who have been pushed to the margins, oppressed, targeted for violence because their sexual orientation or gender is (suspected to) fall outside the Russian idea of 'normal'. Queer is a way to identify those who have been constituted as threatening to society by the government and by various other civil society actors. If the political and theoretical ambitions of queer are in capturing the workings of power, hierarchies, and disciplinary structures that emerge around sexual behaviours/desires and genders that are *made* abnormal and lesser, thereby justifying their oppression or exclusion, using 'queer' to refer to individuals who may identify otherwise is the closest I can come to describing their abject location without imposing an identity upon them (Berlant 1997, 2022; Berlant and Edelman 2015; Butler 1990; Cohen 1997, 2004; Sedgwick 1993; Warner 2000). Used as such, queer works best when attempting to cover an analytical field that crosses multiple boundaries with no coherent term to capture non-normative sex(uality) that 'fits' in every space.

The term queer has been used in many different ways both within and outwith IR. Indicatively, queer scholars both within and outside of IR have focused on a variety of issues. These mainly focus on how ideas about in/appropriate sexuality and gender were/are at the core of: colonialism (Bakshi, Jivraj, and Posocco 2016; Delatolla 2020; Hoad 2000; Massad 2007; Rahman 2014b; Rao 2014a); war (Richter-Montpetit 2007, 2014; Weber 2016); mass atrocity (Biddolph 2022, 2024; Cooper-Cunningham and Kremer 2024; Gifkins and Cooper-Cunningham 2023; Gifkins et al. 2022; Jensen 2002; Waites 2018); terrorism (Gentry 2020; Puar 2007; Puar and Rai 2002; Schotten 2018); global health (Altman 2001; Bersani 1987; Schulman 2021; Youde 2020); sovereignty (Weber 1998, 2016); security (Amar 2013; Bosia 2018; Cooper-Cunningham 2022; Hagen 2016; Leigh and Weber 2019); human rights (Langlois 2014; Picq and Thiel 2015; Rao 2014b; Wilkinson 2014); homophobia (Bosia and Weiss 2013b; Currier 2019); foreign policy (Foxall 2019; Weber 1999); nationalism (Berlant 1997; Peterson 1999; Slootmaeckers 2023); state formation (Peterson 2014a, 2014b, 2021); norm diffusion (Ayoub 2015, 2016; Schulz and Thies 2024); regional integration (Ammaturo 2015; Slootmaeckers 2020, 2023); geopolitics (Wilkinson 2018); peacekeeping and humanitarian intervention (Hagen 2016; Hagen, Ritholtz, and Delatolla 2024; Vernon 2022); and political activism (Bronski 2011; Gould 2009; Schulman 2021).

Because it gets used in so many different ways and for different purposes across all of these studies, I want to be clear from the outset that I use queer with the same theoretical commitments as Lauren Berlant and Michael Warner: 'Queer social theory is committed to sexuality as an inescapable category of analysis, agitation, and refunctioning' (1998, 564). A queer analysis, for me, must also always examine deviance and be grounded in a politics that commits to the endless interrogation of relations to power (Cohen 1997, 2004). In that sense, a queer analysis does not *exclusively* focus on sexuality but always focuses on the politics of sex in some way, be it through an examination of politicised homophobia, heteronormativity, politicised homophilia, or the like. Indeed, as Cathy Cohen (1999) shows in her work on Black Politics during the AIDS crisis in the USA, sexuality is not always the exclusive focus of queer analysis, but it plays a central role.

Similar to how feminist scholars conceptualise 'gender lenses' to identify how gender hierarchies operate, my use of queer is always focused on sex (see also Stoffel and Birkvad 2023). It is an analytic sensibility, a curiosity about, and a set of 'queer lenses' that focuses on hierarchies generated around sex.[14] As such, a queer analysis in my mind always comes with an exploration of sex. Particularly, how ideas about 'normal' and 'abnormal' sex, gender, and sexuality are constituted, mobilised, and politicised. As David Halperin writes, queer is that which is 'at odds with the normal, the

---

[14] The idea of 'queer lenses' echoes Spike Peterson and Anne Sisson Runyan's conceptualisation of lenses as focusing attention selectively: 'selective attention is a necessary feature of making sense of any particular subject, practice, paradox, or social order' (2014, 40).

legitimate, the dominant' (1995, 62). It is this being at odds with, being actively antinormative, that makes queer powerful. Part of a queer analysis therefore involves paying particular attention to whether and how sexual norms are rejected and deviant subjectivity embraced by queer people. In the context of IR, this means paying attention to how actors mobilise homophobia or homophilia in their engagement with the international and in their foreign policy. And it means paying attention to how those constituted as threatening or abject because of their (suspected) sexual practices mobilise this as a means of resistance. These are epistemological-ontological points about 'queer' in that they flow from my understanding of sexuality as discursively constituted along axes of normalcy and deviance.[15] But beyond theory and concepts, queer is also an empirical phenomenon in this book in terms of who is constituted as queer, what types of sexual practices are constituted as queer, and how their defence/oppression is attached to foreign policies and international activism.

Returning to its origin story with the risk of oversimplifying the genealogy of 'queer', the term was initially deployed as a homophobic slur, but over the years it has been reclaimed to do a lot of different work (Ahmed 2023). Annamarie Jagose writes that sometimes queer has been used 'as an umbrella term for a coalition of culturally marginal sexual self-identifications and at other times to describe a nascent theoretical model which has developed out of more traditional lesbian and gay studies' (1996, 1). Similarly, I have argued that queer is variously 'used as a reference to LGBT+ issues or an umbrella term for LGBT+ identities, sometimes it refers to the destabilisation of hegemonic ideas about sexuality and gender, sometimes it references a political project grounded in antinormativity and antisociality[16] that emerged in the 1980s' (2024, 88).[17] My own use of queer is rooted in antinormative and antisocial approaches to queer thought.

In academic circles, it is vogue to talk about 'queer' as something that is amorphous, always on the move, always in flux, contested/contestable,

---

[15] In this text, I use the terms 'deviance' or 'deviant' to refer to general practices or specific subjects' behaviour deviating, diverging, or straying from the prevailing and hegemonic norms of a particular group in a particular context.

[16] 'Antisociality' means the refusal to be subsumed into the norm or folded into the neat and tidy organisations of society demanded by heteronormative sociality. Queer antisociality is contempt for dominant heteronormative organisations of society (Bersani 1987, 1996; Edelman 2004). Thus, it is also antinormative in its resistance to powerful moral discourses about 'normal' sexuality and gender performances (Warner 1999, 2000).

[17] See 'The Routledge Queer Studies Reader' for a genealogy of queer political writing (Jagose and Hall 2013).

plural, and open to reconfiguration (Butler 1993a, 228; 1993b; Richter-Montpetit 2018; Weber 2014, 2016; Wilcox 2014). While I see the benefits of this in activist practice, I am not particularly persuaded by this conceptualisation as a theoretical endeavour because it leaves queer susceptible to depoliticisation and deployment as plurality and multiplicity alone. I do not think queer should be reduced to an ontology of multiplicity or plurality. I am also not persuaded by scholarship that seeks to queer non-human entities such as drones (e.g., Clark 2018; Daggett 2015; Wilcox 2017a). I am quite uncomfortable with a conceptualisation of queer that is detached from questions of sex, gender, and sexuality, which the indeterminacy of theorising queer-as-plural has at times enabled. To detach queer theory from questions about sex, gender, and sexuality means cutting the political roots of 'queer' out from underneath it.

Queer's political roots are in gay and lesbian liberation and AIDS activism (Gould 2009; Jagose 1996; Seidman 1993). Just like feminism and post-colonial and decolonial approaches, queer as an intellectual project cannot be detached from these roots, which predominantly focused on sex and ideas about normalcy (see also Stoffel and Birkvad 2023). In particular, what moralising projects about sex do and how to liberate people from oppressive normative structures. AIDS activists, lesbian feminists, and gay liberationists all argued that homophobia and other anti-queer projects are rooted in sexism and moralising about the types of sex one is allowed to have (or desire) and legitimately pursue (Berlant and Warner 1998; Cohen 2004; Warner 1993, 2000). These moralising projects, such as the Russian one extensively engaged above, produce and sustain hegemonic orders: cis- and hetero-normative understandings of gender and sexuality are core organising principles of (international) society that sustain hierarchies and dominant power relations that privilege the cisgendered and/or hetero-sexual subject (Bersani 1987; Foucault 1978; McIntosh 1968; Rubin 2011; Warner 2000).

To think about queer analysis as always intimately bound up in questions about sex, sexuality, and gender, as I do, is not to say that only queer theory can ask such questions as Wilcox (2014, 612) suggests it might. Rather, it is to give some analytical and political substance to queer theorising such that it is not left unanchored as an approach of simply destabilising all sorts of norms or boundaries unrelated to sexuality. Returning to Berlant and Warner's emphatic position that sexuality must remain the category of analysis of queer work, sexual shame and stigma are what I focus on when I say

I am using a queer approach. This accounts for the power structures and normative organisations of society that flow from what is, at a meta level, arbitrary moralising[18] about sex, pleasure, and desire (Cooper-Cunningham 2024, 89). When one focuses on the politics of sexual shame and stigma, this entails a queer curiosity about the way stigmatising and shaming practices about supposedly 'deviant' sexuality and gender are mobilised for violent hierarchical, exclusionary, and disciplinary social and political projects. In the context of IR this means paying attention to how such projects of sexual moralism 'go international' and get organised into a sexualised geopolitics.

The focus of this book, as I have emphasised many times, is not just on Russian homophobia and its geopolitical project, it is also on international contestation of these projects. Russia's heteronormative project has been met with staunch resistance (and acceptance) both domestically and internationally. Reading this resistance through a queer lens is important. Given that resistance is such a central part of the empirical material, it is important to recall the political and more activist origins of 'queer' in liberationist thinking. In this type of queer activism and queer scholarship, antinormativity was a core theoretical agenda. Queer politics and queer theory emerged out of a resistance to the stigmatisation of non-normative object desire and sexual behaviour. It emerged in opposition to the moralism of straight culture about appropriate, acceptable, and normal sexual practices (Berlant and Warner 1995; Bersani 1987, 1996; Butler 1993b; Cohen 1997; Warner 1993, 2000). And it took on a particularly potent form as the AIDS crisis unfolded and the moralists wheeled out the 'gay menace' and 'divine retribution' discourses that further stigmatised non-normative sexual behaviour, especially sodomy and promiscuity (Gould 2009, 74–6, 194).

Deborah Gould writes that identifying as 'gay, lesbian, or queer' during the onset of the AIDS pandemic was 'to travel close to, and sometimes fall over, the precipice of abjection' (2009, 74). It remains so today. Writing in this antinormative vein, Lauren Berlant argues that 'a politics that advocates the subaltern appropriation of normative forms of the good life [bound up in and reproduced through norms] makes a kind of (often tacit) peace

---

[18] When I say arbitrary moralising about sexual pleasure and desire, I refer to the meta argument that any attempt to police the wayward workings of desire is futile and therefore all normative constitutions of moral/appropriate sexuality are arbitrarily drawn lines in the sand. As Warner writes: 'Sex has a politics of its own. Hierarchies of sex sometimes serve no real purpose except to prevent sexual variance. They create victimless crimes, imaginary threats, and moralities of cruelty' (2000, 25). This does not mean that the lived experience of sexual norms and the political context in which heteronormativity governs is negligible and without adversity.

with exploitation and normativity' (1997, 9). In this regard, the political-theoretical work of queer is to refuse to make peace with normativity. The antinormative in queer is about resisting normativity and not differentiating between legitimate and illegitimate ways of living or (sexual) orientation: it maintains 'discomfort with all aspects of normative culture' (Ahmed 2013, 426). Antinormativity is not, therefore, always about transcending norms, about being free from their touch/grasp, or about pure destabilisation, but about undermining their power exactly through non-transcendence. By shifting the analytical focus of queer from multiplicity or a banal disturbing of gendered and sexualised binaries, my use of antinormative queer thought in this book marks a significant political and epistemic shift for Queer IR. Refusing a heteronormative epistemology within which deviation from the heteronorm is constituted or perceived as undesirable, queer as an antinormative project commits to embracing and flaunting 'deviance' because that deviance is not undesirable when one's epistemological position starts from a place where sexual shame is bedrock and there are no hierarchies of sexual legitimacy and value.

Refusing to defend one's sexual orientation or gender identity as 'normal', refusing to conform to normative sexuality or gender, and actively embracing one's constitution as an abject subject—as comes through in my empirics—are antinormative practices and they are generative, antagonistic practices that stock the shelves of queer's political pantry. Queer antinormativity is powerful 'precisely in the face of the persistence of forms of life that endure in the negative attachment of "the not"' (Ahmed 2013, 437). This version of 'queer' positions queer existence and some forms of queer-supporting activism as 'fierce pride in bucking political, emotional, and sexual norms' (Gould 2009, 264). A queer politics that invites radical transformation of society and politics is eternally oppositional, anti-assimilationist, deliberately antisocial, attendant to every relation to power, and adopts an ethics that 'cuts against every form of hierarchy' (Warner 2000, 36). This may seem out of place when read in the abstract and without empirical anchoring, but the antinormative strand of queer activism and theory—almost completely dismissed by Queer IR scholars without any substantial debate—becomes important in this book's empirical analysis of visual and bodily resistances to Russia's heteronormative domestic and foreign policy projects. Antinormative queer theorising is the lens—admittedly not the only one possible—through which I unpack the political in these resistances and how they agitate the Russian project and dominant normative structures in ways that have hitherto been unexplored.

Plan of the Book

In Chapters 2 and 3, I outline the theoretical foundations of the book, speaking specifically to my use of queer and visual theories. Drawing on queer theory and IR literature about stigma and shame, Chapter 2 outlines how I theorise the international politics of sex and the practices of shaming and stigmatising that sit at its core. My main argument in this regard is that states actively shame particular sexual practices and that these shameful sexual acts get attached to particular groups of people, marking them with an abject identity, thereby becoming stigmatising. This stigmatisation often operates simultaneously across international and domestic spheres as this stigmatisation of queer people, which manifests in politicised homophobia, is mobilised by that state in its foreign policy that marks other states as abject for their acceptance of queerness. I call this *heteronormative internationalism*: when heterosexism and homophobia become explicitly articulated parts of an actor's foreign policy and geopolitical strategy. A similar process occurs, sometimes simultaneously with domestic politicised homophobia, when homophilia is used as part of foreign policy to stigmatise homophobic states for their violence against queer people.

In Chapter 3, I theorise the relationship between words, images, and bodies, as well as the political work that different visual genres do. Chapter 3 outlines a poststructuralist theorisation of the social and political before introducing a tripartite word-image-body approach to studying international politics. Where Chapter 2 focuses on how sex is a matter of international politics, Chapter 3 is more about the epistemological and ontological moves I make to study the international politics of sexual shame and stigma and its contestation. The principal move I make here builds on some of my earlier work on the British Suffragettes' (2019) and AIDS activists' (2025) use of images and their bodies to set out a tripartite word-image-body approach for studying international politics. In so doing, I show how my approach captures a wide range of actors and cuts through traditional levels of analysis in IR.

In Chapter 4, I introduce visual genealogy as a method of social science research. Drawing on archival work conducted at the New York Public

Library, I offer an analysis that traces the evolution of several globalised symbols of queer activism and resistance, situating them in relation to contemporary activism. The purpose of this chapter is to unfold the genealogy of queer symbols, which enables a more thorough and contextualised interpretation of the images used in international contestations of Russian state homophobia. The empirical material engaged in this chapter is primarily from New York's gay and lesbian liberation movements and AIDS activism. The genealogy is important for the book because it allows me to trace the visual dis/continuities in queer activism as well as the different politics that the various symbols appearing in queer activism against Russia represent. Importantly, this genealogy not only traces the evolution of queer visual activism but also offers a genealogy of queer politics. It brings out the tension between rights-based activism and more radical queer politics. Had I not gone to the archive to trace the visual patterns and practices in earlier forms of queer activism, this book would have looked drastically different in terms of the analysis offered in the empirical chapters.

The second more empirical half of the book is structured in line with the theoretical and methodological argument I make about words, images, and bodies requiring equal onto-epistemic standing. In the empirical chapters, I shift the emphasis between words, images, and bodies in order to show how my tripartite approach can be mobilised. Importantly, I cover multiple visual modalities and genres, moving from more traditional press photojournalism (Chapters 5 and 6) to visual-bodily acts of contestation (Chapter 7) to more playful visual artefacts such as memes (Chapter 8). Across these different genres, there is some trace of the body. Be that the visualisation of actual bodies protesting in the street or more abstract representations of their disciplining. While all of the chapters engage with words, images, and bodies, they each have a slightly different emphasis. Covering several visual genres means that I am able to include a series of different voices and actors that contest Russia's heteronormative geopolitical project over a six-year period between 2013 and 2019.

The material engaged across Chapters 5 through 8 ranges from reports and statements issued by international institutions; international media reporting and statements by international sport bodies; visual images (e.g., photographs, memes), and visual artefacts (e.g., flags, parades). Bringing this variety of material together enables a wide-ranging exploration of the visual politics of queer international activism and includes important actors that would disappear if one only focused on 'official' sources. I vary the empirical material not only with the theoretical ambition of establishing the different political work different genres of image do, but also to bring in and think about the way marginalised actors engage in international politics—in this case activism around a heteronormative domestic and foreign policy agenda. All of their responses can be broadly considered activist: political activism can take many forms from service provision to lobbying to applying diplomatic pressure to direct action to marching in the street (Gould 2009, 51). I focus specifically on responses that come from outside Russia in order to understand how international activism unfolds in response to a geopolitical project rooted in moralising about appropriate sexual behaviours and erotic desires. Given that Russian politicised homophobia has international ambitions, how that normative internationalist agenda is contested from without is key.

2

The International Politics of Sexual Shame and Stigma

Wendy Brown argues that 'political power does not come in only one variety' (1995, 175). Brown's argument resonates with how I think about international politics: there is not only one variety of power; rather, it has many diffuse, intersecting, and sometimes surprising vectors. While my work is rooted in an amalgam of queer, feminist, and poststructuralist epistemologies and ontologies, I am not particularly invested in advancing one vector of power—be it material capabilities, institutions, rules, norms, economy, class, gender, culture, racial, and ethnic domination, identities, discourse— as more important than another for understanding international politics. What I offer here is a framework that accounts for the role that moralising politics—particularly that about 'normal' and 'appropriate' sex and sexualities—plays in states' foreign policies, as well as the way that sexual shame and stigma are mobilised as part of a Russian geopolitical project that carves the world into decadent, uncivilised queer spaces versus traditional, moral, civilised spaces. There is currently no framework that handles *sexual* shame and stigma in international politics so, drawing on works from across IR and queer studies, I build one.

To begin, I want to highlight two observations emphasised by queer theorists Gayle Rubin (2011), Michael Warner (2000), and Lauren Berlant (1997), using them as points of departure for an analysis of international politics. First, sex has achieved such a prestigious and privileged position in many societies that its governance, management, and regulation seem totally necessary and natural. Second, sex often gets constituted as nationally concerning (Essig 1999; Lazarus 2011; Nagel 2003). We see these in play when governments legislate around reproductive freedoms or appropriate forms of consensual sex, when politicians make discursive moves to constitute reproduction as some form of national duty, or when powerful social and political figures begin to argue that the sexual politics of another state threatens the cultural sovereignty or national

The International Politics of Sex. Dean Cooper-Cunningham, Oxford University Press.
© Oxford University Press (2025). DOI: 10.1093/9780197792544.003.0002

security of theirs. Generally speaking, though, sex is usually constituted as a 'private' matter; as something entirely unrelated to foreign policy or geopolitics. Despite this façade of privateness, the regulation and management of sex are important parts of international politics. This was the case during European colonialism in the nineteenth and twentieth centuries and it is the case with Russia's contemporary attempts to reconfigure international order using arguments of Western civilisational decay in the twenty-first.

The privileging of some forms of sex (i.e., sex that is reproductive and between those of opposite sex/gender) usually involves complex and sometimes plain bizarre moves by state actors to link sexuality to international hierarchies of cultures, societies, nations, states, and civilisations. This operates in a similar fashion to how Ann Towns (2010) describes states and their positioning around 'the woman question'. Policing of 'good' and 'bad' sex often comes with some imaginary of national crisis should this 'bad' non-normative sex go unchecked (Berlant 1997; Rubin 2011). This 'good sex' versus 'bad sex' boundary is established through moralising discourses that create a hierarchy between different sexual practices and the subjects engaged in them. It is this hierarchy, which variously empowers and disempowers certain subjects, that makes these moralising discourses political. Like all moral discourses, those about sex usually do not exist in isolation. They tend to be strategically mobilised in service of larger political projects that require some form of bogeyman (Bosia and Weiss 2013a). For example, nobody could argue that the Nazi's campaign during World War Two was entirely about sex, but thousands of suspected queer people (predominantly those suspected of being gay men) were constituted as unnatural, impure threats to the Nazi's ideological project of purification (Heger 1980; Plant 1986; Waites 2018). As such, like Jewish people, they were rounded up, sent to concentration camps, and murdered in service of an imperial project. Policing 'unnatural' sex was part of this.

In queer studies, scholars argue that shame and stigma are sociologically crucial to the way that individuals' and groups' non-normative[1] sexual behaviours and desires become constituted as immoral and abject (Rubin 2011; Warner 2000). Shame and stigma are vital for creating in and out groups. Similarly, practices of stigmatisation between states are

---

[1] Defined in footnote 6 in *Introduction*.

studied by those in IR seeking to understand how hierarchies, norms, and power struggles in the international system play out (Adler-Nissen 2014; Adler-Nissen and Zarakol 2021; Kurowska and Reshetnikov 2021; Zarakol 2014). Between states, they create the 'goodies' and the 'baddies', those deserving of respect (or, at the very least tolerance) and the stigmatised. These works in IR tend not to address sex as part of stigmatising processes or as part of states' foreign policy projects and geopolitical visions (an exception is Rogstad 2022). Nor do they tend to draw on queer theory to understand this phenomenon. The lack of conversation between IR and queer studies scholars is not uncommon but it is surprising because scholars in queer studies, who broadly speaking take sex and sexuality as their object of study, have examined other issues closely linked to some of IR's key foci: states, their formation, and their disciplinary power; foreign policy; order versus anarchy; security; norms and ideas.[2] Bringing together research on shame and stigma from queer studies and from IR helps analyse the geopolitics of sex, sexually normative foreign policies, and how sexual shame and stigma go international.

In what follows, I outline the politics of sex, shame, and stigma. Then, I build on and develop the literature on politicised homophilia and politicised homophobia to theorise an *international politics of sex* characterised by *sexual shame and stigma*. Third, I introduce the concept of *heteronormative internationalism* to capture how some states' foreign policies and geopolitical imaginaries are marked by a discourse of exporting and defending heteronormativity and 'traditional values' internationally. In Russia, as outlined, this has manifested as a discourse about 'saving Europe from itself' and 'defending true Europe' (Gaufman 2017; Healey 2018; Rogstad 2022). In the concluding part of the chapter, I link forward to Chapter 3, pointing briefly to the visual and body politics of Russian heteronormative internationalism and international contestation of it. What follows is a framework to understand *the international politics of sexual shame and stigma* emerging around Russian state homophobia. While I am focused on a Russia-West confrontation, this framework could be applied more broadly.

---

[2] This is something that Cynthia Weber (2014, 597; 2015b, 27–8), and Laura Sjoberg and Cameron Thies (2023) point out.

The Politics of Sex: Shame and Stigma

In this section, I draw on queer theorists who have argued that sex has a politics that operates through shame and stigmatisation, bringing this into conversation with IR scholarship on the ways that stigma works between states. At this point, it is important to reiterate how I use the term queer. Queer is both a theoretical perspective and an empirical phenomenon. Theoretically, I understand queer in a similar way to how many IR feminists think about gender: as a lens. Where gender is the primary lens for feminists, sex/sexuality is the primary lens for me. This means queer is an analytic approach that directs attention to the hierarchies generated around sex, paying particular attention to how ideas about 'normal' and 'abnormal' sex and sexuality are constituted, mobilised, and politicised. A queer approach critically examines societal norms around sexuality and gender and explores how power structures influence and construct sexual categories. In terms of the empirical component, queerness in international politics comes in mainly through the politicisation of sex as part of foreign policy, the embedding of heteronormative ideals in geopolitical struggles, and international actors' activism around state homophobia.

I have suggested above that the primary lens for feminist IR scholars has been gender and the primary lens for the version of queer theory I am using is sex/sexuality. This does not mean that the two are mutually exclusive. Gender and sexuality are connected in the sense that desire for the opposite sexed/gendered body is assumed natural and 'normal', whereas desire for the same is constituted as a deviation from normative sexual and gender order.[3] One of the names given to this normative programme is heteronormativity: that is, the structures of understanding that privilege heterosexuality.[4] Deviating from heteronormativity comes with significant costs (Warner 2000, 38) and is therefore best conceptualised in structural terms as 'a fundamental motor of social organisation' (Berlant and Warner

---

[3] On exactly this, in January 2025, the International Criminal Court recognised how gender and sexuality are intertwined when issuing arrest warrants for Taliban leaders in Afghanistan for committing Crimes Against Humanity against women, girls, and the LGBTI+ community. Using existing international law on gender-based violence, the ICC Prosecutor Karim Khan, included LGBTI+ populations in the ICC's work for the first time.

[4] As outlined in the introduction, I follow Berlant and Warner, defining heteronormativity as 'the institutions, structures of understanding, and practical orientations that make heterosexuality seem not only coherent—that is, organized as a sexuality—but also privileged'. Cisnormativity refers to the privilege and normalcy afforded to those who identify with the gender they were assigned at birth.

1998, 564). Heteronormativity is powerful, it is ordering, and it disciplines people into particular ways of being. The result is often that those (suspected of) practicing sexual behaviours that deviate from the normative programme 'are subjected to a presumption of mental illness, disreputability, criminality, restricted social and physical mobility, loss of institutional support, and economic sanctions' (Rubin 2011, 149). This has led to the persecution and securitization of certain sexualities and genders. When it comes to the state and nationalism, the constitution of sexual or gender deviance is often done in relation to national security or cultural sovereignty, and manifests specifically in practices of state homophobia.

For Michael Warner (2000), who builds on Erving Goffman's work, heteronormativity works through processes of sexual shaming and stigmatisation that simultaneously erect and police the iron borders of 'normal' sex and desire. Warner argues that stigma, shame, and moralism about appropriate sexual behaviour and erotic desire are essential in upholding the aforementioned dichotomy of perverse versus normal sex and gender. It is in this sense that sexual shame is political: 'shame and opprobrium … are political resources that some people use to silence or isolate others' and it 'works as a means to power' (Warner 2000, 16, 18). Whereas shame is linked to specific acts, stigma is much stickier and is 'a mark on the body' that constitutes 'the person, not the deed, as tainted' (Warner 2000, 27–8). To deviate from normative sexuality—which names appropriately gendered objects of desire and types of sex—is to engage in shameful acts. When these desires/acts are constituted as identities and as the very essence of one's being—as has been the case since sexual acts, erotic desires, and bodily pleasures were transformed into social identities one occupies—they invite stigmatisation (Foucault 1978; Warner 2000, 29). Through shame and stigma, sexual normativity forecloses any possibility of sexual autonomy by preventing and punishing any form of variation or deviation from the rule. 'The moralists', Warner writes, 'work very hard to make sure that this happens' (2000, 12). That moralism can be directed at various actors, be they individuals, groups, states, or the like.

Investigating this moralism around sex, queer theorists focus on how shameful acts and stigmatised individuals/groups are constituted as lesser, deviant, abnormal; always measured against and positioned below discursively produced ideas of the 'normal'. It is this hierarchical element that queer theorists emphasise as central to thinking about the politics of sex.

Particularly, how it enables and justifies privilege and oppression. Drawing on Gayle Rubin (2011), Warner argues that:

> Sex has a politics of its own. Hierarchies of sex sometimes serve no real purpose except to prevent sexual variance. They create victimless crimes, imaginary threats, and moralities of cruelty. Rubin notes: 'The criminalization of innocuous behaviors such as homosexuality, prostitution, obscenity, or recreational drug use is rationalized by portraying them as menaces to health and safety, women and children, national security, the family, or civilization itself.' These rationalizations obscure the intent to shut down sexual variance.
>
> (Warner 2000, 25)

Like Foucault in *The History of Sexuality Vol. 1*, Warner is interested in who manages sex and what politics and subject positions flow from that management (see Berlant 2022, 65–6; Foucault 1978). In other words, how people's sexual autonomy is constrained and what sorts of punishment are handed out for deviating from a socially constituted idea of 'normal' sexuality. Following this tranche of work, the conceptual anchor of 'queer' as I use it is a focus on the politics of sex and the power structures that flow from normative, moralistic formulations of appropriate/deviant sexuality and gender. Importantly, as Cathy Cohen points out, '[d]ifference, in and of itself—even that difference designated through named categories—is not the problem … it is the power invested in certain identity categories and the idea that bounded categories are not to be transgressed that serve as the basis of domination and control' (1997, 461). In this sense, binary difference is not *a priori* violent and oppressive, it is only when hierarchies and rigid boundaries are introduced that such dichotomies become oppressive.[5] These hierarchies can be rearranged but never fully eliminated.

Urging queer scholars and activists to take (deviant) sex as a focus rather than sexual identities such as lesbian or gay, Cohen (1997, 1999, 2004, 2023) repeatedly argues that while queer analysis should maintain a focus on sex and sexuality, it must not limit itself to a focus on sexual practices/desires *as identities* (i.e., the LGBTI+ model). To do so is to miss the disciplining

---

[5] This is a reason why I am drawn to the antinormative theorisation of queer I outline in the introduction. To destabilise or think multiply is not always to escape hierarchies and disciplining, especially when binary difference is not always violent. Furthermore, difference is ontologically necessary.

and oppression of all those whose sexual practices/desires fall outside what is constituted as 'normal' and societally acceptable—even if those engaged in non-normative sexual practices identify as (predominantly) heterosexual/straight. Yes, one of the core pillars of queer politics is 'a fundamental challenge to heteronormativity' but 'heteronormativity interacts with institutional racism, patriarchy, and class exploitation to define us in numerous ways as marginal and oppressed subjects' and the 'power and entitlement of normative heterosexuality' does not neatly map onto all heterosexual bodies (Cohen 1997, 445, 446, 447; see also: Rubin 2011). Keeping this in mind, a queer analysis is focused expressly on the politics of non-/normative sex, not on homosexuality *per se*. As such, when I talk about a queer analysis of foreign policy and geopolitics, I follow Warner's 'deliberately capacious' use of the term queer:

> in order to suggest how many ways people can find themselves at odds with straight culture. 'Homophobia' is a misleading term for what they equally resist, because it suggests that the stigma and oppression directed against this entire range of people can be explained simply as a phobic reaction to same-sex love. In fact, sexual stigmas are more shifty than we think. Gay men and lesbians have been a principal target, but a political movement that defines its constituency solely as 'gay men and lesbians' blinds itself both to the subtlety of the oppressive culture and to the breadth of the possible resistances.
>
> (Warner 2000, 38–9)

Relatedly, Cohen's insistence on focusing on *deviance* rather than sexual identities is important because sexual shame and stigma are social, meaning that they are broad, unstable concepts susceptible to change. Just as today's sexual deviants are not always exactly the same as those in the past, tomorrow's sexual deviants are not necessarily the same as today's, and this differs across space too (Bakshi, Jivraj, and Posocco 2016; Cohen 2004; Cottet and Picq 2019; Duggan 2002). Furthermore, sexual shame and stigma are not necessarily directed solely at particular identity groups, even if it befalls them more often:

> The stigma that we call homophobia ... can descend on people for a lot of different reasons, and many of them are not exactly the same as being gay or homosexual ... so even an expanded catalog of identities can remain blind

to the ways people [including heterosexuals] suffer, often indiscriminately, from gender norms, object-orientation norms, norms of sexual practice, and norms of subjective identification.

(Warner 2000, 37, 39)

The effect of sexual normativity is discipline and control of each and every one of us. Every discursive move constituting 'normal sex' is a move to delimit and determine who and/or what we sleep with and how we get bodily pleasure and joy. In this sense, the politics of sex is not just about LGBTI+ people, it is about the sexual autonomy of everyone: shaming certain sex acts and stigmatising particular people/groups infringes upon everyone's (sexual) autonomy. Even if we were somehow able to prove that heterosexuality is the default and only 'natural' (i.e., non-social) orientation, such primordial sex need not be the only legitimate option: the possibility of variation is both a precondition and outcome of sexual autonomy (Warner 2000, 11–12, 17). Normative sexuality, then, affects *everyone* and its main source of power comes from the shaming and stigmatisation of those who do not or cannot be made to conform with so-called normal sexuality. Shame and stigma are discursively produced and have a policing effect.

Focusing on the 'deviant' sexual practices that have been stigmatised as part of a state's domestic and foreign policy, I suggest, opens up the possibility of: (a) studying the loose architecture of the international order envisioned by that state, defined primarily by what it is not and does not support; and (b) being 'witness to the power of those at the bottom, whose everyday life decisions challenge, or at least counter, the basic normative assumptions of a society intent on protecting structural and social inequalities under the guise of some normal and natural [international] order to life' (Cohen 2004, 33). This leads me into the international political dimensions of sexual shame and stigma.

Sexual Moralism and International Politics

We know that stigmatisation plays a large part in creating an 'out group' in international society and that stigma can sometimes be positively reconfigured by the stigmatised party to their advantage (Adler-Nissen 2014; Adler-Nissen and Zarakol 2021; Altman and Symons 2016; Kurowska and Reshetnikov 2021; Warner 1999, 2000; Wilkinson 2018, 2019; Zarakol

2014). But we know relatively little about how *sexual* shame and stigma work in terms of international politics and foreign policy. In other words, for all the scholarship about international society's and the international system's working, how *sexual* shame and stigma are deployed at the international level to carve the world into decadent, uncivilised queer spaces versus traditional, moral, civilised spaces is largely absent.

Writing about international politics, Rebecca Adler-Nissen argues that 'stigmas are the result of historical interactions that produce not just deviant behavior, but deviant identities, which may remain "spoiled" even after behavioral change' (2014, 146). Frédéric Mégret echoes this, arguing that stigma has the sociopolitical role of 'delineating socially acceptable and inacceptable behavior, forming a society's deep sense of self, and constituting a society through the designation of its "other"' (2013, 288). Thus, stigmatisation is always about discursively constituting conditions that bring about respect for particular beliefs, traditions, practices: 'stigma is both an expression of the inherent moral blameworthiness assigned to the perpetrators of certain heinous acts and a way of constituting the society that assigns this blameworthiness' (Mégret 2013, 290).

In this sense, stigma is generative and relational. If the discursive constitution of an Other is ontologically necessary for the production of the Self and for the state's security-provider *raison d'être*, stigma is ontologically necessary for shaping and defining both that Other and the Self. It is, therefore, co-constitutive of Self and Other. Stigma is also important with regard to establishing hierarchies; the successfully stigmatised occupy a lesser position. For example, Russia's *sexual* stigmatisation of both the individuals engaged in/desiring non-normative sex as well as the states defending those individuals—or even just not actively, explicitly, and violently oppressing them—is generative across the domestic and international (see Figures 2.2 and 2.3). Domestically, it orders society, restricting the sexual autonomy of the Russian population, and constituting queerness as deviant and abhorrent, expressing Russia as the antithesis of 'Gayropa'. Internationally, it opens up space for a new international order patterned by anti-queer politics, the attempted eradication of sexual difference, the shaming of non-reproductive/non-traditional/non-heterosexual sex, and the stigmatisation of a collection of states dubbed 'Gayropean' who harbour 'extremist' LGBTI+ organisations.

Sexuality, National Identity, and Politicised Homophobia

As should be clear both from the above and my lengthy discussion of Russian politics in the introduction, national identity and sexuality are often conflated. Albeit a potent example, Russia is just one of many examples that demonstrate the way that polities define their collective identity in sexual and gendered terms. Queer scholars have been exploring how sexuality is tied to the nation for a long time.[6] They argue that one can speak of an implicit national sexuality (Berlant 1997; Berlant and Freeman 1992).[7] Lauren Berlant argues that most of us 'experience the world as permeated by the practices and narratives' of 'heteronormative culture—a public culture, juridical, economic, and aesthetic, organized for the promotion of a world-saturating heterosexuality' (1997, 16). This heteronormative culture brings sexuality and the national fantasy into contact first in 'the regulation of "perversion" on behalf of a heterofamilial citizenship norm' and second when 'the modal form of the citizen is called into question, when it is no longer a straight, white, reproductively inclined heterosexual but rather might be anything, any jumble of things, the logic of the national future comes into crisis' (Berlant 1997, 18). When changes (perceived by some as crises) begin around the economy, politics, and the juridical, when comfortable sexual and gendered subjectivities and identities become questionable, when the constructedness of the 'state' becomes visible and perceptible, 'a virulent form of national heterosexuality [is usually] invented' (Berlant 1997, 19).

Similar to Berlant, Joane Nagel argues that 'the domestic and international politics of ethnicity revolve around the defence of ethnic homelands from sexual invasion and attack' and that 'strategies of competition and domination include the sexual control of ethnic Others' bodies and territories' (2003, 10). She continues that there is:

a[n] often hidden feature of ethnicity and nationality ... its presumed heterosexuality. Part of the reason for this heteroassumptivity is the close connection between family and community in ethnic, racial, and national

[6] One of the most inspiring and enlightening pieces of queer scholarship on state-building and sexuality that I have read is V. Spike Peterson's political history of writing technologies and how they 'materialize the normalization of (hetero)gender binaries in thought ... and practice' (1999, 35).

[7] Depending on how far from the normative a subject is or how vociferously normative sexuality is imposed by state (adjacent) actors, this national sexuality can be explicit too.

groups. Homosexuality does not fit easily into ideologies stressing traditional family life as the cornerstone of ethnic community. Thus, homophobia is a common feature of racial, ethnic, and nationalist ideologies and programs of social control. Unlike racism and prejudice that seek targets *outside* ethnic boundaries, homophobia can be directed *inside* ethnic communities as well, and used to create an internal sexual boundary that excludes or 'disqualifies' a group's own members.

(Nagel 2003, 26)

Engaging in 'abject' sex is not, however, reserved for those who might most readily be understood as 'queer' though (e.g., the LGBT). Nagel demonstrates this and the connection between the nation and sex using French women collaborators with German forces during World War Two. During liberation, those who were suspected of having sexually collaborated with the Nazis during the occupation were marched through the streets with shaved heads (2003, 140–141).[8] The abject sex in this case was heterosexual. What this example neatly captures is that shaming and stigmatising certain 'undesirable' and 'treacherous' sexual practices has the effect of 'strengthen[ing] hegemonic national sexual orders' and shows how 'national and sexual boundaries are mutually reinforcing' (Nagel 2003, 141). Similar to the Russian case, the French case is about the prescriptions and proscriptions around sexuality for 'good citizens' that accompany national imaginaries. The governance of acceptable sexual practices and desires—in peacetime and conflict—involves the permission of some sexual practices and prohibition of certain non-normative practices. This is enforced through stigma, shame, and discourses about 'normal'. When this stigma and shame are directed at individuals or groups we would place under the LGBT acronym, we tend to call this homophobic—something I unpack in the next section.

Speaking specifically to the intersections of Russian nationalism and sexuality, Laurie Essig emphasises that:

In the same way that sexuality employs a language of gender, it also speaks in the idiom of nation … Nationness is not only different among nations, but it also performs differently within a nation. 'Being' Russian, like 'being' a man, depends not only upon geographical and cultural boundaries, but lines of class, gender, ethnicity, education, and of course, sexuality.

(Essig 1999, 123)

[8] Lee Miller famously photographed these women in her role as a (war) photographer and correspondent for *Vogue*. The images of these sexualised-gendered bodies in conflict were printed in *Vogue* in 1944.

Given the connection between (reproductive) heterosexuality and nationalism, we can speak of *heteronationalism*. Highlighting how racism, ethnocentrism, patriarchy, and heterosexism come together in nation building, heteronationalism is a concept that captures how 'nations must always be heterosexualized to ensure the reproduction of citizens, just as they may also be racialized and gendered to ensure the construction of national boundaries and bodies' (Gosine 2009, 98 in Lazarus 2011, 82). Scholarship on 'heteronationalism' emphasises that state homophobia is used to ensure compliance with the heteronormative script that constitutes national identity and the boundaries of the body politic.[9] Writing specifically about Jamaica, Latoya Lazarus (2011, 81) points out that 'nationalist and moral anxieties about the possible implications of legitimisation, visibility, and "spread" of homosexuality' underpin heteronationalism. Heteronationalism is the promotion of virulent heterosexuality, pro-natalism, and commitment to performing 'traditional' gender norms in domestic and foreign policy, and, thus, national identity. It is also an exercise of boundary drawing and establishing the outer limits of national identity, rooted in sexual and gender politics: 'heteronormative nationalism ... relies on the exclusion of [queer people] from the nation' (Slootmaeckers 2019, fn. 3). This brings me to the literature on politicised homophobia in IR, which although it does not often use the language of sexual shame and stigma or that of heteronationalism, is about exactly that.

Politicised Homophobia

Michael Bosia and Meredith Weiss (2013b) encourage Queer IR scholars to direct their focus to homophobia. Homophobia is rooted in sexual shaming and stigmatisation. Focusing on homophobia analytically is a useful way to identify when sexual shame and stigma are in play. In the most general sense, *homophobia* involves moralising about sex, desire, and bodily pleasure in ways that produce, sustain, and secure heteronormativity as the norm and

---

[9] Unlike homonationalism, where some non-normative sexualities are brought under the protection of the state, heteronationalism is heteronormative nationalism that rests on the exclusion and/or elimination of queers from the nation (Slootmaeckers 2019). This, in Russia, is paired with a desire to spread this heteronormative worldview externally—hence, heteronormative internationalism. Vis-à-vis Russia, this might actually be described as anti-homonationalism: 'a refusal of the EU's and the West's supposed promotion of the virtues of their human rights regimes for LGBT citizens. These contests play out in a context of geopolitical jostling for influence over the region between Russia ... and the European Union, which sharpened drastically after the Ukrainian crisis of 2014' (Healey 2018, 201).

that which should be universally shared. *Politicised homophobia* is a little different: it is the strategic use of homophobia in service of some political end, regardless of any 'real' hatred of those who deviate from heteronormative sexuality. Bosia and Weiss conceptualise *politicised homophobia* as a modular phenomenon that can be attached to various political projects. For them, politicised homophobia is an actively mobilised practice, 'a purposive strategy adopted by state and social actors' with no innate qualities (2013a, 15). It is 'the totality of strategies and tools, both in policy and in mobilizations, through which holders of and contenders over state authority invoke sexual minorities as objects of opprobrium and targets of persecution' (Bosia 2013a, 31).

The political ends sought by mobilising homophobia can range anywhere from gaining election votes to underpinning an internationalist project that pits itself as a rival to the liberal international order. It involves the disparaging and constituting as deviant those sexualities that do not align with heteronormative prescriptions of good, normal, natural sex and desire (Bosia and Weiss 2013a; Currier 2019, 11; Rubin 2011; Warner 2000, 25). Essentially, it is fear of the queer, that which is at odds with straight culture, and which crosses the line between good and bad sexual practices and gender performances. For example, the gay propaganda law—a type of legislation not unique to Russia but now increasingly popular globally—prohibits any positive public representation of non-heteronormative sexuality and gender. It is a key part of Russian state homophobia that polices the boundaries of Russianness. The law is simultaneously the product of a strategic use of homophobia for political gain and crucial to the sustenance of the heteronationalist project.

Both homophobia and politicised homophobia require some element of shame around specific acts and stigmatisation of entire collectives for permitting or engaging in those acts. Understanding how sexual desires and pleasures are legitimised and policed, as well as how homophobia is often mobilised for political gain is vitally important as we enter a post-liberal international order characterised by deep culture wars and a polarising debate about appropriate sexual behaviours, eros, and gender expressions (Ayoub and Stoeckl 2024; Cooper-Cunningham and Kremer 2024; Gifkins and Cooper-Cunningham 2023). States have always policed the types of consensual sex and desire their population are allowed to engage in and seek out; who they are legitimately allowed to desire. These projects of disciplining are not only oriented domestically towards states' own populations. In some cases (increasingly more), the constitution of certain sexual behaviours as 'decadent', 'unnatural', and 'non-traditional' has started to form the basis of foreign policy, taking a prominent place in the advancement of a moral geopolitics centred around ideas about so-called traditional values and protecting the family.

Looking across Europe alone, one can find several examples of politicised homophobia from Hungary to Italy, the United Kingdom to Poland, Serbia to Lithuania, Russia and beyond. While scholars of politicised homophobia argue that its *modularity* (Bosia and Weiss 2013a, 5–7) precludes the specification of 'an exhaustive typology for when, how, and why political elites turn to this strategy' (Currier 2019, 20), in the contemporary moment there are several elements that are common across instances of politicised homophobia. These commonalities form a very loose anatomy of politicised homophobia, including some or all of the following: targeting queer visibility (e.g., propaganda laws); emphasising traditional values (e.g., religious, family, cultural); constituting queerness as a foreign imports (e.g., discourses of 'foreign agents' or 'foreign influence' or 'Western imposed values' or 'cultural sovereignty'); crafting a narrative of queer civilisational decay (e.g., 'Gayropa'); a turn towards more authoritarian, sometimes populist, politics and the decay of democratic institutions (e.g., when Hungary used executive orders to change the constitution during the Covid-19 pandemic); and, increasingly, targeting trans individuals.

Homophobia, broadly defined, 'remains not just alive, but aggressively kicking' (Bosia and Weiss 2013a, 7; see also Currier 2019). Focusing on sexual shame and stigma as it manifests in the particular practice of *politicised homophobia* is incredibly useful for examining how sexuality has been used as a tool in geopolitics. In the case of this book, looking at Russian state homophobia opens a window to its carving out of a vision of an illiberal world order that is deeply tied to traditional Christian, family values (Foxall 2019; Holm 2020; Wilkinson 2018) and how Western actors contest this. Focusing analytically on practices of politicised state homophobia leads me to theorise, in an empirically driven fashion, *heteronormative internationalism* as part of a broader *international politics of sexual shame and stigma* characterised by competing discourses about sex, rights, culture, morals, and, more often than not, security.

Heteronormative Internationalism

In Queer IR, there has been a recent tendency to focus on how other societies and cultures have been variously constituted as Other because of their homophobia or their 'deviant' sexual practices. This branch of work, while not using the language of shame and stigma, looks at the way homophilia has been politicised and used as a tool in international power games and the maintenance of global hierarchies (for an excellent example, see Slootmaeckers 2020, 2023). Rather than shaming or stigmatising other states for accepting or condoning queerness, a homophilic practice has emerged where state homophobia becomes stigmatised (Delatolla 2020; Duggan 2002; Puar 2007). This literature focuses predominantly on how Western actors use this homophilic strategy (see the Western side of Figure 2.2). Such research has been fundamental to reconfiguring how we understand the way international hierarchies and identities are constituted through polities' purported queer friendliness.

Inspired by this work, which I would argue is looking at stigmatising practices, I caution that we not forget homophobia and must remain attentive to political strategies of state homophobia, how they obtain an international and geopolitical dimension, and how they enable the production and visioning of a particular world order. We see this crystal clear in the Russian example where politicised homophobia has been used to enforce heteronormativity domestically and to project heteronormative values, embodied in traditional family values, internationally. Bosia and Weiss made a similar argument in their edited volume on politicised homophobia, where they wrote that the focus on 'the influence (or not) of Western models of sexuality spread by global LGBT activists or tourists' has started to eclipse 'the politics of the homophobia local sexual minorities increasingly face on their own streets' (Bosia and Weiss 2013a, 6). Circumspect about the shift in focus to the globalisation of LGBTI+ human rights and state homophilia, Bosia argues that:

> such approaches undervalue the role of state homophobia in both the constitution of identities and the adoption of a rights framework through which sexual minorities increasingly engage in politics and contestation. Much research neglects the role of the state in articulating either a 'gay peril' or a 'normal sexuality' against and through which sexual minority politics is then organized.
>
> (Bosia 2014, 257)

The study of LGBTI+ rights as human rights and on strategies of state homophilia are important, but studying them alone risks overlooking state-directed politicised homophobia as if it has somehow been relegated to history. It also risks sidelining an emergent international characterised by a politics of sexual shame and stigma.

So, how does sexual shame and stigma go international? As outlined above, politicised homophobia is 'modular' in the sense that it can be transplanted to a variety of different social spaces and combined with a huge variety of political and ideological positions.[10] When connected to nationalist projects, we can speak of heteronationalism (outlined above) where homophobia is used to ensure compliance with the script that constitutes national identity and the boundaries of the body politic. When politicised homophobia is directed outside a state's borders, with the intent or effect of privileging heteronormativity or policing its borders, we can talk of *heteronormative internationalism*. Heteronormative internationalism involves the state (or other actors) deploying politicised homophobia as part of its foreign policy and/or as part of an internationalist political project. The differences between these homophilic and homophobic moralising projects are captured in Figure 2.1—note that none of these practices are mutually exclusive and can co-exist.

Heteronormative internationalism builds from heteronationalism and involves a sexually normative, moralistic foreign policy (i.e., an outwardly

	Homophilic	**Homophobic**
Domestic	Advocating and institutionalising LGBT+ rights, protections, and equality *(e.g., civil rights, equal marriage, protection from discrimination)*	State(sponsored) homophobia *(e.g., gay propaganda laws, legal discrimination)*
International	Homonormative internationalism *(e.g., homonationalism, pinkwashing, homocolonialism)*	Heteronormative internationalism *(e.g., foreign policy based on traditional values, civilising missions)*

Figure 2.1 Homophilia and homophobia across domestic and international spheres.

[10] Homophilia is also similarly modular.

anti-queer stance with a view to exporting that view elsewhere) and/or the constitution of a state's position in the international system as staunchly against homophilic states and organisations. For example, when a State pursues a foreign policy agenda that fundamentally opposes (the existence of) non-heterosexuality and/or rights and protections for sexual and gender minorities. Or, when a state is outwardly critical of, even hostile towards, states and organisations who purport to be queer friendly. Where heteronationalism is the practice of moulding national identity to the exclusion of those practicing queer sexualities and genders, heteronormative internationalism is the directing of a heteronormative agenda outwards and internationally. Both combine as political practices that constitute a state's status in international politics on the basis of being a heterosexual space amongst a group of queer states. Neither can be fully separated out since national identity is always bound up in foreign policy and there is no constitution of the national Self without reference to an Other/series of Others (Campbell 1992; Derrida 2009; Hansen 2006).

In the case of Russian policy, this takes form in a quasi (re)civilising mission to restore (gender) order and tradition in Europe. Russian politicised homophobia is manifest in the *explicit* institutionalisation of heteropatriarchal family values as 'normal', as 'traditional', as 'Russian', and 'true European'. The latter two are constitutions of collective identity, which are incredibly important conceptually: they confirm Russian policy as both heteronormatively nationalist and internationalist. The government under Putin constitutes Russia as a proudly heteropatriarchal state, a society with 'traditional Christian values'. Russians are encouraged, forced even, to follow hypermasculine, hyperfeminine gender norms (Wilkinson 2018). This heteronationalist turn—where Russian policy leaders constitute Russia's national identity against a queer 'Gayropa' using anti-Western, anti-Globalist discursive strategies—is maintained through strategic deployment of a heteronormative foreign policy (captured in Figure 2.2). Heteronationalism in this case is founded on a so-called return to conservative and traditional values, but it also has a predominant external factor linked to the discursive constitution of 'Gayropa' and a stated intent to re-traditionalise and re-civilise Europe, saving it from itself (Foxall 2019; Gaufman 2017; Healey 2018; Holm 2020; Riabov and Riabova 2014; Wilkinson 2018). This vision of a violently heteronormative international is not necessarily new

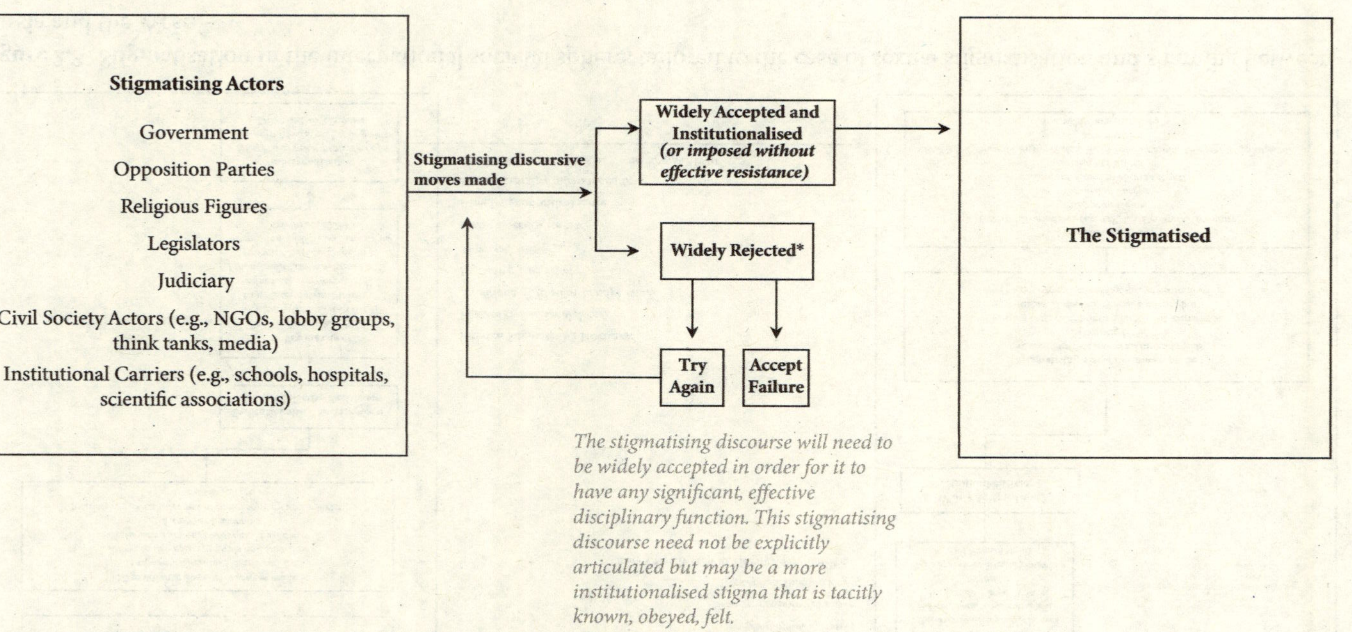

* Rejection or challenge does not need to happen at the initiation of a stigmatising discourse. It can be resisted, rejected,challenged, overcome at a temporally different location.

Figure 2.2 Stigmatisation in the domestic societal sphere.

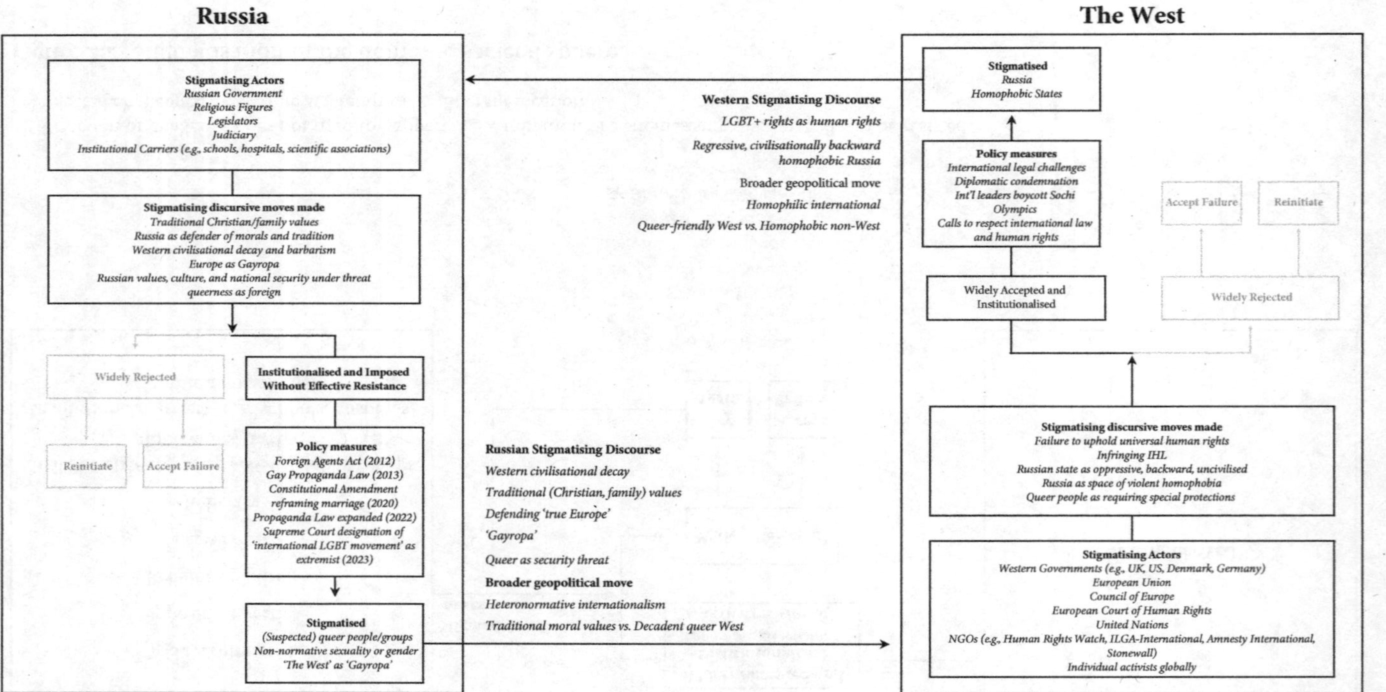

Figure 2.3 Stigmatisation in the international societal sphere, tailored to the case of sexual stigmatisation and shaming between Russia and the West.

and the concept also captures international practices of enforcing heterosexuality during European colonialism, where colonial powers linked specific versions of morally acceptable sexual behaviours and gender performances to 'civilised' status and established mechanisms to manage sex and gender in order to legitimise imperialism.

This has included colonial projects starting in the nineteenth century that used heteronormativity and cisnormativity to establish colonisers' (moral) superiority, as well as a more recent 'homocolonial' turn where the emancipation of queer people in the global south from legal, social, and political oppression has become a standard of civilisation used to legitimise various forms of violence and domination (see inter alia Atshan 2020; Delatolla 2020; Duggan 2002; Hoad 2000; Puar 2007; Rahman 2014b; Rao 2020; Schotten 2018; Vernon 2022).[11] That is to say, European colonialism, like Russian state homophobia and the international activism[12] responding to it, both involve moralising on appropriate and civil sexual behaviour. This is what I am calling an *international politics of sexual shame and stigma*. This international politics of sexual shame involves the marking out of certain non-normative sexual practices, erotic desires, and bodily pleasures as abhorrent, decadent, threatening, to-be-cured, uncivil, and/or immoral, and exporting that particular constitution and ordering of sex internationally; be it through state-to-state dialogue or through transnational, non-governmental institutions and networks such as the International Organisation of the Family (formerly World Congress of Families), National Conservatism (NatCon), and Conservative Political Action Conference (CPAC).

Ontologically, when states use moralising and stigmatising discourses to constitute 'appropriate' and 'normal' sexual practices as part of their foreign policy, they fold the sexual behaviours/desires of individuals into the realm of international relations such that the boundary between the public/private and domestic/international domains dissolves. Russian discourses about the immorality of queerness, its connection to 'Western' culture, and the threat that it poses to (Russian, European …) civilisation are all attempts at stigmatisation and shaming that focus on individuals'

---

[11] In the current context of international politics, it is possible to question whether homophilic policies are transitioning to more homophobic ones given the increased resistance to rights and protections for queer people globally.

[12] As Deborah Gould points out, political activism can take many forms: service provision, lobbying, direct action, protests, and so on (2009, 51). Political activism can be individual or collective, it can be organised or spontaneous.

acts but simultaneously ontologically conflate those people's sexually non-normative acts/desires with state, regional, or bloc identity. In short, the shame and stigma directed at individuals/groups internally is inseparable from the shame and stigma directed externally towards other states and their populations internationally.

Stigmatic Encounters

Adler-Nissen argues that 'norm-violating states are now routinely denounced as "pariahs", squarely positioned outside the company of "civilized states"' (2014, 144). She goes on to say that 'states that are unwilling to conform to "normal" standards are not merely objects of (failed) socialization. Rather, they are active agents, able to cope strategically with the shame they are subjected to and, in some cases, may even challenge a dominant moral discourse by wearing their stigma as a badge of honor' (144). She also argues that it is important to take Goffman's concept of stigma 'from the domestic sphere (and its microsociological application in analyses of, for example, disabled, homosexuals, and unemployed) to the international sphere' (144). The interesting thing about the Russian case, and specifically in relation to its heteronormative geopolitical project, is that Russia is simultaneously a stigmatising actor targeting homophilic states and a receiver of stigmatisation from international society and various non-state civil society actors for its homophobic projects (see Figure 2.2).

Adler-Nissen also argues that 'international society is in part constituted through the stigmatization of "transgressive" and norm-violating states' (2014, 143). Keeping this in mind, we might consider the way politicised homophobia and homophilia enter states' foreign policies as a mechanism for imposing (sexual) stigma and differentiating between the 'civilised' and 'normal' in much the same way as sexual stigma is imposed on queer individuals as 'deviants' in a domestic political setting. Since politicised homophobia and homophilia are modular in the sense that they take on different qualities and look different in given contexts, the international politics of sex—understood as various moves of stigmatising and shaming directed at other (collections of) states and rooted in particular understandings and moralising about the 'normal' and 'deviant' sexual practices, desires, and bodily pleasures sought out by individuals, by states' citizens—is always in process, repeatedly negotiated, and tumultuous as homophobia/homophilia become either strategically advantageous/detrimental to states' political projects.

Russia's foreign policy is predicated on the potential sexual activities and desires of both Western and Russian people. Western activism contesting Russian homophobia reveals that defending non-normative sex is important to a whole array of state and civil society actors, usually framed in a human rights discourse. The actions of both sides transform individuals' sexual practices and preferences into components of international relations and power struggles, leaving sex neither personal nor separate from international politics. This manifests as a sort of 'our state's sexual order is more morally legitimate than your state's' contest. For Russia, this is part of an attempt to forge a new international order patterned with negative norm diffusion around sexuality and gender: that is, 'when States emulate discriminatory and restrictive legislation curtailing freedoms of expression, peaceful assembly and association based on sexual orientation and gender identity' (United Nations Independent Expert on protection against violence and discrimination based on sexual orientation and gender identity 2024, §23). For Western actors, it seems to be more about defending defining features of liberal democracy and liberal international order: equality and human rights. At least until the Far Right's recent rise.

I conceptualise these competing discourses about sexuality between Russia and the West as a *stigmatic encounter* in which competing ideas about sexual morality, progress, and civilisation that structure two competing visions of international order come to clash. In the same way that projects such as ILGA's Rainbow Maps that demarcate 'queer friendly' and states with 'progressive' or 'outdated' policies towards LGBTI+ people are potentially stigmatising and shaming, Russia's discoursing about a morally decadent and civilisationally regressive 'Gayropa' is also potentially stigmatising and shaming (Ammaturo and Slootmaeckers 2024). Both mark out 'failed' or 'failing', 'rogue' or 'outlaw' civilisations because of their political homophilia or their homophobia. Sexuality then becomes a vector through which 'certain peoples, nations, practices, or utterances get marked as beyond the pale of tolerance' and how 'lines between tolerable and intolerable [are] drawn' (Brown 2006, 19).

Stigmatisation 'helps clarify norms and achieve conformity by distinguishing between "us" (the normal states) and "them" (the transgressive ones)' (Adler-Nissen 2014, 149). And as we know from Iver Neumann:

> The role of external 'Others' for the identity formation of nations and states reveals the relevance of these processes for the student of international relations. The making of Russian policy is dependent on what sort of political project its politically leading citizens want Russia to be. Since the fight about this is conducted as a question of how it should relate to Europe, ideas about Europe emerge as a key background determinant for both domestic and foreign policy.
>
> (Neumann 2017, 3)

In the case of Russian foreign policy, national identity, and sexuality, there is a shaming and stigmatisation of non-normative sexualities and genders whether they appear within or without its borders, and a concomitant stigmatisation of 'the West' or 'Gayropa' for its homophilia, its acceptance and accommodation of these deviant behaviours and identities. This is all part of a visioning of a political project that enshrines traditional values and seeks greater geopolitical influence. In opposition to this constitution of 'Gayropa' and Russian homophobia, a particularly visual form of international activism has emerged to contest state homophobia, painting a much different vision of future international order.

Figures 2.2 and 2.3 illustrate how shame and stigma as well as this particular *stigmatic encounter* operate. Figure 2.2 captures how shame and stigma work within a more narrowly bounded social sphere—in this case national. Figure 2.3 builds on Figure 2.2, expanding it to capture the way shame is directed at the policies or actions of other polities in the international system as well as how stigma attaches specific identities to those polities as tainted. It shows how, in the domestic sphere, shame is directed towards non-heterosexual sex and stigma towards deviant homosexual identities within. In the international, it shows how Western and Russian actors have used different discourses to stigmatise one another. Whereas queer theorists point to sexual shame and stigma being directed at individuals or collectives based on their sexual behaviours/sexuality, what I am highlighting with my concept of heteronormative internationalism and the international politics of sexual shame and stigma (as well as Figures 2.2 and 2.3) is the additional element where states direct that sexual shame and stigma towards other states. State-to-state stigmatisation does involve individuals, but the shaming and stigmatisation are more about the Other state's permission/tolerance/support of queerness within its borders.

Sexual Geopolitics

Neumann and Adler-Nissen's points above echo Charles Tilly's classic (1985) argument that having defined the boundaries of belonging, the state—in exchange for obedience to disciplining, taxes, and resource extraction—promises protection from a series of threats so defined by the state. On this, Michael Bosia and Meredith Weiss argue that the:

> homophobic state and social actors create a gay peril against which they seek to organize state efforts. In the process, those elites secure their own privileges. Indeed, political homophobia often takes root before a critical mass of sexual minorities even begins to think of itself as 'lesbian', 'gay', or 'transgender', let alone to endow these identities with any collective, political significance or policy claims, threatening or otherwise.
>
> (Bosia and Weiss 2013a, 16)

Signing the propaganda law into force Putin institutionalised stigma of non-normative sexualities and genders, both at a domestic level but also at an international level by constituting deviation from heteronormativity as 'foreign' and a matter of societal security. This pandered to Putin's conservative domestic supporters and diverted attention away from a faltering economy and widespread corruption (Healey 2018). It also positioned Russia as a defender of traditional values not just at home but internationally (Wilkinson 2014, 2018). Looking towards the West, Russian foreign policy constitutes its place in the world as the saviour of 'Western civilisation' and the defender of not just traditional values and a particular heteronormative version of the family but of 'true Europe' that risks imminent demise as it extends human rights to LGBTI+ people and opens up traditional, heteronormative institutions like marriage to (some) queer people (Healey 2018, 200; Michel 2017; Ministry of Foreign Affairs of the Russian Federation 2023; Neumann 2017, 170–171; Putin 2013a; Riabov and Riabova 2014; Savelau 2018; White and Feklyunina 2014, 104, 112–114). Constituting itself as the defender of traditional values, Russia has begun to carve out a role for itself in the international system it has constituted as populated by decadent, threatening 'Gayropean' spaces and traditional, moral ones. This is a decidedly internationalist project, which Rita Abrahamsen (2020) argues is a geopolitics of the family wedded to 'traditional values'.

Geopolitically, non-normative sexual behaviour and object desire have become one of many points of stark political conflict between Russia and mainly Western states. One where Russia positively constitutes itself as a bastion of traditional (heteronormative) values and the defender of the civilised (heteronormative) world. For those same reasons, some Western states have negatively constituted Russia as homophobic, regressive, and uncivilised while positioning the West as the apex of human rights and positively constituting itself as a space of sexual liberation and freedom. This is powerful because, as Wendy Brown notes, discourses of civilisation 'configures the *right* of the civilized against a barbaric opposite that is both internally oppressive and externally dangerous, neither tolerant nor tolerable' (2006, 204). Who are the civilised and who are the barbaric differs between the Russian and Western actors involved in the stigmatic encounter outlined above. All of this speaks to there being not only a domestic politics of state homophobia but an *international politics of sex* that is rooted in practices of shaming and stigmatisation around non-heteronormative sexual desire, pleasure, and behaviour. We cannot understand our current geopolitical moment, where we are in the throes of an emergent post-liberal order, without paying attention to the work that the politics of sex and heteronormativity are doing here.

Vis-à-vis traditional values, in recent years, the issue of non-normative sexual behaviour and desire has become an accelerant in a deepening moral panic about sexuality and gender that cuts across traditional Left/Right political stratifications internationally (Abrahamsen 2020; Gifkins and Cooper-Cunningham 2023; Mudde 2019).[13] All of this is about 'what people and practices will count as national' (Berlant 1997, 21) but—and this is the value of adding an IR analysis to a queer one—it is also a discursive battle about what 'Europe' and 'international society' should look like. We

---

[13] Citing Erich Goode and Nachman Ben-Yehuda (1994) in our work on atrocity prevention, Jess Gifkins and I note that a moral panic is characterised by: 'a "heightened level of concern over the behaviour (or supposed behaviour) of a certain group or category and the consequences that that behaviour presumably causes for the rest of the society"; "an increased level of hostility toward the category of people seen as engaging in the threatening behaviour"; widespread feeling in society that the defined group is deviant, dangerous and/or threatening, though this need not be a majority consensus; a disproportional response to and "wildly exaggerated" claims about the so-called threat; and volatility' (2023, 2068).

know from studies of genocide and other mass atrocities that the discursive moves outlined above and the persecution of queer people are often the starting point in and legitimacy cover for broad geopolitical projects replete with violence against all manner of groups, not just queer people (Cooper-Cunningham and Kremer 2024; Gifkins and Cooper-Cunningham 2023; Gifkins et al. 2022; Nellans 2020; Waites 2018; Warner 2000, 20). Recognising the role that discourses about 'normal' sex play in states' domestic and foreign policies is vitally important for understanding the current state of international politics and an emergent international where rights, protections, and democratic institutions are being violently challenged. We cannot understand Russian foreign policy or its geopolitical imaginary without understanding how 'normative' sex has been constituted. Nor, for that matter, can we understand the politics of the international activism emerging around Russian state homophobia without thinking about how discourses of 'normalcy' and 'civilisational decay' are being resisted with another, more homophilic, discursive move.

Conclusion

Sex is part of international politics and the politics around it is rooted in stigmatising and shaming practices whereby states' actions are called out either for their homophobia or their homophilia. The international politics of sexual shame and stigma affect every individual on the planet and are therefore crucial to the study of IR. Using a queer analytical lens, IR scholars can learn much about the international order emerging around (Russian) politicised homophobia and (international) activism against it, as well as how our bodies are international. Russia's heteronormative internationalism has provoked an international response from queer activists in Russia and elsewhere and from formal international institutions. To understand what activists are doing, it is key to understand exactly what they are responding to: hence, I introduced my conceptualisation of *heteronormative internationalism* and an *international politics of sexual shame and stigma* above.

The international politics of sex cannot be attributed to or studied purely at the level of states or international organisations; those deemed the big players in international politics. Since political homophilia and homophobia are forms of moralising about sex, erotic desire, and bodily pleasure, the international politics of sex is always about individuals, how their sex(uality) conforms or deviates from the norm, and how their bodies perform in and negotiate the social world. Queer bodies are politicised, disciplined, and mobilised in various homophilic and homophobic ways as state and state-adjacent actors moralise about sex and use this as a geopolitical tool that differentiates the 'civilised' from the 'barbaric' and 'deviant'. When homophobic/homophilic projects go international, they not only begin to structure relations between (collections of) states (e.g., the West and Russia) but affect individuals' lives as their supposedly 'private' behaviours, desires, and intimacies become part of the justification for geopolitical moves that come to affect all of the stuff we lump into 'high' politics (e.g., diplomacy) *and* the lives of all the queer individuals who bear the brunt of states' moralising about sex. As Berlant and Warner (1995, 1998) put it: sex is public. And I would add, international.

Sexuality, something that is embodied (in the sense that it is felt and practiced by human bodies and minds) is without any doubt a battleground upon which international politics is played out through moralising, civilisational, war-legitimising discourses. If the politics of sexual shame marks bodies as deviant for the pleasures it seeks, desires, has, and disciplines bodies into appropriate ways of being, then the international politics of sexual shame and stigma is about constituting the states who support those deviants as despicable, deviant, and disruptive of the normal (international) order of things. In this respect, sex is not only public but international; it is connected to policy and everyday life. Heteronormative internationalism, as a project that promotes and secures heteronormative sociality internationally, is thus a political and stigmatising means to power that deploys shame and opprobrium to silence, isolate, and ostracise others internationally.

Historically, we have seen moralising foreign policies about sexuality and gender as part of colonial 'civilising' missions that go on to carve up the world in the image of the moralising powers (Delatolla 2020; Hoad 2000). Today, this is exemplified by discourses about supposedly impermissible sexual practices in states' domestic and foreign policy projects as well as the whipping up of national debates about 'normal' gender and sexual behaviours. More and more governments bake moralistic and normative positions about appropriate sexual behaviour and gender performances into their foreign policies, which means the types of sex and pleasures people pursue and are allowed to engage in are informing broader geopolitical visions and projects for like-minded politicians and sympathisers to rally around.

What I outline above is not *just* about attacks on LGBTI+ rights or the rolling back of protections for LGBTI+ people, which would be a legitimate focus even if it were. It is about how sexuality is mobilised a part of a Russian geopolitical project specifically as well as how the international politics of sexual shame and stigma more generally limit the possibility for everyone, every subject, in certain spaces to use their bodies the way they desire. It is about how heteronormativity is mobilised as a geopolitics and in a security discourse. In this sense, heteronormative internationalism is an anti-democratic international project that forecloses the possibility of (sexual) autonomy by preventing and punishing any form of variation or deviation from the rule. None of this is limited to one sexuality-based identity group, it affects everyone who may succumb to the wayward working of sexual desire such that it invites sexual stigma and shame, and everyone who may find themselves on the receiving end of a foreign policy project that involves establishing boundaries around appropriate sex. Acts of sexual stigmatisation are political, they are often politicised and strategic, and they affect both individuals and international politics.

3

Words-Images-Bodies

A Tripartite Approach

In this chapter, I offer a theorisation of the connection between words, images, and bodies, as well as the political work that different visual genres do. To do so, I outline the epistemological and ontological moves that I make to study—or perhaps more fittingly, *see*—the international politics of sex I outlined in the previous chapter. This happens in three steps. First, I outline a classic interpretation of poststructuralist theorisations of discourse, which leads into a discussion of what is at stake when we think about discourse analysis as exclusively focused on words. Second, I outline how I theorise the visual and the body. Third, I explore the interconnection between words, images, and bodies, arguing that we cannot neatly separate the three out, particularly in the context of activism. For me, discourse is not just words-based but also visual and corporeal. Therefore, I propose a tripartite words-images-bodies approach that treats words, images, and bodies as a dynamic triad of equals in epistemological and ontological terms. By treating words, images, and bodies as such, this framework offers a new way to explore the political through the complex interrelation of linguistic, visual, and corporeal discursive practices. This expanded understanding of discourse encompasses all three as sites of knowledge about international politics that, in this case, reveals how queer political activism and the emergent international politics of sexual stigma it contests means rethinking the spaces of international politics, the actors we count, and the mediums/genres of international political intervention we turn to.

What should be clear by the end of this book, by weaving the different threads of the theoretical and the empirical chapters into a tapestry that will invariably look different for each reader, is that the body and the visual help shape and are shaped by international politics in complicated ways. In the case of the international politics of sex, queer bodies are

The International Politics of Sex. Dean Cooper-Cunningham, Oxford University Press.
© Oxford University Press (2025). DOI: 10.1093/9780197792544.003.0003

co-opted by governments as props in their homophilic/homophobic foreign policies, being variously endowed with meaning as normal/abnormal, safe/threatening. Some of the very bodies targeted by those in power move into the streets to protest this co-optation through activism and to challenge the limitations imposed upon how people use their own bodies. In the case of Russia, the very visibility of queerness in public is constituted as a security threat. We see this in the various legislation outlined in the introduction. Images have been used to represent this homophobic political project across traditional and social media, but they have also been a means of resisting those political projects by creating queer visibility and contesting the seeking invisible of difference by the Russian authorities. Those same images (e.g., the Gay Clown Putin meme) are also met and constituted by governments as a security threat, a foreign ideology in visual form. These dynamics confound the epistemological and ontological privilege afforded to discourse—and therefore knowledge—as written/spoken.

That this project started from a photograph is testament to the power and utility that images have in terms of engaging with international politics: they can open up theoretical questions and inspire new ways of thinking (Cooper-Cunningham 2024; Hansen Forthcoming). In this case, that image opened up theoretical questions about the connection between words, images, and bodies, as well as those about the politics of representation more generally. The visual, the body, and words are all part of the responses to and activism against Russian homophobia that I analyse in Chapters 5 through 8. In each case, they come in in complex and overlapping ways that reveal the analytical utility of a broadened epistemological and ontological terrain for studying international politics. Especially when dealing with non-state actors, the politics of sex, and international activism, which are issues not often so explicitly present in the more classic empirical material used in IR. These come into view through bodies on the streets, photographs of people, memes of Vladimir Putin, speeches about decadent sexuality, and much more. To be clear, I am not arguing that every project about international politics needs a visual analysis or that every analysis needs to pay attention to bodies. But, I am arguing that it is always worthwhile asking: what might paying attention to the body and the visual change about my analysis? What can these vessels of knowledge give my analysis? How can they help me theorise?

Discourse

Language has become one of the primary ways international politics has been studied. There is an abundance of theory and methods detailing the how and the why of studying language in IR (e.g., Campbell 1992; Doty 1993; Edkins 1999; Hall 2021; Hansen 2006; Neumann 2002; Shepherd 2008). Scholars frequently analyse written and spoken texts such as policy documents, speeches, government debates, newspapers, popular culture, and the like (Campbell 1992; Doty 1993; Hansen 2006; Shepherd 2008). Discourse analysis has been the primary method for studying language in IR, and while approaches to discourse vary, I draw on poststructuralism because it is the primary theoretical route through which discourse has come into IR.

Generally speaking, discourse is usually studied through texts and words (Williams 2003). Since language is the main vehicle through which we come to understand, represent, and organise the world, it is also the primary means through which we share, negotiate, and debate our understandings of and positions in the world (Foucault 1972; Laclau and Mouffe 1985). In this sense, language is not just description. It is social and political. It is a shared, ever-evolving, and unstable system of signs or codes through which meaning and identity are constructed (Doty 1993; Hansen 2006). How global issues and events are articulated shapes what and who becomes visible, how they are met and understood, as well as what is deemed important. It structures understandings of international politics, defines security threats, determines who has rights, establishes what is legitimate action and who has legitimate authority to act on behalf of collectivities such as the nation and state, and it constitutes identities of all kinds (Doty 1996). Language, therefore, not only orders and gives meaning to the world but also produces it in specific ways.

Discourse is a practice that organises, orders, and structures the world and our ideas about it (Foucault 1972). It produces subjects, objects, states, and all manner of other 'things', and bestows upon them meanings and identities (Hansen 2006, 18). In this sense, to study discourse is to focus on the politics of representation (Shapiro 1988). As Stuart Hall writes, representation is different from reflection because the former 'implies the active work of selecting and presenting, of structuring and shaping: not merely the transmitting of already-existing meaning, but the more active labour of *making things mean*' (1982, 60). The state and national identity, for example, are both constituted discursively—most often in reference to other states or nations—rather than being something innate that 'just exists'. There is no world in which states, or even the idea of states, just exist a priori. This means that identity is not something that states, or other objects of discourse, have independently of the discursive practices that formulate and make 'identity' possible and seem 'natural' (Laclau and Mouffe 1985). Neither Scottishness nor queerness, for example, are identities that exist prior to their construction in language. They are constructed and stabilised through discourse. While this is most obviously done through words, visual objects such as a national flag reinforce identities and give them stability through repeated performances of the 'nation'.

Taking all of this into account, discourse is decidedly political. It is a vehicle through which power is exercised in the construction of political issues and social order, laying the foundations for and legitimising certain policies, and producing—or challenging—dominant social and political structures. Even with all this power, discourse is neither entirely stable nor incontestable. Discourses can endure relatively unchallenged for a period, but they must always be reproduced, even if only through acquiescence or acceptance. In this regard, there are always possibilities for contesting and destabilising hegemonic discourses. Theoretically and methodologically, focusing on discourse enables a rethinking of the spaces and sites of international politics (Hansen and Spanner 2021). It is not just attentive to what is explicitly stated or politicised but also to what or who gets silenced, pushed to the margins, made invisible (Hansen 2000b; Shepherd 2008). The discourse analyst seeks out ways to deconstruct, destabilise, and interrogate power; to question knowledge that is taken for granted and to open up spaces for different interpretations. This aligns neatly with a queer analysis, where a relentless interrogation and resignifying of discursively constituted power structures is core (Cohen 1997, 2004).

Poststructuralist discourse analysis is not limited to examining language or deciphering what has been said or written. It focuses on power and the politics of representation—how language constitutes subject positions, (re)produces specific understandings of issues, events, or groups, and legitimises certain policies. This involves analysing the emergence, transformation, and disappearance of discourses, the ways they are contested or resisted, and the connections between their constituent elements. Dichotomies play a central role in this process, creating binary oppositions like good/evil, normal/abnormal, and natural/unnatural. These binaries discipline thought and action, sustaining hierarchies and shaping identity construction, such as 'Russian' versus 'non-Russian' or 'normal' versus 'abnormal' sexuality (Foucault 1978; Rubin 2011; Warner 2000). These shape social orders and justify consequences for deviation.

As Hansen observes, 'identity is always given through reference to something it is not' (Hansen 2006, 6). Identity—who 'we' are, who Others are, and the relationship between us—is constructed in discourse and linked to (state) policy (Doty 1993). Communities, nations, social movements (a 'We') are constructed through a dichotomy where an external Other (a 'Them') is constructed in language as different or similar to the collective Self (Campbell 1992; Shapiro 1988). The construction and representation of a collective Self and its Other(s) is central to identity formation and has direct political implications: it shapes states' (foreign) policies and social movements' activities (on foreign policy and social movements, respectively, see Hansen 2006; Tilly 2004). Policy is thus conditioned by representations of identity, which enable some actions and constrain others.

While words are indeed incredibly powerful, we can theorise discourse more expansively. Replacing 'language', 'words', 'speak', and 'write' with 'the visual', 'images', 'illustrate', and 'visualise' or 'the body', 'movements', 'actions', and 'doings' opens up an expanse of data sources for the study of international politics. The empirical sites available for generating knowledge expand far beyond texts and words. They include the bodies and images that, while anchored by words in terms of meaning and identity, simultaneously anchor, co-constitute, and give meaning to words. Here, I theorise the social and political as emergent in discourse and I theorise discourse as not just words-based but also visual and corporeal (Cooper-Cunningham 2019, 2024; Hansen 2000b). Yes, words shape ideas and work upon bodies and anchor images. But, the body and the visual are also important parts of discourse that can stabilise, disturb, and/or contest power structures that are primarily expressed in words. The visual and the bodily also make the world and, in turn, international politics. This is particularly clear and pronounced when one studies political activism.

International politics is not just speeches, policy documents, parliamentary debates, and newspaper articles. It is protests, marches, making and sharing images, placing the body in harms way, satirising a politician's face, waving a flag, and contesting foreign and domestic policy in a whole manner of ways; any way possible really. A whole spectrum of actors engage in international politics through the visual and with their bodies. Sometimes because they have no other choice; this is the only way to get 'heard'. The absence of written/spoken words around a political issue does not mean there are no images. Similarly, it does not exclude the possibility of corporeal responses articulating an issue's importance, whether marching in the streets or on hunger strike, for example. Adopting a broader understanding of discourse and opening up a larger data pool does not require privileging visuals or bodies over language. Instead, their epistemological and analytical significance should be regarded as equal, at least in theory, even if not always in practice.

Visual Politics

Over the last decade, IR scholars have made significant inroads to establish how the visual—both as representative practice and ways of seeing—impacts and shapes international politics. Images 'surround everything we do' and therefore 'shape international events and our understanding of them' (Bleiker 2018, 1). In this sense, we can be said to live in the age of images, where the visual has fundamentally altered how we interact with, understand, interpret, and are affected by political events (Callahan 2020; Williams 2018). Despite the visual only recently gaining status in IR as an important empirical site for understanding society and politics over the last decade or so, 'imagery has been important throughout history and to all societies' (Shim and Nabers 2013, 293). This is an important point, captured in work on aesthetics and politics (Bleiker 2009, 2017; Lisle 2007; Moore and Shepherd 2010; Rancière 2004, 2009). The social and political significance of visuality—a broad term that includes visual artefacts (i.e., images, monuments, sculptures) and visibility (i.e., what is allowed to appear and be seen)—is not something new. Indeed, my work on the Suffragettes (Cooper-Cunningham 2019) and the visual genealogy of the US-based queer and AIDS movements in Chapter 4 are indicative of the power and politicality of the visual, particularly in terms of historic and contemporary activism.

Images are created and disseminated by a whole range of actors from activists and journalists to governments, NGOs to IOs. They are, therefore, part of a massive discursive field in which we make sense of the world and come to 'know' things. Recognising this, IR scholars increasingly turn to the visual as an empirical site for generating insights about the machinations of international politics. As Rune Andersen and Juha Vuori (2018) demonstrate, this takes place in three ways: visuality as *modality*, where images represent the political; as *practice*, where images construct something as a political issue; and, as *method*, where images are used as a research tool (e.g., photo elicitation or auto-photography) or produced as output (e.g., film or photoessay). The first two are the most common ways of engaging images in IR and are where this book sits in the visual IR landscape. These first two approaches treat images as artefacts through which we come to know, make sense of, and act in the world; as artefacts through which we 'see' and 'do' international politics.

This type of work emerges predominantly from the so-called pictorial and aesthetic 'turns'. Examples of this work include: Lene Hansen's work on the Muhammad cartoon crisis (2011) and comic books engaging the Bosnian War (2017); Axel Heck and Gabi Schlag's study of a TIME magazine cover and the Afghanistan War (2013); Roland Bleiker's work on representations of HIV/AIDS (Bleiker and Kay 2007) and the dehumanisation of refugees (Bleiker et al. 2013); semiotic, chromatological approach, which argues that colour enacts and makes security intelligible (Guillaume, Andersen, and Vuori 2016; Andersen, Vuori, and Guillaume 2015); Simone Molin Friis' (2018) combination of digital ethnography and visual approaches to study militant imagery; Helen Berents' (2019) work on images of dead children and the 'telegenic dead'; Constance Duncombe's (2019, 2020) work on images, emotion, and social media; my work on the use of posters (2019) and comic books (2020a) to constitute and/or contest gendered-sexualised-racialised insecurity; Megan MacKenzie's study of soldier-generated illicit images, which shows how images are 'central to, and reinforce aspects of, military band of brother culture' (2020); and David Campbell's work on the visualisation of mass atrocity (2002a, 2002b, 2004, 2007).

In the less common but growing strand of visual IR, visuality as *method*, Sophie Harman's (2019) pathbreaking work uses narrative feature film as a 'method of seeing those who are invisible from politics, policy, and global health research', challenging how we 'see' international politics and global power structures. Others using visuality as *method* include: Sara Särmä (2018) who uses collage to rethink the spatiality of international politics; Elena Barabantseva and Andy Lawrence who use participatory filmmaking to explore the international politics of the everyday (2015); Debbie Lisle and Heather Johnson (2019), Roland Bleiker (2019), and Lene Hansen and Johan Spanner (2021) who use their own photographs to sight, trouble, and rethink international power structures; Frederik Windfeld, Marius Hvithamar, and Lene Hansen who create a comic as part of an academic article to 'to engage critically with the ways in which "Aleppo" has been brought to Western audiences and how the West responded' (2024, 6); Jonna Nyman who uses auto-photography and photo-elicitation as a method for researching security and invisibility (Ferhani and Nyman 2023; Nyman 2021); Cynthia Weber (2011) and William Callahan (2015) who make films as research output; and Benjamin Dix, who engages with issues such as conflict, migration, and asylum, to produce comics in collaboration with those individuals affected (positivenegatives.org). Works from all three not-always-separable strands of visual IR form part of ongoing and productive discussions about how we approach the visual ontologically and methodologically. In other words, what images 'do' and how we engage with them in research.

On this point, to date, most visual scholarship situated within the discipline of IR has been qualitative. However, that is not to say a quantitative approach cannot be used. In fact, there are merits to quantitative and mixed methodologies that allow scholars to ask different types of questions of the visual (Bleiker 2015). A quantitative approach may, for example, be well suited to identifying different patterns in large data sets of images. Bleiker et al. (2013) use a quantitative content analysis to analyse newspaper coverage of asylum seekers, which opens space for different, more nuanced, qualitative study of those images. Hansen et al. (2021) use a quantitative visual content analysis to identify shifts and continuities in the way the European migrant 'crisis' was depicted in newspapers between 2013 and 2015. And Møller et al. (2024) use computer vision methods to over analyse 55.000 images on diplomatic Twitter to examine how 'images uploaded by diplomats … contribute to the symbolic authority of their profession, ritually conveying ideals of international mediation and sovereign equality'. These studies show how different methodologies can be combined to get at the political work images do.

While there is no end to the ways that the visual can be brought into the study of international politics, and debates rage on about the 'best' way to think about visuality, I primarily deal with the visual as a discursive, representative practice and analyse mainly images in this book. What I offer here is, therefore, *one* of many departure gates that researchers can embark on the metaphorical visual aeroplane from. It is not intended to be a blueprint for visual analysis but instead to theorise the interrelation between word-image-body in a way that provides fruitful inspiration for those who wish to study international politics as it unfolds in discrete, often overlooked spaces.

The approach I offer particularly equips those who are researching political activism and the way marginalised actors intervene in international politics with the tools to analyse interventions that take place in ways traditionally overlooked or dismissed as 'low politics' and thus outside IR's purview. I also theorise different visual genres and the different political work they do. Within the burgeoning, interdisciplinary subfield of visual IR there has been an overwhelming focus on the politics of photorealistic genres. This has been challenged by scholars who are asking how illustrated genres—mostly cartoons and comics—also speak to the questions we engage in IR (Aradau and Hill 2013; Cooper-Cunningham 2019, 2020a; Dittmer 2005; Dodds 2007; Hansen 2011, 2017; Särmä 2018; Shim 2017; Wedderburn 2019).

While photorealistic images are given documentary status and regarded as more objective and 'realistic' than illustrated images (Barthes 1977, 17–9), (digitally) drawn images also aim to accurately represent 'nature or the real' in order to convey 'meanings about people…and events' (Sturken and Cartwright 2009, 146). Creators of illustrated media and, by extension, visual artefacts like flags and monuments, use memory and lived experiences to inform their depictions, actively repeating and reconstructing traumas to counteract them (Chute 2016, 3). Both camera-created and illustrated images are all *representations* of the world, not copies, that stake a claim to truth (Aradau and Hill 2013; Bleiker 2018). Whether through photorealistic or illustrated media, thinking about how state policy and activism are represented or contested in relation to queer individuals/groups means thinking about the 'work' particular genres of representation do, in what context they are used, and for what purpose. Each of the empirical chapters in this book engages with different types of visuality for this reason. First, though, a more general theorisation of the image.

Theorising the Image

In previous work, I have taken up Hansen's (2000b, 300) call to include the visual and bodily as additional epistemological lenses through which international politics—particularly security speech and activism—can be studied (see also: Williams 2003). How I theorise the visual in this book builds on and is an extension of this work. It is the culmination of reading, thinking, theorising, questioning, and being intrigued by the way images were being used to contest gendered, racialised, and sexualised power structures by a whole variety of actors, often across borders.

Inspired by feminist and queer activism as well as visual theory, I have explored: how comic books contested and disrupted gendered-racialised-sexualised discourses in post-9/11 security politics (Cooper-Cunningham 2020a); how British suffragettes used political posters as a means to resist the government discourse that women were not political subjects and did not possess the capacity to engage in the public sphere on the basis of their gender (Cooper-Cunningham 2019); and how the visual can be conceptualised as a queer method that centres marginalised voices and opens up new ways of seeing queer subjectivity beyond pure victimhood, even in times of widespread persecution (Cooper-Cunningham 2024). What links these works to what I do here is a focus on political activism, particularly the visual and body politics of activism that crosses (or ignores) borders of all kinds from the national to the linguistic. My theorisation of the visual is therefore the product of thinking and developing my understanding of words, images, and bodies through an engagement with queer, feminist, and visual literatures as well as different instances of political activism.

Epistemologically, I start from the position that images matter politically but that their meaning is always in process and unstable. They are visual representations that are important for policy debates as part of the discursive environment within which political decisions are made. While it is hard to assess direct causal effects, images, like other discursive modalities such as words, impact policy by constituting 'interpretive dispositions' that enable and preclude certain actions/policies and ideas (Cooper-Cunningham 2019; Hansen 2011). Visuals construct 'truths', produce meanings, and structure how we perceive political problems (Andersen, Vuori, and Mutlu 2015; Bleiker 2018; Callahan 2020). Images can therefore be said to constitute 'international' spaces and subjects in politically significant ways, delineating who and what 'appear as subjects, objects, actors, threats and opportunities, and with which identities and responsibilities' (Hansen 2015, 273). Approaching 'the international' from the visual, thus, means asking what meanings are visually attached to 'the international', to the subjects and objects populating that discursively produced space, and what visions of world order are emergent and made possible, thinkable, and thus realisable and authoritative, through the visual.

Taking a broad view of discourse as words, images, and bodies, not only can images entrench power relations, but they can also resist, contest, and reconfigure them. The visual, therefore, plays an 'important role in challenging political narratives' such as Russian heteronormative internationalism 'and pushing the boundaries of what can be seen, thought, and done' (Bleiker 2018, 28). In this sense, images do 'not only represent the world but also condition [and challenge] how we perceive it' (Crone 2020, 576). They do not just 'illustrate international events as visual texts' but 'actively create international politics as nonverbal and nonnarrative experiences and performances' (Callahan 2020, 2). As such, 'visual artifacts are sites of multisensory, performative experience in which the personal, the political, and the international collide' and can thus 'provoke new social orders and world orders' (Callahan 2020, 308, 305). This potentiality was something recognised and embraced by those engaged in gay and lesbian liberation as well as AIDS activism (Finkelstein 2018; Gould 2009; Riemer and Brown 2019). This is evidently also recognised and harnessed by Western activists contesting Russian homophobia who use similar visual practices to those of earlier AIDS and gay and lesbian liberation activists.

As Jacques Rancière (2004, 2009) argues, images are political because they determine what is seen and what is not; they establish the boundaries of the sensible, what can be thought, imagined, and made possible. The visual, thus, affects the ways that politics is 'perceived, sensed, framed, articulated, carried out, and legitimised' (Bleiker 2018, 4). Images can be used by activists to visualise and thus make sensible that which the state loathes and seeks to render invisible, unknowable, and unthinkable. Speaking to this, W.J.T. Mitchell (1987, 1994) argued that major sociopolitical events come to be known and perceived primarily through images, not words. One cannot, for instance, think of or remember the Vietnam War without Nick Ut's iconic 'Napalm Girl' photograph or of the Global War on Terror without thinking about the images of prisoner torture (Hansen 2015).

Images are incredibly political in that they can also provoke those invested in sustaining dominant configurations of society and its structures to react. Images, in this sense, can challenge or reinforce the status quo. This is partly why actors fight to control or stabilise their meaning—as the Russian government did with the Gay Clown Putin memes (Chapter 8). For me, I cannot remember the institutionalisation of Russian politicised homophobia without thinking about the photographs that alerted me to the issue in 2013. Images, then, can be understood as windows to the world. We understand the world, the actors within it, and the structures creating 'order' through the visual. When 'times of protracted crises—migrant crises, pandemic outbreaks, beheadings, racist attacks [arise] images can provoke emotional response and in some instances change' (Harman 2019, 48). This much is indicated by the fact that social media is dominated by overwhelmingly visual platforms (e.g., Instagram, TikTok, Facebook, Twitter/X, Snapchat) through which people share information, present narratives, explore identities, and discuss politics (Duncombe 2020, 2024; Harman 2019; Williams 2018).

This is not just the case on social media, though. News outlets' digital and mobile platforms—including major outlets such as *the Guardian, BBC News, al Jazeera, and the New York Times*—are decidedly visual. Few stories do not have an image illustrating the story. Through these various media, users are bombarded 'with images of world events and issues of current affairs in a way that can desensitize them to violent acts, poverty, poor health, and humanitarian crises, mislead them with images out of context, and mobilize them into action' (Harman 2019, 48). Today, people overwhelmingly and increasingly get information about international politics from visual media, meaning that images literally 'shape our view of the world, by making some things visible' and others invisible (Callahan 2020, 1). The visual has become a 'language of how societies engage in and understand international relations and their own politics' as well as 'a way of creating affect and impact' be that positive or negative (Harman 2019, 48). As such, international politics and, more broadly, the social take shape through the visual. This is why we must pay due 'attention to the politics of framing—who and what are included inside the frame of the political, and how people and issues are excluded from the international' (Callahan 2020, 1).

Similar to Hansen (2011), Bleiker suggests that, while images have been part of the fabric of sociopolitical life 'from the beginning of time', it is the speed with which they circulate and the potential (global) reach they have that has changed (2018, 5). This, alongside a supposed 'democratisation' of the visual is what distinguishes the age of images according to Bleiker. While it is true that a colossal amount more people have access to the technology to take a photograph and immediately share it online to a potentially global audience than was previously possible when states and media had a monopoly (Bleiker 2018, 5), the notion of a democratisation of the visual is problematic (Andersen and Vuori 2018). The viral-potential and global reach of 'new media' has vastly increased the *size of the audience* subjugated minorities can (potentially) reach, but the use of the visual to engage in politics and resist oppression is not new.

Activists have been using visual strategies to enter political discourse for a long time and with great success *without* digital media. One example is the prolific visual strategy—spanning posters, stickers/buttons, flags, marches, videos, and media coverage—adopted by global AIDS activist group ACT UP from the late 1980s. This raises the question: has digital media so radically altered strategies of visual resistance and political activism or are we simply seeing a new instantiation of old visual practices, albeit modified for the digital era? Nevertheless, it is worth noting that the increasing ease with which one can produce and distribute images of all types has significant sociopolitical effects. One of which might be the ability of minorities to 'have a voice they did not have before, or, at least the potential to circulate this voice and perhaps have it heard' (Bleiker 2018, 8; Campbell and Shapiro 2007).

Susan Sontag wrote that every image is 'an invitation to look' (2003, 40). In this regard, every image is also an invitation to ask the political questions: what is not represented, what is excluded, who does this visualisation and framing serve, and to what potential ends is this produced and shared? The visual is a site in and through which international 'political processes, institutions, logics, and myths are reconstituted, stabilised and naturalised' as well as challenged and destabilised (Tidy and Turner 2020: 124). We miss a lot when we do not analyse how the international is visualised and seen.

Visual Polysemy

Images, like all practices of representation, ought not to be treated as innocent conductors of objective truth. They can—like words—misrepresent, mislead, be dismissed, repurposed, and taken out of context. What is important about the visual and aesthetic is that they have the capacity to 'provoke or challenge how individuals and collectives see politics and reimagine political possibilities or the boundaries that stop them from seeing' (Harman 2019, 49). Read through multiple different intertextual and intervisual locales, our interpretations of images and what they are said to represent, the emotions they are said to invoke, and the power they are given, thus constitutes them as a site of politics (Adler-Nissen, Andersen, and Hansen 2019; Duncombe 2020, 621; Hansen 2015). To echo Callahan, the visual is social-ordering and world-ordering in the sense that images are used to 'actively visualize the world [people] want to live in, as well as the societies that they don't want to see and feel' (Callahan 2020, 2). The visual, thus, creates, structures, and performs international politics in incredibly complex ways that are entangled with words and body politics.

It is the possibility for multiple interpretations, for disagreement, for debate, for being affected by, and for having contested meanings—in short, their polysemy and affective qualities—that make images particularly politically potent. They are, as Hansen (2006, 16) argues of language's politicality, 'site[s] for the production and reproduction of particular subjectivities and identities', for a negotiation of power. There is a reason that the Muhammad cartoons became a diplomatic issue for Denmark (Hansen 2011). That said, when it comes to understanding the political significance of visuals in international politics, there is no single answer. Indeed, this is why the politics of the visual has been debated so extensively in recent years (Andersen, Vuori, and Guillaume 2015; Andersen, Vuori, and Mutlu 2015; Bleiker 2015, 2018; Callahan 2020; Campbell 2007; Cooper-Cunningham 2019, 2020b; Hansen 2011; Hansen, Adler-Nissen, and Andersen 2021; Harman 2019; Heck and Schlag 2013; Shapiro 1988). Images are complex and operate on many intersecting levels. There are multiple genres of image, each with their own aesthetic qualities and each with different relations to the political—as should become clear in each of the different empirical chapters.

Ontologically, there are various approaches to theorising the image. Some view images as having an 'auto-activity' and as 'speaking' in and of themselves (e.g., Bredekamp 2010; Heck and Schlag 2013). I do not theorise images in this way. I conceptualise images, like text and bodies, as not 'speaking' alone, in their own right. Rather, their meaning, again like words and bodies, is always mediated by other signs, other parts of discourse. None work in isolation, which is to say that 'neither the word nor the image can speak in the absence of linkages and differentiations to other signs' (Hansen 2017, 588). As such, I follow Roland Barthes (1977) who theorises the image as polysemous. This means that, in principle, all images can be read be received and interpreted in multiple ways, depending on the cultural codes and stock of knowledge those reading them have. This polysemy is generally decreased by text on, near, or surrounding an image, or by some other text(s) and uses of the image that anchor its meaning in some way. As images circulate and move out of the original contexts in which they were printed, posted, and let out into the world, their meaning becomes less stable and more susceptible to vastly differing interpretations—especially when other textual or visual anchors are missing.

Images are also situated within aesthetic regimes that determine how they are read, establishing what is in/visible and, therefore, im/possible (Rancière 2004, 2009). Something recognised by powerful actors such as the state that 'promote ideology by making some things visible and other things invisible' (Callahan 2020, 5; see also: Kennedy 2008). In this sense, images do not communicate independently. Rather, they are always situated within a broader discursive environment that includes various texts, other images, and bodies. Images are also 'read' in particular contexts, in ways shaped by different sociocultural factors, and by people who draw on different cultural and experiential 'stock' to interpret an image—we all have different ways of seeing. How you and I interpret an image is not necessarily the same because we draw on different personal experiences and knowledge to read it. Therefore, how images 'speak', what they 'do', and their ontological status is a large and ongoing debate that cannot and should not be settled definitively (see Andersen, Vuori, and Mutlu 2015). One point of convergence amongst visual IR scholars is that images are irreducible to words. They have an excess and an affective quality that cannot be captured or mediated by words (Hansen 2011; Panofsky 2009; Vuori 2010, 260–1). Images and words, while interrelated, work differently. How they are treated, talked about, and the effects they have are different from words. That said, they are neither superior nor entirely separate from the written/spoken.

A theorisation of images as polysemous and obtaining meaning only through linkages and differentiations to other signs has implications for how one understands the political work images do and how one engages with the visual methodologically. I argue that the meaning of an image cannot be pinned down definitively, that images do not have a single universally received message, and that images cannot be understood as telling a story in and of themselves. We therefore need to include other texts and images in our analysis because these help to attribute meaning to the image(s) under study—as I do with Chapters 5 and 6. This is what Hansen (2011) calls an intertextual/intervisual approach to studying images and it is one I embrace in laying out a word-image-body approach to the visual. I think of this as 'intermodal' in the case of the words-images-bodies approach.

Following an intertextual/intervisual/intermodal approach to visual analysis, images always need to be interpreted: they only obtain meaning by being read through other images, texts (Barthes 1977; Hansen 2011), the practices around their use (MacKenzie 2020) and through 'personal and societal assumptions and norms that surround us' (Bleiker 2018, 16). On this, Bleiker argues that: 'when we look at a photograph we never just look at a photograph alone. We actually look at a complex relationship between a photograph and ourselves'. I argue that this holds regardless of the visual genre we are confronted with (Sontag 1977; Zelizer 2010). As we bring ourselves to engage with an image of any genre, that engagement is 'intertwined not only with experiences, such as our memory of other [images] ... but also with the values and visual traditions that are accepted as common sense by established societal norms' (Bleiker 2018, 16; Hansen 2011). In practice, all of this means that each of the different chapters in this book bleed into one another: the analysis in one is pollinated by my assessment of the politics emerging from different images and texts and activist bodies in the others.

Other texts and images are not the only important things to consider in visual analysis, we must also consider what Megan MacKenzie calls *visual practices*—how an image is produced, circulated, and how it is used—and *visual patterns*—the common visual motifs and styles (MacKenzie 2020). We come to know certain political issues such as war through certain, repeated, aesthetic and visual registers (Malmvig 2016, 262; Sontag 2003, 21). This (re)produces particularised ways of knowing and even structures research by constituting what we 'see' as representative of 'war', 'revolt', 'peaceful protest', and the like. All of this affects how an image might be read, what political status an image is attributed, whether an image is considered a matter of international politics or not, and thus the arguments we can make of an image. When a particular visual motif is used in protest marches (e.g., the pink triangle) or a similar visual pattern (e.g., satirising politician's faces) is used in activism, they acquire a particular status that cannot be read in isolation or ahistorically.

Images, then, do not have their own, universal 'voice' but are instead 'multivocal with audiences determining what they say through their interpretation(s)' and uses or re-imaginations of the image (Cooper-Cunningham 2019, 389). The meanings attributed to images, what they are said to 'do', and the texts ascribing them meaning must come into any analysis (Hansen 2011). The discourses surrounding images, including the practices associated with them, determine what they are perceived as doing, what responses are required or legitimated, and what the image makes politically possible (Adler-Nissen, Andersen, and Hansen 2019, 78; MacKenzie 2020). No image is inherently socially significant and, in this case, inherently homophilic or homophobic: an 'interpretation needs to be established, the image needs to be "anchored"' (Adler-Nissen, Andersen, and Hansen

2019, 80). Embracing polysemy rather than fighting to secure meaning is analytically fertile ground, especially when considering political activism.

As Richard Ashley wrote: 'A text's meaning and limits are ceaselessly dependent upon never finished processes of intertextual production—practices of interpretation and inscription involving the enflaming and opening of contexts—that at once connect each text to and differentiate each from the other texts of a culture' (1988, 233). There is politics in polysemy and the struggle over meaning. For this reason, I use the term *polytics* to capture the various different politics evoked by images on accord of their polysemy. A theorisation of images as polysemous requires an epistemological strategy that is not committed to providing *the* reading of an image (or a set of images) but to exploring the multiple different political possibilities and readings an image presents—their polytics—without attempting to tie meaning down. Our readings inevitably will shape how others interpret those images, too.

What readers will encounter throughout this book, then, is multiple and often competing interpretations of the same (sets of) images and embodied actions. This is intended to capture the complexity of the work images do, but also to illustrate the trickiness of working with the visual. What we offer as researchers is an informed and careful interpretation of the worlds that we study and while some readings might merit more weight than others, there is always the possibility for another, and another, and another. Instead of a monolithic approach, I advocate leaning into polysemy because this is where a more complex politics can be found. Embracing the polysemy of images is important for understanding the different potentialities for and methods of activist contestation and resistance, especially as images freely cross borders and can easily be read without linguistic proficiency or knowledge of the context in which they were produced.

Body Politics

Bodies feel, experience, endure, are affected by, and do politics. Perhaps the easiest example of the body as political is one also taken up by prominent theorists of the body in IR: war and political violence (Dauphinee 2007; Fierke 2013; Wilcox 2015). Clausewitz famously argued that war is the continuation of politics by other means. If war is indeed the continuation of politics by other means then even the most rationalist IR scholar should recognise that bodies are the bread and butter of politics, that they are sites where the international manifests, and that they act internationally. War is conducted by human bodies: they shoot guns, fly war planes, dig trenches, burn towns, rape, pillage, give medical assistance, and lay siege. And war impacts human bodies: they are annihilated, torn apart, shot, raped, starved, tortured, mutilated, and eviscerated.

Outside war, Karin Fierke (2013) has shown that the body is a site where perhaps the most political move/intervention of all is made: that of the body's destruction through the act of self-sacrifice. Theorising the voluntary destruction of the body as political, Fierke argues that the voluntary placement of the body in harms way or its destruction is similar to a 'theatrical performance, in that there is a deliberate, self-conscious "doing" of a highly symbolic act in public' (Fierke 2013, 43). Embodied forms of resistance communicate 'a political message on behalf of a marginalized community, which potentially contributes to its regeneration' (54) and particularly spectacular acts, such as suicide terrorism, have an extraordinariness to them that 'disrupts routine reality, raising questions about what could be so important that an agent would sacrifice his or her life for it' (43). While Fierke's work is focused on more extreme forms of political intervention than, say, the Hidden Flag project in Chapter 7, her argument about the body as a vector of political intervention that communicates the suffering of a particular community to a wider audience is important.

Drawing on queer insights, a different illustration of how politics plays out on people's bodies is the imposition of sex/gender upon people at birth. Reading certain bodies through a male/female sex binary based on their *visual* appearance, their shape, their genitalia, certain norms and expectations are imposed on those bodies (Butler 1990, 2004; Wilcox 2015, 7–9). From that point onwards, social and political power structures work upon those bodies and determine what is and is not possible for that particularly sexed and gendered individual. A whole set of expectations is imposed on us because of the shape of our body, because of our *visual* appearance:

> The received wisdom in straight culture, is that all of its different norms line up, that one is synonymous with the others. If you are born with male genitalia, the logic goes, you will behave in masculine ways, desire women, desire feminine women, desire them exclusively, have sex in what are thought to be normally active and insertive ways and within officially sanctioned contexts, think of yourself as heterosexual, identify with other

heterosexuals, trust in the superiority of heterosexuality no matter how tolerant you might wish to be, and never change any part of this package from childhood to senescence. Heterosexuality is often a name for this entire package, even though attachment to the other sex is only one element. If you deviate from at any point from this program, you do so at your own cost.

(Warner 2000, 37–8)

As Foucault argued, power shapes and disciplines the body (Fierke 2013, 21; Foucault 1977), meaning that bodies are 'important sites for moral regulations and discipline' (Gosine 2009 in Lazarus 2011, 83). So, from the very moment that one's body is sexed/gendered a whole host of expectations and disciplining of the body occur. One such form of moral regulation and discipline comes in the form of appropriate and acceptable sex, object desire, erotics, and corporeal pleasures—as outlined in the previous chapter and by multiple queer activists and writers. How we express our gendered personhood, how we situate ourselves in society, what desires we can legitimately have, what bodily pleasures we can legitimately enjoy or seek out, what careers we can pursue, what role we take on in the family, and so on, flow from that most political and almost quite mundane of moments: our being sexed/gendered and a series of norms thrust upon us.

As Kandida Purnell puts it, bodies are the 'contested sites of global politics that are acted upon and act relentlessly' in ways that trouble our understandings of 'the international' and international politics as spheres separate from and/or unaffected by the personal (Enloe 1989; Purnell 2021). And Ali Bilgiç writes that 'Bodies are racialised, gendered, sexed and commodified, and the "otherness" of certain groups is reproduced through/on their bodies, making them targets of physical and non-physical violence' (2016, 55). The body, then, is a battleground over which actors vie for control, that is disciplined into particular ways of being, and that is allowed to live or marked for death. Bodies are made to live and made to die in very particular ways (Foucault 1977; Mbembe 2003). They are sites of the political and can, thus, also be sites of resistance and contestation of dominant order.

In the case of Russian heteronormative internationalism, the body becomes international through activism and geopolitical posturing around sexual behaviour and erotic desire—two deeply embodied and affective things. Activist bodies become internationalised when they actively challenge Russian homophobia—in whatever space. By flaunting one's queerness or by putting one's queer body 'out there' into public space, the queer body aggravates and confronts Russia's geopolitical strategy of invisibilising—and making unthinkable—the joy and pleasures of a queer life. The bodily pleasures of queer people are made public by the actions studied in this book. From Mads Nissen's photographing of the intimate (Chapter 6) to the Hidden Flag's claim to public space using the rainbowed body (Chapter 7) to the memeification of Putin's face (Chapter 8).

While bodies are arguably the frontline of politics, feminist IR scholars have argued that the discipline's traditional analyses have a habit of pushing 'people to the sidelines of the international instead of foregrounding them as key agents of relations of power and change' (Sylvester 2013, 613). Studying corporeal interventions such as the Hidden Flag and the photographic representations of queer bodies poses an opportunity to centre on modes of international political activism that use the body and the visual to contest foreign and domestic policies. Feminist IR has long held that 'elite decision-makers are not the only people whose positions, knowledges, resources, and sources of information count in international relations' (Sylvester 2013, 619). By examining the body politics of the international through the lens of an international politics of sexual shame, we gain new insights about the way international power games play out and get contested, as well as the different meanings attached to queer bodies—that is, whether the agents are understood as foreign criminals or progressive activists.

Speaking specifically about the way the tortured body is represented in images, Elizabeth Dauphinee highlights how the visualisation of tortured subjects can transform their bodies into 'canvases for the torturer's inscription of pain' (2018, 33). Dauphinee's work is important in that, just like Susan Sontag's (2003), it forces us to think through the ethics of visualising the body in pain and the way that brutalised bodies become aestheticised in problematic ways (see also: Adler-Nissen, Andersen, and Hansen 2019; Berents 2019, 2020). However, Dauphinee approaches the question of the body's place in international politics in a slightly different way than I do here. To view the body only as a site upon which disciplinary power operates is at odds with a theorisation of the body as a (visual) site through which political activism takes place. Such a theorisation builds on K.M. Fierke's (2013) argument about the agentic status of political self-sacrifice and the visuality of pain as well as queer activism that uses the body as a political weapon (see Bargu 2017; Butler 2012; Cooper-Cunningham 2019; France 2012; Gould 2009; Wilcox 2015).

While the body is a site of violence and violation it can also simultaneously be a site of empowerment and resistance. It is a site that is harmed and possibly destroyed, but also one through which agency and power can be (re)directed in service of a new political order—even in death (Fierke 2013; Purnell 2021). We see this most profoundly in the political funerals of people with AIDS whose bodies—whether in the form ashes or corpses in coffins—were used to bring attention to the government and scientific community's negligence through spectacular events such as ACT UP New York's 'ashes' actions at the US White House in 1992 where the ashes of people who had died with AIDS after 'twelve years of genocidal AIDS policy' were spread on the lawn of the White House (ACT UP/New York (1992) in Gould 2009, 230; see Chapter 4 here and Schulman 2021, 331).

Social and political processes not only shape the body 'but the body also forms the basis of social experience and action. On the one hand, we attribute meaning to bodies and use the body as a symbol for social objects and worlds. On the other hand, bodies create meaning by acting within and upon their environment' (Fierke 2013, 21). If the body is a battleground that is actively being worked upon by powerful political actors and the (normative) structures that they support, uphold, and (re)produce then the body can equally be radically transformed into a weapon and anti-normative vehicle that works against those powerful actors and structures in service of a new form of politics. A queer politics, perhaps, that ceaselessly interrogates all relations to power and rejoices in flouting the norm, showing the gaps in the (heteronormative) system and exploiting them for their liberationary potential (Cohen 1997; Gould 2009). This theorisation of the body as political opens up the potential for a radical re-imagination not just of (international) subjectivity but of dominant sociality.

If the political is about the establishment of 'social order which sets out a particular, historically specific account of what counts as politics and defines other areas of social life as *not* political' then theorising the body not just as a passive site upon which the world (and politics) acts but as acting upon and affecting politics is to potentially reconstitute social order (Edkins 1999, 2, 5). Quoting Claude Lefort, Jenny Edkins argues that: 'the political is concerned with the "constitution of the social space, of the form of society"' (1999, 2). This aligns with Chantal Mouffe's theorisation of 'the political' as referring to the ontological level and 'the very way in which society is instituted … a space of power, conflict and antagonism' that constitutes human societies (2005, 9). This antagonism and conflict should not be read as necessarily violent but as events that constitute the organisation of society. If the queer body and the pleasures it seeks out antagonise and provoke societies, including international society, into reinforcing and doubling down on heteronormative sociality then those bodies are political in the most fundamental sense of the word: they expose the fragility of dominant social order and the potential for its reconfiguration.

Not only does this recall the lessons from queer political thought that emerged out of gay and lesbian liberation and AIDS activism—that homophobia is always arbitrary moralism about appropriate, acceptable, and 'normal' sexual behaviour and the management of bodily pleasures and erotic desires (Rubin 2011; Warner 2000)—but emphasises how bodies are 'the world's battleground, the contested terrain on which politics is played out' (Glassner 2012). Russian state homophobia and heteronormative internationalism bring to the fore the extent to which bodies are the end points, the sites that endure and experience every single political move and event, the surfaces upon which the political plays out—be that in relation to war, terrorism, imperialism, poverty, welfare, famine, health, pandemics, patriarchy, heteronormativity, white supremacy, human rights, or the ecological disaster we face. It also shows how bodies 'do' politics, how they can provoke dominant orders through various forms of activism, how they can disturb hegemonic orders and cause chaos around established norms and dominant (heteronormative) forms of sociality by showing their fragility and arbitrary boundary drawing (Bersani 1987, 1996; Butler 2012, 2020; Warner 1993). Bodies are the sites where new organisations of society and subjectivity can be made.

Russia's anti-West, anti-globalist posturing is deeply entangled with a discourse about European and Western (Gayropean) sexual decadence and immorality. We cannot disentangle this sexualised and moralistic foreign policy discourse from the events unfolding domestically around the issue of non-normative sex and/or gender expressions, including state-sanctioned violence against (suspected) queer people. Russian politicised homophobia might, thus, be understood as a transversal phenomenon that destabilises predominant spatialisations of politics as domestic/international—as if these 'spaces' can be separated out and disentangled analytically, and as if individuals' lives and bodies have not always been affected by politics across all levels (Butler 1993a; Gould 2009; Mbembe 2003; Purnell 2021;

Wilcox 2015). Bodies are sites that upend what we think of as the locations of international politics: all of these policies have the human body as their endpoint. Including them troubles IR's narrow focus on nations and states. Starting from the position that bodies are battlegrounds through and upon which (international) politics plays out opens up the possibility that the body is also a site of political activism and contestation where particular politics can be advanced or contested, and (racialised-gendered-sexualised) structures of domination can be entrenched or destabilised (Butler 2012; Cooper-Cunningham 2019; Fierke 2013; Hansen 2000b).

As Judith Butler (1990, 1993a) argues, the body exists materially but is only made intelligible through discourse. The body is not prediscursive but is assigned meaning and identity through language. If we theorise language and discourse more broadly than words—as I do—then the visual is not only fundamental in assigning meaning to bodies but to reconfiguring those meanings and the subjectivities enabled by them. The body stabilises/contests these meanings in the way it moves, positions itself, fails, and acts within and upon the world. Yes, discourses 'systematically form the objects of which they speak' (Foucault 1972, 49). However, this always comes with the possibility of failure or refusal to 'be' as expected or mandated; as in the case of bodies, especially queer bodies, that often embrace abject subjectivities and use deviation as a political strategy of undermining power structures.

Word-Image-Body

Bringing words, images, and bodies together and theorising them as a dynamic, inseparable triad, my words-images-bodies approach sits predominantly within a poststructuralist philosophy. A recurring critique of poststructuralism is that it overemphasises language at the expense of materiality, which might make some sceptical of whether a poststructuralist-inspired framework can adequately capture the complexity of bodies and images. These critiques, to me, rely on a fundamental misreading of the performative element of poststructuralist theorisations of discourse in which the material and the discursive are not ontologically separable but co-constitutive.[1]

---

[1] Laclau and Mouffe (1985, 108) and Judith Butler (1993a, 1997) provide a fuller engagement with this debate than I can here.

Referencing poststructuralist thinkers such as Foucault and Butler, feminist technoscientist Karen Barad demonstrates how a performative theorisation of discourse does not deny materiality but rather emphasises the co-constitution of the discursive and the non-discursive.[2]

> Discursive practices and material phenomena do not stand in a relationship of externality to one another; rather, the material and the discursive are mutually implicated in the dynamics of intra-activity. But nor are they reducible to one another. The relationship between the material and the discursive is one of mutual entailment. Neither is articulated/articulable in the absence of the other; matter and meaning are mutually articulated. Neither discursive practices nor material phenomena are ontologically or epistemologically prior. Neither can be explained in terms of the other. Neither has privileged status in determining the other.
>
> (Barad 2003, 822)

Firmly rooted in a performative theorisation of the visual[3] and the body, the words-images-bodies approach does not reduce bodies or images to words. Rather, it highlights how discursive practices—including all three of words, images, and bodies—are performative, thereby enacting and shaping social worlds in concert. From this vantage point, bodies and images are not passive objects of discourse but active discursive elements. They are all interconnected and working off one another for power. Put simply, while bodies and images are not linguistic entities, they are nonetheless part of the discursive field.

Discourse, theorised as such, is the words, images, and corporeal practices we use to constitute, articulate, and think about international politics. Political activism, contestation of state policies, and intervention in geopolitics might not always manifest in words—they may happen through the visual or the bodily. In this sense, discourse ought to be understood as something more expansive and complex, enacted through and exceeding words: words, images, and the body 'speak' together. Just because there are no words articulating a political issue, or if those words are ignored outright or dismissed,

---

[2] Barad is not a poststructuralist, but her work on the ontological inseparability of discursive practices and the material build on and extend earlier arguments put forth by both Foucault and Butler, connecting them with Niels Bohr's quantum ontology of mutual entanglement (Zanotti 2017, 372–3).

[3] For a full performative theorisation of the visual, see Lene Hansen's book *Images and International Security* (Forthcoming).

does not mean there are no other discursive planes in which political work is being done. None of the visual, the body, or words should be privileged: they must have equal analytic footing. We must think about the other epistemological sites through which we can understand and explore (international) political phenomena. It is important to look at a broad range of materials because this can provide insights about the world that we or others may have missed due to epistemological predilections that create a hierarchy of knowledge sources.

My argument here, then, is a relatively simple but important one: that discourse, contrary to the ways it has been studied to date, is never purely verbal/textual but in fact includes a whole set of other practices from the visual to the bodily and beyond. Visual and bodily practices show and tell stories in conjunction with and/or separately from text/word—as should emerge as the empirical analysis of the book progresses. These forms of representation constitute identities wherein certain bodies, actors, objects, and ideas get meaning(s) attached to them through discourse (Butler 2004; Said 2003). This predominantly takes place through the processes of linking and differentiation that poststructuralists have highlighted (Derrida 2009; Hansen 2006; Laclau and Mouffe 1985; Wæver 2002). Discursive representations establish and impose (sexualised-gendered-racialised) subject positions that certain bodies can occupy (Butler 1990; Said 2003) and they are world-ordering in that they actively shape the world we live in and establish the interpretative dispositions through which we see and understand the events taking place in the world around us (Callahan 2020; Doty 1993; Hansen 2015).

Words may anchor the meaning of and work upon images and bodies (i.e., AIDS as gay plague and queer bodies as incubators of disease and decadence), but images and bodies can also be vehicles for disturbing meanings, contesting established power structures, and powerful sites of political activism. And although texts '"anchor" the meaning of images … they do not determine it. Visuals might communicate differently from texts that accompany them' (Hansen, Adler-Nissen, and Andersen 2021, 7; see also Williams 2003). To proceed with a focus on language as written and spoken means that other ways of speaking and intervening in international politics, and thereby queer politics in general, get disregarded and left out of our understanding of the international politics of Russian homophobia. As Callahan writes: 'visual artifacts [are] sensory spaces in which international politics is represented, performed, and experienced through more embodied, affective, and everyday encounters on the local, national, and world stages' and we must look 'beyond icons and ideology to the pragmatic politics of everyday life' (Callahan 2020, 3). Images perform and constitute identity and community in many registers.

Importantly, the body is also visual. On this, Linda Åhäll argues that gender is 'a social practice that constantly refers to bodies, to what bodies do (or don't do) and to how bodies matter, visually' (Åhäll 2018, 150). The body is, Åhäll continues, 'informed by a visual, gendered logic' in the sense that it is 'sexed' on the basis of its visual appearance, it is visual matter that we see and make assumptions about (dress, body language, mannerisms, etc.), and bodies performatively reproduce sex/gender by either conforming or flouting sex/gender norms. Given that from the gendering and sexing of the body at birth flow the norms—including sexual—that unrelentingly work upon us, disciplining us into conformity with particular constitutions of 'normal', the visuality of gender structures the social and the political in important ways that link to (the contestation) Russian politicised homophobia and heteronormative internationalism.

The visuality of the body matters because it determines the intelligibility of its identity and political subjectivity in a gendered society that can restrict and marginalise particularly sexed-gendered-racialised bodies. Gender is a 'visual language of meaning-making, formed through processes of learning and unlearning' (Åhäll 2018, 156). As such the body, through its visual styling and appearance, can become a vehicle for resisting, in this case, heteronormative politics and ideas that usually obtain disciplinary power through their articulation in words. Like words, the visual and the bodily open up and shut down certain sociopolitical possibilities and they condition how individuals understand and represent themselves and others. What emerges in the genealogy and in the political activism against Russian homophobia analysed in the second half of this book is the interconnection and co-constitutedness of words, images, and bodies. This points to a more complex relationship between words, images, and the body. My aim here is to break down epistemic barriers by showing the degree to which all three collide and intersect with international politics.

When written/spoken forms of discourse are attached to bodies—for example, ideas about gender and sex—the visual and material-corporeal elements of the body get defined and sublimated to words. Bodies, though, have the power to displace that epistemic privilege by messing with normative ideas and structures that attach themselves to those bodies and are most often studied as they emerge textually/orally. As a visual 'thing', the body and visuality are ways to contest and disrupt 'the normal' that is textually/vocally produced and coded. For example, when the body intentionally refuses to conform with socially mandated ways of presenting itself, or engages in object desires outside those that are socially sanctioned— as was the case in AIDS and gay and lesbian liberation activism. Taking a poststructuralist approach to international politics means examining what is included and excluded in theories of the world and the political. Key questions centre on what and who is included/excluded; not just in analytical and theoretical terms, but also in terms of methodological and epistemological predilections.

Considering words, images, and bodies as equal parts of 'discourse' might seem a controversial move. Nonetheless, the body is part of discourse in the sense that it can comply with norms, dominant power structures, orderings of society, and follow—or refuse—the established rules of the game. Compliant bodies reify and recirculate discourses about, for example, sexuality and gender. Defiant bodies fail to conform, buck the trend, and in doing so demonstrate the fragility and malleability of discursively constituted power structures. Bodies, then, are not merely objects of discourse, they actively participate in, reconfigure, contest, reify, stabilise, destabilise, and/or undermine discourses. If the body is also visual in the sense that it is read and interpreted through its visual shape and how it behaves, and if ideas about appropriate behaviour and ways of being in the world, which are usually articulated and expressed in language, attach themselves to bodies (and then get reified and circulated by those bodies conforming or not), then sex and heteronormativity are, by extension, also visual. We invest a lot of stability in the body—for instance, gendering the body, reading gendered bodies— which constitutes it as something stable, fixed, and outside of discourse or social construction; this is ultimately false.

By thinking about discourse as something more expansive and complex, enacted through and exceeding words, looking at how the visual and (representations of) bodily practices construct the international and enable marginalised actors to intervene in international politics is a way of navigating the narrow epistemic parameters established for the creation of 'scientific' knowledge about international politics (Foucault 1980, 'Two Lectures'). It also allows an exploration of the ways that words, images, and bodies are sites of international politics that intervene in and constitute the world independently and concertedly. Particularly important in this case is that images can function as outlets for voices that have been marginalised, silenced, and/or ignored (Campbell and Shapiro 2007, 132). Locating and analysing textual, visual, corporeal forms of resistance and contestation to heteronormative systems and politicised homophobia/homophilia is particularly important in cases where there is a struggle to keep an issue such as Russian homophobia on the political agenda accompanied by attempts to silence or invisibilise it.

Hansen (2006) wrote that a discursive approach to the study of international politics necessitated a methodology of reading. What is needed, building on the theoretical work done here, is a methodology of looking, seeing, and reading that also accounts for the body and the visual as sites of knowledge about international politics—especially the international politics of sexual shame. This book contributes to the study of international politics through the breadth of genres covered, the different types of actor brought into international politics (primarily non-state) by turning to the visual, and the queer politics used to read the images, all of which complicates and nuances our theorisations of the international and the ways that visuality orders world politics.

W.J.T. Mitchell famously wrote that 'all media are mixed media' (2005: 260). Supporting the approach I outlined above, Mitchell continued that: 'the very notion of a medium and of mediation already entails some mixture of sensory, perceptual and semiotic elements'. In this sense, I want to make one important point that visual scholars might engage with moving forward: if texts anchor and give visuals meaning, then visuals can also be said to anchor and provide meaning to text. Seeing and studying international political issues requires more than words. While it is fair to say that visual scholarship has made a veritable impact on IR, there is still much to be done in terms of thinking expansively about the connections between images, bodies, and words. Because words and images and bodies are inextricably linked, all must be addressed in order to unpack the intricate processes through which (international) activism takes place and calls attention to political issues such as state homophobia. The visual and/or bodily, in conjunction with and/or separately from words, show and tell stories (Cooper-Cunningham 2019, 401). Like the Suffragettes and AIDS and queer activists before them, there is ongoing political activism against Russian heteronormative internationalism taking place across linguistic, visual, and bodily planes. This is an effective combination for challenging sexual and gender norms.

My tripartite word-image-body approach does not isolate or privilege visuality above or apart from other discursive planes such as the written/spoken or the bodily. Instead it acknowledges that the visual and bodily can complement our understandings of the social and political in IR by creating space for new ways of thinking about who and what counts as a subject of international politics as well as how words, bodies, and images combine to make international politics and to make interventions. What I offer above is some reflection on how the words we take for granted as the bread and butter of foreign policy and geopolitical analysis ought to be accompanied by some reflection on visual and body politics. Using this tripartite and queer inspired approach to studying international politics allows students and researchers to interrogate how the world comes to be understood as it is, how it is constructed, and how the people and places in that world are not only made to appear in certain ways but disciplined into particular ways of being, feeling, and living (Foucault 1972, 1978; Hansen 2006, 2015). It also allows us to see the representations that justify and legitimise particular policy positions and how power structures are (re)produced and contested. In the second, more empirical half of the book, I show how political activism takes place across all three visual, linguistic, and corporeal terrains where they combine and work together in important ways that cannot be studied in isolation without missing some of the politics at stake in the queer activism against Russian heteronormative internationalism.

4

There Weren't always Rainbows

A Visual Genealogy of Queer Activism

"Bring banners, balloons, mother and dad, posters, love, your best friend, pride ..."

(Christopher Street Liberation Day Committee 1973)

In Autumn 2019, I worked from the Brooke Russel Astor Reading Room using the New York Public Library's (NYPL) *Gender and Sexuality* archives. The Brooke Russell Astor Reading Room sits on the top floor of the library's Stephen A. Schwarzman building, located at the end of the Rose Main Reading Room. The two spaces juxtapose each other quite starkly. The latter is colossal, filled with people, and has incredibly grand decor. The former is intimate and more understated with books and artefacts from floor to ceiling. It is a cool and relatively quiet room except for whispered ordering of material, the occasional hum of a rewinding/fast-forwarding cassette tape deck, clicking keyboards, and, more often than one would expect, mobile phone camera noises. The camera blunder is always followed by a speedy fumbling to silence the device and a quick look round to smile, pull a 'whoops!' face, wave a hand, or some combination thereof.

Despite the quiet, it's a lively space that operates a strictly 'no photos of the room' policy. I overhear Tal, one of the reference archivists, tell another researcher who pleads for a photograph that this is in case of would-be robbers 'casing the joint'. It's a real shame that you can't photograph the room because it is beautiful with its book-lined walls, huge skylight, decorated ceiling, and mahogany furniture. Working in this part of the NYPL, which is off limits to the general public—something many tourists discovered after being buzzed in, quickly clocked, and then ushered out—is one of those rare privileges that academe affords. It also fills you with the sense that you're doing 'real' research, getting your hands dirty, working with physical, tangible artefacts. Proximity, it seems, matters. Proximity not only to the things you are studying, and by extension, the people whose lives you are engaging with

The International Politics of Sex. Dean Cooper-Cunningham, Oxford University Press.
© Oxford University Press (2025). DOI: 10.1093/9780197792544.003.0004

and writing about, but also to other researchers. None of us made friends—a hard task when it's a silent space—but there were always smiles, glances at the material someone else had ordered, and a sense of camaraderie.

When people asked why I was going to New York, I would vaguely reply that I was 'going to the archive'. This was met with intrigue, envy, and lots of questions. Non-academic friends and family asked what 'going to the archive' meant, what you do there, what I would do there, why New York, and so on. Even those familiar with the debates and questions I address in this book puzzled over why I was going to the US to look at a historical archive (mainly 1960s–90s) as part of a project focused on visual international responses to Russian politicised homophobia and heteronormative internationalism after 2013. People wanted to know what I was going to look at, what exactly I was looking for, and why I was looking for it. What purpose did this archival work serve? I wasn't entirely sure about the answers beyond a rather vague response about exploring 'visuals' and 'symbols' used in queer activism. That vagueness, while at times uncomfortable and seemingly unscientific, was intentional and something to get used to: part of doing a genealogy is knowing where you will end but not what path you'll take to get there.

For clarity, when I said 'visuals' I meant artefacts of a visual nature: photographs, badges, posters, banners, drawings, stickers, and so on. With the adage 'queer', I meant any symbol used in activism by and/or on behalf of queer people—that is, those whose sexuality and/or gender do not align with hetero norms.[1] For me, the archive was not only a space for exploration, discovery, wrong turns, and inspiring finds but a space to sit with the politics and magnitude of researching queer activism. For the people whose lives are connected to the material in the NYPL and for those being persecuted in Russia today, sexual behaviour, erotic desires, and gender expressions quite literally mean(t) life or death.

This book explores how visuals have been used in international activism against Russian homophobia. The rainbow is a prominent feature in every chapter. Occasionally, the pink triangle pops up. What does it mean that these symbols are used within and without Russia to resist state

---

[1] A symbol is: 'any object used by human beings to index meanings that are not inherent in, nor discernible from, the object itself' (Elder and Cobb 1983, 28–9; see also Olesen 2017). This aligns with a poststructuralist understanding where symbols—be they in the form of flags, logos, and the like—are discursively constituted and their 'meaning' always unstable (Derrida 2016; Laclau and Mouffe 1985). 'Icons' and 'symbols' are similar in that both ought to be understood by most people who see them (Hariman and Lucaites 2007).

homophobia? What politics is invoked by their presence? How can one read and understand photographs (Chapter 6; Figure 4.1), memes (Chapter 8), or embodied activism (Chapter 7; Figure 4.1) containing these symbols without a thorough understanding of the politics of the rainbow, the pink triangle, and their evolution? Beyond activism contesting Russian homophobia, what does it mean that the rainbow flag is plastered everywhere during Pride month? How did the rainbow achieve such iconicity, what is its political baggage, and is it potentially depoliticised as it moves beyond the spaces it was intended to be used in?

Returning to the questions asked of me before I went to the archive: What was the point in going to New York? Why did I need to work with archival material from US-based gay rights, queer liberation, and AIDS activism? What did any of that have to do with Russia's heteronormative domestic and foreign policy project and the visual international activism contesting it? What purpose does a visual genealogy serve for this project? Well, gay and lesbian rights, Pride, and LGBTI+ politics are often associated with and/or represented by a rainbow flag. The rainbow is taken for granted as a symbol of queerness and queer friendliness; used almost unthinkingly without acknowledging its politics or history. The rainbow flag didn't emerge out of

Figure 4.1 'Gay Pride parade in St. Petersburg' by Roma Yandolin (2013). Image courtesy of Getty Images (ID no.: 176000085).

nowhere: it was designed by Gilbert Baker and made its activist debut in the USA in 1978. While the rainbow flag has become a global icon, there weren't always rainbows in queer or LGBTI+ activism. Thus, it is important to go back and explore the social and political context at the time of its emergence, as well as the various different politics the rainbow flag has been constituted as symbolising. Why New York? Anyone who knows even the least bit about queer history and activism knows that the Stonewall Riots were incredibly important. Stonewall is iconic in popular imaginaries of contemporary LGBTI+ movements—at least in the West. The NYPL hosts one of the largest collections of material specifically related to queer liberation and gay and lesbian rights post-Stonewall. It also hosts a huge collection of AIDS activist material, particularly ACT UP/NY records.

Knowing all of this, I decided that in order to understand contemporary queer visual politics and the iconicity and politics of the rainbow flag— which, given its presence in all of the chapters, is clearly an important part of activism against Russian state homophobia within and without—it was fundamental to go back to one of the key spaces and times that helped constitute (the idea of) a global gay and lesbian rights and liberation agenda, which morphed into what is now a global LGBTI+ rights movement.[2] For this reason, the genealogy is spatiotemporally located in the USA from the late 1960s onwards. What I went to look for in the archive was first and foremost the visual strategies used in queer activism starting from a period that is widely regarded as a 'flash point' in queer history, as well as changes in the visual patterns and visual practices of earlier forms of queer activism.

Following my queer curiosity, I went off to New York with a feeling that something was missing in current understandings of queer icons/symbols and their internationalisation. I was particularly uneasy with the narrative

---

[2] In the NYPL archival material, various organisations and individuals differently refer to their activism as either part of a *rights* or *liberation* movement. I try to honour each organisation's terms as far as possible. In this sense, I offer somewhat of a conceptual genealogy using the material I engaged with; which term is used depends on which actor employs it. The liberation movement had a more radical politics that sought more than civil rights, focused on the politics of sex, and was closely linked with AIDS activist groups. The liberation movement adopted the more antinormative type of politics outlined in the introduction. The rights movement is closer to contemporary LGBT+ movements' desire for social, political, and legal equality (i.e., gay marriage, adoption, etc.). The radicalism of gay liberation's call for a 'wholesale sexual revolution' of the sex/gender system was diminished as the movement grew; the sexual revolution versus civil rights rift settling in the latter's favour (Gould 2009; Jagose 1996, 58). Lesbian and gay liberation activism aligns closely with a queer political commitment to 'challenging the determinism of LGBT identity politics' whereas lesbian and gay rights is more aligned with contemporary LGBT politics (Altman 1993, 128; Cottet and Picq 2019, 4; Gould 2009).

that the rainbow had become too commercial and, thus, depoliticised. I had a hunch that I was going to see a lot of rainbows and some pink triangles in the archive, and I left with the goal of seeing how these symbols and their variations were used over time. I hoped to see their emergence as icons of queer celebration, protest, activism, and resistance; to see how they got to their present—albeit always unstable and contestable—meaning. I also sought to trace visual patterns, symbols, and/or icons that I hadn't yet come across in contemporary activism, that had disappeared or had not diffused and been appropriated—generally and in the particular case of Russia.

What I didn't expect was that I would come away with a quite different understanding of queer politics than I left Copenhagen with. I had no idea that the archival work and my engagement with the radical queer politics of the 1980s would not only force me to rethink my mobilisation of queer but to rethink the politics of the images and the embodied forms of activism that I was engaging with in my analysis of queer international activism against Russia's heteronormative domestic and foreign policy projects. Not only are there similar visual patterns and practices in US-based queer activism from 1960s to 1980s and contemporary activism against Russian homophobia, but similar strategies of using the body as a political weapon that reconfigures subjectivity and political space.

As to the value added of genealogy for this book, genealogy enables a different analysis than would otherwise be possible without it. For visual scholarship, which is anchored in symbolism, metaphor, and context-bound meaning, understanding the historicity and evolution of symbols is crucial and makes for better political analyses of the present. This is particularly the case in queer activism, which has a rich tradition of using visual and embodied practices as part of activism (Finkelstein 2018; France 2012, 2016; Gould 2009; Riemer and Brown 2019). For a queer political analysis, which unapologetically holds a transformative agenda, genealogy also helps reignite the fire of older political agendas and/or shows how they have lost their transformative potential.

Visual genealogy and the historical visual activist strategies brought out here are thus part of an important archaeological exploration of the inter-texts/intervisuals that ascribe meaning to and inform analysis of the visuals being studied here as well as an exploration of queer politics more generally. The genealogy allows me to trace the visual dis/continuities in queer activism as well as the different politics that the various symbols appearing in queer activism against Russia represent(ed). We need to be able to understand where queer symbols come from in order to be able to read the politics of visual activism in the subsequent chapters fully. The rainbow flag and pink triangle are not just random visual symbols, they are politically loaded in their emergence from early gay/lesbian and AIDS activism. It is crucial to reveal that historicity and connection to a queer politics of the antinormative and joy in abjection (on joy in abjection, see Bersani 1987).

Genealogy helps visual scholars unpack the political work images and other forms of visuality do. It is, therefore, a key tool for those who embrace the polysemous theorisation of the visual and seek to demonstrate the instability of meaning and various politics (the polytics) emerging from different interpretations of images. As one of the key figures in AIDS artivism, Avram Finkelstein, writes:

> examining any Gran Fury image without the full context of the years of work by scores of activists absorbed in the issues it articulates completely unplugs it from its power source ... concrete insights into what made these images tick can only come in long form ... once these posters are isolated from the environment they were created for, they become oddly mute. When they are stripped of the native meanings that were activated in situ, their social proportion can't be approximated on a gallery wall with any degree of accuracy ... This work becomes activated in its performance, in its doing.
>
> (Finkelstein 2018, 4–5)

For this very reason, we cannot read the use of rainbow flags or pink triangles or queer political interventions that draw on similar visual-embodied tactics to ACT UP, Gran Fury, or early gay liberation groups without situating them within their genealogical context and asking how their earlier meanings were lost and changed character along the way. Failing to do so renders them mute: their native meanings get stripped away and with it their politics. There weren't always rainbows. There weren't always pink triangles. Queer activists didn't always target politicians' faces. And contemporary queer activists challenging the Russian government didn't invent visual-embodied activism. How we interpret the politicality of visual activism cannot be disentangled with its use in other contexts and times. Genealogy is useful for getting closer to the visual, narrowing the interpretation gap, and exploring how the visual communicates in all its complicatedness without resolving to simplification.

Genealogy

Foucault (1977) understood genealogy as a 'history of the present' that shows the contingency of the present on pasts. Genealogy can be used as a 'historical, interpretative research tool' and is a method for 'historicising social items' and asking questions about how a social artefact or phenomenon has become constituted in its current form (Price 1995, 84, 87; Vucetic 2011, 1296). The social items under study here are symbols, icons, and visual practices associated with queer liberation, lesbian and gay rights, activism, and celebration. Methodologically, genealogy uses historical material to provide an account of a particular sociopolitical phenomenon, event, or issue (Vucetic 2011, 1306).

One can, for example, ask how the rainbow flag came to be understood as a symbol/icon of LGBT+ pride, gay rights, and non-normative sexuality more broadly, how it has achieved a global visual hegemony, to the exclusion of other symbols/icons and, thus, potentially other people and forms of sexuality. Genealogy begins from something current—a practice, discourse, symbol, icon—to ask how present understandings have been shaped and which knowledges have been forgotten, silenced, invisibilised, or have fallen out of the dominant discourse. Genealogy thus occupies a double role in that it stands alone as detailed historical insight but is simultaneously intended to inform and be mobilised in subsequent political analysis.

This chapter examines the evolution of symbols and icons associated with queer politics, paying particular attention to those that have diffused and been appropriated globally as well as the different politics that they have been used to represent. I do not understand 'evolution' in the teleological sense but rather as a diverse, multilayered, and multidirectional process with various criss-crossing and overlapping temporalities (Buzan and Hansen 2009, 3). Genealogy is not about explaining through law-like, linear patterns, but about asking how a phenomenon comes to be understood in a particular way and what that constitution enables/disables. This specific genealogy enables me to trace the galvanising visual nodes that structure queer activism globally and across time. Here, I show how the visual has always been important in queer politics. The visual is not just important today or in a certain space (e.g., Russia), it has been a fundamental part of queer activism across time and space.

One of the advantages of taking a genealogical perspective is that it brings under scrutiny common, generally ahistorical assumptions. For instance, that the rainbow flag is and always has been the symbol of a global LGBT+ rights movement. A visual genealogy offers one of many histories of the present and can provide an understanding of what has happened, which visuals have come in and out of use, the politics they were dis-/associated with, and how their uses and meanings have evolved (c.f. Buzan and Hansen 2009, 4; Foucault 1984, 78; Price 1995). This has the dual role of informing my analysis of visual international activism against Russian domestic and external heteronormativity by tracing the evolution of the symbols associated with queer liberation and activism, as well as fighting the historical amnesia of queer identifications and subjectivities that comes as a result of dominant culture's perpetual 'denial of [queer] history' and 'erasure of [queer] existence' (Riemer and Brown 2019, 16). Visual politics is as much about what is unseen, forgotten, and suppressed as it is about what is and can be seen.

Importantly, this genealogy not only traces the evolution of queer visual activism but also offers a genealogy of queer politics. It brings out the tension between rights-based activism and the more radical queer politics that emerged from queer liberation and AIDS activism. Thus, the genealogy not only serves as an exploration of the visual practices and patterns in queer activism but also how I position myself in terms of queer. A first in visual IR, the visual genealogy traces: the route to rainbow flagged rights, Pride, liberation, and resistance; what has been sidelined, lost, and invisibilised along the way; and the different styles of activism that emerged in the fight for queer liberation and rights. Visuals are always tied to a particular politics and this must be brought out as well. No symbol 'means' in isolation. Meaning always comes from somewhere, is always contextual, intertextual, and unstable.

Doing the Visual Genealogy

The research for this chapter was conducted after I had selected the empirical material included in the main analytical chapters of the book. It was, however, written before the analysis in those chapters. This is a crucial analytical and methodological point. The abundance of rainbow flags and the presence of other queer symbols in the empirics of Chapters 6 through 8, as well as their presence in my experiences watching and participating in Pride marches over the years confirmed the necessity of looking historically to understand these symbols' political status and their iconicity. The added bonus of doing the genealogy was the revelation of how a radical antinormative queer politics emerged in response to identity-based 'rage for respectability' approaches (see Cohen 1997, 2004). These political projects also have distinct visual strategies with their own symbols.

In terms of carrying out a genealogy, Richard Price (1995, 89) and James Keeley (1990, 96–9) advocate a three-step approach similar to Srdjan Vucetic's 'three E' approach (2011, 1300). The overall goal is not to provide a comprehensive explanation but to illuminate key moments in the evolution of queer symbols/icons. The 'three Es' are: episode, examples, and effectiveness. An *example* is something illustrating and supporting the point you make. Here, I use images from the archive, personal photographs, and desk research as examples. An *episode*—or event, moment, epoch—identifies a key period that has shaped the 'present' being historicised. For this period, the competing (visual) discourses and how they changed over time must be identified (Price 1995, 89). In this case, the *episode* I am interested in is the period from around 1969 in the US, primarily New York City. There is a general consensus amongst activists and those writing on LGBTI+ and queer issues that the mid to late-sixties constitute a turning point for—though not necessarily the definitive start of—queer and LGBTI+ activism (Amin 2017, 7; Bronski 2011, 1; Gould 2009; Marcus 2019; Riemer and Brown 2019). Particularly important are the Stonewall Riots.

The Stonewall Riots refers to a series of activism by queer people in New York City in summer 1969, named so because of the place they started. The Stonewall Inn was a gay bar on Christopher Street in New York City's West Village. One June night in 1969, police raided the bar for its supposed infringement of liquor laws. This was not uncommon and police frequently raided gay bars. That night Stonewall's clients—especially trans people—resisted and fought back over an entire weekend, asserting their presence, pride, and anger at being perpetually harassed and brutalised by the police (Altman 1993, 126–7; Jagose 1996, 31). The result was the emergence of a gay liberation movement founded not in quiet, assimilationist tactics but in an antinormative, antisocial[3] politics of acting up and declaring wholesale inaptitude for heteronormative sociality. This moment is widely referred to as simply 'Stonewall', a moment Kimberlé Crenshaw calls a 'multi-racial, gender diverse insurgency' against police brutality and discrimination (2019, 11:30.00).

---

[3] See footnote 16 from introduction.

Many artefacts—press releases, letters, posters, and banners at demonstrations—produced by activist organisations in the US also constitute Stonewall as ushering in a new period and fervour in gay and lesbian activism. It is variously characterised as: 'the time when angry homosexuals first fought back police in a raid on one of their bars' (Christopher Street Liberation Day Committee 1976 emphasis added), 'the start of the contemporary lesbian and gay male liberation movement' (Dykes Against Racism Everywhere 1982), and an event that 'sparked the beginning of the modern Gay Liberation movement in the United States and *throughout the world*' (Christopher Street Liberation Day Committee 1983 emphasis mine). Describing the evening of 28 June 1969, Sylvia Rivera recounts that after years of police and mafia extortion and brutality:

> It just [snaps fingers], everything clicked. Everybody just like, why the fuck are we doin' all this for? The people at them bars, especially at the Stonewall, were involved in other movements and everybody just like, alright, we gotta do our thing. We're gonna go for it.
>
> (Marcus 2016, 05:20)[4]

The NYPL's 'Love & Resistance: Stonewall 50' exhibition called it 'a flash point in LGBTQ ... history' (New York Public Library 2019) and the New York Historical Society referred to Stonewall as 'the dawn of the gay liberation movement' (New York Historical Society 2019).

The 'newness' of the post-Stonewall lesbian and gay activism and the spectacle of mass mobilisations seems to be confirmed by a French onlooker to an unsanctioned 'Stonewall 20' march along Fifth Avenue. Asked by an AIDS activist if they had 'ever seen anything like this?', they respond: 'No, no. We don't have anything like that in Europe, in France, or anywhere else in Europe' (DIVA TV 1989, 00:12:00). Be this 'sparking point' true or false, there is a widespread sense—demonstrated not only in activists' accounts, queer histories, and queer scholarship but also by the number of exhibitions and events commemorating Stonewall's 50th anniversary—that what happened in New York from 1969 onwards was agenda-setting and revolutionary. Michael Bronski suggests that Stonewall happened during a period characterised by 'a new kind of homosexuality that was, first and

---

[4] The Stonewall Riots took place in the context of rising antiwar sentiment during the Vietnam war, increasing racial tensions, and a new wave of radical feminism (Bronski 2011, Chapter 10; Rayside 2020, 47).

foremost, a form of political resistance' (2011, 204). However, Stonewall is not unproblematically regarded as the first time queer people—I say queer because of the diversity of people involved and problems of anachronistically applying current terminology—rose up and rioted against social and politicised homophobia (Bosia 2020a). As such, I do not take Stonewall as a definitive starting point for global gay and lesbian liberation and rights movements—as if establishing one is even possible. In fact, there are also good reasons to trace a European influence on pre-Stonewall, pre-gay liberation, US homophile organisations such as the Mattachine Society and Daughters of Bilitis (Bosia 2020a; Jagose 1996; Rayside 2020).

The various splits and regroupings of the gay and lesbian movement are many and near impossible to trace, but Stonewall almost universally stands in as a symbol for a break from conservative, liberal, assimilationist politics and polite protest that characterised earlier homophile movements (Altman 1993, 127). On this, Annamarie Jagose argues that 'Stonewall functions in a symbolic register as a convenient if somewhat spurious marker of an important cultural shift away from assimilationist policies and quietist tactics, a significant if mythological date for the origin of the gay liberation movement' (1996, 30). US gay and lesbian culture and dissent held (and still hold) significant influence on similar movements globally, which can, in part, be attributed to post-World War II US hegemony (Adam 1987; Altman 1993; Jagose 1996, 34–6). Consequently, the symbolic position of Stonewall as a pivotal moment in gay and lesbian dissent rippled across much of Europe, Canada, Australia, New Zealand, and parts of South America.

More important than Stonewall's status, the late 1960s mark a time when the first seemingly coordinated visual strategies emerged as part of gay and lesbian activism. Both in terms of visibility by being openly 'out' (Altman 1999, 577) and in terms of creating visual materials with unified, coordinated designs (Finkelstein 2018; France 2016; Gould 2009). Figure 4.2—one of the many remixes of Barbara Kruger's works (in this case 'I SHOP THEREFORE I AM') used by queer activists—captures both strategies and two distinct, if overlapping, politics: to be visibly out, proud, and to have visibility as the basis of one's queer subjectivity; and to produce and circulate visuals as a mechanism of resistance and claim to public space.

Returning to the last 'E' of genealogy, an *effective* genealogy focuses on a 'problem' (Vucetic 2011, 1301). That problem is generally how something came to be understood as normal or true. The aim is to uncover the historical situatedness of and common assumptions underpinning that phenomenon.

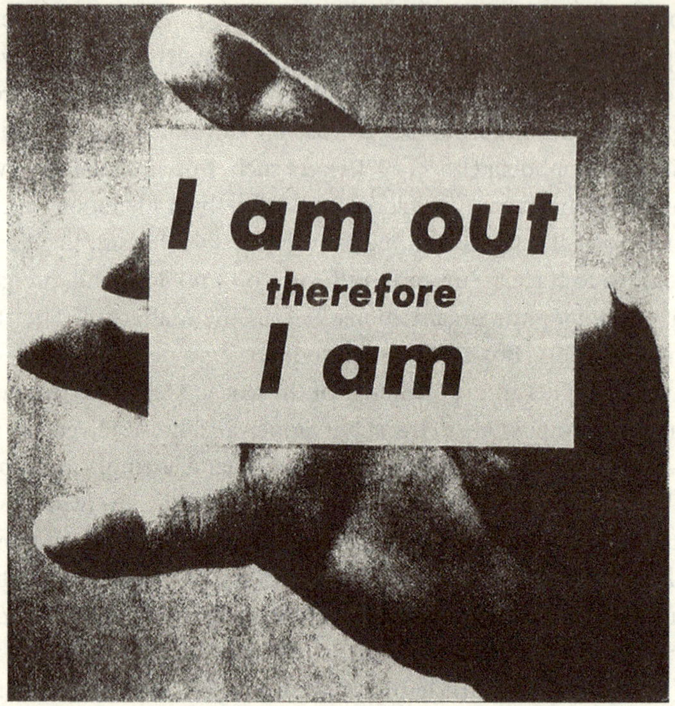

Figure 4.2 'I am out therefore I am' by Adam Rolston (1989). Image courtesy of the artist.

Here, this is about identifying features that were critical in shaping current visual practices. Take the rainbow flag, for example, which is understood and widely recognised as a global icon of equality and the LGBT+ rights movement. This genealogy shows a different story: the rainbow (flag) has not always been visually hegemonic. The lambda (λ) and pink triangles held important positions in the visual politics of queer, AIDS, and gay and lesbian rights activism. There is much more of a complexity to the use of the rainbow that also highlights a rift between queer and LGBT+ activism from the 1980s. Visual genealogy is important in this respect because it provides 'important knowledge of the sedimentation of current representations as well as a critical means through which the … naturalness of these representations can be contested' (Hansen 2006, 83).

Like good discourse analysis, genealogy requires a vast amount of material. Although I spent a month in the NYPL archives and studied many miles of primary sources, this is and can never be the full story. The archive is a constructed entity, reliant on people submitting things to be archived and, here, there is a particular bias towards New York-based groups. A good set of historical artefacts and background texts can be useful for filling in the gaps and identifying alternative discourses. I supplement my analysis of the NYPL material with insights from Reimer and Brown's beautiful tome 'We are Everywhere' (2019) as well as the histories written in Bronski's 'A Queer History of the United States' (2011) and visual stories told by Finkelstein, a founding member of the *Silence = Death* artivist collective (2018). Reimer and Leighton's volume traces queer imagery from 1867 to 1994 using artists' and photographers' work from multiple archives across the US. The visual story they show is consistent with the story I saw both in the NYPL and back in Copenhagen when working with the material again.

Visual Genealogy as a Methodology of Looking

Returning from the archive with a catalogue of photographs of the visual artefacts I had engaged with in the archive, I was confronted with the problem of actually doing the analysis. Initially, I used NVivo to code and organise the visual material. This made the process far too complicated. The analysis could be more easily carried out by manually organising the material. NVivo made it tricky to get a big-picture overview of the visual material, which made tracing appearances and particular uses of rainbows or pink triangles harder than it should be. I found myself adding more and more codes, getting more and more lost in individual images, and with an increasing inability to 'zoom out' and actually see the bigger picture. A high-level view (literal and metaphorical) is crucial for a visual genealogy.

NVivo helped me see the trees (individual artefacts) but not really the forest (the entire collection). Genealogy is not about each individual tree but the cultivation of the forest: which parts grew and eclipsed the others and which parts were deforested or outgrown. So, instead, I opted to identify patterns by sight and not code. To analyse the material from the NYPL, I spent four days printing and organising the visual materials I had engaged with in the physical archive in New York and the digitised collection by decade. The total number of images I had taken hovered around 2000, but having eliminated poor quality, duplicate, and completely irrelevant images, I printed roughly 1400. There were some collections I could not photograph. In these cases, I relied on drawings and descriptions from my notebook. After printing and organising my material by decade—a process that included going back-and-forth between the archive's finding aids, my personal notes, and internet searches to roughly date certain artefacts (e.g., when Bill Clinton was president or Ed Koch in office)—I took over a meeting room for two days and spread all of the material across the floor chronologically, trying to group visual motifs (e.g., pink triangles, lambda symbols) together to identify patterns and shifts. In the process, I eliminated images that showed the same visual artefacts (e.g., rainbow protest banners) being used in the same way and at a similar point in time or at the same event.[5] This still left a huge number of images. In order to reduce the number of images and concentrate the genealogy further, I identified key visual nodes (i.e., those symbols that appeared most often and most consistently): the lambda symbol, two versions of the pink triangle, the rainbow, and the 'Bloody Handprint' from Gran Fury's 'The Government has Blood on its Hands' poster in Figure 4.3. Removing other visual artefacts such as 'Read my Lips' posters by Gran Fury from the late 1980s and images that targeted politicians (the dominant visual strategy from the 1990s; see Figure 4.13) allowed me to move from the floor onto tables. By day two, I was left with a couple of hundred visuals including photographs, posters, stickers, stills from VHS recordings, and badges created by different actors.

Carrying out the visual genealogy this way and addressing such a mix of visual genres proved useful and tricky. Two similar but slightly different stories emerged when I removed photographs and VHS material from the spread and included only posters, badges, and stickers. The photographs and VHS material were mostly created at protests and showed a lot of rainbow flags. When that material was removed, a less complex narrative is depicted, one where the rainbow flag is largely absent until the 1990s. This raises various questions about: designing the genealogy and what material one engages with, the constructedness of archives, and the political status of the rainbow, which media it was portrayed in, which contexts it was mobilised in, and how it was used visually.

All of this experimentation presented a methodological opportunity. If discourse analysis entails a methodology of reading and most genealogies are founded on reading textual artefacts then, methodologically speaking, visual genealogy must entail a dual process of reading and looking. All

---

[5] Some of the images were undated so an approximation was made. My familiarity with the archive, the materials' relationship to one another, and the key actors and events made organising the material quicker and easier.

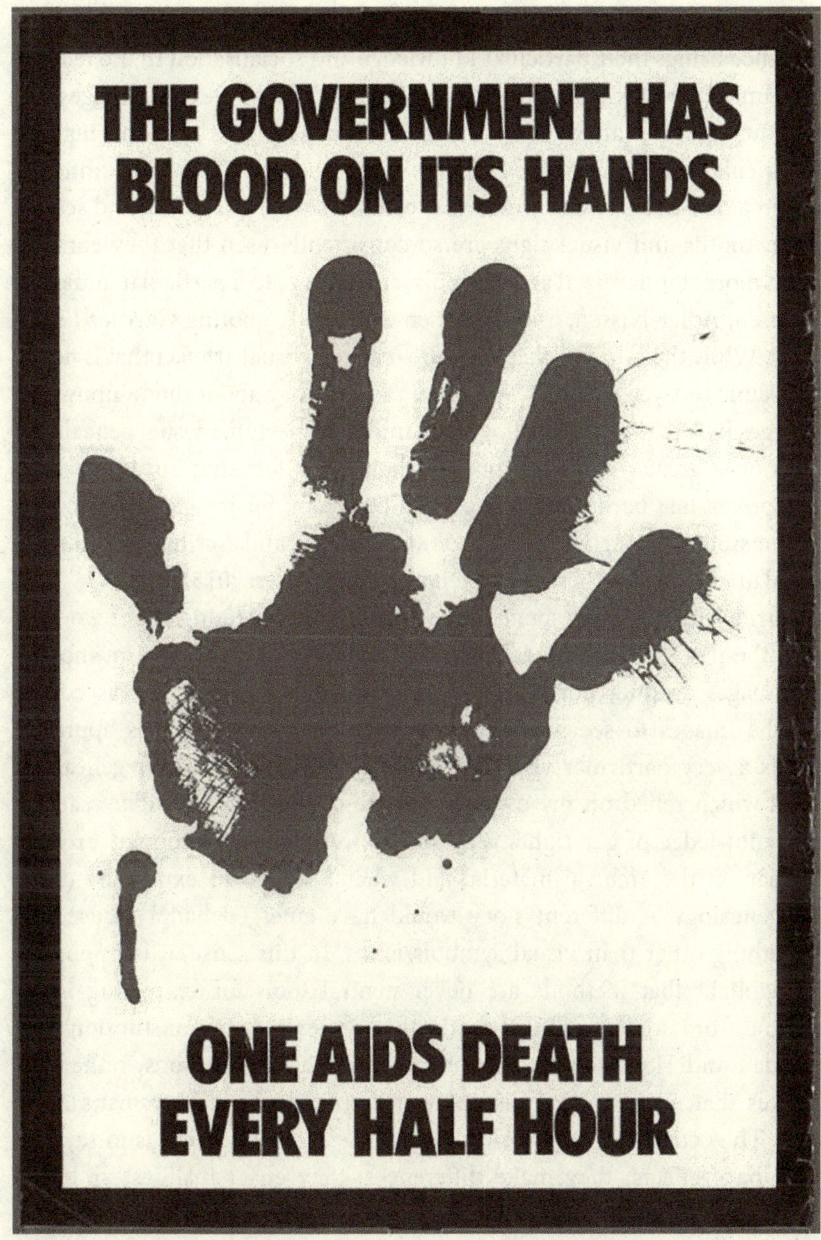

Figure 4.3 'The Government Has Blood on Its Hands. One AIDS Death Every Half Hour'. By Gran Fury (1988) in Manuscripts and Archives Division, New York Public Library Digital Collections. Image ID: 1577320.

images, like texts, can be interpreted in multiple different ways as a given audience brings their particular knowledge and socialisation to the reading of an image. The texts surrounding an image—and also the other images surrounding them—narrow down the meaning of an image by anchoring it in a particular way. This means that all images are constituted and communicate in a discursive environment that produces ways of reading and seeing. Some 'motifs and visual signs are so consistently used that they come to "tell a more standardized and less polysemic story" to a particular audience' (Hansen, Adler-Nissen, and Andersen 2021, 6–7, quoting Gartner (2011, 548)). While the rainbow flag might be read as a visual artefact that is not so polysemic today, a different and more radical story about the rainbow flag emerges by situating it genealogically. In this respect, the visual genealogist takes on a greater empirical burden than those focusing on purely written/spoken text because they must not only look for images but also find their textual anchors (i.e., those texts surrounding and ascribing meaning to visual artefacts) (Barthes 1977; Bleiker 2018; Hansen 2015).

During the two days spent in the Copenhagen meeting room working with the images I had taken from the archive, my focus was on moving the images around, positioning them together and apart. I was collaging the images to see how they related to one another. This approach builds a very particular vision of queer activism, a particular genealogy, all of which relied on my own knowledge of the archive, wider reading, and knowledge of gay rights activism, as well as the questions I brought to bear on the archival material and what I sought to expose by doing the genealogy. A different story would have emerged had I focused on something other than visual symbols/icons. In this sense, it is important to highlight that methods are never neutral tools for 'extracting information' from some empirical world that pre-exists our constitution of it (Aradau and Huysmans 2014; Aradau et al. 2015). Methods, rather, are devices that enact and/or disrupt worlds (Aradau and Huysmans 2014, 603). They constitute the world they are used to study. That is to say that they 'have effects; they make differences; they enact realities; and they can help bring into being what they also discover' (Law and Urry 2004, 393). The practice of visual genealogy, here, was an experiment in combining archival work, discourse analysis, and collage (see Kangas et al. 2019 on collage). It is close to what Aradau et al. might call 'bricolage', where empirics, methods, and concepts are experimentally brought together (2015, 8–9).

Collages, according to Anni Kangas et al. (2019, 5), offer possibilities for disruption and representation of the ways that multiple and often competing discourses intersect. Inspired by their work on student collages and argument that collaging 'allows for a seemingly paradoxical combination of themes and surprising connections made visible through composition and layering' (5), I made my own large-scale collage with a view to seeking out the connections, patterns, and developments in queer activism. This visual genealogy, therefore, emerges out of a 'bricolage' of archival work, discourse analysis, and genealogical collaging that allows for identification of the visual patterns MacKenzie (2020) identifies as crucial to understanding the political work of images.

Collaging is particularly apt as part of a visual genealogy because it not only problematises assumptions of temporal linearity and can illuminate the intense relationality of the present on pasts (Kangas et al. 2019, 6) but also highlights previously unseen connections across spatiotemporal boundaries. In part, this is because the visuals are removed from their original (archival, indexed, organised) context. While I am writing the genealogy for this book—a product of scholastic conventions and disciplinary epistemologies (see Callahan 2015; Harman 2019)—the collage is better placed than writing to capture the vast and complicated visualities of queer activism.[6] This is especially so given that there is an excess to the visual that words/speech cannot capture. It makes sense, then, to do the collaging to bring out key themes and linkages.

The Politics of Seeing

Every archive or museum collection is constructed in the sense that it is a collection of materials brought together—sometimes donated, other times taken, stolen, or looted—that might otherwise never have been situated in relation to one another (Featherstone 2006; Lisle 2007; Sylvester 2009). The archive is thus constructed politically. Having been archived, artefacts obtain a new meaning and tell a story; they are considered important and worth memorialising (see Lisle 2007, 236 on art curation). Being donated to, looted, or otherwise curated for the archive and deemed worthy of being

---

[6] My 'collages' are so large—even when transferred to tables—that I had to use a ladder to photograph them. I have neither the artistic nor photographic skills to make these aesthetically pleasing in a book format.

kept, archived material moves from an everyday object to an historical sociopolitical artefact, archived data, that researchers ought to pay attention to. This process entails a subjective judgement on the part of the archive's staff and also requires people to donate. The archive is not a neutral space where artefacts are stored: it has deeply entrenched racialised, gendered, sexualised, colonial, voyeuristic logics (Featherstone 2006, 591), and it is replete with absences and silences (Murphy, Marshall, and Tortorici 2014). This raises questions about what gets excluded, what we cannot see, touch, read, or feel.

The NYPL's Sexuality and Gender archive is vast. It comprises many individual collections brought together under one banner. The specific collections I looked at were: the ACT UP New York records (1969–97), AIDS Activist Videotape Collection (1983–2000), AIDS Poster Collection (1986–93), Barbara Gittings and Kay Tobin Lahusen Gay History Papers and Photographs (1855–2009), Bettye Lane Gay Rights Movement Photographs (bulk from 1971–1989), Christopher Street Liberation Day Committee Records (1973–86), Diana Davies Photographs (1969–78), Fierce Pussy Collection (1991–94), Gay Men's Health Crisis Photographs (bulk from 1982–93), Gran Fury collection (1987–95), International Gay Information Center (IGIC) collection (1951–94), and the Women's Action Coalition (WAC) (1989–2003).

The breadth of material covered in these collections is huge. In the Sexuality and Gender archive, there are newspapers, leaflets, photographs, posters, banners, clothing, badges, stickers, diaries, meeting minutes, videotapes, cassette tapes, CDs, condoms, match boxes, personal notes, correspondence, club cards, boardgames, permit requests for marches, artwork, and a whole host of other things. I could not look at everything in a month. That said, I ordered as much as possible from the aforementioned collections that contained some visual element. Some of what I looked at (e.g., the Bettye Lane photographs) could not be photographed or reproduced. Some of the material was kept in plastic covering that I could not remove. Some photograph collections had no negatives and so had to be protected as far as possible, others had restricted access, and sometimes viewing the original images and not photocopies required approval from the curator. These are important methodological points on how one does archival work that also speak to questions of how we see, show, and engage with images.

The biggest sources of insight into the life of visual symbols were the 'AIDS Activist Videotape' collection and photograph albums of demonstrations and marches. The photorealistic genres showed many of the posters, button badges, stickers, and banners I had ordered from the vault in use and painted a broad picture of the galvanising visuals that struck a chord, made it into 'action', and achieved a visual hegemony during certain periods. The VHS tapes and photographs showed the dominant visual practices at activist actions (e.g., marches and 'die ins'), how symbols were used and circulated. Returning to my earlier point about removing the photographic material from the 'big picture' collage, had I only engaged with posters, badges, banners, and the like, I would have missed the entire story of where and how certain symbols—the rainbow flag in particular—were used throughout the 1980s. The rainbow flag would only have entered the visual discourse in the 1990s according to an arrangement of the material that excluded photographs and VHS recordings. Hence, it was important that I included visuals of all kinds and did not delimit my genealogy by image genre.

Writing about photographs from the Gay Liberation era, Steven Dansky argues that photographs 'make visible what is concealed and become evidence of reality—a photograph is a powerful record of social space' (in Riemer and Brown 2019, 17). I am less inclined than Dansky to claim that photographs evidence some unconstructed truth or reality. However, photographic images are the least abstracted versions of and closest one can get to an event without physically being there—at least in terms of 'sight'. Photographs, in particular, 'allow the viewer to be brought back to the same time and place as when the image was captured' (Adler-Nissen, Andersen, and Hansen 2019, 80). I am confident that the various videotapes and photographs of marches created by a host of different actors give a good indication of which visual motifs triumphed and when. For this genealogy, photorealistic material has a certain epistemological edge on posters and banners because I not only wanted to see how visual symbols were used in print material but also their life/prevalence beyond; that is, the visual practices around galvanising visual symbols.

Now, after a lengthy but necessary set up, I address the symbols I identified as central to queer activist politics as well as how their meanings evolved or how they fell out of fashion. This comes in three overlapping but distinct visual phases: the lambda symbol; pink triangles; and rainbow flags.

Lambda

Amidst all the attention that the pink triangle and rainbow flag receive, the lambda symbol is the lesser addressed symbol in queer politics. Perhaps this is a symptom of its fall from use as a symbol of 'Gay and Lesbian Liberation' in the late 1970s/early 1980s, as it was gradually replaced by the more visually exciting rainbow and politically loaded pink triangle. The lambda symbol entered the visual discourse in 1970 when Tom Doerr chose the Greek character as the symbol of New York's Gay Activists Alliance (GAA). Its status was reinforced in 1974 when the first International Gay Rights Congress, which later became the International Lesbian and Gay Association (ILGA), pronounced it as the symbol of lesbian and gay rights. That lambda fell out of use—even with official endorsement and sponsorship—is indicative of the instability and impermanence of the visual and meaning.

As the 1970s progressed, the gay liberation movement increasingly focused on achieving equal rights, decriminalising sodomy, and normalising non-heterosexuality. This is clear from the visual material: the lambda symbol is frequently paired with specific bills that promoted civil rights for 'gay people' and there is an overarching message that 'gay is good', normal, and non-pathological at this time (Figure 4.4). A message that made inroads to changing US Americans' attitude towards non-heterosexuality before the legal battles and culture wars between gay liberation activists and the Church (1970s), and the onset of the AIDS crisis (1980s) (Bronski 2011, 221–4).

In the archival material, despite its use by various actors, it is clear that the lambda symbol was primarily associated with the GAA as it most often appears on baseball caps, pin badges, posters, banners, and flags created by or associated with the organisation (Figure 4.5).[7] Its association with the GAA is one possible explanation for its fall from popularity in the 1980s. The GAA explicitly targeted homophobic sentiment in media, law, and society (Bronski 2011, 211). It used a tactic—later adopted by AIDS Coalition To Unleash Power (ACT UP)—called 'zaps', which are public confrontations of people and organisations promoting homophobic sentiment. While zaps gained significant public and media attention, as GAA grew,

[7] The extent of the use of the lambda symbol can be seen by searching for 'International Gay Information Center collection. Photographs' in the NYPL's digital collections search engine. It is available at: https://digitalcollections.nypl.org/collections

Figure 4.4 Left: Scanned image of a sticker from Box 1 (*Stickers, Buttons, Leaflets*) of the International Gay Information Center collection, Manuscripts and Archives Division, The New York Public Library. **Right:** Scan of pin-badges from Box 155 (*Buttons 1960s–2000s [?]*) of the Barbara Gittings and Kay Tobin Lahusen gay history papers and photographs, Manuscripts and Archives Division, The New York Public Library.

it strayed from more radical, anarchistic, and revolutionary 'overthrow the system' politics and became increasingly conservative and reformist (Bronski 2011, 214–5); less liberation, more assimilation. By the 1980s, GAA was more or less defunct, but its political influence was carried on through messages of pride, celebration, promoting inclusivity and sexual diversity, and combatting homophobia in society.

The uses of the lambda symbol and the types of politics it was associated with were at first liberatory and with a goal to countering sociopolitical anti-gay sentiment, but then increasingly normative and about conformity and being folded into heteroised society. As the AIDS crisis hit in the 1980s, the political focus of the GAA and associated organisations on gay rights and equality moved to the back burner. So too did the use of lambda. While the common enemies of activist organisations remained the same, the context of activism 'was nearly unimaginable' as the stigmatisation and demonisation of male homosexuality—now no longer simply associated with sexual

Figure 4.5 Photograph by Richard Wandel of Gay Activists Alliance Actions (1970s) in Box 17 of the International Gay Information Center collection, Manuscripts and Archives Division, The New York Public Library. Image courtesy of The Lesbian, Gay, Bisexual & Transgender Community Center (New York).

degeneracy and immorality but also with fatal illness—rapidly took hold across the US in the media and politics (Bronski 2011, 224–5; Youde 2020, 307).

Just after the tenth anniversary of Stonewall, the pink triangle starts to come into its own as an icon of queer activism and resistance, pushing lambda out of the frame. As lambda is phased out, so too are the hand-drawn posters, stickers, and other ephemera characteristic of 1970s activism. This was replaced with a more sophisticated, artistic, and design-led visual strategy (e.g., Figures 4.7–4.13). The drawn, homemade aesthetic of banners and posters made by the Gay Liberation Front and GAA was replaced with sophisticated, high-quality printed works—including t-shirts, posters, banners, and the like—that engaged a wider audience. This was a far cry from the mimeographed flyers the GAA distributed. With the AIDS crisis and an increased momentum against social and politicised homophobia, the pink triangle enters as a symbol of resistance, hope, and death that challenged the assimilationist politics the GAA resorted to and that lambda came to symbolise.

Pink Triangles

The story of the pink triangle is actually a tale of two triangles: one pointing up, the other down. This is an important distinction that marks two different, if overlapping, political uses that are clearly identifiable from the visual material in the NYPL. The downwards pointing triangle originates from the Nazi practice of marking (suspected) homosexuals in concentration camps. This triangle was appropriated and used from around the late 1970s as a symbol of the lesbian and gay movement. The upwards pointing triangle is a repurposed version used by the *Silence = Death* art collective, which was closely associated with ACT UP, to call attention to AIDS-related issues.

Triangle of Pride: From Homophobia to Reclamation

The pink triangle was first introduced under Hitler's Nazi regime as a way of marking (suspected) male homosexual bodies. The politicised homophobia of the Third Reich was by no means new: Paragraph 175 of German law already prohibited 'unnatural sex acts committed between persons of the male sex or by humans with animals' (Kaczorowski 2015). However, Hitler's government expanded this law and made acts such as kissing, embracing, and 'gay fantasies' illegal (Stevens 1999, 748), thereby installing a form of Nazi heteronationalism and heteronormative internationalism that is different from but has parallels to Russia's heteronormative project. During the Holocaust, thousands of men were convicted of homosexuality and imprisoned. Like other prisoners, they were made to wear marks identifying the reason for their conviction. The pink triangle marked a conviction for homosexuality (Figure 4.6).

During World War Two, the pink triangle not only marked queer bodies but also symbolised their impending elimination, their murder. In the 1970s, the pink triangle was reclaimed and repurposed as a symbol of 'pride, solidarity, and the fight against oppression' (Stevens 1999, 734). This is clear in the archival material where the downwards pointing pink triangle is used to identify bodies as non-heterosexual in a celebratory fashion, as a symbol for pride, solidarity, and community, and in the fight against homophobia (Figures 4.7 and 4.11). It has been reclaimed to such a degree that the triangle is used as a symbol of memorialisation. For example, the *Homomonument* in Amsterdam and the *New York City AIDS Memorial* (Figure 4.14). What I call the Triangle of Pride, unlike the lambda and *Silence = Death* triangle, was not attached to any specific organisation or group, and is hence more unstable in its use. Notably, it is abundant on stickers and badges that would be fixed upon activist bodies that, in another time and space, would have been marked for death. This points to the politics of visibility, outness, and the occupying of physical and political space by openly being queer and celebrating queerness with a previously persecutory symbol.

While some criticised the reclamation of this symbol because it cannot be 'extricated from [its] original horrific uses', those using the pink triangle retort that it 'speak[s] to the invisibility of gay history, recasting symbols of victimhood into a warning against complacency' (Stevens 1999, 748). The political power of this symbol, I argue, lies in the inability to extricate it from its history: without this politically charged history, the pink triangle would be nothing more than a randomly selected emblem of a gay movement, like lambda. Its intervisuality with the past Nazi version is crucial to its political

Figure 4.6 Prisoners in the concentration camp at Sachsenhausen, Germany, (19 December 1938). US National Archives I.D. No.: 540175.

effect. In this sense, the triangle is political in declaring a pride in shame and what is/was derided as the filth of homosexuality. Figure 4.7 is demonstrative of this queer politics: the t-shirt in the image declares that 'Pride = Power' alongside the triangle, thereby also alluding to a more queer political commitment to rejoicing in stigmatic abjection.

As Andersen, Vuori, and Guillaume (2015) note, the pink triangle was reappropriated throughout the 1970s in the USA and Western Europe as a symbol of resistance to and memory of homophobic persecution. Their analysis of the pink triangle is excellent and aptly demonstrates how it functioned to unite the diverse and often fractured queer community under a symbol of historical memory and contemporary struggle. Nonetheless, their analysis requires partial correction since there are two pink triangles linked to queer activism. The significance of there being two versions is only clear upon a more in-depth, genealogical study of queer activism and resistance.

It is unclear which pink triangle Andersen and Vuori are discussing when they write about the triangle as an 'emblem of male homosexual pride through its effect of making past and contemporary insecurities visible, and thereby sayable' (Andersen, Vuori, and Guillaume 2015, 452). From my work in the archive, it seems that they are referring to the downward

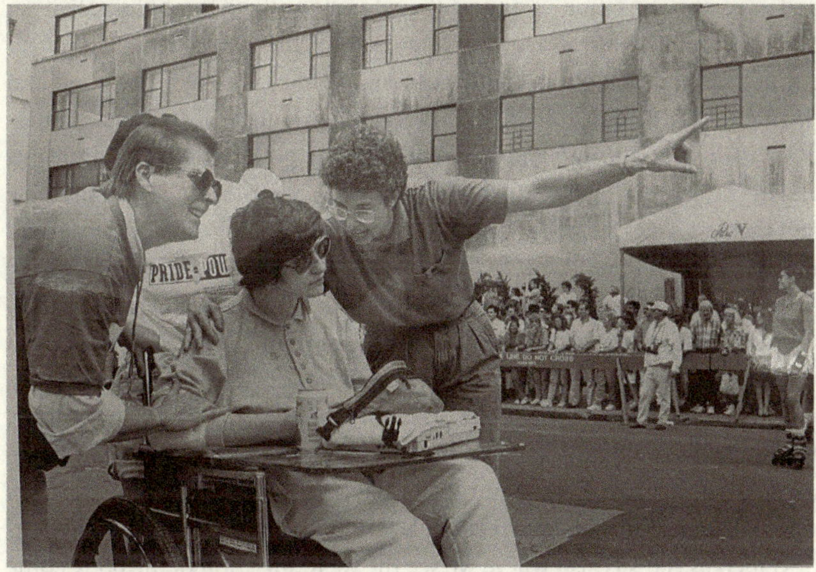

Figure 4.7 Dyke March NYC (1992) in Box 3, Folder 3 of the International Gay Information Center collection, Manuscripts and Archives Division, The New York Public Library. (Gifted by Robert Wilkinson.)

pointing triangle, which, although less celebratory and assimilationist than the lambda became, was still used by some activist projects that embraced heteronormative sociality and a politics of respectability. This is, in part, due to the Triangle of Pride not being attached to a particular group, which meant it was almost a free-floating symbol used by radical queer groups and more assimilationist, respectability-seeking groups simultaneously.

While the difference in direction appears small, there is a different politics attached to each. The optimism and hope of the 1970s as well as the focus on being out, loud, and proud (Altman 1999, 577) is visible in the increased visual presence of the down-point triangle. It was used beside and, although more prominent, almost interchangeably with, rainbows during rallies, parades. It functioned similarly to how the rainbow flag does at contemporary Pride events: as a celebration at marches, as a proclamation of political subjectivity, and as a way of marking 'outness' and queer space. It was not a symbol of total submission to a gay rights and rage for respectability agenda, but it had less of an antagonistic politics than the subsequent *Silence = Death* triangle, which was more firmly rooted in a quasi-anarchistic punk politics.

The politics of the later *Silence = Death* Triangle (Figure 4.9), which, although deeply entangled with the history and politics of the Nazi triangle and its re-appropriation, is quite different in its use and symbolism. Figures 4.8, 4.12, and 4.16 show that the 'Triangle of Pride' was often a marker for gay and lesbian liberation, rights activism, celebration (of Stonewall), and the fight against discrimination alongside the rainbow flag, thereby intertwining their politicality and differentiating the politics of the rainbow flag and the Triangle of Pride with the Triangle of Death. Meanings are not stable and there was a clear struggle around symbolism and what a queer politics was.

As we move into the mid-1980s, two distinct visualities emerge: (i) AIDS activism; and (ii) Gay Rights, Pride, and Liberation. The former was dominated by the *Silence = Death* triangle, bloody handprints, and the deliberate targeting of politicians. The latter by rainbows and the Triangle of Pride. While the Triangle of Pride also shifts towards a politics of pride in being constituted abject and an embrace of deviance, the Triangle of Death is where the most radical, intersectional, and antisocial version of queer politics emerges. This is also where we see the weaponisation of the body come into queer activism through die-ins and political funerals: bodies became symbols of loss and despair as well as provocateurs of radical social change (Figure 4.10).

Figure 4.8 Pride Marches in NYC (1986) in Box 4 of the International Gay Information Center collection, Manuscripts and Archives Division, The New York Public Library. Gifted by Jay Schneider.)

Figure 4.9 *Silence = Death* Poster (*Silence = Death* Collective 1968) from Manuscripts and Archives Division, The New York Public Library. Image ID: 1577322.

Figure 4.10 ACT UP at FDA Oct 11, 1988 by J. Scott Applewhite 1988. Image courtesy of AP/Ritzau Scanpix.

Triangle of Death: AIDS Activism and Queer Resistance

It was really in the 1980s that there was a cohesion of visual motifs and a streamlining of the visual strategy amongst queer and AIDS activists. This is visible in Figures 4.9, 4.10, and 4.13, where the *Silence = Death* triangle features prominently, particularly in connection to AIDS activism. The visual material produced during the AIDS crisis—specifically when it was clear that gay men were being scapegoated and demonised by society and the government—was dominated by the activist art group *Silence = Death's* take on the pink triangle. From the mid-1980s, visual material produced by activist groups ACT UP and Gran Fury dominated in terms of defining the visual aesthetics of the time and in the sheer amount of material they disseminated. In the archive material from the mid-1980s, there is rarely an occasion when the *Silence = Death* triangle is absent. This is not to say that there weren't any rainbows or Triangles of Pride, but *Silence = Death* dominated. As one activist states: 'This symbol has now been turned on its ear and is now a symbol of gay resistance in the AIDS epidemic' (Unknown ACT UP Activist DIVA TV 1989, 00:17:10).

The rainbow certainly had a place, but its politics was a little different. In terms of 'into the streets' demonstrations (Figures 4.10 and 4.13) and material produced to resist homosexual demonisation (Figures 4.9, 4.11, and 4.12), the *Silence = Death* triangle was visually hegemonic and brought with it a politics committed to direct action, radical antisociality that contested all instantiations of power, and turned bodies into weapons not just disciplined objects upon which norms are imposed. The Triangle of Death is also used in different spaces from the Triangle of Pride and the rainbow flag: the latter two usually at celebratory events and the former at events that refused to celebrate and party while parts of the queer community were being allowed to die around them.

Unlike the Triangle of Pride, the *Silence = Death* version (in use from April 1986) was not an exclusively queer symbol and it invoked a politics of fear and anger rather than hope and joy. ACT UP was an explicitly single-issue organisation that sought to tackle AIDS-related issues and stigmatisation. And while AIDS overwhelmingly affected the queer community—particularly men who had sex with men—ACT UP was not an LGBT organisation. Even if its members were overwhelmingly white men, it held intersectional values at its core (Bronski 2011, 232; Gould 2009), which can be seen in the translation of its key messages into Spanish (*Silencio = Muerte*)

Figure 4.11   Scans of lesbian and gay pride badges (1991–93) in Box 1 (Stickers, Buttons, Leaflets) of the International Gay Information Center collection, Manuscripts and Archives Division, The New York Public Library.

and the group's focus on previously neglected groups such as women with AIDS.[8]

As the *Silence = Death* triangle comes into being, the term 'queer' is also reclaimed and becomes an increasingly popular term to describe the coming together and coalition of people with a huge variety of sexual predilections (Cohen 1997; Gould 2009; Queer Nation 1990; Schulman 2021). One of the major distinctions between the original pink triangle and this later version is its status as a symbol for AIDS activism, not just queer issues. As such, the Triangle of Death functions not just to contest the exclusions of queer people but also all forms of ostracism and exclusion. Its use in contemporary activism thus comes with that political baggage: none of us is free until we all are. Liberation means no exclusions, no moralising, no disciplining, perpetual interrogation of power, and a distinct mistrust of normalisation and assimilation.

The onset of the HIV/AIDS epidemic was rapid and facilitated the constitution of queer people, especially gay men, as dangerous (Youde 2020, 303–4). Antigay sentiment increased exponentially and the flames of homophobia were fanned by religion and the political Right (Bronski 2011, 226; Rayside 2020, 58). With the increase in religious- and political Right-fuelled antigay sentiment, AIDS transformed into an issue about reinstating and legislating for traditional values about sexuality (Bronski 2011, 227; Gould 2009; Rayside 2020, 53; Schulman 2021). This is similar to what has

---

[8] You can see various examples of ACT UP's engagement with the issue of women with AIDS at the permalinks below:

https://digitalcollections.nypl.org/items/510d47e3-8335-a3d9-e040-e00a18064a99
https://digitalcollections.nypl.org/items/510d47e3-1cba-a3d9-e040-e00a18064a99
https://digitalcollections.nypl.org/items/510d47e3-1c84-a3d9-e040-e00a18064a99

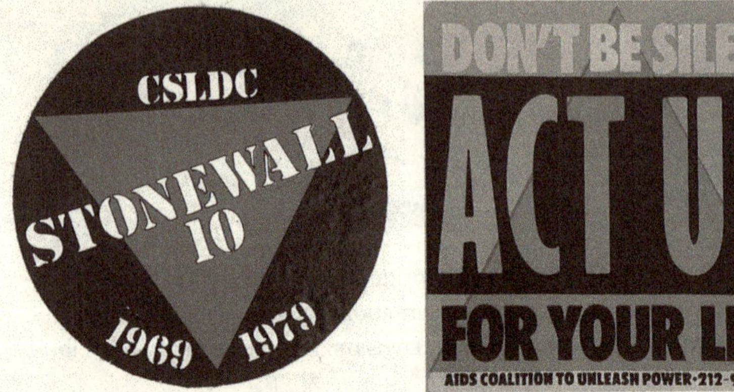

Figure 4.12 Left: Scan of CSLDC 'Stonewall 10' Sticker. **Right:** Scan of ACT UP 'Don't Be Silent' sticker. Both from Box 1 (Stickers, Buttons, Leaflets) of the International Gay Information Center collection, Manuscripts and Archives Division, The New York Public Library.

happened in Russia since the introduction of the gay propaganda law and Putin getting (back) into bed with the Russian Orthodox Church (Altman and Symons 2016, 53, 58; Riabov and Riabova 2014; Wilkinson 2014). The US Supreme Court had also, in 1986, ruled that there was no constitutional protection for male-male intercourse, adding fuel to the already burning antigay fire. This paved the way for suggestions to tattoo AIDS positive individuals, in a similar vein to Nazi practices. It is in this context that ACT UP and the iconic *Silence = Death* pink triangle emerged (Finkelstein 2018, 43; Schulman 2021, 318–27).

With its single-issue approach and multi-community coalition, the organisation model of ACT UP was founded in a firmly queer politics and drew on lessons from other social movements. ACT UP adopted the most successful aspects of the women's and civil rights movements using direct action as well as 'zaps' (a GLF and GAA tactic) in pursuit of civil rights, healthcare, and legal protections (Bronski 2011, 231; Gould 2009). ACT UP's deliberately 'theatrical' approach, with its coordinated visuals, into-the-streets actions, and transformation of the body into a visual-material weapon follows a pattern in US history where the arts have been used to incite a re-imagination of the 'American' identity and its possible constitutions (Bronski 2011, 254). It was the combination of a unified visual aesthetic and embodied direct action that cemented ACT UP's position in US culture and society, allowing

Figure 4.13 Silence = Death Banner with AIDSGATE posters of Reagan in the background (1987). Still taken from VHS 01099-A by Catherine Gund in AIDS Activist Videotape Collection, Manuscripts and Archives Division, The New York Public Library.

it to reframe the debate on not just HIV/AIDS but gender and sexuality (Finkelstein 2018; Gould 2009). One particularly important tactic was the use of the body as a political canvas: through die-ins, political funerals, mass protest, and direct action, ACT UP turned its activism into a spectacle that could not be ignored. Through die-ins and political funerals, the body communicated politically; especially through its destruction and wilful killing through government inaction.

While I separate the 'Triangle of Pride' and 'Triangle of Death' in this genealogy, the two are inextricable; as were AIDS and gay liberation activism (Altman 1999; Youde 2020, 306). However, identifying the distinctiveness of and interactions between the two triangles—linked to two different but overlapping politics—is important for the analysis of queer visualities. By using the Triangle of Pride over the Triangle of Death, the activist photographed in Figure 4.1 invokes a politics that sits somewhere between a desire for inclusion and a radical anti-sociality and inaptitude for hetero-sociality. Whether this is intentional or not isn't the subject of a poststructural analysis, but the political symbolism, polysemy of, and work that this specific triangle does is important in considering the political space opened and closed by its presence.

On the Triangle of Death, I owe space to the *Silence = Death* collective, which was instrumental in the solidification of the pink triangle as a symbol of queer liberation and AIDS activism:

> We tore through, debated, and rejected every agreed-on symbol for the lesbian and gay community: the rainbow, the labrys, the lambda, and the triangle. All of them had baggage, and on some level we were uncomfortable with each of them. The pink triangle seemed an obvious way to connect Buckley's suggestion of tattooing to the concept of genocide, but to the extent it might be a signifier of victimhood, it felt potentially disempowering to us. In the context of fears about segregation, quarantine, and internment of HIV-positive people, even a strategic appropriation could become a double-edged sword. We were uncomfortable with this aspect of the pink triangle. We liked the inclusiveness of the rainbow. But it also had a little hippie baggage, and its brightness seemed inappropriate and somehow lacking in gravitas. Ultimately, however, it was the graphics that disqualified it. We decided it would make an ugly poster … So we resigned ourselves to the use of the pink triangle, convincing ourselves that the codes activated by the triangle were open-ended enough to be useful, signifying lesbian and gay identity to some audience members, maleness to others, and referencing the historical meanings of genocide to audiences familiar with that history. But we gave the familiar symbol a makeover. Changing its color from pale pink to a more vivid fuchsia, Pantone 212 C, seemed an acceptable reinvention that reflected graphic trends and suited the poster's aggressive tone. Turning it upside down was another gesture of reinvention that was inadvertent but worked out in our favor. Chris, who had recently visited Dachau, was certain it pointed upward. Oliver volunteered to 'research' it and later confirmed the direction without actually checking it. We discovered it was incorrect after the printing, but decided it answered one of our concerns, superimposing an activist stance by borrowing the 'power' intonations of the upward triangle in New Age spirituality, further skewing its relationship to the death camps.
>
> (Finkelstein 2018, 44–5)

While the Triangle of Pride is re-appropriated and used for celebration and being visibly 'out' and proud, the Triangle of Death is a painful reminder that selected bodies, human lives, were being left to die because of their sexual practices and assumed danger to society. Rather than committing resources

Figure 4.14 Author's Photograph of the New York City AIDS Memorial (12 October 2019).

to saving and protecting queer lives, the government and many in the medical community wilfully left them to die. The *Silence = Death* collective chose the pink triangle because of its graphic qualities and because of its political baggage. Finkelstein's words show why genealogy is key: we cannot assume the stability of symbols nor can we assume that accidental transformations don't occur.

Both pink triangles are equally important, even if the queer politics I advocate is closer to that of ACT UP, which is symbolised by the Triangle of Death. The *Silence = Death* version visually equates the former Nazi practices of extermination with the US government's ignorance of AIDS as a public health crisis because it was a 'gay plague'. It is, in this regard, a more radical and queer(er) critique of society and politics that demands not only sexual liberation and respect of queer people but wholesale revolution against the heteronormative sociality that enabled powerful actors such as the church and state to authorise the eradication of queers through wilful inaction on AIDS. In the case of Russian homophobia, this manifests in the constitution of queer people and queer culture as propaganda and the sanctioning of their extermination, literally and metaphorically.

Both triangles were used alongside one another and are inseparable. While both had different politics, which emerged primarily in the visual practices around them, it is probably the case that some people and groups used one version of the triangle without really realising the different politics surrounding their use. The visual power of the pink triangle is that it conveyed organisation and coalitional power in the queer community: 'Without its visual message of sleek, defiant power, ACT UP would not have been as coherent to the outside world' (Schulman 2021, 327). Both triangles are still used today, albeit less frequently, which means care must be taken in any analysis of queer visual patterns to understand and acknowledge these symbols' pasts. In one of its most recent outings, *Voices4*, an activist organisation campaigning for those who are silenced and persecuted, used both versions, appearing somewhat oblivious to their former uses (Dorfman 2019). Now, I turn to the rainbow flag, which often featured alongside the Triangle of Pride at more celebratory events.

Rainbow Flag

Flags are complex. They are not just physical pieces of cloth or simply logos. They are visual artefacts that communicate instantly and usually without words (Baker 2015b). They are visual symbols, ways of representing and visualising 'the desires, histories, and identities of specific communities' (Stevens 1999, 747). They are also distinctly international and a way of making something international. Flags are used in various ways to represent states, IOs, NGOs, social and political movements, and even abstract ideas/concepts like peace (Andersen, Guillaume, and Vuori 2016). In this respect, flags help create communities and establish boundaries between who is 'inside' that which is represented by the flag, and those who are 'outside' what is represented: the most obvious example is a national flag, which represents all those of a certain nationality. Flags are things 'around which assemblies gather out of a common concern' be that 'to burn the flag, to raise it, to march with or against it, or to rally around it' and can thus unite and/or divide (Andersen, Guillaume, and Vuori 2016, 138). They can also erase difference and diversity in favour of unity (Stevens 1999, 747), which can be problematic and something that sits uneasy with the politics of queer approaches because these symbols, such the rainbow flag, may end up performing 'exclusion[s] of the sort that the term "queer" was envisioned to avoid' (Weber 2014; Wilcox 2014). Regardless, critique of the flag is not the goal of this chapter and it is more important to discuss the rainbow flag in the context and political spirit with which it was created; to deal with its historicity.

During my first few days in the archive I was surprised by the lack of rainbows and the dominance of pink triangles. I was twenty-five when I visited the NYPL archives and for me—a white, cisgender, newly middle-class, queer man—the rainbow flag was synonymous with the LGBT+ movement and queer activism. Growing up, it's what I associated with the LGBT community and it's what I saw used to celebrate the legalisation of civil partnerships (2004) and same-sex marriage (2013–14) in Scotland, England, and Wales. In a moment I remember clearly because I was by then actively following queer political developments since it concerned my right to exist, the White House was lit up in rainbow colours after the landmark civil rights case *Obergefell v. Hodges* (2015).

Today, the rainbow flag is more ubiquitous than ever. It is on Absolut vodka bottles, Brooklyn Beer bottles (Figure 4.15), Apple Watch straps, McDonald's fries packaging, Nike and Adidas trainers, clothing by high-end brands such as Burberry, Gucci, and Calvin Klein and high-street chains like H&M and J. Crew; national banks jump on the bandwagon with one Australian bank, ANZ, even creating rainbowed, glittery 'GayTMs'; emergency services rainbow their uniforms, vehicles, and logos; Coca Cola and Listerine have released rainbow bottles for pride; and food retailer Marks & Spencer released a controversial rainbowed 'LGBT sandwich' (that's Lettuce, Guac, Bacon, and Tomato). In the political climate in which this book comes out, many of these companies are critiqued for being too 'woke' and putting the rainbow on their products and marketing. This has led several to sever ties with Pride and to stop Diversity, Equity, and Inclusion programmes, proving right many who called their initial uses of the rainbow and allyship pinkwashing.

The rainbow flag is so omnipresent in some spaces that it almost blends into the background. For as long as I can remember, since I became aware of 'queer stuff' the rainbow flag has been there. In hindsight, and now as an academic more privy to politics—to power—that flag was not simply a symbol of inclusivity or a sexual liberation battle won. It has come to symbolise particular forms of acceptable 'queerness' and has become somewhat exclusionary through its attachment to a politics wedded to identity claims, respectability, and assimilation. This has led many people to argue that its

Figure 4.15   Personal photograph of The Stonewall Inn (7 April 2019).

This is not a beautiful or particularly well-shot image but I include it to invite the reader to see the 'sparking' point and the rainbow's commercialisation. Note the passerby who I noticed slow down and take time to look at/acknowledge the site.

commercialisation has detached it from the politics out of which it was created: that of community-building, resistance, activism, and a celebration of queerness in all of its abjectness (Baker n.d.).

That the rainbow flag is so all-pervasive today is part of the reason for this chapter. It is everywhere. And it is all over the activist images in the latter half of this book. The NYPL archive enabled me to see where it came from, what its politics are, how it has been used historically, and the political projects it has been attached to. As mentioned above, the political possibilities of the following analysis are that the activist histories, meanings, and politics of symbols such as the rainbow flag might be recovered and remobilised. In tracing such symbols' historicity, a metaphorical spanner may be thrown into the works by problematising the argument that the rainbow flag is too commercial, redundant, depoliticised, and, thus, no longer relevant for radical, liberatory, and antinormative queer politics. Its current usage does not mean that the antisocial, antinormative, coalitional, unbounded, and queer politics that surrounded its creation and early use cannot be reclaimed.

Returning to my surprise at the lack of rainbows in the archive: that the rainbow flag is newer and not as present in early activism as I'd expected could be attributed to the archive's constructedness and focus on ACT UP. However, the dearth of rainbow flags compared to other symbols holds true in other photo albums of queer activism (see Riemer and Brown 2019). This puzzled me because one of the organisations at the forefront of queer artivism—Visual AIDS—produced a broadsheet reflecting on the fifty years since Stonewall plastered with rainbow colours (Visual AIDS 2019). The broadsheet imposed a version of the rainbow flag alongside the iconic *Silence = Death* visual and the Red AIDS Ribbon on a contact sheet of photographs taken by Eric Stephen Jacobs at the 'Gay Liberation Day' in New York City, June 1970 (Visual AIDS 2019).[9]

Another explanation for the lack of rainbows in the earlier decades of the archive is ACT UP's rejection of the symbol because it was too 'hippie' and 'its brightness seemed inappropriate' at a time when the queer community was being decimated by AIDS and government inaction (Finkelstein 2018, 45). Another still is that the rainbow flag was only created in the late 1970s, just before the AIDS crisis took prominence. The darkness and punchiness of the black and pink design of *Silence = Death* it seems captured the mood of the 1980s better than the celebration of liberation and rights movements. In truly queer political fashion: how can we celebrate when others are dying because of their sexual behaviour and erotic desire? This is perhaps a reason to question the use of the rainbow flag in contemporary activism: how can we possibly celebrate when so many are still persecuted for their object desire, sexual practices, and erotic pleasures?

That said, even the rainbow flag is dense with layers of meaning. While it has today become synonymous with Pride and LGBT+ rights advocacy. It is by far the most visually hegemonic symbol associated with sexuality politics; be this good or bad. While there are many discussions around the commercialisation of the rainbow flag and its depoliticisation, it is important to look back to the entry point of the rainbow flag to trace the discourses around and uses of the flag during that time. Its creators' intentions and statements about the rainbow flag are texts that attribute meaning to the flag and thereby influence how it is read as a symbol of queer liberation, activism, and a celebration of difference. Tracing the historicity of the rainbow flag shows that there is a radical politics of inclusion and equity at the core of its creation; one that celebrated the abjectness of being queer

---

[9] I came across this exact contact sheet by Eric Stephen Jacobs in the NYPL (Jacobs 1970). It is located in the Barbara Gittings and Kay Tobin Lahusen collection.

and *not* normal. This politics, although now overshadowed by criticism of commercialisation, may be reclaimed.

Looking historically, it is important to ask: what is the politics of the rainbow flag and the fighting that has gone into the rainbow flag? What was invested politically in this symbol (that has now been lost, marginalised, silenced)? The archival material complicates and problematises the discourse that the rainbow flag is corporatised and non-radical, arguing that its more radical, revolution-inspired politics might be reclaimed as a mechanism of resistance. This politics is particularly acute in the Russian setting featured in Figures 4.1, 6.3, and 6.4. There is a particular critical status to the rainbow flag and its politics, a critical history, that comes out in this Russian context; one where any public display of non-traditional sexuality is forbidden. The rainbow flag, globally understood as a symbol of non-normative sexuality and/or gender, becomes a clearly political move to subvert the Russian government's anti-gay laws. That critical and radical activist politics is something that might be brought (back) out today.

In 1988, the *North American Vexillological Association* noted two 'interesting flag designs' from Gay Pride Week (Carrier 1988). One was the rainbow flag, which had been adopted by the International Association of Lesbian/Gay Pride Coordinators in 1985. The second, a white flag with a black rhinoceros over a pink triangle. The rhinoceros was apparently used because of its 'tough hide' but peaceful nature, which supposedly contrasted against the Nazi German pink triangle, though I don't see it. By 1994, the rainbow flag had been solidified as a symbol of queer community and resistance. On 26 June 1994, Gilbert Baker and Cleve Jones' project 'Raise the Rainbow' saw protestors carry a mile-long rainbow flag—the world's largest flag—during the Stonewall 25 March on the United Nations to commemorate the 25th Anniversary of the Stonewall Riots (Guenter 1994, 1; Klein and Freiberger 1994a, 1994b).

From my archival work, moving into the 1990s I can see ACT UP's domination of the visual landscape start to diminish and its visual strategy take on a new approach. This is consistent with Carrier's analysis of the dominance of the rainbow flag at Pride Week in 1988. The hegemony of the *Silence = Death* triangle begins to drop out in the NYPL material and there is a turn to demonising and targeting specific politicians and their policies. This is visible in the background of Figure 4.13 and in many images that can be

Figure 4.16 Two stills from VHS01066 by Catherine Gund: 'DIVA TV—Pride 69–89 in NYC' (1989).
Source: AIDS Activist Videotape Collection, Manuscripts and Archives Division, The New York Public Library.

found by searching for 'ACT UP New York records' in the NYPL Digital Archive. Where each symbol is used is also crucial in constituting meaning: the rainbow was mostly used at pride events, which although political and more resistive back then, were less antagonistic than the ACT UP (or even early GAA) zaps where the Pink Triangles were the main visual symbol.

Baker designed and hand-crafted the first rainbow flag in the late 1970s with a group of friends and fellow activists in a Gay Community Center in San Francisco (DeGenaro 2013; Stevens 1999). In 1977, his friends Harvey Milk, the USA's first openly gay politician elected, and Artie Bressan, Jr., a filmmaker, challenged him to design a symbol for the gay rights movement (Baker n.d.; DeGenaro 2013, 733). Inspired by the tricolour of the French Revolution and the way flags had been used to mark a distinct change in politics, Baker decided that a flag was the most fitting symbol. Like national flags, Baker writes, a flag for the gay rights movement was a way of saying 'we are a people, a tribe' and visually proclaiming power (Baker 2015b, n.d.). He wanted his flag to become the symbol of a gay revolution 'a tribal, individualistic, and collective vision' where non-heterosexuality is not demonic but something to rejoice in (Baker n.d.).

This particular political origin is important, especially when telling the story of queer visual politics. In contrast to ACT UP's pink triangle, which was envisaged as a resistance against the scapegoating of people with AIDS as infectious and demonic members of society, the rainbow flag emerged out of a desire to symbolise community and pride as well as revolution and, to a degree, absolute joy and pride in those stigmatic associations attached to queer sex, erotics, and desires. Again, this is clear from its use as demonstrated in the material in the NYPL, where Pride was not conformist but the marking out of a new, queer sociality; all under the rainbow flag banner (Figures 4.8 and 4.16).

The rainbow flag is important when thinking about queer in/visibility. Baker and Milk, like many gay rights activists in the 1970s, were determined to make queerness visible, to de-stigmatise it in public discourse and end discrimination and violence(s) directed at the gay community. In this respect, the notion of unity and coming together as a 'tribe' under a new symbol is important. The last time the queer community were united under one visual symbol was when they were marked with, and subsequently reclaimed, the pejorative pink triangle, which some deemed an oppressive symbol 'put on us by Hitler and the Nazis' (Baker 2015a, n.d.; Heger 1980; Jensen 2002; Plant 1986; Waxman 2018). It is this newly created symbol, positioned starkly against the politics of the pink triangle and its Nazi legacy, that makes it a significant departure from other symbols being invoked at the time. The idea of this new symbol, a flag, was to bring people together under a less murderous symbol: the rainbow. The rainbow was a conscious choice, selected because it represents the diversity of the queer community (Baker 2015b; Stevens 1999) and because it has previously been used as a symbol of hope, change, and revolution by the hippie and racial equality movements (Baker n.d.; Conradt 2017; DeGenaro 2013, 733). It was to be a 'symbol of liberation' that represented a local and international community 'in the midst of an upheaval, a battle for equal rights, a shift in status' (Baker n.d.).

This is why the first flags were debuted in United Nations Plaza, San Francisco, on 25 June 1978 as part of the Gay and Lesbian Freedom Day Parade. This space was deliberately chosen because—for Baker, Milk, and their associates—the gay rights movement was a 'global struggle ... a global human rights issue' (Baker 2015b). Speaking to this idea of community, common struggle, and internationality, the rainbow flag has come to be a generic symbol for the queer community and something that, for Baker, connects queer people across the globe (Baker 2015b). In this respect, the rainbow flag was radical for its celebration of the abject but created with a seeming intention to defuse the antinormative power of non-heterosexuality (c.f. Bersani 1987, 1996).

Importantly, the rainbow flag has become attached to a sense of community and safety. In its many different forms from stickers to mugs, the rainbow is often displayed to mark spaces as 'queer friendly'. This is even advocated by Baker, who states that: 'if I see a rainbow flag, I feel like that's someone who is a kindred spirit or [that it's] a safe place to go. It's sort of a language, and it's also proclaiming power' (Baker 2015b). The flag has been used in many guises by a multitude of actors since its creation; most obviously in Pride parades and marches (DeGenaro 2013, 734; Sawer 2007, 45). In this sense, the rainbow flag has contemporarily and historically been deployed as a symbol of queer solidarity and visibility.

Throughout the 1980s, the rainbow flag grew in popularity. It was appropriated and refashioned in many different ways (DeGenaro 2013; Sobel n.d.). In fact, different groups with differing politics even added symbols to the flag in a similar fashion to that which we see happening today: watching hours of footage in the AIDS Activist Videotape collection there were countless modifications of the rainbow flag. Some imposed the rainbow on a US American flag, some added a pink triangle, among other symbols. The adaptation of rainbow flags at ACT UP events has a clear visual resonance with the multiple iterations of the Rainbow Flags we have today. For example, Daniel Quesar's Progress Pride Flag from 2018. The incorporation of the pink triangle with the rainbow was relatively common at Pride and AIDS activist events. The desire to bridge the AIDS triangle and its politics with the rainbow flag and 'pride' has largely failed according to Stevens and DeGenaro: HIV/AIDS activist Leonard Matlovich unsuccessfully tried to add a black stripe to commemorate those lost in the HIV/AIDS crisis (DeGenaro 2013, 734; Stevens 1999). I, however, can see genealogically, that this is false. There has been a consistent and long-lasting interaction of the rainbow flag and the pink triangle in its various guises. In many of the activist actions captured in the VHS collection, there are modified rainbow flags flying alongside ACT UP's pink triangles, suggesting that the rainbow flag had started to enter AIDS activism as well. The 'Triangle of Pride' in particular has been used alongside and almost interchangeably with the rainbow flag in activist circles, and as we move into the late 1980s even AIDS activists are using the rainbow flag alongside the *Silence = Death* motif.

The rainbow flag has been consistently present in queer political activism despite its political attachments changing over time. Attempts to modify it, to make it more inclusive, and to make it hark back to the politics of the late 1980s queer movements, are becoming increasingly common. Particularly as discourses about its commercialisation and selling out to conformity abound. The practice of modifying the rainbow flag is part of its revolutionary politics. And it is an important part that Baker embraced and welcomed: the debates about 'playing' with the rainbow are incredibly detached from the more fluid politics of Baker's original design. It is only recently that there has been increasing condemnation and joke-making towards 'editing' the flag with jibes that it is a symptom of the 'woke' 'Alphabet Mafia', where there has been a shift to so-called overly politically correct culture and too many letters.

Perhaps it is time to reconsider the status of the rainbow flag and return it to its previous politics of revolution, resistance, celebration, and promotion of difference and inclusivity; as in Quasar's Progress Pride flag, which includes brown and black stripes as well as the colours of the trans flag. This return of a more radical queer politics to the rainbow flag may be exactly what is needed to shift away from the currently popular rage for respectability that has led many to abandon their fellow queers as they get 'normalised' and accepted into heteronormative sociality as tolerable (for now). As the identities attached to the rainbow become 'normal' and acceptable, it might actually be the most queer, revolutionary, antinormative, and antisocial thing to screw with the design and shift its parameters so that it becomes too hard to pin down. The continual reinvention of the rainbow flag makes it queer in the sense that it is an artefact that is continually evolving as its relations to power are interrogated—especially vis-à-vis the power relations and divides it creates and/or sustains within the queer community.

Conclusion

The success of a movement's framing of its activism depends on how well it resonates culturally with the wider audience(s), including the values of oppressor and oppressed (McAdam 1994, 38). Movements will often tap into highly resonant ideas already embedded in a particular society, or even more global ideas, to legitimate and motivate protest activity rather than present new and somewhat alien ideas. To use the rainbow flag today thus invokes all of its social and political baggage: community, pride, outness, visibility, and most importantly, resistance and revolution. These last two are almost entirely eliminated in academic and activist criticism of the appropriation of the rainbow flag and its commercialisation. Perhaps instead of critique we ought to be doing the work to bring out its critical politics and remind people of the queer politics it is rooted in.

It is not just the visual but the body that connects queer thinking, queer liberation, and AIDS activism from the 1980s/90s, as well as the radical antisocial queer politics from that time, to what's going on in terms of international activism against Russian homophobia. In this regard, the genealogy is incredibly important because it reveals the link between the visual practices of AIDS, gay and lesbian liberation activism, and the contemporary visual practices and activism studied in the subsequent chapters. It unravels and connects the radical queer politics of antinormativity, negative sociality, and delight in abjection to the contemporary international activism against Russian homophobia. It is critical not just in revealing the (continuation of) visual patterns and practices across space and time, but also the radical visual and body politics of queer. The body was a vehicle for resistance and activism throughout the gay and lesbian liberation movement and particularly so in ACT UP actions, as shown most clearly in Figure 4.10.

What I found in the archive was quite different from what I expected. The story I tell above is about the visual evolution of queer symbols and galvanising visual nodes that, since Stonewall have structured visual queer activism, how queer visuality has come to have its present structure, what has been included and excluded along the way, and what this means for subsequent analyses of queer visual material. To reiterate what one activist said 'Stonewall was a riot. Now we need a revolution' (DIVA TV 1989, 11:45). That revolution includes reinstalling the queer political baggage of the rainbow into present forms of activism.

The visual-embodied activism against Russian heteronormative projects has deep connections to a radical queer politics that makes it something of a continuation of a queer project in part tied to US sexual liberation and AIDS activist politics (see Amin 2017, 7; Gould 2009, 256; Warner 1999). The analytical and political implications of this visual genealogy, including beyond the book, are, thus, that the activist histories and radical politics of the queer symbols included in this analysis—even those forgotten/hidden/suppressed symbols uncovered in the archive—may be remobilised and reappropriated.

The rainbow flag takes on a distinct new role as a symbol of resistance and not purely celebratory in the activism against Russian politicised homophobia because of the gay propaganda law, how the flag and its colours are mobilised to contest the law, and because of the political baggage explored in the above genealogy. The implications of the rainbow flag's—and other symbols'—political activist history provide for the possibility that these roots be remobilised. Rather than throw out all the rainbow flags, perhaps they should be taken back to their political roots. The rainbow flag and pink triangle, as they are used in Russia, do something quite different to when they are used in a Western context. This opens up questions of queer (visual) imperialism,[10] but more importantly, draws attention to the original revolutionary, liberationist, and resistive politics that sat at the core of the rainbow flag in particular.

Today, although versions of the pink triangle appear in some protests, including in Russia (e.g., Figure 4.1), the rainbow flag is much more prominent. This raises a particularly important point: the rainbow flag has taken over from the pink triangle as the go-to symbol of queer politics. One potential reading is that the rainbow depoliticises. Another is that in taking over from the triangle, the rainbow flag thereby also incorporates the politics of the pink triangle. This latter reading, I think, given the status of these symbols that have emerged in the genealogy, is much more appropriate. It also creates the political space to recognise and see a different story than one wrapped up in commercialisation and depoliticisation, so intent on critique that it cannot see the radical political potential of the flag. There is an ambiguity to the rainbow flag. Its politics are murky and complex. It is this that makes it particularly politically powerful: it adapts, changes across space, context, and time. Plus, it has stood the test of time for over forty years. Its critical and radical activist politics—most prominently emerging through its use alongside the pink triangle and repeated modifications—is something that can be brought back out today as a mechanism through which to resist aspects of commercialisation that queer communities are so radically opposed to. Genealogy helps reignite the flame of older political agendas and/or shows how their transformative potential withered and needs revitalised.

That the rainbow flag had less of a resistance or activism connotation and more of a celebratory function in the 1970s and 1980s (if not in intent, at least in use) is significant when it comes to analysing how the rainbow is

---

[10] Laurie Essig's *Queer in Russia* is wonderful at illustrating the influence of 'Western' (mostly US-American) influence on queer activism, organisations, and tactics in the 1980s–90s. Essig notes that: 'Queers in Russia … are trapped between the rock of Western imperialism and a hard place of the Russian state' and '[a]ttempting to make Russian sexualities over in Western drag has alienated some, even while it has been useful to others' (Essig 1999, 155–6).

mobilised as a means of resisting Russia's heteronormative internationalism. That law, which prohibits the propagation of non-traditional sexuality, is about the visibility of queerness. The very presence of a rainbow, because of its association with Gayropa and queerness, is prohibited. This endows the rainbow flag with a quite different status than in the lesbian and gay movements of the 1970s/80s. Therefore, this genealogy enables a much different analysis in terms of understanding and unpacking visual queer politics and resistance to state homophobia.

Ultimately, the genealogy enables a more radical, queer reading of political activism taking place internationally and in response to Russian heteronormative internationalism and its domestic persecution of queer people. Without the genealogical work here, the politics of the rainbow flag and its intertwinement with that of the pink triangle would have been missing, and the lineage of visual activism around the (international) politics of sex would have been absent. The resulting analysis in the subsequent chapters would have been much poorer for that. This is not to demand of all visual analyses a genealogical approach, but rather to highlight the analytical depth that can be gained from taking such an approach.

5

Dominant Representations of Queer Life in Russia

This chapter maps the Western discourse about Russian state homophobia as it emerged in EU documents and the media between 2011 and 2018. The analysis focuses on two periods during which major social and political events led to increased international attention: the passing of regional and federal gay propaganda laws and the Sochi Winter Olympics (2011–2014); and the FIFA men's World Cup (2018). The aim of the chapter is to understand the (visual and linguistic) discourse in Western debates about Russian state homophobia before proceeding to an analysis of the news media images used to represent it. As outlined in Chapters 3 and 4, understanding the wider context and discursive environment within which images are situated is key to unpacking the political work they do. The first part of this chapter therefore establishes the wider policy discourse, background, and context that enables the subsequent visual analysis of images used to represent Russian homophobia in news media in the second part. Since the main analysis is about representations and activist responses to Russia's heteronormative domestic and internationalist projects, including attempts by Western actors to create the conditions for change at home and abroad, what follows is an analysis of the discursive terrain in which Russian state homophobia and visual activism against it took place.

A thorough discourse analysis should engage with texts from various sources, including those beyond official texts, to assess how widely dispersed basic discourses are across society (Hansen 2006). In order to establish how widely discourses about state homophobia have traction across the West, this chapter analyses a variety of texts that capture a spectrum of debates: EU documents and news media. Important here are the policy discourses that emerge around state homophobia and what they do in terms of constituting international objects and subjects (Shepherd 2008), the interpretative dispositions through which people understand and negotiate the world (Doty 1996), and the carving out of international hierarchies that emerge through

The International Politics of Sex. Dean Cooper-Cunningham, Oxford University Press. © Oxford University Press (2025). DOI: 10.1093/9780197792544.003.0005

stigmatising notions of modernity/backwardness. The texts studied here work together to constitute an idea of Russia and the West as respectively backwards and modern.

To reiterate, I do not use 'the West' uncritically or understand it as some fixed space, place, and idea that exists outside its constitution in discourse, detached from relations of power and hierarchies. 'The West' is a fundamentally malleable and unstable idea that takes on different forms depending on how and when it is invoked (Hellman and Herborth 2017). Discourses about 'the West' are often part of a power move that establishes hierarchical relations between spaces, actors, and times by constituting the 'non-West' as Other and reinforcing a Western imaginary of exceptional modernisation and development (Weber 2016, 51). However, as is the case here, the idea of 'the West' can also be weaponised by non-Western actors as a means of rallying support for alternative internationalist projects (see Neumann 2017). Thus, 'the West' takes various forms depending on how it is constituted in the research context.

This chapter is divided into two parts: the first focuses on words, the second on images. In the first part, I start by building on established literature about how international institutions have approached LGBT+ rights to unpack the EU discourse on (Russian) state homophobia. The documents analysed here, by and large, confirm how LGBT+ issues are often mobilised strategically, producing ideas of a civilised modern West and uncivilised backward non-West (Ammaturo 2015; Delatolla 2020; Kulpa 2014; Rahman 2014a; Slootmaeckers 2020). Then, I analyse the textual discourse in news media, which overwhelmingly focuses on the safety of Western queers in Russia. The main policy positions and identity constructions are summarised in Figure 5.1. In the second part, I turn to news media images accompanying articles about Russian state homophobia in order to analyse the visual representation of Russian homophobia and how this aligns/jars with the textual part of the media discourse.

Part One: Words

Official EU Discourse and LGBT+ Rights

In this section, I briefly outline the results of my analysis of EU documents that deal with Russian state-directed homophobia between 2011 and 2014.[1]

---

[1] The geopolitical context in 2014 was dominated by Russia's annexation of Crimea so the EU's external engagement with Russia centred on this, which perhaps accounts for the decrease in news

Source	Discourse	Identity	(Proposed) Policies
European Union	LGBT rights as human rights	Modern, sexually liberated, civilised Europe	Quiet diplomacy, multi/bilateral dialogue Partnerships for Modernisation
	Homophobia as archaic and backwards	EU as LGBT security guarantor	Enforce International Human Rights Law
	Homophobia as unEUropean	Sexually backward/ undeveloped 'third countries' (predominantly non- Western)	Economic support for activists, NGOs, and other civil society actors Public denouncement of state homophobia
News Media	Russian homophobia as threat to Western athletes/tourists	Modern, sexually liberated, civilised West	National olympic committees and international sports bodies as arbiters for Russian compliance with human rights law
	Homophobia as non-Western, backwards, and barbaric	Sexually backward, undeveloped, uncivilised Russia	
	West as modernised bastion of sexual liberation	Regressing Russia	Economic and political sanctions

Figure 5.1 Overview of key linguistic discursive positions in Western representation of Russian homophobia.

It is brief primarily because there is nothing hugely surprising: it confirms previous research that finds that EU identity constructions often claims '"women's equality" and "gay rights" as symbols of its superior "modernity" and "civilisation"' (Haritaworn, Tauqir, and Erdem 2008, 79; also Bracke 2012). It is for methodological reasons that I started by looking at the EU: it is the main actor and Europe the primary territorial space that are constituted as morally decadent 'Gayropa' in Russian policy discourse (Foxall 2019; Healey 2018; Holm 2020; Riabov and Riabova 2014; Wilkinson 2018). In other words, I do not start in Europe because I think the continent of Europe or the EU is representative of some stable idea of 'the West'. Rather, it is important to understand the policies of this 'Gayropean' space and how it responds to the state homophobia and heteronormative internationalism justified by reference to 'Gayropa'. I focus on this three-year period specifically because it covers the introduction of regional gay propaganda laws, growth in Russian state homophobia, and the subsequent passing of the propaganda law at federal level.[2] I analysed 238 documents

coverage about state-directed homophobia identified in the next section (Council of the European Union 2015).

[2] The first regional versions of the gay propaganda laws were implemented in October 2011 (see Healey 2018, 10 fn.35 for an extensive list of implementation dates).

in the EU Journal and EU Document Register that contained the terms 'gay' *and* 'Russia' published between 1 October 2011 and 31 December 2014.[3] To guide my analysis, I asked several questions of the documents: How is (Russian) state homophobia constituted? What moral judgements are made of homophobic states? What relationship is constituted between the EU and Russia?

Two main intertextual references recurred throughout the EU documents referencing Russian homophobia: the *Toolkit to Promote and Protect the Enjoyment of all Human Rights by LGBT People* (2010) and the *Guidelines to Promote and Protect the Enjoyment of all Human Rights by LGBTI Persons* (2013). These documents commit to the advancement of and respect for LGBTI+ rights in external relations and are frequently invoked as guides for country-specific actions. The European Parliament, for example, 'expects EU delegations and diplomats to actively implement the Toolkit' in their work (European Parliament 2012b). And the European Council stated that the *Guidelines* were 'the basis of the EU actions during 2014' (Council of the European Union 2014a, 75). The *Toolkit* and *Guidelines* contain explicit policy positions, spatiotemporal constitutions of the EU as a modern and exceptional world leader on LGBTI+ issues, and ethical articulations of the EU as *the* global defender of LGBTI+ people (see Figure 5.1). These collectively produce an identity of sexually liberated and modern EUrope, which has implications for EU foreign policy by setting the interpretive disposition of the individuals using these documents and framing their understanding of sex (or in most cases sexual identity) in international politics. Since the *Toolkit* and *Guidelines* are general policy guides, neither mentions Russia by name. Nevertheless, they provide the foundations upon which official EU discourse around LGBTI+ issues was based during this period. Both documents advocate the promotion of LGBTI+ rights as human rights in external relations (including actively denouncing state homophobia) and the EU acting as an LGBTI+ norm diffuser internationally (e.g., Council of the European Union 2010, 14–21). Responsibility for action is placed squarely on the EU's shoulders in terms of 'progressing' third countries and showing them the way to a sort of queer enlightenment.

Beyond overarching strategy documents, those that specifically mention Russian state homophobia reiterate that: 'Promoting human rights is the silver thread which runs through the core of the EU's foreign policy

[3] The search terms 'LGBT' *and* 'sexuality' returned fewer results so I chose 'gay' for a broader picture.

and external action' and that the EU is 'actively engaged in efforts at the regional and multilateral level to tackle discrimination on the basis of sexual orientation or gender identity' (Council of the European Union 2014b, 14, 168). When the gay propaganda law was passed, the Commission stated that it would monitor the situation, noting that the law is 'in contradiction with Russia's national and international commitments to uphold fundamental rights of all individuals' (European Parliament 2013c). Such moves situate responsibility ambiguously between the Russian responsibility to protect all citizens equally and the international community's obligation to ensure it does so; even if through relatively weak measures such as monitoring (see European Parliament 2012a; European Parliament 2012b, 2012c, 2013a). The EU, in this regard, is reproducing common language around states' responsibility to protect their citizens and reifying a commitment to the principle of international society's responsibility to uphold that protection should a state fail to do so (see Gifkins and Cooper-Cunningham 2023).

In 2012, the European Parliament declared that it would consider halting further cooperation with Russia unless there was an improvement in human rights protections (2012c). And in 2013, it condemned Russia's non-compliance with international human rights law, stating that pursuit of a closer EU-Russia relationship was predicated on 'compliance with rule of law and universal human rights' and that the EU '[r]emains concerned about Russia's lack of commitment to the rule of law, pluralist democracy and human rights, as demonstrated by recent legislation that hinders the work of civil society organisations and targets minorities, including LGBT communities' (2013b). Continuing with a policy discourse laden with themes of modernisation and sexual liberty, it states that collaboration beyond the EU-Russia *Partnership for Modernisation* relies on 'progress in areas such as human rights' of which LGBTI+ rights are part (European Parliament 2013b). Here, sexual freedom and LGBTI+ rights became one of many pawns in the game of international power politics and the contours of EUropean shaming and stigmatisation of Russia for being out of step and engaging in state homophobia are coming into play. The constitution of Russian state homophobia as conflicting with international standards is a new iteration of the West's stigmatisation of Russia as 'backward' and 'inferior', but in this case, that stigma is not received negatively by Russia. Rather, it is received positively as recognition of the moral validity of its heteronormative internationalism (see Figure 2.3). This is a sort of stigma rejection, sort of counter-stigmatisation by Russia where its 'homophobic backwardness' is not in fact backwardness at all but rather is reconstituted as respecting traditional values, securing cultural sovereignty, and its heteronormative internationalism a source of pride.[4] Thus emerge two competing visions of international society in Russian and EU discourse.

Generally, EU discourse about the lack of protection of LGBTI+ people centres on: regression, democratic immaturity and anti-democratic values, societal and cultural backwardness, and an international responsibility to protect LGBTI+ individuals as part of a commitment to universal human rights. This is often accompanied by constructions of the EU as the lead defender of LGBTI+ people through its external engagement. Articulations of an 'international responsibility' are powerful discursive moves that shift an issue 'out of the realm of the strategic and "selfishly national"' to 'the "higher grounds" of the morally good' (Hansen 2006, 45). In this regard, the EU positions itself as the 'morally good' supranational force that will protect LGBTI+ people from persecution not just within the bloc's borders but abroad through its foreign policy (Figure 2.3). While this is admirable and opens up space for change in the world, some would argue that it masks the continuing anti-queer agenda within the EU's borders by presenting the LGBTI+ question as solved in EUrope. These core themes in the EU documents referencing Russia are no different to previous research about the political and strategic importance of LGBTI+ rights to the EU's global mission and self-positioning in international hierarchies (see inter alia: Ammaturo 2015; Kulpa 2014; Slootmaeckers 2020, 2023).

While unsurprising, it is important here to recall that Russia's heteronormative domestic and internationalist politics are rooted in an anti-Western, anti-liberal geopolitical project, part of which is the constitution of Europe as going morally bankrupt and regressing civilisationally because of its extension of rights and freedoms to LGBTI+ people. The Russian discourse about Gayropa and the EU's recent doubling down on LGBTI+ issues as sitting at the core of the EU project and its external relations may be partly responsible for the continual strengthening of Russia's heteronormative projects

---

[4] Russia's reception of Western stigma on the basis of its violent enforcement of heteronormativity domestically and internationally sits uncomfortably between stigma rejection and counter-stigmatisation. It is possible to conceptualise this as an extension of what Kurowska and Reshetnikov (2021) conceptualise as Russia playing its trickster role in international society, but this is not a perfect fit. The main takeaway is that there is a conflict between visions of a *liberal* and *illiberal* international order at play, part of which involves a focus on gender and sexuality in Russian foreign policy, but rooted in a discourse supportive of *some* of international society's underpinning features: for example, sovereignty, which is here recast in cultural terms.

domestically and internationally (on homocolonialism see Delatolla 2020; Rahman 2014b). As the EU pushes its LGBTI+ rights model internationally, this inadvertently solidifies and 'proves' Russian discourse about the EU as morally decadent queer utopia, which Russia must fend off. This enables further moves grounded in a discourse that: (a) the government must prevent Russia from becoming a queer 'utopia' modelled on European standards; and (b) it must rescue Europe from itself. The EU's foreign policy and external engagement around LGBTI+ issues risks inadvertently bolstering 'traditional family values' projects in Russia and global far right circles. This is very much what we have seen in the case of Russia's campaign in Ukraine, where Russia has legitimised its invasion of Ukraine through a discourse of European sexual decadence (Edenborg 2022; Gifkins et al. 2022). Russia's recognition of Western stigma on the basis of its homophobia (amongst other policies) works much differently to the stigma recognition practiced by the so-called 'new joiners' to Western-dominated liberal international society that Ayşe Zarakol (2010) wrote about a decade ago (see also Adler-Nissen 2014). Rather than being received as proof of Russian 'backwardness', those stigmatising moves, made above by EU institutions and below by Western media, are, taking Russian discourse to its logical conclusion, positively received as recognition of Russia's moral superiority. They support Russia's internal and external policy discourses about the ethical nature of its civilising project directed at 'Gayropa'.

'Worlds Apart': Russian Homophobia in Media Discourse

Moving to news media allows me to trace the hegemony of EU discourse and the dis/continuities between official and wider policy discourse. Negotiated texts such as those above are usually more subtle in their articulation of identity so turning to media texts aimed at national audiences one can expect greater variation and clearer identity formulations (Hansen 2006, 85; Hansen, Adler-Nissen, and Andersen 2021, 6). Here, I focus on whether media representations reinforce/contradict the idea of a sexually liberated, modern West, and the policy positions formulated in official discourse. Importantly, the EU *Toolkit* and *Guidelines* documents refer EU officials and member states to several empirical sources to guide them in determining the situation for LGBTI+ people in any given country. This material includes news coverage, blogs, websites, personal testimony, and NGO reports. EU decision-makers rely on these sources to inform their assessment of a country's LGBTI+ rights record, thereby guiding and shaping EU policy. Beyond this, media representations are important sites for analysis because they affect policymaking by shaping the interpretative dispositions of policymakers and by being cited as evidence of LGBTI+ abuses. They also contribute to broader policy debates that destabilise/stabilise official discourse.

Given the globalised media environment we live in, the outlets included below are not limited to EU countries but to major international outlets publishing in English.[5] I used *LexisNexis* to search for news articles published between 2011 and 2018 with 'LGBT' *or* 'gay' *or* 'homosexual' *and* 'Russia' in the title and leading section. This returned 759 results. Even with this strict search, not all articles were relevant and some were excluded (e.g., those about sprinter Tyson Gay). The distribution of news coverage over time is shown in Figure 5.2. Overall, the picture that emerges in the material analysed is one of two spaces that are worlds apart. It is in this regard that we can talk of a sexual geopolitics and an international discursively divided into queer utopias and dystopias. This sexual geopolitics is rooted in two competing visions of international society.

The majority of news coverage between 2013 and 2014 focuses on Western responses to antigay persecution in Russia and condemnation by various actors from organisations such as the IOC (e.g., Goldstein 2013c, 2013d; Longman 2013; Pengelly 2013; Washington Post 2013a), politicians such as David Cameron, Angela Merkel, and Barack Obama (e.g., Augstein 2013; Herszenhorn 2013; Hughes 2013), world-class athletes (e.g., Broadbent 2013; Gibson 2014; Ingle 2013), and celebrities such as Stephen Fry, Clare Balding, Lady GaGa, Madonna, and Elton John (e.g., Denham 2013; Flood and Walker 2014; Goldstein 2013d; Hoyle 2014b; Hughes 2013; John 2013; Michaels 2013, 2014; Selby 2014; Walker 2013; Wright and Luhn 2014).

---

[5] *The Independent, The Guardian, The Times, Politico, The New York Times, The Washington Post,* and *Der Spiegel International.* While it would have been interesting from a sociological and political perspective to include tabloids, they have poor online records making it difficult to find articles published between 2013 and 2015 on their online platforms. This only presents an issue when working visually: *LexisNexis* has the text of tabloid articles but does not show images, which requires using the original publications' websites. I excluded outlets where I was unable to expand my analysis beyond text to include the visual for purposes of continuity.

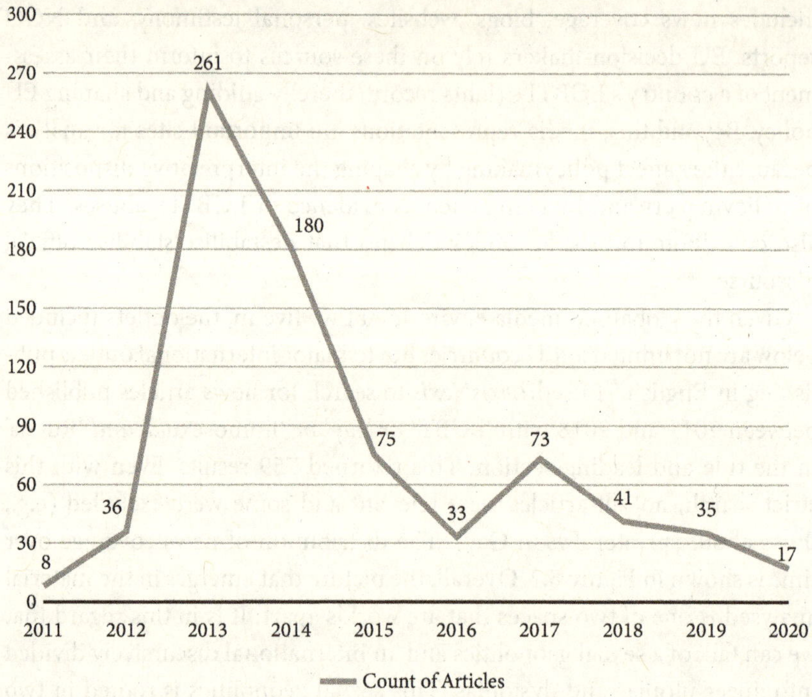

Figure 5.2 Count of Articles published between 1 Oct 2011 and 31 Dec 2020.

From the end of 2013 until March 2014, after the intense initial criticism of the gay propaganda law, the media focus shifts to Russian politics more broadly and the upcoming Winter Olympics, subsuming gay rights and LGBTI+ persecution under more general concerns about corruption, freedom of the press, freedom of expression, Russian geopolitics, and what Olympic sponsors would do in response to human rights abuses (Applebaum 2014; Boyes 2014; Broadbent 2014; Elliott 2014; Flood and Walker 2014; Gibson 2013c; Hoyle 2014a; Nunn and Foley 2014; Sweeney 2014). This pattern is repeated in 2017–18 as the FIFA Men's World Cup approached (Batchelor 2017; Chan 2017; MacFarquhar and Smale 2017). As the Olympics drew close, the focus shifted towards who would represent states at the Opening and Closing Ceremonies. Several outlets reported on the composition of national delegations, particularly the Obama Administration's, noting the refusal to send anyone from the President or Vice President's family but instead two openly queer athletes: Billie Jean King and

Caitlin Cahow (Baker 2013; De Piero 2014; Epstein 2013; Harding and Ebel 2013; Nakamura 2013a; Politico 2014a; Walker 2014). One went so far as to call this 'the soft power swindle of the year' and demanded '[t]hree cheers for the infinite wisdom of US presidents' (Charlton 2013b). Another took a less celebratory tone, calling it a politically motivated and instrumental act of state homophilia (Goldstein 2013a).

From March 2014, coverage of the propaganda law became relatively sparse and the persecution of queer Russians is but a side note, included only in introductory remarks about Russia or in relation to other issues such as geopolitical tensions between Russian and the EU (specifically over influence in former Soviet states), Russia's annexation of Crimea, and reports about the LGBTI+ rights situation globally. Bizarrely, many reports feature the propaganda law or LGBTI+ rights in the headline and leading text, but the rest of the article is focused on something completely different. In one instance, the opening paragraph leads with the controversy of the propaganda law before moving on to the politics of table tennis (Politico 2014b). It seems the cliché that 'sex sells' applies.

While the number of articles mentioning gay propaganda or the persecution of queer people—especially gay men—in Russia remained high in 2014, it was not the primary concern of reportage once the Winter Olympics were over. After the Games, the fate of queer people was no longer a major concern in Western media. The Games went off without any issues for Western queer people and activists, so Russian LGBTI+ issues fell off the agenda and coverage of queer persecution dropped dramatically. In itself, this is not surprising given that attention spikes due to major international events. Between 2017 and 2018, similar foci to the 2013–14 coverage emerged. Particularly, there was a focus on athletes and World Cup attendees as well as celebrity and sportsperson activism (e.g., Alabaster 2018; Austin 2017; Broadbent 2018; Staples 2018; Tatchell 2018; Walker 2017; Walker and Kelner 2018; Winter 2017; Ziegler 2017). Yet, compared to 2013–14, the focus on Western fans and athletes was almost equalled by the focus on the 'gay purge' in Chechnya (Dearden 2017b; Remnick 2017; Rubin and Breeden 2017; Walker 2017). Another point of divergence from the coverage in 2013–14, is that Western outlets spoke to and/or shared more stories from queer Chechens, enabling their voices to emerge and shape the coverage of the situation for queer people in the space being discussed (e.g., Amos 2017; Dearden 2017b; Kramer 2017a; Remnick 2017; Sokirianskaia 2017; Walker 2017). This is a welcome change from the 2013–14 coverage, but it is still outflanked by concern for the West's queer population travelling to Russia.

Regress and Forgettings

Just after the propaganda law was passed, one recurring reference in the UK press was to Stephen Fry's open letter to the Head of the International Olympic Committee (IOC), President of the International Association of Athletics Federations (IAAF), and the UK Prime Minister. Fry (2013) calls for '[a]n absolute ban on the Russian Winter Olympics of 2014 on [sic] Sochi' arguing that 'Putin cannot be seen to have the approval of the civilised world. He is making scapegoats of gay people, just as Hitler did Jews'. Focusing solely on the persecution of Jewish people during the Holocaust, Fry goes on to compare the Sochi Olympics to the 1936 Berlin Olympics, which took place in Nazi Germany. Unlike the AIDS activists who similarly compared governments' inaction on AIDS to the Holocaust (Chapter 4), Fry's letter ignores queer histories such as the Nazi targeting of suspected homosexuals and the legacy of British imperialism by focusing on religious persecution over that of sexual behaviour. Several outlets—including those outside the UK—make this same comparison to the Holocaust, framing the debate around queer persecution as one about humanity, ethics, and progress in the face of regressive, fascistic, anti-gay politics that mimics 'Third Reich-style politics' (e.g., Fierstein 2013; Goldstein 2013b, 2013c; Herszenhorn 2013; Pengelly 2013). The problem is that, in making this comparison, they fail to acknowledge the actual persecution of queer people during the Holocaust (see Gifkins and Cooper-Cunningham 2023; Waites 2018).

While the comparison is not unwarranted, the Holocaust comparison inadvertently adds fuel to the Russian homophobic fire by framing this as an international culture war in which only one side can prevail and dominate. This is the emergent international politics of sexual shame and stigma that I outline in Chapter 2: equating Russian state homophobia with one of the critical 'never again' moments in international political discourse is a marked stigmatising move. This inadvertently strengthens rather than destabilises the Russian discourse of a morally corrupt and deviant Gayropa—a foreign threat that seeks to infect and undermine Russianness and 'true European values' by supporting morally dubious queer sex. While Russia's persecution of queer people is abhorrent, framing it as a clash of cultures—as

'Russia vs. Europe' (Keller 2013)—plays into Russia's hands by 'proving' its Gayropean discourse and bolstering its position as the saviour of 'true Europe'. Intentional or not, this is dangerous. It does nothing to destigmatise or showcase the existence of those queer people who are marginalised in Russia and it plays straight into Russia's stigma management strategy: rather than attempting to overcome the shame and stigma that potentially comes with state homophobia, there is a doubling down and embrace of this as well as a recasting of Western pride around sexual progress as shameful.[6]

An important part of the media discourse about Russian homophobia is that it is not predominantly constituted as a *lack of progress*, which is commonly the case in discourses about homophobia in the non-West (Delatolla 2020; Hoad 2000; Puar 2007; Rahman 2010; Ritchie 2014; Weber 2016). Instead, it is constituted as *regress* (e.g., Beaumont et al. 2012; Essig 2013; Schwirtz 2012; Walker 2012). In this case, it is a regression to the Soviet era, suggesting that Russia is regressing backwards rather than being developmentally stunted or permanently located in some homophobic past temporality. This framing implicitly sets up a sort of new cultural Cold War clash of civilisations, shaping the type of viable policy responses available. This theme is present not only between 2013 and 2014, but also between 2017 and 2018 (e.g., Chan 2017; MacFarquhar 2018). In many ways, this discourse brings with it a complacency to the threat of Russia's heteronormative internationalist foreign policy gaining any traction in the West: the discourse unfolds as a sort of *we prevailed in the ideological and political clash last time, so we will again*. The complacency that comes out of the discourse is perhaps why we see projects grounded in Russian discourses of tradition and anti-wokeness making in-roads across the West: it's a sort of *we have been exposed to that homophobia before and are now immune to it* attitude that nurtures the idea that preventive measures are unnecessary in the West because homophobia is 'solved' (Cooper-Cunningham and Kremer 2024; Gifkins and Cooper-Cunningham 2023).

On the whole, news media amplify many of the implicit identity constructions in the EU's institutional discourse. A vision of Western cultural and moral superiority, and of the West as a global leader in LGBT equality, is produced. The shadow of Europe's own past identity-based violence plays a

---

[6] See Adler-Nissen and Zarakol (2021) on stigma management with particular reference to Russia.

central role throughout 2013–14, but importantly, the history of European states' violent enforcement of heteronormativity is missing:

> Russia's treatment of gay people is not just historically disgraceful, but, *unlike almost everywhere else in the world, getting considerably worse … Violence against homosexuals and lesbians is commonplace, and horrifying in its scale … Stephen Fry, in a measured open letter to the [UK] Prime Minister, compared the position of gay people in Russia in 2013 to the position of Jews in Germany in 1936.* That seems fair enough. In both cases, laws have been passed limiting their freedom, and concerted acts of violence mounted with the connivance of the state against their persons and businesses. *An organised Reichskristallnacht against gay bars in Moscow hardly seems an implausible prospect … Everyone knew that it would not be right to engage with South African sport in the years of apartheid.* Would it really be right to go to a country that, in recent years, has taken such steps to prevent any expression of the rights of its gay and lesbian citizens? Where appalling anti-gay violence is not only commonplace, but in many instances not prevented by the forces of law and order?
>
> (Hensher 2013, emphasise mine)

This refrain about the uncivilised *Reichskristallnacht*-esque horror of Russian homophobia—equated with the genocide of the Holocaust and, although less frequently, South African apartheid—supports the temporal othering and stigmatisation of Russia as backwards, regressing, and in need of modernisation. While Nazi antisemitism and South African apartheid are frequently invoked as comparisons, not once is Nazi persecution of (suspected) gay men. Reference to racist and anti-Semitic violence, while important parts of world history, is indicative of a 'forgetting' of the history of the extremely violent enforcement of heteronormativity in Europe and the former colonies as well as more recent examples such as the UK's Section 28 and Lithuania's gay propaganda laws (see Gentry 2020 on forgettings). Despite the obvious similarities, coverage of the Chechen gay purge—which includes the literal rounding up of (suspected) gay men and lesbians, their torture, and murder—never makes the historical comparison to Nazi concentration camps. These forgettings are important in moralistic international commentary about sex. But, they again carve out a policy terrain in which the potential influence of the Russian heteronormative internationalist project is not a core concern. Only now can we see the extent to which such complacency has enabled this project to seep into the political projects of so many powerful figures across the West.

The story of Western sexual exceptionalism and liberty, while not always explicitly articulated, recurs throughout press coverage. The absence of reference to its past history of homophobia sanitises Western histories of queer persecution and produces a narrative where the West has apparently always been a reasonably safe place for queer people. Indicatively, in what started as an apparent critique of homonationalism and pinkwashing by Western states, one reflection on an Olympic Games marred by state-directed homophobia quickly reverts to clichés of Western leadership on LGBTI+ rights and the unliveability of a queer life elsewhere:

> The focus on Russia has been intense, but we mustn't forget that homophobia can be found in all countries on all continents. Most recently in India the nation's top court re-criminalised gay sex and Uganda's parliament has passed draconian laws which will ... further criminalise homosexuality. *The lives of LGBT people in those countries, and many many more, tell the story of daily homophobia and transphobia without recourse to justice ...* Stonewall was founded 25 years ago to challenge injustices in Britain and it is as a result of the hope, passion and bravery of so many, that we stand on the eve of the first same-sex marriages and full legal equality for lesbian, gay and bisexual people ... *We'll continue to work with human rights defenders from across the world during their own long journeys until they can realise their goals.*
>
> (Hunt 2014, emphasis mine)

It is important that the media derides the persecution of queer people across the world and gives space to organisations like Stonewall, but it is concerning to see Western exceptionalism so ubiquitously promoted without any reflection on the track records and histories of anti-queer violence. Forgetting Europe's past creates an impression of the impossibility of the current, ongoing, and future persecution of queer people and anyone considered 'woke'. It enables denialism.

Demonstrating exactly this point, Libby Purves extols the benefits of including the gays in the onward march of progress in liberal democracies: 'Across all continents, nations with most ticks [next to their names on human rights] correlate exactly with democracy, relative prosperity, peace and self-confidence. Which should tell Mr Putin more than any number of rainbow flags' (2014). Purves argues that the socioeconomic benefits of adding gays and stirring is enough of a 'convincing argument against homophobia' (Purves 2014). This argument—which captures the position of a significant amount of the press coverage about corruption and issues of democratic backsliding in Russia, especially with regards to freedom of assembly and banned Pride marches—sidesteps any attempt to liberate non-normative sexuality from oppressive and violent straight culture by reinforcing existing social and economic hierarchies, simply arguing that prosperity follows the normalisation of queerness and folding it into already existing and oppressive structures of 'the normal' that have gone global through the Western LGBT model (Bersani 1996; Warner 2000). The narrative is essentially: include the gays and everything will be great—better even. This discourse is decidedly not about liberty or (sexual) autonomy as a cornerstone of liberal democracy.

Protecting Our Own

One of the most important points to emerge from the textual analysis was the overwhelming focus on Western athletes and Olympic/World Cup attendees. As might be expected given the periods covered, most news stories between 2013–2014 and 2017–18 cover the propaganda law in relation to the Olympics and the FIFA Men's World Cup. While one expects the press to make links to these large international sporting events—or, nation-branding events (Eggeling 2020)—the extent of their centrality in Western press was surprising. Especially since they were periods of heightened queer persecution—both through the propaganda law and vigilante violence in 2013, and the Chechen gay purge in 2017. The propaganda law only maintains its prevalence in the media because Russia was/would be hosting two major sports events, with some suggesting attendees 'make Sochi 2014 the gayest Olympics ever' (Moran 2013). The sharp drop in news coverage after the Olympics demonstrates this most clearly (Figure 5.2). The focus sat squarely on the impact the propaganda law would have on foreign attendees to the Games and was also the central focus of reports about lobbying national governments and the IOC. This is clearest in the concern by Western media, civil society, and political elites on whether the propaganda law would be enforced for foreign tourists or athletes during the Games since this violates the Olympic charter (e.g., Gibson 2013c; Goldstein

2013d; Longman 2013; Washington Post 2013a, 2013b). This shift clashes with earlier discursive patterns reifying ideas about international society's responsibility to protect people when a state fails to do so. In effect, the protective backstop is removed.

After the propaganda law was passed in 2013, *Politico* reported that '88 members of the House sent a letter to Secretary of State John Kerry asking the U.S. to protect LGBT athletes, staff and spectators at the games' (Kopan 2013a). Other outlets were similarly Western-centric in their reporting about Russian homophobia in the build up to and during the Sochi Games: 'Confusion over what will happen to athletes has fuelled the row' (Brown 2013b); 'Mr Putin says the new law does not harm anybody and there is "no danger" for homosexual competitors or spectators at the forthcoming Winter Olympics' (Wright and Luhn 2014); 'the I.O.C. had received assurances from the Russian authorities that its antigay law would not have an impact on athletes or officials at the Games' (Clarey 2013); 'NBC assured gay employees who may cover the Winter Olympics in Sochi that it would do everything possible to keep them safe' (AP 2013); 'Passed just six months before Russia is slated to host the 2014 Winter Olympics in Sochi, the law also allows foreigners to be arrested and detained for up to two weeks should they choose to "propagandize" homosexuality while visiting' (Washington Post 2013b); 'Under Russian law, gay people attending the games as athletes or spectators will not be allowed to "spread propaganda of non-traditional sexual relations" to anyone under 18. This means that they will not be allowed to behave or speak in any way that equates straight and gay relationships, or distribute material on gay rights' (Pengelly 2013); 'the International Olympic Committee (IOC) [announced] that it has "received assurances from the highest level of government in Russia" that the country's draconian new anti-LGBT policies "will not affect those attending or taking part in the games"' (Goldstein 2013c); and '[the Merkley Bill] will be a nonbinding resolution asking Russia to ensure those traveling to the games "will not experience anti-LGBT discrimination"' (Kopan 2013b).

The same thing happened between 2017 and 2018 in the build up to the World Cup. The concern was about those attending major sports events, not on the people who live permanently under laws that condemn their sexualities and gender performances, and seek to make them invisible (e.g., Austin 2017; Buchan 2018; Mohn 2017; Panja 2017; Walker and Kelner 2018; Wintour 2018). Notably, some of the focus during the World Cup centres on the closing down of Diversity House, a site for celebrating diversity in football

(Walker and Kelner 2018), and whether fans can wave or wear rainbow flags (Austin 2017; Slater 2017). This all prompted UK MPs to voice concerns 'about lack of "specific provisions" to protect LGBT+ football fans, who already face additional risks of attack and persecution in a country whose government has taken "little action to combat homophobia"' (Buchan 2018; see also: Wintour 2018). And it led the UK Foreign Office to specify guidelines for LGBT+ fans attending the World Cup because 'Public attitudes towards LGBT+ people are less tolerant than in the UK' (The Football Supporters' Federation 2018; UK Foreign and Commonwealth Office 2018). Several news outlets warned against public displays of queerness such as holding hands or waving the rainbow flag (Carroll 2018; Kelner 2017; Panja 2017).

The concern for Western audiences and athletes attending these major sports events is astonishing. Answering the classic Feminist Security Studies question 'whose security matters?' After reading these articles is easy: Russian queer people's security is outranked by Western athletes and spectators attending these international sports events. Such was the concern in the media and by National Olympic Bodies about what would happen if fans or Olympians did something considered gay propaganda that Putin issued a statement saying that: 'athletes or fans who made statements or gestures that could be considered as propaganda would not be punished' (Charlton 2013a). And the 'mounting pressure [on the IOC] from around the world to strip Russia of the right to hold the Games, where it is feared openly gay athletes, coaches, fans or media could be arrested or fined under the new legislation' forced the IOC to emphasise that 'all Olympic visitors should be allowed to speak and act openly … at the Games' (Brown 2013c; see also The Times 2013).

The same happened before the World Cup. FIFA was forced to issue a statement that they had received assurances 'that everyone will feel safe, comfortable and welcome' (quoted in Panja 2017) and that 'Fifa [sic] has a zero-tolerance approach to discrimination and we have mechanisms to ensure that the atmosphere in the stadiums is one of celebration and respect' (quoted in Ziegler 2017). Director at Football Against Racism in Europe, Piara Powar, issued a statement saying that they 'have been given forceful assurances that people's safety in and out of stadia would be taken care of' (quoted in Carroll 2018). To all of this, Russian World Cup ambassador Alexei Smertin said: 'You can kiss all you like, and hug one another, within the bounds of normal reason' (quoted in Carroll 2018). All of this not only exemplifies the ethical element of the discourse—FIFA and IOC as responsible—but the primary concern with Western audiences travelling to Russia, over the people who live through state-directed homophobia on the daily. More recently, similar discursive patterns have emerged around Qatar and Saudi Arabia's hosting of the FIFA Men's World Cup.

All of this is accompanied by chest thumping self-congratulations in many of the articles constituting the situation in the West as radically different. In comparison to Russia, we are led to believe that the West is a queer space where LGBT+ people are free to live untroubled lives, despite the odd spot of homophobia by a few *individual* bad apples (see Rifkind 2014 for a particularly potent example). The temporal positioning of the media discourse—Russia's active regressing—concomitantly produces the West as advancing, a beacon of LGBTI+ hospitality, that legitimises 'forgettings' about the West's history of homophobia, relegating it to the past, facilitating pinkwashing, and enabling homonationalist power projection. It also enables the idea that prevention at home is not necessary in the West (Cooper-Cunningham and Kremer 2024) Ethically, the focus on athletes and visitors shifts the realm of resposiqikity to protect queer Russians away from international society (as a backstop) and back solely to Russia; a more classic interpretation of sovereignty and responsibility that challenges existing norms around violence against a state's own people.

Attributing Responsibility

While the media discourse reproduces the EU discourse that LGBTI+ rights are human rights, one additional emphasis is made. That a country set to host such a prestigious international event should follow established international legal obligations, particularly those on human rights: 'the dignity with which gays are treated has been recognized as a fundamental human rights concern in much of the world. No country, especially not one on the cusp of hosting the Olympic games, should expect such bigotry to go unnoticed' (Washington Post 2013b). This questioning of Russia's suitability to host major international events continued during the World Cup (Staples 2018; Tatchell 2018).

On this issue, the ethical dimension of media discourse is most pronounced. Throughout the course of 2013–14 and 2017–18, the IOC, and to a lesser extent FIFA, Olympic sponsors, and the IAAF are constituted as arbiters for gay rights changes in Russia (e.g., Goldstein 2013d; Hoyle 2013; Kelner 2017; Longman 2013; Staples 2018; Walker 2018; Washington Post 2013a):

> This double standard, whereby the IAAF or the IOC awards major sporting events to nations with gross human rights violations in defiance of their own charters, and then mandates that athletes to [sic] shut up and behave like nothing's happening - so long as they don't see any LGBT people being beaten bloody, arrested, or tortured within the stadium walls - has begun to wear thin ... the Kremlin's own 'Berlin 1936 redux' must not be aided and abetted by sporting organizations or corporate sponsors, particularly not by those who ignore their own anti-discrimination policies or profess liberal values at home while propping up a homophobic dictatorship abroad.
>
> (Goldstein 2013d)

Non-governmental organisations are most frequently called upon to encourage change and compliance with international human rights law; something that has been recurrent in media coverage of Qatar and Saudi Arabia's hosting/being awarded the FIFA Men's World Cups. In the case of the IOC, the media encourages establishing a precedent for the Olympic Games (and other sporting events) to be used as a carrot for coercing states into respecting/advancing human rights: 'The Russian law clearly violates the Olympic Charter, said Ty Cobb, director of global engagement for the Human Rights Campaign ... "We're going to call on our members and on sponsors to say the IOC has to change this"' (Lally 2013) and 'the new IOC president, said when he was elected in September that the organisation would have to take a realistic approach to the overlap between sport and politics' (Gibson 2013b).

These major events, which frequently shout about their political neutrality, become constituted as tools for modernising non-Western countries by shaming them just enough to encourage change. International sports events are repeatedly constituted as tools for diplomacy and soft influence by Western powers (e.g., Gibson 2013a; Lally 2013; MacFarquhar 2018; Panja 2017; Staples 2018; Walker 2018; Walker and Gibson 2014). To constitute non-government actors as ethically charged with enforcing international legal regimes is powerful. It transforms international sports bodies into potentially very powerful policy actors. And it reproduces the idea that the world can be easily divided into modern and antiquated queer spaces. In this case, the former is charged, through its institutions and control of/influence over major international events, with leading on LGBT+ rights and 'civilising' missions globally.

A Different Brand of Homophobia

Notably, from 2017, there is a significant shift in media coverage of Russian state homophobia. As coverage is dominated by reports about the 'gay purge' happening in Chechnya, a new religious element is introduced. The Chechen gay purge involved the Chechen authorities kidnapping, torturing, murdering, and disappearing suspected queer people in Chechnya, an autonomous Muslim majority republic of Russia.[7] The addition of a religious element to the discourse in many cases took the spotlight off Russia and allowed tropes of Muslim conservatism, backwardness, and staunch homophobia to rise to the surface (Amos 2017; Kramer 2017a, 2017c; Porter 2017; Sokirianskaia 2017; The Independent 2017). The focus on Chechen homophobia as a distinctly *religious* (Islamic) brand of state homophobia—set apart from Russia's *political* state homophobia—has a similar function to the narrative of Western queer exceptionalism between 2013 and 2014. It masks and renders invisible the homophobia in mainland Russia that laid the discursive foundations enabling Chechnya's gay purge and its leader's statement that: 'We don't have those kinds of people here ... We don't have any gays. If there are any, take them to Canada. Praise be to God. Take them far from us so we don't have them at home. To purify our blood, if there are any here, take them' (Kadyrov in Amos 2017).

Almost letting Russia off the hook for being comparably less violent, the media focuses repeatedly on Chechnya being a 'conservative Muslim republic' (Porter 2017) whose leadership 'press agendas of traditional Muslim values' (Kramer 2017b), and whose 'Muslim clerics' have 'announced jihad against all the staff of Novaya Gazeta', the Russian newspaper first reporting on the gay purge (Dearden 2017a). Unlike reporting on the gay propaganda law, which mentioned in passing the influence of the Russian Orthodox Church and the discourse of a return to 'traditional' values, Islam and religious conservativism is a primary feature of many articles between 2017 and 2018 (e.g., Kramer 2017d; Savelau 2017; Vasilyeva

---

[7] More on this can be found in Human Rights Watch's (2019) and ILGA's (2019) reports.

and Roslyakov 2017). The attribution of homophobia to Islam constitutes Chechen homophobia as qualitatively different to Russian and reifies popular Islamophobic discourses, in effect conflating two objects of stigmatisation (Islam and the Russian Federation). There is in fact only one mention of the influence the Russian Orthodox Church exerted in advancing anti-queer discourse in Russia (Parfitt 2018) and some coverage differentiates the extreme brutality of Chechen homophobia against Russia's comparative 'tolerance' (Staples 2018).

Part Two: Images

Having established that the official EU and news media discourses reinforce and potentially legitimise the queer utopia/dystopia spatialisation of international society present in official Russian discourse, in this second part of the chapter, I address how Russian state homophobia is visually represented and contested at the level of the international. I specifically attend to the way Russian and Western identities are visually produced through the issue of each space's treatment of their queer populations as well as the implicit stigmatisation at play. Doing so, I analyse the visual aspects of sexual geopolitics and how visual media representations order the world and international politics. The aim is to understand the political work of visual representations of Russian homophobia and queer (in)security to answer two fairly straightforward questions: What are the dominant representations of Russian homophobia? And how do they play into an international politics of sex characterised by practices of shaming and stigmatisation?

To get at these questions, I study published images representing Russian homophobia by coding and analysing images in news media between 2011 and 2014. The images analysed in this part of the chapter come from the same textual corpus as in the part above although I narrow the focus to the peak period of news coverage (i.e., until end of 2014) because I was interested in how the issue was represented during the period of most international attention. Only 211 of the articles contained images (Figure 5.3). For those unfamiliar with the mechanics of doing visual analysis, the images that accompany news articles are not shown in textual databases (e.g., *ProQuest* or *LexisNexis*). As such, having analysed the textual part of the dataset, I used each individual news outlet's website to find the publisher's version of the articles I had analysed from *LexisNexis* and check whether an image accompanied the story.

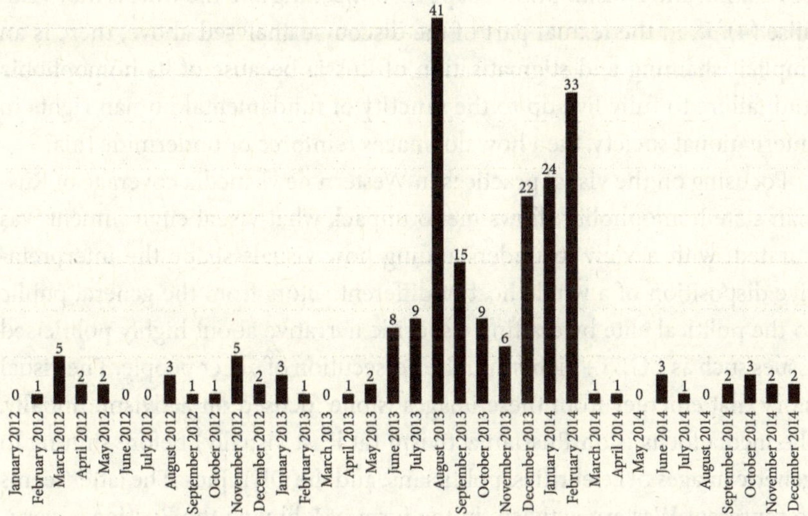

Figure 5.3 Count of articles *with* images published each month between 2012 and 2014.

My approach here is inspired by Megan MacKenzie (2020) and Lene Hansen's (2011) work, which emphasises the importance of seeing which (types of) image gain traction and how they circulate. MacKenzie (2020) in particular argues that visual research must not only focus on the content of images but *visual patterns* and *practices*:

> *Visual patterns* are ... regular poses, gestures, framing, subjects and activities captured across multiple cases of images that can construct a visual vernacular, or a form of visual grammar that has the potential to convey meanings beyond the individual content of the images. Moreover, the *regular practices* associated with producing, circulating and consuming images can reveal a great deal about the politics, power and significance of images within a particular group.
>
> (MacKenzie 2020, 4, emphasis added)

The *practices* surrounding images are incredibly important because images are 'involved in a seemingly endless array of practices; they are produced, deleted, edited, published, exchanged, viewed, censored, replicated, captioned, copied, tweeted, shared, filtered and archived' (4). To treat images as standalone artefacts that convey information overlooks how 'the practices associated with images and the politics involved in the[ir] production, circulation and consumption' shape their meaning and the worlds they visualise (4). If, in the textual part of the discourse analysed above, there is an implicit shaming and stigmatisation of Russia because of its homophobia and failure to fully live up to the sanctity of fundamental human rights in international society, then how do images reinforce or undermine this?

Focusing on the visual practices in Western news media coverage of Russian state homophobia allows me to unpack what visual environment was curated, with a view to understanding how visuals shape the interpretative disposition of a whole host of different actors from the general public to the political elite by crafting a specific narrative about highly politicised issues such as LGBT+ rights and the persecution of queer people. The visual story that emerges from these images is one focused on activism. Initially, the media focus is on Russian activism (at least visually) before shifting to generic images of celebrities, politicians, and the Olympics. The latter seems to represent Western activism in the form of lobbying the Russian government to halt its abhorrent treatment of queer people. While I do not study Russian activism per se, it does appear sporadically in the empirical material covered in this chapter.

Photography and the Politics of Representation

Since the predominant visual medium in news media is photography, it is important to outline the political and epistemological status of photography. This will be important to recall in the next chapter as well. Photography is often attributed documentary status and regarded as more objective and realistic than illustrated images such as comics or cartoons (Barthes 1977, 17–19; Bleiker 2018; Hansen 2017; Sontag 1977). For that reason, photography is powerful in convincing audiences that what is shown is the closest one can get to the truth, to what exactly happened at the moment the image was shot without having been there (Shapiro 1988, 124). Because photography is widely understood to collapse the representation/reality divide photorealistic images are endowed with an epistemic privilege over other genres. Speaking to this, Butler writes that 'although narratives might mobilize us, photographs are needed as evidence' (2010, 69).

The idea that photorealistic images have a greater truth value than their 'more constructed' counterparts has been widely disputed by visual scholars (see, inter alia, Andersen 2020; Barthes 1977; Bleiker 2018; Butler 2010;

Campbell 2007; Chute 2016; Cooper-Cunningham 2020a; Hansen 2017; Shapiro 1988; Shim 2017; Sontag 1977; Vuori and Andersen 2018). Photographs are no less produced and manufactured, no less a mediation of 'the real' sought represented, than illustrative genres. They may be closer to 'reality' in the sense that a camera captures what is in its shot closest to how it is seen by the eye—and even that is disputed (Sontag 1977)—but it also does not tell the whole story. Photography's authority as a conduit of transparent, complete 'truth' is a product of social processes; powerful but also contestable. Camera-created images *represent*, they do not make absolute like-for-like copies. This means accounting for the political work photographs do in terms of setting, contributing to, and/or (re)shaping debates as a result of their epistemic power. Because of this epistemic status, photographing homophobia is generally received as documentation of fact rather than the mediation of events. This claim of being closest to the 'real' means photographs produce particular forms of knowledge that organise the world (Foucault 1980, 93, 102).

For me, *representations* of the international, (in)security, or homophilia/homophobia constitute that which they claim to represent. This is a performative understanding of representations. What is represented is therefore inseparable from its representation since 'we are only able to know things by virtue of their representation' and as such 'meaning, truth or politics do not exist prior to, or independent from, their discursive representation' (Shim 2014, 17). This means, we only know 'Russia', 'the West', and 'the international' and its inhabitants through their representation. Those representations are always profoundly political with particular effects for people, states, and organisations. In this case, the world is geopolitically organised into spaces of sexual liberation/autonomy (modernity) and sexual control (archaism). If sexual politics is a key feature of state identity, foreign policy, and the structuring of international hierarchies, then how we come to know about and understand it, and how it is represented is important. In this case that is through photographs.

While it is important to question the status of photographs and their political function, the problem I address here is that of in/visibility, how issues become internationally concerning, and how international subjects are made to appear (or disappear). What I uncover is the dominant *visual patterns* (ways of representing) and *practices* of showing Russian homophobia and Russian queer people in Western media, which shape how problems are understood and therefore responded to. Photographs are *chosen* to represent a particular idea, story, or issue from a huge visual pool. News outlets mostly use image agencies—Getty Images, for example—with thousands of photographs from which editors select an image deemed to represent a story (Gursel 2016; Hansen, Adler-Nissen, and Andersen 2021, 3). During the period covered in this chapter, traditional media was not as challenged by social media as the predominant source of news as it is today. In this regard, while media professionals were no longer the primary proprietors of visual power by the early 2010s in the sense that smartphones and social media were ubiquitous across the West, they were still the predominant arbiters of how issues were framed to a mass audience. What news outlets publish and what they leave invisible was important then and remains so today: it sets the course of debate by constituting what is socially and politically important, it structures truth-claims and knowledge about an issue, and it establishes authority for handling an issue (Shim and Nabers 2013, 297; see also Van Veeren 2018; Vuori and Andersen 2018). To echo Herman and Chomsky (1988), those who control the media control the minds and imaginations of the public by establishing what is visible, sayable, thinkable, and doable (see also Callahan 2020; Rancière 2004).

What is (not) used to represent an issue is political in the most fundamental sense: it is a selection of what matters and how it matters. To draw on an example from the material here, choosing to represent a story about state homophobia with a photograph of Putin addressing the UN, Madonna performing in Moscow, or queer Russians being attacked by vigilantes sets the parameters for understanding the negotiation of queerness in Russia and it establishes the types of agency available to particular groups of people. While images function differently from words, they too establish the ethical, temporal, and spatial arrangements of international politics, conditioning our perceptions of the world and establishing who is responsible for solving an issue. Given that visuals can represent identity to tell us 'who we are (and who we aren't)' (Callahan 2020, 23; Neumann 2018), news images shape how a collective such as the nation understands itself and how people relate to or recognise Other countries by reproducing/destabilising powerful discourses about those places.

Images of Russian Homophobia in International Media

Until August 2013 news outlets primarily published images of queer Russians, protests, and anti-queer violence (e.g., Beaumont et al. 2012; Kramer 2013). Then, around the IAAF World Athletic Championships in Moscow

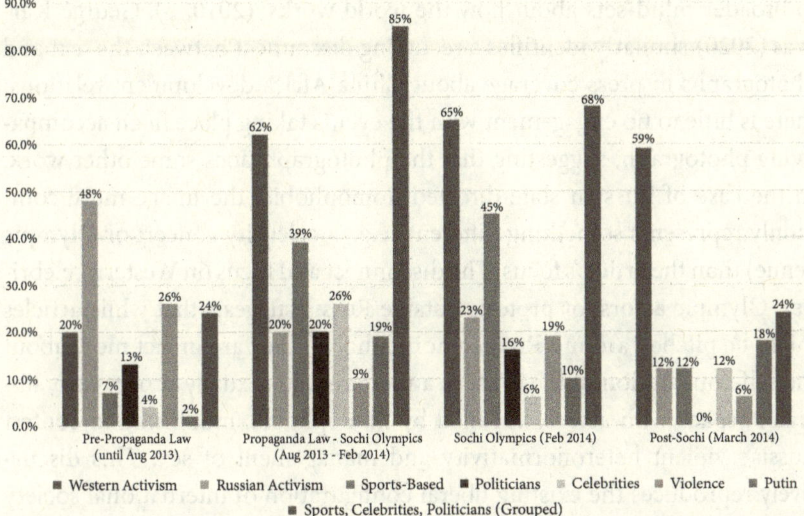

Figure 5.4 Percentage of news images in each category during time period.

(10–18 August 2013) the visual representation of Russian homophobia changes. From then, the queer people written about in news reportage disappear. They are replaced by athletes, celebrities, Olympic symbols, and politicians (e.g., Brown 2013a; Gibson 2013b; Lally 2013). As the representation of queer Russians drops, the representation of athletes, celebrities, and politicians rises and photographs of violence and arrests decrease. Over time the visual and textual discourse in the media ignores the very people it talks about. Then, Putin emerges as an icon of regression, the symbol of unreason and human rights abuses (see Gibson 2013b) and Western athletes and celebrities become the embodiment of progress and respect for human rights. Instead of the queer people featured in the main body of the reportage (even if briefly), the visual focus shifts to the Western actors, their (in)security and potential role as mediators of change in Russia, and (representatives of) the institutions that are being encouraged to do something. That is to say, there is often a stark disconnect between what appears in news images (e.g., celebrities) and the content of the article (e.g., vigilante violence against queer Russians). I illustrate the visual patterns in Figure 5.4—note that the chart columns follow the order of the legend alongside.

Speaking to this type of visual practice, Barbie Zelizer writes that 'pictures [in news media] are frequently used in ways that depict not the core of a news story but its peripheral, symbolic, and associative sides—scenes removed from those described in the text but valuable because they play to broader mind-sets about how the world works' (2010, 5). George Karavas (2020) similarly identifies a recurring disconnect between the text and photographs in press coverage about China-Africa development relations: there is little to no engagement with the events taking place in an accompanying photograph, suggesting that the photograph does some other work. In the case of Russian state-directed homophobia, the image more commonly represents something different (e.g., a celebrity concert or Olympic venue) than the article's focus. The disconnect and focus on Western celebrities, Olympic actors, or protests outside Russia suggests that while articles might be pitched around Russian homophobia, they are in fact more about the self-constitution of the West as a modern and sexually progressive, liberated, space with actors, appalled by homophobia, mobilising to contest Russia's violent heteronormativity and management of sex. This discursively reproduces the existing liberal configuration of international society and its norms as the best possible and most ethical configuration: continually visualising celebrities and athletes implies their relative security in the West compared to their insecurity in Russia as well as their responsibility to do something about Russian homophobia. This works visually to carve out that sexual geopolitical map in a similar way to ILGA's rainbow map (Ammaturo and Slootmaeckers 2024). And, again, it narrowly answers the question of whose security matters and who is responsible for ensuring it.

While the visualisation of Russian state homophobia changes over time, the text-image interaction repeatedly (re)asserts Western sexual exceptionalism, modernity, and progress. Paired with the media articles' text, images of protest and violence are initially used as evidence that Russia's queers need protection, confirming Russia's status as not just the epicentre of global homophobia but a shining example of regression, corruption, and inhumanity. Importantly, images of protest and demonstrations that get printed in the media predominantly contain anti-queer violence and/or police detention, which more than simply showing the violent persecution of queer Russians—an undeniably important move—also renders invisible moments of collective action and more complex queer subjectivities than simply 'the victimised'. This raises concerns about how agency and subjectivity are constituted. Based on the media images, it seems that queer life is fundamentally unliveable in Russia, and that queer people experience no joy or agency. This is a contrast with the more complex subjectivities and queer life that emerge in Mads Nissen's photographs studied in the next chapter. All types of visualisation are important in the sense that we need to have different forms of intervention that reveal stories about violent state-enforced heteronormativity in Russia. However, that does not mean we should not question and problematise media portrayals for the relations to power and subjectivities they entrench and reproduce.

Later, as images of celebrities/athletes/politicians come to accompany textual representations of Russian homophobia, those images reorient the focus from the insecurity of queer Russians to the potential insecurity of Western athletes and visitors to Russia. This not only highlights how homophilia is equally as politicised as homophobia, but carves out a hierarchy between the queer friendly West/homophobic Russia by showcasing the variety of Western institutions and actors condemning the situation in Russia as well as how queer people become insecure by crossing borders and leaving the West. These images become representative of a story about just how far the West has come on LGBTI+ issues rather than Russian homophobia, which legitimises and further enables Western states' management of our bodies, pleasures, and sexual opportunities through sheer ignorance and/or denial of heteronormativity's persistent power.

After August 2013, we rarely *see* the queer Russians risking everything to fight oppression, to fight for their right to exist in public space, and carving out their own queer subjectivities. It is not that images of resisting Russians suddenly become unavailable, that images of a queer movement in Russia do not exist. They were just not used in the media and images depicting Western actors' activism were more prevalent. The visual absence of Russian queer activism in Western media invisibilises and removes agency from Russian activists, constituting them as victims in need of Western defence or rescuing without reflecting on what shape that assistance ought to come in or how queer organisations/people in Russia mobilise. Neither text nor image fully captures Russian activism: it is silenced/invisibilised. The spatialisation of resistance and responsibility for action thereby shifts from within Russia to the international sphere as news media, the EU, and NGOs begin to constitute Russian homophobia as an international political issue. But there is something of an ambiguity around whether international society has any responsibility to ensure the protection of queer Russians or only their own citizens. This raises a visual provocation around the international norm of a responsibility of protection that starts with the state and ends with international society should a state fail in its responsibility to ensure the security of its citizens.

This is the emergent international politics of sex I wrote about in Chapter 2, in which Russian homophobia—rooted in a geopolitical confrontation with the West—becomes a recognised terrain of confrontation between the West and Russia (the developing and the regressing) in which the West must act immediately not only to assist the queer Russians living under the law but to secure its position as a global LGBTI+ defender and space where people can live their non-normative sexuality (narrowly defined as LGB) freely and without harassment. This shift in spatiality and ethical responsibility coincides with the increasing concerns in the media over whether foreign athletes and Games attendees would be subject to the gay propaganda law.

Lene Hansen, Rebecca Adler-Nissen, and Katrine Andersen note that the generic images of European politicians, civil servants, and political buildings used to represent the 'refugee crisis' are politically polysemous in that they could be read as 'remov[ing] the plight of refugees from sight' and/or 'visually connecting politicians to the refugee crisis, thus accentuating their political responsibility for solving the crisis' (2021, 10). A similar reading could be made of the images used to represent Russian state-directed homophobia. Queer people and defenders of sexual minorities in Russia are undeniably pushed out of the picture by images of celebrities, politicians, and Olympic symbols used in the media, but there is a complexity to these generic images, which could represent a huge range of political issues. They do not solely invisibilise the queer people being persecuted but also reinforce one of the major ethical dimensions emerging in the textual documents analysed above. They visually place responsibility for finding a solution to Russian homophobia and assisting those Western queers endangered by the propaganda law and increased societal hostility to non-normative sexualities at the feet of the IOC and Western states. The media visually calls upon Western institutions to back up their commitments to equality and protecting minorities—particularly the IOC, whose Olympic Charter proclaims to forbid discrimination of any kind.

There is the possibility that these types of generic images are clickbait and thus generate increased public attention and awareness of Russian homophobia by virtue of audiences simply being more drawn to topical news stories such as the Olympics or the World Cup. This visual pattern, however, edits the international in such a way that 'reality' becomes distorted and our view of the world detached from actual goings on. This edits both what is in/visible and the politics that are able to emerge around certain issues. Yes, one expects the media to focus on the Olympics and Western athletes, but a different representational practice is possible and necessary; one that doesn't switch to a 'protect our own' but documents queer life in all its guises and also gives visual space to non-violent resistance against Russian state homophobia.

Given that much of the media coverage (e.g., Herszenhorn 2013; Kopan 2013a; Riach 2013) and some EU debate (e.g., European Union 2013) was tinged with questions about the treatment of Olympic fans and athletes in Sochi rather than the treatment of queer Russians, the West's concern for queer Russians' (in)security appears empty and a political strategy to out-manoeuvre Russia in the international political sphere. The (visual) story is rarely told from the perspective of queer Russians and after August 2013 there are so few images of what is actually happening that debate is shifted towards a comparison of Russian homophobia versus the 'freedom' of queers in the West. This ultimately reproduces notions of Western superiority and the West as queer safe haven, masking the power of heteronormative structures and increasing anti-LGBTI+ hate crimes in many parts of 'the West' (see Cooper-Cunningham and Kremer 2024; Gifkins and Cooper-Cunningham 2023). All of this makes me question how Wiedlack arrives at the conclusion that 'victimized young gay men' became 'symbols of Russian backwardness' (Wiedlack 2020, 67). Actually, they were not really in the media at all.

The *visual practices* in international media are powerful and ordering. The photographs published in international press divide the world into a much too neat dichotomy between good/bad states, which fails to capture the complexity of states' strategic use of homophobia and homophilia, which are not necessarily mutually exclusive. By using generic images of celebrities, athletes, politicians, and Olympic symbols, they fail to represent the full story of queer life in Russia from the exceptional violence to the underground queer communities and mundane moments of joy and delight in one's queerness. The result is a one-dimensional representation of queer life that reinforces a hierarchy of nations based on ideas of sexual liberty in the West and control in Russia. This points towards both homophilia and homophobia being one of many pawns in a broader geopolitical struggle.

This neat binary, as Slootmaeckers and Ammaturo argue 'displaces the lived experience of queer people' such that 'when those living in so-called LGBTQI+ friendly countries experience violence, their experience are interpreted as random instances and systemic structures of oppression are ignored, whilst at the other end of the spectrum queer people are imagined as eternal victims, and positive stories and individual/collective tools of resistance and abilities to create safe space are rendered impossible' (2020). The result is the invisibilisation of queer subjects living under the propaganda law and the establishment of an incredibly low bar for Western states to judge their 'success' in advancing protections for queer people against Russia and other homophobic spaces. The political effect of these photographs is to establish a hierarchy of 'liberated' queers and persecuted queers, and states their treatment represents.

Conclusion

What should be clear from the above is that there are two competing visions of international society, part of which involves the use of queer issues as a measure of morality and legitimacy to lead internationally. This is demonstrative that there is a politics of sex and that it has gone international, informing foreign policy, underpinning internationalist political projects, and turning sexual behaviour and erotic desire into a geopolitical issue. States and state adjacent actors are using sexuality to position themselves within an international hierarchy; there is a sort of selfish solidarity that comes out of the discourse above, both visually and textually. The amount of attention around sexuality and Russia's heteronormative project is indicative of how something deemed by so many to be the most personal and apolitical thing—sex—is international and highly politicised. Russian homophobia and Western condemnation of it are part of an international jostling and moralising around acceptable forms of sexual behaviour, erotic desire, and bodily pleasures.

Russia is clearly not an objectively good place to be queer—as if such a place existed—and there is no denying that politicised homophobia is a huge problem in Russia. Yet, the way the material above authorises a modernising project by taking the moral high ground on the issue of non-normative sexuality is troubling. As is the lack of attention to those who bear the brunt of Russian homophobia: queer Russians. All of this carves out hierarchies through notions of modernity and backwardness. This is an international political game, part of which is structured around the question of sex. The EU and Western media condemn Russia and advance a modernising discourse in which Russia must be brought in line with the West's 'tolerant' LGBTI+ model. Russia condemns the West's 'modernisation' project as a sort of abhorrent queer utopia in which sexual decadents are destroying the foundations of European civilisation. And Western media fans the flames of a geopolitical confrontation around non-normative sexuality. Instead of reflecting on the West's historic role in a global heteronormative project, the power that normative sexuality has on us all, or for that matter on the queer Russians experiencing the brunt of a geopolitical conflict attached to sex, the media focuses on: the potential threat faced by Olympic athletes, the 'progress' of the West on all things LGBTI+, and badgering the IOC and FIFA to become enforcers of modernising processes for non-Western countries.

These discursive moves (re)produce international hierarchies using sex as a vehicle. Just as Russia's domestic gay propaganda law and its heteronormative international project are 'exercises in official [national] storytelling and the production of mass political experience' (Berlant 1997, 177), representations of Russian state and societal homophobia occupy a somewhat similar position in Western states. The text and images of Russian homophobia actually recognise Russia as the type of queer dystopian space it wants to be recognised as. These representations actually reproduce and strengthen the Russian discourse. As Zelizer notes, what emerges visually is often an indication of a broader conceptualisation of how the world works and ought to be structured. Some years on from the period analysed here, the struggle over which version of international society will prevail is very much still playing out and this remains replete with shaming and stigmatising moves, including about gender and sexuality. In the next chapter, which is methodologically and analytically twinned with this one, I focus more specifically on photographs of queer Russians, reading their activism and visual presence as non-violent resistance to the Russian authorities' homophobia that hovers between rejection and embrace of stigma.

6

Alternative Visualisations of Queer Life in Russia

In this chapter, I focus on what photographers' images do politically and what a queer analysis of photographs of Russian homophobia enables in terms of thinking about the international politics of sex and the individuals affected by geopolitical projects such as the heteronormative internationalism of the Russian government. In the main analysis, I analyse 369 photographs created by three photojournalists, all of whom covered Russian state homophobia from the outset of Western media attention on the issue.[1] I do so with a view to seeing how alternative representations of Russian homophobia and queer life were possible. And to see whether there is an alternative visualisation that destabilises—or at complicates—the sexually modern/backward hierarchy emerging in Chapter 5. While Chapter 5 deals with what was shown/published in news media, I focus here on a visualisation that was largely absent: the activism of queer people in Russia. This involves a comparison of the three photojournalists' images with those published in the media. In this regard, the following analysis is twinned with that in the previous chapter. Before I do this, I want to return to the personal account with which I opened the introduction.

▲

My first encounter with Russian state homophobia was through the photograph of three individuals at a Pride event in St Petersburg that I introduced at the beginning of the book. The trio were surrounded by police officers who wore riot gear. One of them had blood streaming from their nose and mouth. Several photojournalists photographed this and other similar scenes (e.g., Figures 1.1, 6.1, and 6.2). Many of the photographs from that event contained the same

---

[1] I analysed 369 images from these photographers: 94 by Dmitry Lovetsky available on AP Images/Ritzau-Scanpix, 94 by Mads Nissen available on Panos Pictures/Ritzau-Scanpix, 181 by Roma Yandolin from Flickr (169) and Getty Images (12).

The International Politics of Sex. Dean Cooper-Cunningham, Oxford University Press. © Oxford University Press (2025). DOI: 10.1093/9780197792544.003.0006

Figure 6.1 'Russia Gay Clampdown' by Dmitry Lovetsky, 29 June 2013. Image courtesy of AP/Scanpix-Ritzau.

four individuals identifiable from Figures 6.1 and 6.2. Three of the photojournalists who captured the 2013 Pride event in St Petersburg are the focus of this chapter: Mads Nissen, Dmitry Lovetsky, and Roma Yandolin.[2] Lovetsky's image (Figure 6.1) is incredibly similar to Nissen's image (Figure 1.1) with which I open the book. The many images of this scene say something about the importance attributed to this particular scene by the photojournalists who were present. Lovetsky's photograph was chosen as one of the Associated Press' Top 10 Images of 2013 and it circulated globally.

Those images have stuck with me. Encountering them, as I recounted in the opening pages of this book, was incredibly provoking and affective. From what I recall, looking at those images was the first time I had an intense loathing of another country. Having never lived in the context of the Cold War and not growing up in a household where Russia was frequently discussed, Russia became saturated with an identity as some backwards, barbaric, and

---

[2] I could have chosen many photojournalists for in-depth analysis. I selected these three for various reasons: Nissen because his images are internationally acclaimed, particularly 'Jon and Alex', which won the *World Press Photo* award; Lovetsky because their images circulated widely with Figure 6.1 included in *AP's Top Images of 2013*; and Yandolin because a large selection of photographs of events not covered elsewhere were available on Flickr, giving a less polished insight into the events photographed. Notably, Yandolin has since made their Flickr page private.

uncivilised place. If I am being completely honest—which I think is warranted in the context of a book that deals with the way images work politically to shape how we meet international political issues—back then, at the very start of my university education, I thought of Russia as a country populated by deplorable homophobes. Seeing the Russian state sanction and encourage the persecution of queer people because of who they desire sexually was incredibly uncomfortable for me because I had never really thought of desire as governed, controlled, or directed before. I had no idea what should be done at a policy level, but I supported an international response—be that granting asylum, issuing state sanctions, taking Russia to court, I understood Russia's queer population as needing help, the country's government as needing redirection, and the West as playing a key role in this.

All of this is indicative not only of the power of the visual to illicit affective, political responses but also illustrative of how they are intertextually/intervisually situated. There is nothing in these photographs that suggests any of the individuals are queer, nor is there anything—at least to the unfamiliar eye—that suggests the photographs were taken in Russia. They could have been taken anywhere and could be of any group of people being beaten up and surrounded by some militarised force. The headlines accompanying them and the articles in which these images are embedded are also doing a lot of work. The text and the image work together to narrow the interpretive gaps and to reinforce the discourse that the LGBTI+ question—like the woman question— was settled in the West, the supposed apex of queer liberty and security to be imitated elsewhere. This text-image interaction is clearest when one compares Figures 6.1 and 6.2 with how Figure 6.1 was used in The New York Times *(see Herszenhorn 2013).[3] The text-image interaction is powerful and crucial to how the image's polysemy (i.e., the ability to interpret an image in multiple ways depending on the library of knowledge and stock of symbols that one has to draw upon) gets reduced and obtains meaning. There is also a conflict between what we can see in Figure 6.1 when it was used in* The New York Times *(Herszenhorn 2013) and how it was captioned. The caption suggests that the police officers are 'guarding' protesters. Are these laughing and joking police officers really 'guarding' the protesters while they wield truncheons and laugh?*

My response to those images (simply put: why isn't the West doing something to Russian, to save these people?) not only verges on that Western saviour

---

[3] I encourage readers to look this article up. Unfortunately, the copyright costs for the New York Times article and accompanying image were too high to include in the book.

Figure 6.2 'Supporters try to protect LGBT activist, Kiriee Fedorov, from further attacks' by Mads Nissen, June 2013. Image courtesy of Panos Pictures. Image ID: MNN01266RUS.

and superiority trap[4] that I discuss into in the previous chapter, but it also speaks to the way that an entire country and its population's identity can take on (new) meaning through an image. Particularly for those unfamiliar with the general machinations of international politics or domestic affairs in other states, but also for those who don't have the time, energy, or wherewithal to seek out and triangulate information from different sources. What we see does something politically and is a part of how we are socialised into viewing the world geopolitically. It is these qualities that make images—and specifically these particular images of 'deviants' and their punishment—geopolitical and ordering. They create hierarchies and tensions. In the same way that Vladimir Putin had been setting up an image of the West as this morally bankrupt Gay-ropean space, the Western representation of Russia as a similarly morally and ethically bankrupt homophobic dystopia does something in terms of establish-ing hierarchies and ordering the world into distinct, neat spaces characterised by insurmountable difference.

That image, those linked to it, and the text accompanying them established the interpretative dispositions that make certain ideas and practices possible.

---

[4] In the sense that I viewed queer Russians as 'victims without the capacity or means to resist the state.

In that moment, to me Russia was a place that was stuck in the past and full of homophobes. There was no space for nuance or questioning the political work that media representations do; at least not at first. That image reduced Russia and its place in the world to a single snapshot and in so doing reduced the complexity of Russian politicised homophobia, constituted queer Russians as victims of extreme, ignorant, hate-fuelled violence, and masked the heteronormative politics of sex still persistent in the West—the self-professed pinnacle of sexual liberation where moralising about sex was a thing of the past and we had reached the sexual autonomy Warner (2000, 7) discusses. While everyone's reading of an image or text is to a certain degree unique, I cannot have been the only one with this interpretation since the images were anchored by text(s)— those discussed in Chapter 5—that worked to construct Russia as stuck in the past and regressive.

I use my experience as a tool for demonstrating how powerful the words and images we use to represent political issues are. But this encounter is also a lesson in what critical approaches, especially queer and poststructuralist approaches, offer to the study of international politics. It is only now, some twelve years after my first engagement with those photographs that I can reflect on the political, world ordering moves those images make. These images matter because through them we come to know Russian state-directed politicised homophobia, because they constitute 'international' spaces and subjects in politically significant ways, and because they are constitutive of a security discourse that encompasses Russian and Western queer subjects.

Like words, images shape and orient social and political outlooks, constitute identities, and justify, delegitimise, or even demand certain actions. Beyond this and at a more abstract level, as Lene Hansen (Forthcoming) writes, images can also be tools for IR scholars to think with theoretically and conceptually in the sense that they can provoke and inspire. The images in this chapter occupy both roles, but do critical work in making visible the queer Russians and their spectacular and everyday resistances to state homophobia. In the rest of this chapter, I look to other, less prominent images of Russian state homophobia, which arguably have an activist potentiality insofar as they open space to see queer counterpublics and resistance in Russia in ways that were otherwise invisible in the media.

▼

The rest of this chapter will unfold in two parts. I first outline my approach to studying this alternative visualisation of 'queer dystopia Russia', the dominant discourse that emerged in the previous chapter's analysis. Then, I turn to two types of visualisation centred around the activism and resistance of queer (allied) actions in Russia that emerged in Nissen, Yandolin, and Lovetsky's photographs: *Public Spectacle* and *Everyday Personal*. I explore the politics of these two visualisations and pay particular attention to the potentiality of the everyday personal in Nissen's images as a visualisation through which to think through antinormative queer politics and the visualisation of an immanent queer counterpublic in Russia that is more subtle than the into-the-streets activism that appeared in early press coverage of the gay propaganda law and in Yandolin and Lovetsky's images. Not only does this focus complicate how we think of the spatialisation of international politics and the spheres in which international security and power politics play out, but also how we think of activism and resistance to geopolitical projects.

Photojournalism, Alternative Visualisations, and Queer Counterpublics

Like in the previous chapter, I coded the photojournalists' photographs inductively using Microsoft Excel. The aim was to establish and analyse the *visual patterns* (i.e., what was commonly photographed) in a series of mainly unpublished images to see if they aligned with the visual patterns in the media. Essentially, was there an alternative visualisation that was possible? While I had no pre-established coding scheme, I did, of course, have an idea about what I was looking for: violence, protest, rainbows, police, counter-demonstrators. Given that I had seen numerous images with the four individuals in Figures 6.1 and 6.2, and keeping in mind visual theory on the identifiable victim effect (Adler-Nissen, Andersen, and Hansen 2019; Bleiker et al. 2013), I was also particularly interested in whether they featured heavily or not. Further codes were developed inductively and based on the analysis in the last chapter. Comparing the three photographers' images with the images published in news media between 2011 and 2014 provides a unique contribution to the study of visual politics in that I assess the discourse crafted across seven news outlets against a wider selection of images that could have been used to represent the same issue. This specifically unravels the politics of representing and speaks to the ordering work that images do in terms of setting the frame through which international political issues are received and understood.

I divide the three photojournalists' images into two categories: *Public Spectacle* and *Everyday Personal*. These distinctions are mainly analytic and are not a theoretical or conceptual distinction between the public/private, which many queer and feminist academics have critiqued (Berlant and Warner 1998; Peterson 2014a). Rather, emerging from the empirical material, it is the contrast between the *visual patterns* in the photographers' work—in terms of image content, aesthetic, and the politics they invoke—that lead me to make this distinction, rather than any theorisation of the public/private as ontologically separate or political/apolitical spheres. Lovetsky and Yandolin predominantly photograph spectacle events such as protests, demonstrations, and violence whereas Nissen takes a more personal approach, capturing subjects over an extended period of time, adding depth and context to the representation of Russian homophobia; even producing two photo essays about his engagement with people holding both homophilic and homophobic politics in Russia (Nissen 2013/14, 2014). Nissen photographs people in their everyday lives—at home, commuting to work, in the club—and visualises queer Russians in a more intimate setting than Lovetsky and Yandolin. He is the only photographer to purposefully photograph and interview people with explicitly anti-queer politics (Figures 6.12 and 6.13).

Through *public spectacle* and *everyday personal* images, queer people and their (in)security are brought into international politics and constituted as a matter of international concern, but they do not arrive as actors devoid of agency. Primarily because their strategies of resistance and coping with their persecution get visual space. There is therefore the possibility of reading the photographed subjects as reconstituting their abject subject position as something to be embraced, celebrated, and weaponised by being visible and by being photographed in spaces where it is differentially safe and unsafe to be openly (suspected of being) queer (allied). These visual embodied acts work in such a way that allows spectators to see an otherwise invisible oppositional queer counterpublic. If we move from a heteronormative epistemology where non-normative sexuality reads as negative and towards an antinormative queer epistemology where deviance from normative structures is celebrated as a liberatory move, these images and the embodied act of being photographed read as a positive embrace of queerness and refusal to be made invisible and *unqueer*.

There are images of hope and joy here, which I argue represent the less acutely violent aspects of queer life in Russia as well as the immanent queer counterpublic they inhabit (Edenborg 2017, 191; Muñoz 1999, 5). Counterpublics, following Nancy Fraser, are public arenas in which exclusionary norms are contested by marginalised groups. Fraser specifies that subaltern counterpublics are 'parallel discursive arenas where members of subordinated social groups invent and circulate counter discourses, which in turn permit them to formulate oppositional interpretations of their identities, interests, and needs' (1990, 67).[5] The subaltern counterpublic, here, can be conceptualised as queer and antinormative in its rejection of dominant, oppressive normative structures. But also in the sense that to emerge as a counterpublic requires some degree of internalisation and recognition of the stigma directed at oneself as part of a social group for diverging from norms, in this case sexual: 'The subordinate status of a counterpublic does not simply reflect identities formed elsewhere; participation in such a public is one of the ways its members' identities are formed and transformed. A hierarchy or stigma is the assumed background of practice. One enters at one's own risk' (Warner 2002, 87). All counterpublics, as Warner continues, are thus only public insofar as they 'try to supply different ways of imagining' society and all types of hierarchical relations of power between people (88).

Reading these images through a more queer theoretical lens as antinormative and as visualising a queer counterpublic is possible firstly because queer people are knowingly appearing as subjects of stigma (i.e., as queer) in public in these photographs, and secondly because there is a clear refusal to be made completely invisible and to abide by heteronormative and docile ways of comporting oneself in public (e.g., Figures 6.3 and 6.4), which acts as a challenge to the dominant discourse of 'queer Western threat' propagated by Russia's political establishment. Thus, an imminent queer counterpublic is given visual space. Whether queer counterpublics are seeable and knowable is a matter of *visual practices:* they were decidedly not possible or seen in Chapter 5.

Taking all of this into account, the focus of this chapter is on exploring what it means to bring queer theory to the study of the visual in international relations. One that builds on the antinormative politics outlined in the introduction and takes seriously the possibility of an immanent queer

[5] Note that counterpublics differ from countercultures where the former are constituted by socially, politically or economically marginal groups/individuals opposing mainstream culture and the latter by those who are not marginalised (Clark-Parsons and Lingel 2020; Jackson and Kreiss 2023).

counterpublic in Russia. This is about seeing those individuals and groups sought invisible and marginal, as well as seeing the everyday and spectacular resistances they are engaged in to challenge and bring attention to the daily insecurity they face just by being. Those resistances are most complex in Mads Nissen's images of his interlocutors' everyday lives, which are pivotal in representing the everyday insecurity of queer Russians: this is not just about acute threats but also the systemic/structural violence that threatens people's autonomy and basic civil rights in service of an internationally reaching heteronormative agenda.[6] In particular, what comes out of these photographers' images is queer Russians resisting, not just remaining passive and victimised. In these images of activism, many of the individuals deploy similar visual symbols to the social movements in Chapter 4 and that which we see across the West today: namely, rainbows and pink triangles. This is not to say the activism in Russia is a copy of other forms of queer activism, but that there is an intervisuality at play.

This alternative set of photographs to that which were printed in Western media both eschew dominant depictions of non-Western minoritised groups as in need of Western assistance but also demonstrate how (visual) tactics are globally mobilised and how their politics travels (Figures 6.3 and 6.4). Using the rainbow and pink triangle in Russia reproduces and alters their queer politics in important ways. It emphasises the liberatory and anti-normative politics of queer over more identity-based LGBTI+ rights approaches such as those advocated by the EU, some Western governments, and human rights NGOs. That the pink triangle, in particular, is used enables a reading of Russian queer activism as not just about respectability, assimilation, or rights, but more about a radical reimagining of politics, dominant sociality, and the distribution of power in Russia. It situates queer activism as a fight for more than civil rights, but a broader reconfiguration of politics, specifically vis-à-vis autonomy and liberty. Read through an antinormative lens, I argue that the individuals

---

[6] Following my work with Detmer Kremer, where we follow Galtung's typology of violence, I use the following definitions: '*acute violence* … [is] personal or immediate violence committed with the intent to harm individuals based on their actual or perceived sexual orientation or gender identity … [including] killing, physical attacks, and verbal harassment … *Systemic threats* are forms of violence that are intrinsic to a particular system, often going unnoticed by those who are not impacted by them. Heteronormativity is a form of such violence that affects LGBTQI+ people. Heteronormativity is an ingrained norm shaping social and institutional fabrics in ways that exclude or discriminate against non-heterosexual individuals'. The latter often has no single identifiable perpetrator. Both types of violence 'are often legitimised and sustained through cultural means such as religion, ideology, language, art, science, and so on' (2024, 6 emphasis added).

in these photographs—particularly visible in Nissen's images of community and kinship but also in public spectacles of rainbow flag waving at Paratroopers Day—take up 'the challenge to invent forms of radical, post-national counterpublicity' (Berlant 1997, 23).

So, what is the alternative visualisation of queer life in Russia that emerged from these photographers' photographs? Across the three photographers' images, queer Russians still come into view as victims of violence and oppression by the police and other citizens: just under half of the photographers' images contain some form of physical violence or the threat of it (e.g., Figures 6.1–6.3, 6.5, and 6.6). Those individuals/groups featured do not necessarily get a voice or the chance to express themselves in words, however, their visual presence does something. Running my argument about words-images-bodies to its logical conclusion, visual presence is equally as important as vocal/textual. At first, this seems to encourage a reading of queer Russians as needing to be rescued and Russia modernised to Western standards of sexual 'liberation'. However, most of their images are taken at protests, which encourages a reading of these images that refuses to reduce queer Russians to wholly victimised subjects: they are also agentic resisters carving out their own queer spaces and radically reimagining their relationship with society. In many instances, they voluntarily place their bodies in harms way. Such acts have been theorised as powerful, non-verbal acts of resistance and proclamations/reclamations of agency (Bargu 2017; Fierke 2013; Scarry 1985). This is a strategy that has been central to queer activism in the past and is critical for reconfiguring the disciplinary, normative regimes in Russian society that work towards the elimination of queer people and their visibility across society (Chapter 4; Finkelstein 2018; France 2016; Gould 2009; Schulman 2021).

That most of the photographs are taken at protests or demonstrations shows how the Russian queer community is mobilising to resist and demonstrate against the propaganda law, often putting themselves in danger and making themselves temporarily more insecure in service of a longer-term political project that is broadly about securing the right to exist openly, freely, and visibly queer in public—should one choose to. In these photographs, there is more space to read moments of resistance than in the images used to represent Russian homophobia during the peak news reportage. When reading the media texts and images through the three photojournalists' images, it becomes clear just how invisible Russian activism was in the news media over the period studied. In the latter, there was a drastic indifference to Russian activism compared to Western-based activism. Choosing a photo of Elton John or Billie Jean King is political and in many ways reads as a representational politics rooted in Western exceptionalism—a chest-thumping self-congratulation of Western progress on the inclusion of some 'deviant' sexualities and genders (namely the LGBT) into the folds of the national community that produces 'uneven geopolitical temporalities' (Heimer 2019, 177). The invisibilisation of queer Russians and queer activism in Russia denies those individuals the possibility of coming into view as victims who are bludgeoned, beat up, and targets of violence but also equally—if not more so—as powerful, active, brave, and determined people resisting vehement homophobia in their struggle for space, sexual and gender autonomy, and social and material wellbeing. This is a struggle on two fronts to undermine a domestic and geopolitical strategy whereby queer people within Russia are scapegoated, demonised, and oppressed as part of an illiberal internationalist project set on constituting a good, leading, moral Russia against a bad, woke, imperial, immoral West.

Public Spectacles: Protest and Violence

The images I include in this category capture a moment in broad terms, are not necessarily aesthetically beautiful, and are shot in the moment, hastily, to capture large, spectacular events (e.g., protests such as Pride marches or the like). These photographs are those most commonly assumed to document an event exactly as it was and reproduce that moment for those not present. When it comes to protests or demonstrations, these photographs—when viewed as a collection—appear to tell the full story of an action: how it moved, what happened, and who was there. The people who appear in public spectacular images become somewhat objectified; they are photographed to illustrate a story. The subjects of the photograph are not as actively involved in shaping the visual story as one might be in a portrait session or in what I am calling *everyday personal* images. While they may feel the presence of cameras and play to them, using them to advance their cause and gain publicity, the camera is less definitely trained on one person/action.

Photographs of protests and demonstrations make up the majority of the images in the three photographers' collections: 284 (77%) of the 369 photographs. These types of photographs were also prevalent at the very beginning of news coverage of Russian homophobia. Most of those protest images involve some form of confrontation and 52% of the protest images include violence. It is no accident that photographers choose to focus on violent confrontations between protesters and vigilantes and/or (riot) police:

> Protest imagery disseminated by the mainstream media can be ideologically charged ... and therefore generate specific visualizations of power ... that can serve to either encourage mobilization in support of protests and the protestors' cause, or to delegitimize the protesters' causes, aims and objectives.
>
> (Veneti 2017, 280)

As with other images of violence, when they circulate these types of images make the violence globally visible and 'can put governments in a position where they are forced to "do something"', even if only condemning the violence (Duncombe 2020, 613).

So, how do queer Russians come into view in public spectacle images? And what do those images 'do'? To answer this, I analyse some of the key visual nodes—those that broadly represent the collection in its entirety—in Lovetsky and Yandolin's image collections.[7] As outlined in Chapter 3, there is no universal logic in the way we read images: everyone interprets them differently, drawing on subjective experiences, ideas, and knowledge. Despite the trickiness of giving a single reading or interpretation of an image, I opened this chapter with the story of how all the images like Figure 6.1 'pricked' me and sparked a connection with those subjects photographed. Zelizer (2010) asks under which conditions images work most powerfully. This is a question I've asked myself a lot in writing this chapter. Particularly when trying to capture, unravel, and theorise the emotional pang that photograph triggered. Barthes argues that news images often do not have a *punctum,* that is, something in the image that provokes the spectator (Barthes 1981, 41). I disagree. Lovetsky's photograph, as well as the variations by other photojournalists, have been imprinted in my mind, an emotional prick ever since I saw it.

Without caption or explanation, this photograph could be an image of any three people surrounded by police anywhere in the world at any time. They could be criminals on the run. They could be in the United States.

---

[7] Of their images, Figure 6.1 and similar were widely circulated, and Lovetsky's photograph was listed among AP's top images of the year.

Figure 6.3 'Gay Pride Parade in St. Petersburg' by Roma Yandolin. Image courtesy of Getty Images. Image No.: 175893577.

This could have been taken yesterday. The image is ambiguous and only becomes about queer political issues and Russia when read in the context of the album, alongside the caption/text or with some prior intervisual knowledge. Contextualised by its database title ('Russia Gay Clampdown') and its publication, the photograph works to convey the idea of a backwards and barbaric Russia where queer people are threatened just for existing and/or demanding the right to exist in public space, contra the propaganda law.

The contrast between brutalised, beat up bodies and smirking police officers underscores the dehumanisation of queer people as well as the institutionalisation of homophobia in Russia. But it also recalls one of the key lessons from the lesbian and gay liberation movements in the USA: that the police are a state apparatus implicated in anti-queer violence not only through their turning a blind eye but also in their unblinking enforcement of homophobic laws that uphold heteronormative structures (Bosia 2020b; Gould 2009). The unfamiliar might ask: Why are the police laughing? Why does it look like they're about to beat them up? For many oppressed groups, this image is incredibly relatable and poignant *because of* the police violence. The story of police complicity and the important reminder that the state can withdraw its support for marginalised groups at any moment is absent when all we see are celebrities and symbols of the Olympics. There is a complexity therefore to the visual story that is missing in the more prevalent news media images where the persecution of queer people in Russia and the violence they face is reduced to an issue that simply requires some lobbying from Western celebrities and key figures during an international sports event.

In the caption that *AP Images* gives for Figure 6.1, we are told that the police are guarding the three activists. Yet, the wider series of images and news reportage tells another story: police stand idly by while queer people are beaten by violent homophobes. The *New York Times* article using the image writes that: 'When some gay people protested the propaganda law by kissing outside the State Duma, the lower house of Parliament, police officers stood by and watched as the demonstrators were doused with water and beaten by antigay and religious supporters of the bill' (Herszenhorn 2013). Whose safety are the police securing? These scenes of police coercion and violence recur throughout the images at protests and they bear a striking intervisuality with the photographs from the NYPL archive, which saw huge police presence at ACT UP demos and almost always extreme police brutality. This opens up political space for reflecting on how we can overcome heteronormative sociality by drawing on similar lessons and tactics from past activism that succeeded in large part to prevent the erasure of queers. Such photographs' politics is complex: they tell important queer lessons about policing but also reify the 'barbaric Russia' discourse. Perhaps there is no real way around this, but giving appropriate visual space to those sought invisible is one way to undermine the Russian government's discourse of queerness as a Western phenomenon while also giving visual space and acknowledgement to those risking their lives for the potential to be in public, to challenge a political project intertwined with a Russian geopolitical challenged to the West on the basis of sexual politics.

Given that there is a relatively high presence of police officers at the protests/demonstrations, the levels of violence may at first seem surprising until one situates this intervisually within a genealogy of queer activism. While the images are a stark contrast to the peaceful and celebratory scenes we now see at Pride in Copenhagen, London, New York, Sydney, and Paris, these photographs bear a close resemblance to the images of the Stonewall Riots of 1969 (Riemer and Brown 2019) and ACT UP actions (Gould 2009, 277; New York Public Library 2002). Figures 6.5 and 6.6, where there is a violent confrontation between queer and anti-queer protesters, when read beside Figures 6.1–6.4, demonstrate the extent of the violence and the escalation from peaceful (albeit intense and passionate) protest to violence and fighting, including with police. The contrast between Figure 6.4 and Figures 6.5 and 6.6 is also important in emphasising just how little time it takes for queer individuals, activists in Russia to become targets of violence. While Figures 6.1–6.6 are demonstrative of the anger and hatred directed towards (public demonstrations of) queerness in Russia, they also disturb the media's visual discourse: only on rare occasions were images that show queer people *fighting back* published.

Figure 6.4 'Russia Paratroopers Day' by Roma Yandolin. Image courtesy of Getty Images. Image no: 175895746.

Situating the images within a history of queer activism, they destabilise the dominant discourse emerging in the media where queer Russians are cast as victims in need of some international intervention. Yes, these photographs of queer protest function as 'evidence' of the brutality of Russian homophobia and the violence queer Russians encounter when they assemble to protest. Yes, they 'confirm' the stories queer Russians have told about the difficulties of living queerly in Russia (Gessen and Huff-Hannon 2014); admittedly, these were not often printed in Western media, as highlighted in Chapter 5. But, they also reconstitute queer Russians' subjectivity by capturing moments of resistance to state-imposed order and control, to state-imposed sexual and gender norms, and state-imposed regimes of visibility. These photographs not only display Russian activism but also take on an activist status by showing queer resistance to the regime and encouraging mobilisation/giving space to queerness; their intervisuality with previous forms of queer (visual) activism, which had that intention, helps.

This is the visualisation of a counterpublic emerging—a counterpublic constituted by different forms of political behaviour and ways of speaking than in dominating, heteronormative Russian society. One where the stigma and shame thrust upon the queer population is both simultaneously rejected and used as the basis through which to challenge normative, disciplining politics and the violent domestic and international society sought (re)produced by Putin. As Fraser puts it, this form of 'discursive contestation' is a fundamental and crucial move towards eradicating the 'unjust participatory privileges enjoyed by members of dominant social groups' by forcing the 'assumptions that were previously exempt from contestation . . . to be publicly argued out' (1990, 68, 67). This echoes Butler's (2015) argument that appearing and laying claim to public space is politically important, particularly when documented and transmitted through media, in that it challenges who is allowed to be visible but also because it challenges the definition of 'the people' (see also: Edenborg 2019). To photograph this immanent counterpublic also implicates the photographers in this counterpublic as spectator, participant, and nourisher.

Between Figures 6.3 and 6.6, there is a clear willingness by those protesting to put themselves in harms way by fighting for the right to exist in public space, brandishing and wearing queer symbols that contravene the gay propaganda law (see Chapter 4). Images like these are, again, strikingly similar to images of activism in the US, particularly those of ACT UP whose distinctly queer politics was all about refusing to be respectable queers who submit to dominant sociality, who refuse to be made invisible or downplay their difference from the norm, ultimately taking 'fierce pride in bucking political, emotional, and sexual norms' (Gould 2009, 264). The queer activists in these images are angry and fired up. They are using the stigma attached to them as a mechanism to carve out a different social system invested in challenging the Russian state as a security threat. The refusal of visual space to these actions in Western media when there is a clear demand for visibility is not only a gross oversight but the doubling down on the suppression of queer visibility not just in Russia but the West as well.

Figure 6.5 'Russia Paratroopers Day' by Roma Yandolin. Image courtesy of Getty Images. Image no: 179619783.

When visualised, the performative practice and reproduction of embodied resistance—protesting, being beaten and arrested, turning oneself into 'gay propaganda', and photographs of it—is turned into a spectacle and audiences must decide whether to interpret these bodies as 'witness to injustice' or as per the propaganda law 'criminal' (Fierke 2013, 103). The act of embodied resistance and the visual representation of suffering and vulnerability make the body a site of resistance through and upon which (homophobic and homophilic) politics plays out. The embodied act and its visual representation are important political expressions for those stigmatised by the Russian government and marked as dangerous, foreign threats. Images of such actions and the reality of the injured, attacked body communicate 'a larger experience of social suffering' against the oppressive, queerphobic Russian government thereby materialising 'the injustice experienced by the community' and creating 'conditions for its restoration' or, in this case, its public manifestation (Fierke 2013, 79, 83). These images are invisible after August 2013 in Western media, ergo reifying the very discourse of the Russian government: queerness is not a Russian thing, but a Western thing.

Moving away from mass confrontations, many of the public spectacle images capture the same individuals across multiple events. The result is

Figure 6.6 'Russia Paratroopers Day' by Dmitry Lovetsky, 2 August 2013. Image courtesy of AP/Scanpix-Ritzau.

a powerful connection with those photographed in a qualitatively different way than Bleiker et al.'s (2013) analysis of refugees. These individuals become 'identifiable victims' who spectators can empathise with: photographs of the same people experiencing violence across multiple events create personal connections to those suffering. In these particular images, there is, I would argue, a lingering incompleteness to these images, a lack of resolution that makes this even more powerful: Are they alive? Are they in prison? Did they leave Russia or did they stay? One of those people whose stories are never finished is Kirill Kalugin (Figures 6.4–6.6 and 6.10).

Kalugin takes up significant space in the dataset, appearing in 11% of the images analysed. One series of photographs is particularly powerful: those from Paratrooper Day in St. Petersburg in August 2013. They represent a confrontation between hyper-masculine, militarised identity and queerness. What is at first a peaceful protest—flying the Rainbow Flag—escalates to the point where Kalugin is surrounded by former paratroopers and physically assaulted. Given that the rainbow flag originates from US queer activism and that Russia's anti-queer agenda is supported by a discourse of 'Gayropean' corruption of Russian society, flying the rainbow flag is always a potentially risky move; as shown in the Russian government's reaction to the

US Embassy flying the rainbow flag in Moscow during Pride Month (Reuters 2020).

Such public display of queerness by Kalugin could be read as an act of political self-sacrifice: the intentional placing of oneself in harms way in service of a (queer) political project that embraces one's abjection and uses it to confront social norms in politically meaningful ways, which was a common tactic used in AIDS activist 'zaps'. To photograph this move and the retaliation to it, communicates the injustice experienced by queer Russians to a wider audience of potentially millions, while avoiding subjugation and invisibilisation. Contrary to how Russian homophobia is represented in the media, these types of images are important in that they constitute queer Russian subjects as persecuted but not passive. They therefore obtain a queer activist potentiality; one that can only be activated if it is visible.

On another note, Figures 6.5 and 6.6 demonstrate the importance of context, situating different gender norms, and considering how images translate across borders. To a Western audience, it is not implausible that the images on Russian Paratroopers Day read as queer coded. The sailor-style outfits of the paratroopers, with their stripes and hats, echo a famously camp and queer Jean Paul Gaultier aesthetic. This double reading of the subjects in Figures 6.5 and 6.6 points to the way that queerness and queer codes are not universally shared as well as how artificial and socially produced gender norms are. The possibility that these paratroopers become constituted in a Western gaze as camp and queer creates the possibility—as with the Gay Clown Putin memes—for a reading of hypermasculinity and the policing of gender and sexual boundaries as fundamentally absurd, something to be mocked and teased for all efforts to control that which is fundamentally wayward and arbitrarily policed as if defending 'natural' order and not a social construction.

From the perspective of the body, public spectacle images raise questions about embodied resistance and the ways queer people are constituted, represented, and responded to in and outside of Russia, especially when they are protesting. This is about how individuals and collectives can articulate (in)security (e.g., through protest) and how queer bodies are constituted and produced by the Russian government as threats and by other international actors as needing to be saved. The ambiguity and polysemy of the body and the visual comes through clearly in these photographs: how these bodies are read differently (as queer, as insecure, non-/threatening, threatening, resistant) and how these visuals are read differently by different actors has something to do with the way the photographs are circulated, captioned and anchored.

The visual discourse that emerges in these images is, hopefully as is clear from the above, complex. It is one of barbarism and hyper-aggressive institutionalised homophobia, but also one of hope, resistance, and persistence. Overall, queer Russians come into view in two main ways that centre on agency and passivity: as brutalised victims and ardent resisters. As Constance Duncombe argues, images 'can help us to understand another's suffering through the visual representation of causes of pain' (2020, 612). In the case of these protest photographs, pain is not poetically or metaphorically represented as in the Gay Clown Putin memes or Nissen's images discussed below, but emerges as the result of physical violence, making the images incredibly affective/emotionally potent. These images 'do' something. They have a *punctum,* something in the image that cuts through and punctures the spectator.

The tension between agentic resister and passive victim in need of saving is one that emerges most profoundly when reading the media discourse through the photographers' images. Both sets of images condition who is viewed as a worthy subject, how they are viewed, and how Russian homophobia is constituted as an issue of international political concern. However, whereas the photographers' images are accessible primarily to people seeking to publish images to represent an issue or those who follow these particular photographers' work, the printed photographs circulate much more widely and are seen by a much larger audience. Media images are more public thereby conditioning the ideas and imaginaries of the public and policymakers, whereas images sitting in the photographers' archives have a much smaller audience—many remaining unpublished. Our understanding of the issue remains, therefore, limited and the very oppression condemned actually ends up reproduced through Western media by the sheer absence of queer activism in Russia in the Western visual environment.

Images 'can enact powerful effects since governments, international organizations, and the public are almost always pressed to take action when confronted with imagery of human suffering, such as wars and famines' (Shim and Nabers 2013, 292). That we do not see many images of queer Russians being assaulted as they undertake acts of resistance means that the possibility of a visual rallying call to the international community is diminished and that it is near impossible to see the presence of a queer counterpublic in play. The use of Western-centred media images enables a construction of 'the West' as sexually liberated, metaphorically suggesting 'we don't have that here'. Just as Möller and Shim (2018, 4) argue about 'peace' being alluded to through the visualisation of war and violence, the photographing and printing of scenes of homophobic violence and resistance abroad in Western media produces a visual discourse about the absence of homophobia at home. The result is a problematic hierarchy of the sexually liberated West/sexually controlled Russia. This is a powerful discourse that, in Western quests to liberate the Other, makes Western publics ignorant of their disciplining through homo/heteronormative socialities, which queer commentary points out (see Cooper-Cunningham and Kremer 2024).

If 'visual artifacts are sites of multisensory, performative experience in which the personal, the political, and the international collide' (Callahan 2020, 308), then photos of anti-queer violence in Russia are sites where the personal, political, and heteronormative internationalism meet. Not only for those photographed but for those looking as well (Azoulay 2008). They are sites where individuals' lived experiences of homophobia and the international struggle around which state protects their queer population best, or even if queer people should be protected, come together. Russian queer people are constructed by the government as un-Russian, influenced by or infected by decadent Gayropean ideology. As a result of this discursive move, those individuals' lives are affected by a geopolitical struggle between the West and Russia. For that same reason, these individuals become subjects of photographs and subsequently international spectatorship. As their experiences of homophobia go global, it is also possible that they become the object of voyeurism. However, I would argue that the images of resistance here work to open up more visual space for appearance, more space for contestation, in ways that undermine the very logic of the Russian government's stated intent to make all queerness invisible.

Everyday Personal: Seeing and Feeling Everyday (In)Security

Of the three photographers' works studied here, Nissen's is the outlier and sits on the boundary of art and photojournalism. His photographs have an intimacy with those represented that the others analysed here do not. The images of Jon and Alex (Figure 6.7) as well as the photographs of queer couples embracing, friends hanging out, and people generally going about their daily lives (Figures 6.8, 6.9, and 6.14) have a different visual vernacular that communicate insecurity in a potentially more queer way than any of the other images included here. The everyday personal photograph is less about spectacle, big events, and catchy headline stories. It is more intimate and less extraordinary, chronicling subjects over a longer period of time, and inviting reflection. Here, they follow people as they negotiate their queerness in a hostile space where their very existence could be deemed propagandistic and anti-/un-Russian. As a *visual pattern*, these images produce an intimate link and poignant, personal connection between the represented and those looking. In contrast to the public spectacle images, the everyday personal image may be more posed and staged, offering a different but powerful perspective on the story of queer stigmatisation. Similar to the public extraordinary images, though, they give visual space to the aforementioned queer counterpublic not just by visualising queer life in these more hidden spaces, but by quite explicitly visually articulating one of Lauren Berlant and Michael Warner's (1995, 1998) key arguments: sex is public. Even in spaces deemed 'private' the Russian government's assault on queer visibility—queerness in general—these queer bodies and the (potential) queer sex they are engaged in, combined with their visualisation and being photographed, are public and, in this case, international matters.

Nissen often photographs the unextraordinary and these images work in a more poetic way to constitute queer (in)security that eschews western exceptionalist storytelling while not shying away from representing the everyday violence queer Russians face as they carve out their own spaces and constitute non-victimised subjectivities (Figures 6.8, 6.9, and 6.14). His images are more ambiguous and require work to interpret them in relation to Russian anti-queer politics. The everyday personal photograph is less immediate and, to be understood, needs to be read through various intertexts and intervisuals. Nissen's photographs are examples of why visual discourse analysis must examine what is not represented in mainstream media, that which is invisibilised or not widely circulated. We would not have seen such intimate and queer moments, those that destabilise the discourse of passive victimisation, if we only paid attention to the images published in news media. And we could only read the politicality of them and their antinormative immanence when read through queer scholarship on the politics of sex and its management.

Nissen's images are particularly illustrative of the different types of agency that can emerge through images and changing perspective. Here, from

Figure 6.7 'Jon and Alex' by Mads Nissen. Image courtesy of Panos Pictures/Mads Nissen. Image no: MNN01651RUS.

protest and in-the-street violence to the household and queer nightclub. Bringing Nissen's images into the analysis destabilises the victim/agent binary in a powerful way; in part, because they are read in opposition to the media and other photojournalists' images. This is indicative of the way meaning evolves as we bring different texts and images together. His work does not necessarily escape the victim/agent dichotomy completely, but it destabilises it by adding complexity and layers to people's situations. They rewrite heteronormative ways of making victimhood visible.

Most of Nissen's images are clearly about non-normative sexualities—predominantly featuring same-sex intimacy and kinship or some recognisable aspect of queer culture—but their relation to Russia is less explicit. This quality makes them incredibly powerful at destabilising the dominant discourse of passive queer victimhood and Russian homophobia/Western homophilia that emerges in the news media. Many of his photographs could have been shot somewhere in Europe or North America (Figures 6.7–6.14), thus visually confronting the audience with heteronormativity and straight culture in all of its intrusiveness and disciplining force, not just in Russia but everywhere. Capturing sex, friendship, intimacy, violence, parenthood, and recreation, Nissen's photographs, in their everydayness and their relatability show how state-sanctioned regimes of 'the normal' discipline every body into compliance. They visually articulate the intrusion of the state into the 'private' sphere; the impossibility of sexual liberty.

That they were shot in Russia gives them a powerful emotional potentiality that holds the mirror up and provokes reflection on how indiscriminately the arbitrarily drawn 'gender norms, object-orientation norms, norms of sexual practice, and norms of subjective identification' across all times, cultures, societies, and places, work upon every body—even in the West—effectively precluding (sexual) liberty (Warner 2000, 39). The queerness of these images lies in their confrontation of heteronormativity and sexual stigma, which manifests in the persecution of those engaged in 'non-traditional' sex; a Russian internationalist project tied to anti-Westernism and a struggle for recognition as a Super Power (Adler-Nissen and Zarakol 2020). When read against the public spectacle images, Nissen's more intimate images are incredibly powerful in terms of creating a storyline filled with characters whose lives we are forced to think through. Often shot in intimate spaces like the home (Figure 6.8), his photos convey the persistent underlying insecurity queer people face *everywhere* at *all times*; that the domestic laws being passed, the anti-Western/anti-Gayropean foreign policy being adopted in Russia, the Russian/European sexual geopolitics, and their personal lives collide; that what is taking place in these private spaces makes them vulnerable to the violence seen in Lovetsky and Yandolin's photographs and reported in the early media. Not only is the acute violence visible, but the structural and systemic.

Take Figures 6.8 and 6.9 for instance. Both show lesbian couples and both feature children—in one case this is more metaphorical with a pregnant belly pictured. Given that the Russian propaganda law specifically targets children as referents of the state's security discourse, Nissen's focus on children here destabilises that queer threat discourse quite substantially. Here are four individuals, in various ways, occupying caring roles, offering social security to their (unborn) children. Entering these private spaces, encountering those who are constituted as society's aliens, society's threats, Nissen's images show how the personal is not only political but international and how the state is founded on and persists through the heteronormative (re)production of the family and the binding of ideal, 'normal' forms of kinship, erotic desire, and pleasure to the performance of ideal citizenship (Bersani 1996; Cohen 1997; Peterson 1999, 2014a). One could absolutely push the visualisation of

Figure 6.8 'Lesbian couple Lada, 33, (left) and Irina (31) at home feeding their three children' by Mads Nissen. Image courtesy of Panos Pictures/Mads Nissen. Image no: MNN01420RUS.

these queer families even further in the antinormative direction and draw in Edelman's work on reproronormativity and futurity, but what these types of visualisation push to breaking point, to collapse under its own weight, is the government discourse of a global, paedophillic, queer threat to Russia's children. Here are the very individuals charged of being such subjects doing quite the opposite.

Focusing on more everyday moments, even if they are partially staged, these images are visual entry points into queer life. By showcasing the most intimate aspects of queer existence and the persistence of queerness in times of persecution, they make visible the invasion of the state into the erotic, its disciplining of corporeal pleasures and intimacy, and its attempt to constrain and control the waywardness of object desire, pleasure, and sex by arbitrarily delineating boundaries of 'normal' sexuality (Bersani 1996; Warner 2000). Doing so, Nissen's images provoke heteronormative structures by celebrating and visualising the non-normative and abject in a way that—although potentially voyeuristic—puts *sex* back into queer theory and into conversations about Russian homophobia, reiterating that homophobia is fundamentally about policing erotic desire, sex, and bodily pleasures

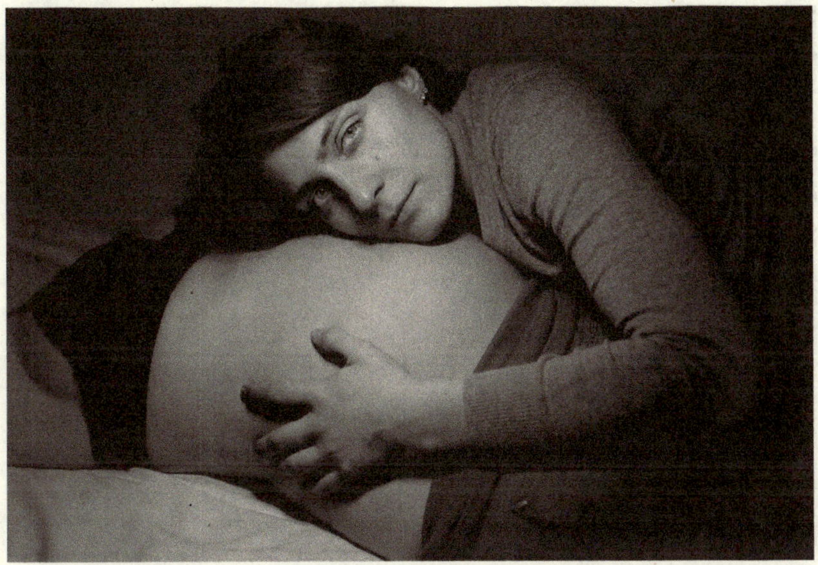

Figure 6.9 'Polina Popova, 25, with her pregnant girlfriend Irina Zinovieva, 37' by Mads Nissen. Image courtesy of Panos Pictures/Mads Nissen. Image no: MNN01403RUS.

(Bersani 1996; Rubin 2011; Warner 2000). The sex is not always entirely visible (as in Figure 6.7), but exists at times in the realm of possibility and metaphor (Figures 6.9, 6.10, and 6.14), meaning that these images also engage with and resist the Russian legislation and geopolitical project on its own terms: the politicisation of sex is not always about what *actually* happens, but about the *possibility* of sex, particularly sex that falls outside of societal norms or expectations happening. The visualisation of this possibility in positive terms invites spectators into the immanent counterpublic: it becomes an advertisement of possibility, albeit by forcing spectators to imagine a different future.

Nissen's most famous photograph, 'Jon and Alex' (Figure 6.7), won the World Press Photo Award in 2015. The politics of sexual shame and stigma come through most strikingly in this image, where two men, Jonathan Jacques Louis and Alexander Semyonov, are photographed having sex in their apartment. Bersani (1996) critiqued the removal of eros and sex from queer theory. This criticism is equally possible of queer IR and global LGBTI+ activism, where the sexual, the erotic, and desire have fallen out of many discussions about the international politics of homophobia

Figure 6.10 'Pavel Lebedev, 23, (orange shirt, facing down) with his boyfriend Kirill Kalugin' by Mads Nissen. Image courtesy of Panos Pictures/Mads Nissen. Image no: MNN01257RUS.

and homophilia. The global push for civil and human rights and an ever-expanding catalogue of *identities*—as well as the many critiques of how these strategies defuse queerness of its power and subsume queer practices under heteronormative structures—by failing to articulate the political work *sexual shame* does, mask how heteronormative institutions such as marriage and the nuclear family are rooted in exploitation, domination, and violence. Ultimately, this failure to focus on the politics of sexual shame has led to a definition of 'freedom and liberation in narrow terms of privacy, domesticity, and the unfettered ability to consume in the "free" market' which effectively 'collaborates with a mainstream nationalist politics of identity, entitlement, inclusion, and personal responsibility' (Eng, Halberstam, and Esteban 2005, 11).

Nissen's images of Jon and Alex offer a way for sex and the erotic to re-enter the picture of queer, refocusing audiences, scholars, and activists on the (geo)politics of *sex* and *sexual shame* not just *sexual identity/orientation*. They resexualise queer activism, resisting heterosexist culture's 'homophobic and erotophobic discourses' that manifested clearly around AIDS when gays were condemned for getting AIDS by having queer sex

(Gould 2009, 74). To reinsert sex, joy, and pleasure into queer politics high-lights how shame operates and squeezes queer people—in Russian *and* the West—to become more inclined to articulate their queerness in terms that constitute them as good moral citizens, legitimate players in politics, dignified homosexuals who can participate fruitfully and productively in the polity and secure its futurity (Edelman 2004; Warner 2000, 31, 39–40).

Rather than submitting to the heteronormative social ordering that Russian queer people are confronted with, Nissen's images show individuals who sit within their queerness, embrace their abjectness, carve out their own communities, their own queer publics, and, like me here in Denmark, can still go to the gay bar, be surrounded by half-naked people, and get drunk (Figure 6.14).[8] I want to be explicit here: these images are over a decade old and the period of study is by now historical. These types of images, these types of activity might not be similarly possible today. However, such images still propose and encourage pride in sexual difference that refuses to sub-mit itself to heteronormative structures, not just in Russia where they were shot but globally. Instead of downplaying sexual difference, Nissen's sub-jects read as instigating a 'righteous rebellion' against sociopolitical norms (Gould 2009, 249), which, in this case, are directly tied to an international politics rooted in sexual moralism.

The wider series of images of the Jon and Alex encounter have an intense affective and emotional potential because they contrast dominant visuali-sations of Russian queers in style, intimacy, and the tenderness they have. Because we know of the violence and hardships endured by other queer people, these photographs are deeply moving. There is an innocence in these photographs, taken during the most intimate and 'private' moments for most, that serves to humanise the individuals spoken about in news cov-erage of the propaganda law, of Russia as queer dystopia. We are forced to focus on their bodies and their faces rather than, as in protest imagery, every-thing that is happening around them. The intimate is powerful here. Jon and Alex could be anywhere in the world, but the power the photograph holds is achieved mostly in knowing this is from Russia—a space where this type of activity, while not illegal, is increasingly condemned. The jarring of that context, its destabilisation, with the scene is where its political power resides.

---

[8] Figure 6.14 is also important politically because it fundamentally undermines the Russian dis-course of a Gayropean queer threat to Russia's cultural sovereignty. That threat in fact emanates from the Russian state itself, which priding itself on the Russian Ballet as a cultural export, threatens to oppress the very people who constitute this emblem of societal and national pride.

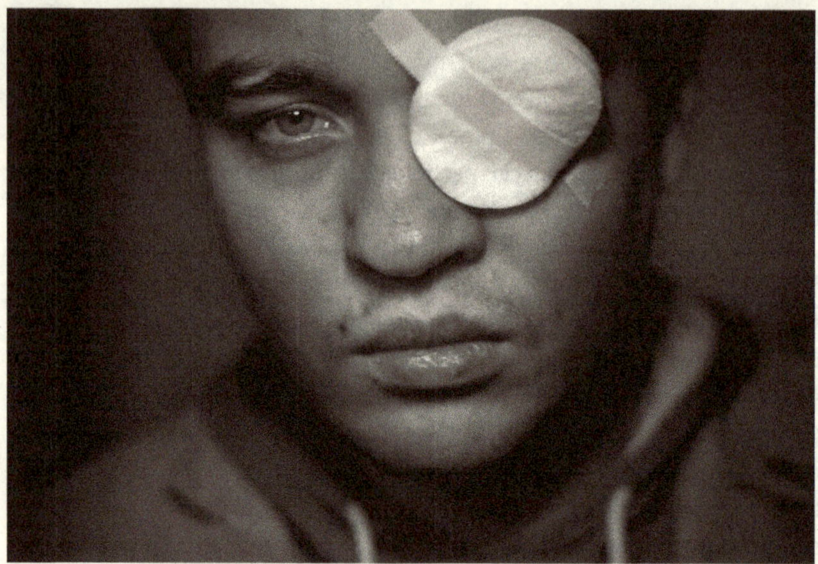

Figure 6.11 'Dmitry Chizhenvskiy, 27, had his left eye permanently destroyed in a homophobic attack on 3 November 2013' by Mads Nissen. Image courtesy of Panos Pictures/Mads Nissen. Image no: MNN01402RUS.

It is possible to make another reading of the Jon and Alex image that is less celebratory. The image could be said to have a fairly typical World Press Photo aesthetic—which I would not necessarily disagree with—and that it is not the most provocative display of sex. This is certainly one possibility and my analysis above does not obliterate the possibility of making this reading: both can co-exist. The political potential of this image for revealing the liminal subjectivity of queer people in Russia and the persistence of queer life in totalitarian times and the presence of a different, vibrant, violated, oppressed, queer counterpublic is not diminished by the fact that this is a safe photograph. Perhaps its ambiguity and that it is shrouded in darkness— are they actually even having sex?!—is what gives it the political potential to challenge the Russian project: it's not really anyone's business, not even the state's.

In general, Nissen's images destabilise the monolithic idea of queer Russians as passive victims. They complicate the story of Russian queerness and show how queer life persists and finds a way. They do not necessarily undermine the discourse of insecurity that circulates but instead complicate it. The posed nature of some of Nissen's photographs raises a question about whether they undermine queer politics. I would argue that they gain more status as queer political interventions in being semi-posed. Acknowledging the presence of the camera, using the camera as a lens to the world is indicative of a clear intent to make oneself visible as an anti-normative figure, as the abject subject. As highlighted by Matthew Riemer and Leighton Brown in their visual history of lesbian and gay liberation movements in the United States:

> For queer people, being the subject of a photograph will always be 'daring and risky,' a 'physical declaration of political and sexual identity that may not fit into simple definitions of political and sexual identity' that may or may not fit into simple definitions and dominant narratives. 'Our visibility is a sign of revolt,' bisexual activist Lani Ka'ahumanu said in 1993.
>
> (Riemer and Brown 2019, 17)

These photographs are a poetic and visual means through which queer Russians carve out their own space, challenge the propaganda law, and declare a particular form of queer Russian subjectivity that is distinct from, even if in many ways connected to Western forms of queerness.

While many news articles mention vigilante violence and torture videos where gay men are tricked into meeting with a potential date by groups of thugs ready to torture them, none show those images or people. In Nissen's work he includes several stills from videos made by members of the vigilante group 'Occupy Pedophilia' (Nissen 2013/14, 2014) and he photographs the perpetrators of violent homophobia. None of the images solely of perpetrators of homophobic violence are, to my knowledge, printed. They do, however, do important work in terms of establishing the types of individual self-identifying with the state's heteronormative project and in terms of showing the ever-present threat of violence. Figures 6.12 and 6.13 only feature men/boys and in both cases there is the threat of violence to varying degrees: in one, a boyish figure raises a fist, in the other a screaming man raises a whip, which looks a little more like a noose in front of a crowd with fists pumping in the air. These photographs are not glorifying. Figure 6.12, at least, is entirely staged and the three individuals appear willing subjects. In both Figures 6.12 and 6.13, there is no desire to hide their homophobia: it is on full, clear, proud display and being photographed is clearly not an issue. Politically, these are potentially Nissen's most important images: they hold each individual here to account and force the spectator, particularly in

Figure 6.12 'Vitaliy Tsimodanov, 20, Filipp Razinskiy (centre), 16, and Artyom Buriy (left), 24, all members of "Occupy Pedophilia"' by Mads Nissen. Image courtesy of Panos Pictures/Mads Nissen. Image no: MNN01396RUS.

Figure 6.12, to sit up: these are not just the classic image of some old, dusty far right bigot, they are young men. The anger in the images of homophobic protestors clashes with the rest of Nissen's more joyful, community-based images of queer people. In this sense, the visual contrast could be read as reiterating the absurdity of the politicisation of non-normative sex as a domestic and foreign policy project.

On their own, Figures 6.12 and 6.13 are not necessarily the most politically or visually striking. Situated intertextuality and intervisuality, however, the relationship between Figures 6.11, 6.12, and 6.13 makes them both visually and politically significant: the metaphorical possibility of violence present in Figures 6.12 and 6.13—symbolised by a raised fist and a whip— can only be read as homophobic and fully materialised when situated beside/against/with Figure 6.11, which shows the real, physical result of a homophobic attack on Dmitry Chizhenvskiy's body, and as part of the wider photo collection on Russian LGBT life. These three photographs, situated together with the wider collection, both reinforce the more poetic elements of Nissen's work by forcing the reader to make the intervisual connections

Figure 6.13 'Ultra-nationalists, wearing Cossack style hats and holding whips, shout abuse at participants taking part in a Gay Pride Rally on 29 June 2013' by Mads Nissen. Image courtesy of Panos Pictures/Mads Nissen. Image no: MNN01240RUS.

between different parts/arms of the Russian government's heteronormative project, but they also emphasise the very literal effects this grand policy strategy has on civil society. Some Russian people have voluntarily become a vigilante police force doing their 'duty' to protect traditional values and eliminate the 'queer threat'. Other Russians' bodies, namely those who are or are suspected of being queer, have become walking targets of violence from these vigilante forces. The ever-present potential of physical, acute violence is made tangible through the intervisuality of these images, which work together. We are never told that Dmitry was assaulted by any of the people in Figures 6.12 and 6.13, but the individuals in those images become the embodiment, symbols of all other perpetrators of heteronormativity-policing violence, but also the wider structural enablers of that violence. This is what I mean when I call many of Nissen's images poetic communication of queer insecurity.

More generally, in terms of composition of Nissen's photographs, many of the subjects stare directly into the lens, giving the illusion that they stare straight at you. These images have more of an intimacy to them, something that humanises the suffering of queer people in Russia. The intimacy and closeness Nissen achieves in these photographs capture much more than just the tales of violence and protest in the media. It destabilises the monolithic vision of all queer existence in Russia as unliveable, as queer life always being existentially threatened. He shows that there is another side to queer in Russia, one that makes the scenes of desperation, protest, and heteronormative violence more devastating. Their intervisual link to protest images and those showing violent attacks is crucial for their effect. The intimate, close-up, artistic shots in queer Russians' private spaces, and the images unpacked above, communicate Russian homophobia but in qualitatively different ways. His style of photograph shows queer Russians as more than victims: they love, they fuck, they have lives beyond protest, they work, they go out, they do drag, they experience joy. It unapologetically shows them in some, if not all, of their queerness.

While images can become radically decontextualised without captions, other images, or texts anchoring their meaning, these photographs show humanity in all its vulnerability. This is a powerful vehicle through which to constitute queer (in)security as an international political concern. Nissen's photographs are situated within and reproduce the discourse of Russia as a bad place for queer people, but they also add complexity by showing the lives of the queer people affected by state homophobia not as passive and eternal victims but people with full lives that re-constitute their subjectivities in particularly queer ways.

While Nissen's work does not get a lot of criticism here, that does not mean that there is no space for a more queer critique of his oeuvre. Some of his images are very normative, emphasising family, reproductive futurism, and reifying heteronormative sociality. The photographs of Jon and Alex are very softly shot, not too explicit in their sexual nature, and thus not too confronting for heteroised society. His nightclub images are perhaps the most risqué in showing queer bodies (Figure 6.14), but overall, his images are very safe and sanitised. That we see queer sex and intimacy is important, but these are still safe and sanitised for straight sociality. But, perhaps it is Nissen's own sensitivity to the public these images would meet that motivates such decisions. Notwithstanding such critiques, these photographs are of course important and political images. We need to have different forms of intervention; even if imperfect. This is part of the queer politics I outlined earlier, which includes a perpetual interrogation of power and norms—especially after queer-allied actions for liberation.

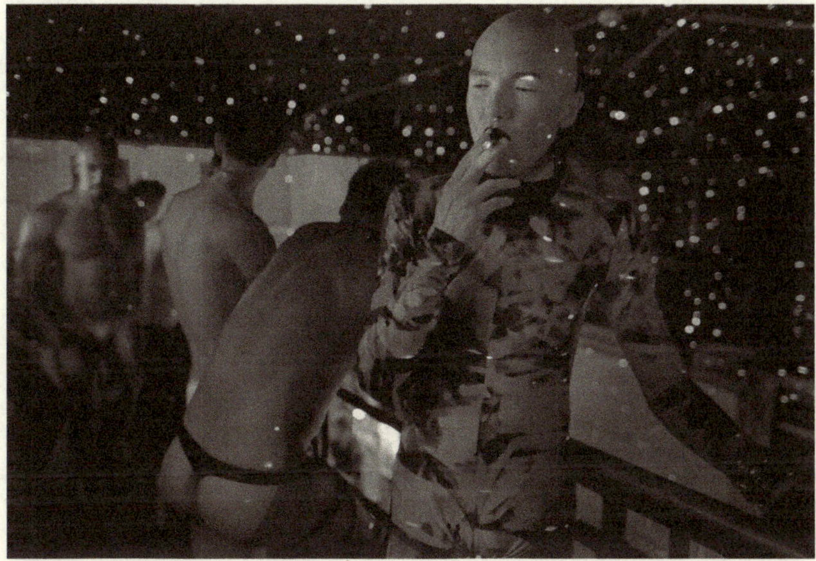

Figure 6.14 '27-year-old Ruslan, a ballet dancer at The Academy of Russian Ballet, smokes a cigarette at the Central Station, an LGBT nightclub' by Mads Nissen. Image courtesy of Panos Pictures/Mads Nissen. Image no: MNN01250RUS.

Conclusion

This chapter was partly inspired by Sontag's (2003, 12) invitation to be vigilant about those pictures, cruelties, deaths, and events that are not being shown. Hence, I offered a kaleidoscope of perspectives that enabled an interrogation of the dominant visual representation of Russian state homophobia in Western media as well as what other representations were possible. This gave space to the polysemous political working of images and different visual perspectives. Building on the analysis in Chapter 5, where I unpacked the discourse in news media, I address what *visual patterns* were present in images that didn't get such public display.

Queer Russians are most visible in news media before August 2013, when the gay propaganda law was passed. From then, queer activism in Russia dissipates and is replaced by images of Western athletes, politicians, celebrities, and symbols of the Olympics. Engaging with the three photographers' images, I show that the turn away from visualising queer Russians makes their activism and an immanent queer counterpublic invisible. This inevitably reproduces the very oppressions the Russian government is engaged in and plays into its discourse about queerness as a purely Western thing. When we turn to the photojournalists' images studied here, a more complicated story of queer subjectivity in Russia is brought into the visual environment. They move closer to a queer(er) politics that centres on the intimate and emotional, moments of joy in abject subjectivity, queer sex and erotics that is different from the press images. Mads Nissen's images, in particular, are a reminder that what we are confronted with is politicised moralising about sex, queer intimacy, and the strategic mobilisation of homophobia/homophilia as an internationalist strategy.

Images are artefacts through which we come to know, make sense of, and act in the world; through which we 'see' and 'do' international politics. What they represent, regardless of its veracity, is powerful in shaping international politics even if only as tacit knowledge of what happens 'over there'. If politics revolves around what and who is and can be seen, visual representations are central to international politics. Images show us (parts of) political pasts and create openings for potential political futures. The absence in news media of these types of images, which visualise instances and moments of queer uprising and resistance *in Russia by Russians* makes possible a sort of Western exceptionalism that constitutes queer Russian subjectivity as passive and solely victimised. It invisibilises the immanent queer counterpublic pointed to above and it blinds Western audiences to their own disciplining, to the politics of sex (be it homophilia or homophobia) that also plays out in the West.

The photojournalists' images studied above provide a different lens through which to read the news articles and their images. This enables a novel analysis of the politics of representation and how *visual patterns* construct a particular story about Russia and the West thereby feeding into the geopolitical confrontation around sex and sexuality. Whether intentional or not, news images produce particular visions of the world and, in this case, divide the international into spaces of sexual archaism or modernity. This is part of a much larger international political practice of delineating friend from foe, good and civil states from bad and uncivilised, and those who lead and those who are led.

Images of violence and resistance paired with the reality of the injured body together communicate the experience of social suffering against oppressive governments and reveal a queer counterpublicity in which dominant structures are contested and undermined not always in dramatic spectacular ways, but through the very refusal to *un*queer oneself, to become invisible and silent, to be pushed out of public entirely. Compared to the images in news media from August 2013, which predominantly focused on symbols of the West and Western actors, the three photojournalists' images tell a different story of Russian homophobia. Yandolin and Lovetsky's images resemble some of the first photographs published between 2012 and mid-2013, and Nissen's destabilise the hegemonic image of 'the queer Russian victim' by showing a less violent side to queer life that speaks to a more antinormative reading of queer life in Russia, enabled through queer theorising on hope, joy, and embrace of being abject through a refusal to fold into a heteronormative system. All of their images show how central the rainbow is to Russian queer activism. And all three photographers' images show moments of insecurity, vulnerability, violence, intimacy, kinship, and desire by centring on queer Russians and not on Western celebrities, athletes, politicians, or the Olympics. In their images, the queer people sought invisible by the Russian government, and pushed out of the frame in news media, are given space to appear in more complex ways than in the news media. The acts of being photographed and of photographing become challenges to the oppression and invisibilisation mandated by the government.

All of this simultaneously confounds and confirms dominant discourses emerging in the last chapter: Russia is a homophobic space where queer people face distinct insecurities that require address, but queer people are not necessarily in need of rescuing to the degree that comes across in hegemonic discourses. These photographs highlight the complexity of sexual geopolitics, particularly in the case of Russian heteronormative internationalism: there is no 'right' representation since many visualisations risk confirming Russia's narrative of Gayropean immorality or embracing homophobia to undermine such a discourse. The alternative visualisation present in these photojournalists' images, however, is one where queer people in Russia exist, they resist, and they inhabit a queer counterpublic that through its visualisation invites others to join in. This pulls the carpet out from under the government's discourse and geopolitical imaginary that queerness is a Western thing, an import into Russia that must be eradicated: there are Russians in Russia who are queer and establishing a counterpublicity against their demonisation.

7

Bodies, Rainbows, and the Politics of Visibility

In recent years, queer Russians have found their bodies transformed into battlegrounds upon which international politics is fought. Since the passing of the gay propaganda law, reports of physical violence directed at (suspected) queer people have poured out of Russia and, more recently, Chechnya and occupied parts of Ukraine.[1] In interviews with queer Russians, Human Rights Watch has documented widespread violence against those in Russia's queer community. This violence usually involves vigilante groups such as Occupy Pedophilia (as seen in Figure 6.12) tricking people into dates by posing on dating sites/apps and asking to meet in public before assaulting and torturing them:

> Such encounters have often involved perpetrators pouring urine over their victims and in some cases forcing them to drink it. Assailants often hit and kicked the victims; in some cases they hit their victims with dildos or forced them to hold and pose with dildos; stripped them naked; painted and drew slurs on them; and/or sprayed them with construction foam in the genital area. Hundreds of such videos have been posted online.
>
> (Human Rights Watch 2014, 2)

The entanglement of 'the international' and 'the personal' could not be much clearer. Queer Russians' bodies are the target of both physical and epistemic violence[2] as the result of a domestic political strategy aimed at reinstalling confidence in the government by pointing to a Western

---

[1] For reports on Russian persecution of queer people in Ukraine, I refer readers to the excellent work of Ukrainian LGBTI+ organisation Nash Svit.

[2] An expanded conceptualisation of violence includes not only physical attacks to the body but also epistemic violence that constitutes certain lives as unworthy, ab/normal, and thus legitimate targets of physical violence or elimination (Butler 2010; Galtung 1969; Mbembe 2003; Warner 2000). Conceptualising violence as a continuum means that practices such as stigmatisation, ridicule, and the making invisible of non-normative gender/sexuality are forms of violence linked to physical attack, albeit qualitatively different (Butler 2004; Shepherd 2008).

The International Politics of Sex. Dean Cooper-Cunningham, Oxford University Press. © Oxford University Press (2025). DOI: 10.1093/9780197792544.003.0007

Figure 7.1 The Hidden Flag activists photographed beside a Russian police officer. Image courtesy of PRIMO BUENOS AIRES S.L.

I and Primo Content made every reasonable effort to contact all individuals in Figures 7.1 and 7.2. While five of the six consented to the image's publication in this book, we were unable to reach the individual whose face is pixelated. Given their inability to provide consent, we have pixelated their face out of respect for their privacy.

'gay bogeyman' (Bosia 2014, 266; Healey 2018) *and* a geopolitical strategy, outlined extensively in the first half of the book (Holm 2020; Holm and Tjalve 2018). Russia's targeting of queer people domestically and internationally recalls lessons from queer theorising that homophobia is always arbitrary moralism about appropriate, acceptable, and 'normal' sexual behaviour and the management of bodily pleasures and erotic desires (Rubin 2011; Warner 2000). But it also points to a more ontological point that has been raised by feminist and queer scholars and activists for decades: bodies are battlegrounds for political struggle (Glassner 2012).

Russian state homophobia brings to the fore the extent to which bodies are the end points of politics—the sites that endure and experience every single political move and event, the surfaces upon which the political plays out. It also shows how bodies 'do' politics, how they can disturb hegemonic orders and cause chaos around established norms and dominant (patriarchal and heteronormative) forms of sociality simply by appearing in public

Figure 7.2 The Hidden Flag activists photographed in Moscow's Red Square. Image courtesy of PRIMO BUENOS AIRES S.L.

and exposing the fragility of the arbitrary boundary drawing at the heart of those normative and disciplinary power structures (Bersani 1987, 1996; Butler 2012, 2020; Warner 1993).

As already shown, Russia's anti-West, anti-globalist posturing is deeply entangled with a discourse about European and Western (Gayropean) sexual decadence and immorality (Gaufman 2017; Healey 2018; Wilkinson 2018). We cannot disentangle this sexualised and moralistic *foreign* policy discourse from the events unfolding *domestically* around the issue of non-normative sex and/or gender expressions, including state-sanctioned violence against (suspected) queer people. Russian politicised homophobia can, thus, be understood as a transversal phenomenon that destabilises predominant spatialisations of politics as domestic/international—as if these 'spaces' can be separated out and disentangled analytically, and as if individuals' lives and bodies have not always been affected by politics at all levels (Butler 1993a; Mbembe 2003; Purnell 2021; Wilcox 2015). It is hard to write about international relations without falling into the analytical trap of using language of levels. Here, this is a purely linguistic device, not a theoretical/conceptual distinction.

Starting from the position that bodies are battlegrounds through and upon which international politics plays out, as I do in this chapter, opens up the possibility that the body is also a site of resistance where particular politics can be advanced or contested, and structures of domination can be entrenched or destabilised (Butler 2012; Cooper-Cunningham 2019; Fierke 2013; Hansen 2000b). Bodies are not only acted upon, they also act upon the world. They do politics. The focus of this chapter is not specifically on biopolitics, necropolitics, and the disciplining of the body into compliance with norms, despite their importance in understanding the political in terms of the body (see Fierke 2013; Purnell 2021; Wilcox 2015). Here, I focus on an instance of embodied resistance that undermines those disciplinary structures, produces new forms of queer visibility, and makes a claim to public space in a way that intentionally violates Russia's gay propaganda law, albeit in a subtle, almost clandestine, manner: the Hidden Flag (Figures 7.1 and 7.2). I use this collaborative project as a heuristic through which to theorise the place of the body in international politics. Through the Hidden Flag, I explore three onto-epistemic questions: What happens when we locate the international at the level of the body? When 'international' political issues are responded to through the body as a (visual) political intervention? When the body refuses to perform in normative ways that align with a nation's imagined citizenry?

Theorising the body as a *visual* site of international politics through which important interventions and resistances are made, this chapter falls in three parts. The first introduces the Hidden Flag and briefly touches upon how I study the bodies that constitute it. In the second, I turn to recent instances where the rainbow flag has been the object of intense politicisation to demonstrate the risky politics of its display, not least in a space where it is prohibited. Lastly, I unpack the politics of the Hidden Flag at two intertwined ontological-epistemological levels: that of the visual (or visibility) and that of the body. In this section, I home in on what it means to use bodies as a visual form of activism by drawing on Chapter 2's theorisation of the body as political, as visual, and as a site upon which politics not only plays out but also simultaneously acts upon the world, thereby reconfiguring relations to power and rebuking heteronormative sociality.

The Hidden Flag

By the time the FIFA Men's World Cup came around in 2018, Russia's homophobic propaganda law had been in place for five years, and the transnationalisation of a 'traditional family values' discourse had taken hold. This has led to a 'geopolitics of the family' in which the protection of the heteronormative family unit has become a key area of the Global Right's political project (Abrahamsen 2020). As shown in Chapters 5 and 6, a lot of international media attention around the World Cup focused on how foreign fans and athletes would be treated under the propaganda law, as was also the case in the build-up to the Sochi Winter Olympics. In the midst of this, 'The Hidden Flag' emerged as a visual and embodied provocation of Russia's propaganda laws. During the World Cup, six individuals turned their bodies into visual canvases for political activism as part of the Hidden Flag campaign. Wearing football jerseys from their home countries (Argentina, Brazil, Colombia, Mexico, The Netherlands, and Spain), six people came together to form the rainbow flag through what I call an 'interbody' visual expression.

Exploiting the fact that Russia was hosting the World Cup, where it would be subject to international attention and scrutiny, the Hidden Flag organisers used this as an opportunity 'to denounce their behaviour and take the rainbow flag to the streets of Russia' in the name of 'a fight that will never be silenced' (Hidden Flag 2018).[3] That the action took place at the same time as the World Cup is important and is part of a well-established practice of using sport mega-events as a space for political activism (Boykoff 2017) and nation-branding (Eggeling 2020). The Hidden Flag is the product of a collaboration between Spanish rights organisation Federación Estatal de Lesbianas, Gais, Trans y Bisexuales (FELGTB) and global advertising agency LOLA MullenLowe. The full details of this collaboration are unclear. However, an agency like LOLA MullenLowe is usually appointed by a client to meet a particular brief, meaning it is likely that FELGTB commissioned it to collaborate with them on a campaign. In this case, that campaign had the stated intent of highlighting Russian homophobia.

When introducing the project on its website, FELGTB referenced Gilbert Baker's original rainbow flag, writing that:

> When Gilbert Baker designed the rainbow flag in 1978, he did so to create an icon for the LGBT community and a globally recognisable symbol that people could display with pride.
>
> Unfortunately, 40 years later, there are still countries in which homosexuality is persecuted, sometimes even by jail sentences, and in which the rainbow flag is forbidden.

---

[3] In 2018, the FELGTB received just over €37.000 from the EU through an EIDHR grant specifically for 'tackling anti-LGBT hate speech and hate crime'. Whether this went towards the Hidden Flag project or not, that the organisation engages in EU-sanctioned activities is important.

Russia is one of those countries.

For that reason, while the rest of the world celebrated Pride Month, we decided to take advantage of the fact that Russia is hosting the World Cup in order to denounce the situation by taking our flag to the streets of Russia. In broad daylight, in front of Russian authorities, for all of society and the whole world to see. And we did it with pride.

How? Using something that wouldn't raise suspicion: football shirts.

Spain, the Netherlands, Brazil, Mexico, Argentina, and Colombia. Six countries. Six LGBT activists that, together, formed our flag and toured prominent sites in Russia, taking a struggle that will never be silenced to every corner of Russia.

(Hidden Flag 2018 [my translation])

As laboured on in previous chapters, the polysemous nature of the visual means that how you and I interpret a visual image or artefact is not necessarily the same because we draw on different experiences, intertexts, and knowledge to read it. We must therefore include other texts and images in our analysis because they attribute meaning to the image(s) under study as the 'stock' that people draw upon to interpret the visual.

The note on the Hidden Flag website is one part of a much broader discursive environment that ascribes meaning to the actions of the Hidden Flag activists. Another intertext, or rather intervisual, is the rainbow flag itself, its status as a political icon, and the evolution of the politics attached to the visual artefact (see Chapter 4). Further intertexts include the Gay Clown Putin meme (Chapter 8), which also used the rainbow as a form of resistance, and the photographs of Russian activists using rainbow flags at protests (Chapter 6). These intertexts/intervisualities encourage a particular reading of the Hidden Flag as an act of international condemnation and resistance to the invisibilising of queer (bodies) in public.

In addition to the text and photographs on the Hidden Flag project's website, a video was published online by FELGTB (2018) that brought attention to its work.[4] The video opens by splicing together a series of widely available clips showing homophobic violence in Russia—some of the scenes and people, including Kirill Kalugin, are recognisable from the photographs studied in Chapter 6. These snippets of protest and homophobic violence are accompanied by text that reads:

---

[4] Video available at: https://vimeo.com/289147132 (English) and https://youtu.be/M8Or-SfzGJY (Spanish).

> Russia is one of the most homophobic countries in the world. Its laws forbid any public show in favour of the LGBTQ community. Something as simple as showing the rainbow flag can be punishable with a prison sentence. This is why, with the world's eyes on the World Cup in Russia, we have chosen to defy the law and fight against homophobia. Nailing [sic] our flag where everyone can see it.
>
> (FELGTB 2018)

Halfway through the video, the focus shifts away from protesting Russians, scenes of police brutality, and homophobic violence to headshots—taken in front of St. Basil's Cathedral in Moscow's Red Square—of the six activists fighting against the invisibilisation of queerness in Russia. The video ends in a rather peculiar way by stating that 'hiding has never been so brave'.

By nudging the audience towards an interpretation of the Hidden Flag action as denunciation, they provide an anchor through which to understand and interpret the type of political engagement taking place through the corporeal formation of the (hidden) rainbow flag in Russia—rather than intertextual relationships between 'texts', I call this interbody relations. Situating this form of resistance intervisually with gender-based activism, this strategy is not dissimilar to the way British Suffragettes used sandwich boards with slogans printed on them to turn their bodies into visual political weapons that confronted dominant societal norms about women's 'nature'. It is also similar to the visual-embodied strategies used by AIDS activists and queer liberationists, giving it a layer of complexity that enables a reading of the Hidden Flag as a claim to queer space that gestures towards, although does not necessarily replicate, the radical politics of AIDS activism and gay liberationists. It also connects to the counterpublic discussed previously.

With regard to the reception of the project, the Hidden Flag was awarded the Bronze Prize for a 'cause related' Public Relations campaign at the 2019 CLIO Awards—an international advertising awards event (CLIO Awards 2019b). Beyond this, the Hidden Flag gained positive coverage from international media (e.g., Brammer 2018; Bratek 2018; BuzzFeed 2018; Martínez 2018; McCallum 2018; Reuters 2018), political groups such as the EU Parliament's LGBTI Intergroup (LGBTI Intergroup 2018), as well as several LGBTI+ and human rights organisations. The response to the Hidden Flag was generally positive and congratulatory, signalling widespread support for its rainbow-based activism, even if tinged with anti-Russia sentiment (Meier et al. 2021). Its reception is captured in an infographic posted on the CLIO

Awards websites, which interestingly only show the positive attention the action received (CLIO Awards 2019b). The Hidden Flag was also the subject of one of the most popular political tweets during the World Cup. Of all political communication on Twitter that piggybacked on the World Cup to highlight international political issues concerning Russia—for example, about Syria and Ukraine—only the Hidden Flag activists were 'able to draw substantial, yet short-termed attention for their issues' (Meier et al. 2021, 11–12, 796–797). Fittingly, I was only alerted to the Hidden Flag when Chelsea Clinton reposted the action on Twitter (now X), calling it 'Courageous & beautiful' (Clinton 2018).

While it is important to highlight the attention that the Hidden Flag received, the point of this chapter is not to assess its reception. That would make this a study of reception rather than a theoretical-empirical intervention about the visual international politics of the body. The Hidden Flag is important in this book primarily because it is about bodies and provokes us to think and theorise about what the body does in international politics; in this case, how it works visually to contest and undermine homophobic policies. Nevertheless, that it generated media, political, and wider societal attention is indicative of the salience of this type of activism, where the body is used as a visual site through which oppressive and discriminatory politics are challenged in non-violent ways that (re)claim public space when it has been denied (see Butler 2020).

To be clear, there are a lot of different ways to interpret the politics of the Hidden Flag project. It centres not on Russian activists but on foreign activists protesting in Russia. It uses the Western-originating rainbow flag instead of an organic, contextually specific, Russian symbol of queerness—if there is one that can take the place of the rainbow flag. It is the product of an advertising agency's collaboration with an LGBTI+ rights organisation that has been paid for and used for business gain. It potentially makes invisible the same people I critiqued the media for leaving out. And it only makes visible 'respectable' bodies behaving in 'respectable' ways: What about displaying bodily pleasure and erotics deemed 'decadent' instead? All of this opens the Hidden Flag up to criticism as the culmination of Western-style LGBTI+ rights activism and a neocolonial 'save the gays' strategy as well as submitting to sanitised ways of displaying the queer body.

I do not deny these potentialities. In fact, they are demonstrative of the polysemous politics of the visual and the body, as well as the difficulty of engaging with international activism. While I am attentive to the arrangements of power emerging from such forms of activism, for the purposes of this chapter, the focus is on what the Hidden Flag does in terms of resisting heteronormative power structures and homophobic politics through the use of the body and its rearrangement of heteronormative structures of visibility. What I argue below is that the Hidden Flag contests the particular politicisation of sex by the Russian government and in so doing disturbs the structures of power that flow from its heteronormative discoursing and attempted structuring of (visual) public space.

Studying Bodies

Given that this chapter is focused on the visual body politics of the Hidden Flag, I must briefly outline how I study and see the body. In methodological terms, I use photographs and videos of the Hidden Flag published online as a way of 'getting at' and 'seeing' forms of embodied resistance.[5] These photographs and videos—just like in Chapter 5's visual genealogy—are a way of 'seeing' the visual-bodily protests in Russia as best as is possible for lack of actually being in attendance and physically present when the action took place (see also: Loken 2021). Through photographic representations and videos of embodied resistance, I theorise what it means to stake a claim to public space through visual-embodied forms of political action. All of the images of the Hidden Flag that I draw on circulated online in 2018 after the action had taken place. BuzzFeed News (2018) reported that the project's work was not published until the activists had left Russia due to safety concerns.

While it would have been quite a different thing to be physically present when these interventions were made, to see how the Hidden Flag bodies were responded to by the general public and authorities, to feel and explore the spaces they protested in, and to see whether the rainbow flag was recognisable or not, whether this was an obvious form of activism or not, photographs of the action are the closest I can get. In many ways, this is no different from the archival work carried out in the visual genealogy. The photographs of the Hidden Flag are my window into activism and allow me to theorise what this form of visual-embodied activism means politically and

---

[5] There are incredibly large ontological and epistemological debates to be had about whether this is a study of the representation of bodies or of bodies themselves. That, however, is beyond the scope of this chapter.

how it encourages a rethinking of the spatiality of intentional politics and the politics of the body.

Dangerous Displays of the Rainbow

As outlined in Chapter 4, the rainbow flag is dense with layers of meaning. The rainbow flag emerged out of a desire to symbolise community and pride as well as revolution and, to a degree, absolute joy and pride in those stigmatic associations attached to queer sex, erotics, and desires. This is clear from its use in the material in the New York Public Library, where Pride was not conformist, assimilationist, or commercialised like it is in many places today but was instead the marking out of a queer vision of the social under the rainbow banner. The rainbow flag, regardless of the intention behind its use, has become the site of intense politicisation in recent years, which requires fleshing out in order to fully grasp the politics invoked by its embodied appearance as the Hidden Flag.

In June 2021, the Covid-delayed 2020 Union of European Football Associations (UEFA) European Football Championship saw the display of the rainbow flag become an intensely politicised issue after the City of Munich sent a request to UEFA to light up the stadium in rainbow colours before the German and Hungarian teams met at the Allianz Arena. This was supposed to bring attention to homophobic legislative moves in Hungary. Both UEFA and the Hungarian Government pushed back on Munich's plans, ironically bringing more attention to Hungary's version of the gay propaganda law than any civil society action had. The request to rainbow the arena was ultimately denied because it was 'political' and targeted 'a decision taken by the Hungarian national parliament' (UEFA 2021). *Politico* called this the 'rainbow wars' with Hungary and UEFA in one corner versus 'everyone' else in the other (Eder 2021). Following UEFA's refusal, several German football clubs lit up their stadiums, and the German Football Association handed out 10,000 rainbow flags before the Germany–Hungary match in a sign of solidarity with Hungary's queer population and as a protest against anti-LGBTI+ laws that have been sweeping across many European states in recent years.

A year prior, the rainbow was also the source of controversy in Ukraine. In June 2020, advertising agency Saatchi & Saatchi partnered with KyivPride to orchestrate the raising of the rainbow flag alongside Ukraine's Motherland

Monument as a form of activism for Pride, which had been moved online because of the Covid-19 pandemic (Figure 7.3; KyivPride 2020; Lang 2020; Little Black Book 2021). The transformation of the statue from a symbol of communism and the USSR into one of pride and celebration was met with mixed political responses. Some completely rejected the stunt whereas so-called pro-Western media and institutions supported it, according to the agency's creative director (Little Black Book 2021).

The same year the Hidden Flag was recognised at the CLIO Awards, Ben&Jerry's also won a Silver Prize for a pro-LGBTI+ campaign called 'The Unbreakable Rainbow', which saw the installation of a water and light rainbow in Warsaw (CLIO Awards 2019a). The Unbreakable Rainbow replaced the previous rainbow installation (*Tęcza*), which was made of artificial flowers and permanently removed after being burned down and rebuilt seven times. Read in the context of increasingly violent homophobia and the explicit targeting of universally recognised queer symbols in attacks, the rainbow can be understood as a powerful visual provocation of heteronormative sociality that comes with the potential of destruction and bodily harm to those who wield it.

It might seem strange to include the contestation of Hungarian state homophobia by the City of Munich, the rainbow activism of KyivPride, and a Ben&Jerry's campaign in a chapter about body politics and Russian

Figure 7.3 Screenshot from video posted to Facebook by KyivPride (2020, 00:38). Image courtesy of KyivPride.

homophobia. Nevertheless, they demonstrate the politics of the rainbow, how it is being mobilised today, and what is at stake in making that symbol of non-normative sexuality/gender and queer politics in/visible. These activist actions highlight the confrontational politics of the rainbow, the controversies arising from its display in public spaces, and why that matters for how we read the (images of) rainbowed bodies discussed in this chapter. They also highlight how the international politics of sex is by no means isolated to Russian homophobia and international responses to it. The international politics of sex is multifarious and Russia's heteronormative internationalism has gained traction globally in right-wing circles, even in the EU: the most recent examples of this being Hungary and Poland's shift towards violent state-enforced heteronormative projects, as well as moves in the UK and Italy.

For all the talk of commercialisation and its endowment as a symbol of LGBTI+ politics, regardless of its roots in more radical queer activism, that the queer rainbow is so often destroyed, torn, set ablaze, and targeted by those who most ardently seek to enforce heteronormativity makes it all the more powerful and all the more necessary to display the rainbow in any and all activism by those who refuse the disciplining of sex, erotics, and gender expression into the 'normal'. If the rainbow so often invites violence and condemnation, its meaning and status not only invoke the politics unpacked in Chapter 4 but are altered and obtain a new, more abrasive quality. Waving the rainbow flag or interbodily constituting it becomes an invitation to condemnation, inviting homophobic reprise in some ways. Being the rainbow, waving the rainbow, wearing the rainbow, or building the rainbow is to actively challenge and provoke heteronormative structures and sociality by virtue of the rainbow's constitution as an affront to straight culture.

Visibility and Queer Politics

The Hidden Flag is a visual-embodied protest that sets itself up as fighting against the silencing and invisibilisation of queers in Russia. This raises questions about the relationship between the body, visuality, public space, and politics as well as questions pertaining to queer and feminist work on visibility. In terms of visibility and its intersection with queer politics, Emil Edenborg's work is instructive. Edenborg asks what role visibility plays in efforts to define 'the people'—the nation—in gendered and sexualised ways (Edenborg 2020 106). Although not explicit in doing so, Edenborg's problematisation of queer and feminist questions around in/visibility links to questions about the visual and its intersection with sexuality, race, and gender that are increasingly taken up in IR (see, inter alia, Ackerly et al. 2019; Åhäll 2018; Chan 2018; Cooper-Cunningham 2020a; Harman 2019; Wilson 2018). This particularly concerns the always-already visual performance of sex/gender (Åhäll 2018; Butler 2010; Wilcox 2017b).

Edenborg argues that 'efforts by states to define and delineate "the people", involve[s] the production of arrangements of visibility' and these arrangements regulate 'what gendered, sexualised, and racialized bodies can appear in public, and how they are seen' (Edenborg 2020, 106). In this sense, racialised-sexualised-gendered state policies are always intimately connected with the visual: they discursively produce competent and failing bodies (Wilcox 2017b) and delineate the subject positions available to non-/conforming bodies. As Rancière argued: 'politics revolves around what is seen and what can be said about it, around who has the ability to see and the talent to speak' (2004, 8). In the case of Russia, the government has made policy moves that constitute queer bodies as decidedly not part of 'the people' and as individuals whose lifestyle should be made invisible and denied an existence. Policies such as the propaganda law and Russia's heteronormative internationalist project that constructs an immoral queer-loving 'Gayropa' establish a traditional-values-driven national identity that is founded in cisgendered heterosexuality where even the potential visibility of gender and/or sexually non-conforming bodies is constructed as a social and political threat to Russian security.

Edenborg's argument that those who subvert and resist 'hegemonic conceptions of community ... by making visible bodies that have been rendered invisible or [by] making already present bodies visible in new ways' (2020, 106) is an important insight for reading the way the Hidden Flag reconfigures queer subjectivity both in Russia and beyond. If particular bodies—in this case, queer bodies—are *sought* invisible through legislation and social norms that prohibit their appearance, this does not mean they actually *are* invisible. They may only be invisible in certain spaces such as the street, at work, or at school. They may only be invisible to individuals who are socialised into, say, heteronormative or misogynist ways of seeing. Likewise, those who are deemed acceptable, 'normal', and are thus free to appear in public without fear of violence or persecution may hide those parts of their subjectivity that would invite stigmatisation: for example, same-sex desire (Ward 2015; Warner 2000).

Queer people in Russia make themselves visible in different and incredibly complex ways that do not necessarily fit into a simple invisible/visible binary. The photojournalists' images in Chapter 6, for instance, show that there is a willingness of some to openly flaunt their non-normativity at protests and in public whereas others suppress their queerness, leaving it only to be displayed in 'safe' spaces such as the queer bar or when amongst friends. The question of in/visibility is therefore incredibly complex. Here, I am focused on the public display of queerness by international actors in Russia and how this undermines the government's homophobic projects.

As Edenborg goes on to argue, 'embodied appearance will not necessarily take the form of antithetical opposition but may be more ambivalent' (2020, 107). The Hidden Flag is a complex combination of visible and invisible queerness that is decidedly ambivalent: whether queerness is visible or not depends on whether the bodies of the Hidden Flag come together and in the correct order. The Hidden Flag is a subtle form of appearance, and we may only even see this as a form of resistance because it is photographed and framed as such. We do not, for instance, 'see' instances when the bodies are out of order, not constituting the rainbow. Nor do we see how the activists were reacted to as photographs were being shot. Nevertheless, the Hidden Flag is a form of appearance that undermines the desired invisibilisation of queerness by virtue of making a distinctly queer and clearly confrontational symbol public in a space where its display is prohibited. The queer counterpublic in Russia expands.

In feminist and queer scholarship, visibility has often been treated in an idealised manner or questioned for its supposed benefits. This is not only the case in academic scholarship but also in activist circles: lesbian and gay rights movements in the United States placed an extraordinary emphasis on being 'out' and publicly visible from the homophile movement onwards. This manifested in chants of 'into the streets and out of the closet', posters declaring 'I am out therefore I am', as well as badges intentionally marking bodies as gay ('gay is good') and others emphasising being 'out' ('out, loud, and proud'). Activism by marginalised groups has often emphasised visibility as a way 'to increase awareness of social injustice and discrimination as well as challenge stereotypes' (Edenborg 2020, 109). On this, Phillip Ayoub (2016) has argued that visibility is an important factor in establishing LGBTI+ activists' ability to demand rights and protection from their state.

Be this as it may, visibility and being 'out' is not necessarily always a positive. Hansen (2000b) has shown how vocalising one's insecurity is not always beneficial or a means through which one might achieve 'security'.

It can, in fact, make one more insecure and render the body susceptible to (further) violence. Those working on queer issues have similarly shown how visibility is not necessarily a means to 'advancing the position of excluded groups' and may augment insecurity (Edenborg 2020, 109). When it comes to queer issues, security is also often dependent on 'passing' as hetero-sexual and/or cisgender (Shepherd and Sjoberg 2012; Wilkinson 2017b). Queer visibility is therefore not necessarily always possible, nor is it always beneficial: it can very often invite violence. In Russia, as we have seen in Chapter 6, there is a clear willingness to put oneself out there regardless of the consequences, and even if one is only 'visible' within the community—for example, trying to hook up or date—that too can be dangerous. In this regard, the Hidden Flag activists' actions can be read as the intentional plac-ing of oneself in harm's way in service of a political project that confronts social norms in politically meaningful ways. That said, this visibility may invite further violence to Russia's queers, thereby doing potentially more harm than good.

Visibility can be thought of as a process through which bodies are regu-lated and (sexualised-racialised-gendered) norms constituted and renego-tiated. Visibility, however problematic at times, can also be a means to the reconfiguration of heteronormative sociality. In this case, making oneself visibly queer through a visual-embodied expression such as the Hidden Flag might be read as showing an inaptitude for dominant sociality by delighting in one's abjection and refusing to submit to the full power of the state and its enforcement of homophobic legislation that promotes and sustains het-eronormative power structures at all costs (Bersani 1996). Openly flaunting dominant arrangements of visibility by marking one's body with something deemed propagandistic and thus illegal is to invite stigma and to welcome all that comes with abjection.

Visibility depends on there being readily available and intelligible sub-ject positions for one to occupy and competently perform; otherwise those bodies that sit outside those available and intelligible subject positions are rendered incomprehensible and failing (Butler 1999; Wilcox 2017b). When queerness is sought invisible, the availability and intelligibility of 'queer', of the different non-normative ways of performing 'being', and the whole spectrum of always-in-process queer subject positions start to disappear. In the next section, I show how the Hidden Flag is a powerful political move that refuses to allow non-normative sexual behaviour and desire to be unintelligible and unthinkable.

Rainbowed Bodies as Visual Political Weapons

In Chapter 2, I theorised the body as a battleground over which actors vie for control, that is disciplined into particular ways of being, and that is allowed to live or marked for death (Foucault 1977; Mbembe 2003). As Ali Bilgiç writes: 'Bodies are racialised, gendered, sexed and commodified, and the "otherness" of certain groups is reproduced through/on their bodies, making them targets of physical and non-physical violence' (2016, 55). Building on this, I argued that while the body is a site of violence and violation, it can also be a site of empowerment and resistance. The body is something that is potentially harmed and possibly destroyed, but it is also something through which agency and power can be (re)directed in service of a new political order, even in death (Fierke 2013; Purnell 2021). The body is a site of the political and, thus, potentially a site of resistance, refusal, and contestation of dominant order.

If the body is a battleground that is actively being worked upon by powerful political actors and normative structures, then it can also be transformed into an anti-normative vehicle that challenges those structures and creates the conditions for a new form of immanent (queer) politics. If we take seriously Deborah Gould's (2009, 74) point that identifying as queer comes with the possibility of falling into abjection, then bodies coming together to constitute the rainbow—the most recognisable and widespread symbol of non-normative sexual and gender politics—are significant visual-embodied sites where international politics plays out and gets contested. By publicly displaying their queerness, the Hidden Flag activists refuse to 'be' as expected and mandated by Russian legislation, they embrace abjection, and they use deviation as a political strategy of undermining heteronormative projects that straddle Russia's domestic and foreign policy, which invites a reconfirmation of normative structures.

In the case of Russian homophobia, the body becomes 'international' through activism such as this *and* homophilic/homophobic geopolitical posturing around sexual behaviour and erotic desire, which are two deeply embodied and affective things. The activist bodies of the Hidden Flag challenge Russian homophobia by flaunting one's queerness and by putting one's queer body 'out there' in public. These queer bodies aggravate and confront the government's strategy of invisibilising the joy and pleasures of a queer life through making visible the most prominent queer symbol we have. The use of the body as a visual site of queer international activism therefore undermines the attempted invisibilisation of non-normative sex and gender in Russia and shows how the politicisation of sex works upon, and can be reinforced/contested through, bodies that (do not) comply. In this sense, bodies stabilise/contest meanings and dominant structures in the way they move, position themselves, fail, and act within and upon the world. In this particular case, six individuals bring their bodies together to form what I above referred to as an 'interbody' visual expression.

Like intertextuality/intervisuality, one might think of the interbodily as the way bodies gain meaning through their relation to other bodies; how bodies co-constitutively make meaning and are read in relation to one another: for example, masculine bodies against feminine bodies against non-binary bodies against trans bodies. None of the football jerseys alone signals a queer or LGBTI+ politics. When arranged in a particular order and positioned together, however, they convey something different and do something politically. This only works through their interbody connection and their collective intervisual link to the rainbow flag.

Chris Rossdale (2016, 201) argues that practices of resistance bring 'subjects into an encounter with the politics of security' as they contest formations of power. In the case of the Hidden Flag, this encounter is with a national security discourse attached to a heteronormative project that is inseparably domestic and international. Because resistance is about disputing, questioning, scrutinising, disrupting, and/or offering alternatives to the ways power is localised (Amoore and Hall 2013, 100; Rossdale 2016), it is both destabilising and productive. It undermines structures identified as problematic and offers alternatives to the status quo. In Russia, those pushing against the government's homophobic politics and challenging hegemonic gender and sexuality structures are constituted as threats. Indeed, they *are* threats to heteronormative power, but not out of malice towards the heterosexual population but to the disciplinary power heteronormativity holds over all bodies.

The power of the state is tied to its ability to draw lines that distinguish different types of subjectivity, determining their place inside or outside the community, and whether they possess political rights (Edkins and Pin-Fat 2005; Walker 1992). If politics revolves around what and who is and can be seen, visual-embodied expressions such as the Hidden Flag are central to resistance and making new forms of politics possible. In Chapter 2, I argued that the body is visual in the sense that it is read and interpreted through its visual shape and how it behaves. Since discourses about appropriate behaviour and ways of being in the world attach themselves to bodies and then get reproduced by those bodies either conforming or not conforming, then sex and heteronormativity are, by extension, also visual.

As a visual thing, the body can therefore be a tool for resistance and a way to 'imagine the unimaginable ... an expression of political hope because it ruptures and transcends the language of habit that surrounds us and circumvents what is and is not politically visible, thinkable and possible' (Bleiker 2018, 29). The body can take aim at, destabilise, and resist power structures derived from sexual moralising. But it can also reproduce them: for instance, by following the rules of the game and submitting to disciplining. The Hidden Flag is a form of visual-embodied resistance that, by refusing to submit to the Russian government's attempts to eradicate every trace of queerness from the face of Russian society and placing the body in harm's way, short-circuits heteronormativity's disciplinary power and embodies the queer political conviction of revelry in the stigmatic abjections attached to non-normative sex and gender. That is the joy that was invested in early uses of the rainbow flag.

In the case of Russia and the Hidden Flag, the constitution of a 'normal' Russian subject and Russian national identity as decidedly heterosexual means that the public display of queerness—or in this case the styling of the body into a queer icon through its clothing—becomes a mechanism of embodied resistance against heteronormative Russian sociality and legislation. By occupying public space, bodies speak, they resist, and they reconfigure the political. If 'collective (heteronormative and queer-exclusionary) bodies are produced through regulating what (gendered, sexualized, and racialized) bodies appear in public' (Edenborg 2020, 107), these queer bodies, then, are not merely a 'tool to carry political messages ... the "protesting body" itself is a political message' (Bilgiç 2016, 55). Their presence serves as a reminder of the disciplining we all endure to assimilate, be constituted as innocuous, and have our lives made acceptable and liveable by the state's standards.

As a coalition of bodies, the Hidden Flag, thus, becomes a site that confronts state power. It confronts the state's ability to draw lines that distinguish different types of subjectivity, determining their place inside or outside the community, and thus whether they possess political rights or not (Edkins and Pin-Fat 2005). Creating visual images and artefacts, circulating memes, pasting posters on walls, flying rainbow flags, pinning rainbow badges to clothes, wearing t-shirts emblazoned with pink triangles, and walking through the streets of Russia in colourful football shirts that collectively form the rainbow flag are political strategies and forms of political intervention that create forms of visibility where otherwise that possibility has been denied.

Here, the body is the main vehicle through which visibility and space are sought. Transforming six bodies into a rainbow is a visual struggle for presence and space where it is otherwise denied. This provokes broader reflections about which types of bodies get to be visible and appear in public, which subjects are allowed to live, which are marked for elimination—be that through the literal annihilation of the body or in a more epistemic fashion through its invisibilisation. With the Hidden Flag, then, there is an outright defiance of established modes of appearance that jams established (heteronormative) matrices of power. The very presence of protesting (queer) bodies destabilises and challenges the oppressive and hetero-internationalist structures of Russian homophobia but also homophobic politics more generally. Given that bodies can redeploy space in order to 'contest and negate the existing forms of political legitimacy' (Butler 2012), protesting the gay propaganda law *in* Russia using a Western-originating queer icon, those foreign queer bodies both challenge their securitization as dangerous national security threats and rearrange the spatiality of international politics from something that happens above the state, the local, and the personal to something that happens transversally through and upon our bodies.

Conclusion

There is a long history of using the rainbow flag in queer and LGBTI+ activism. Regardless of your view on the rainbow flag—whether you regard it as a symbol of commercialisation and normalisation, or one of radical queer resistance—it is an important and historical artefact. UEFA's recent refusal to allow Munich to light up its stadium in rainbow colours to protest against Hungary's doubling down on heteronormative and homophobic legislation and the repeated burning of the *Tęcza* rainbow monument in Poland are political, and they reify the heteronormative structures the flag is supposed to contest. When rainbow flags are constituted as propaganda, thereby seeking to make them invisible, that is a political decision to deny non-normative sex and gender public space and visibility.

In a heteronormative world, the rainbow is often one of the few easily readable, universal, highly visible, and quickest ways to claim public space and contest the exclusion and persecution of those who refuse to submit to the management of something as wayward as erotic desire and pleasure. This is what we see in the Ukrainian action, and it is what we see with the Hidden Flag. Any decision to prohibit the flying of the rainbow flag—in the case of Russia, disguised as being for the protection of children from decadent gay propaganda—is to say that queerness has no place in the world. It is to say that it is okay for queer people to be sought out and persecuted. The world is replete with symbols of heterosexuality, and yet none of these are contested or considered propaganda despite being just that. Take national anthems or national flags, for instance; these are grounded in heteronormativity and the reproduction of the nation.

We can have a debate about the virtue-signalling of the Hidden Flag activists, of FELGTB, or the actors who mobilise the rainbow (usually for political gain), but, parking that for a moment, when you deny the rainbow space, you deny queer people space. When the rainbow flag is banned or people are punished for waving/wearing it, this is one of the most political moves the state can make: it tells queer people they are not worthy of existence, of being, that they are not part of 'the people' and thus are devoid of rights. The presence of foreign queer bodies in Russia also highlights a more subtle element of Russia's heteronormative project: its threat to queer people all over the world through the transnationalisation of a 'traditional family values' based Global Right project. Furthermore, it highlights the extent to which moralising about and the politicisation of sex and gender expression is by no means over: internationally, even as LGBTI+ rights spread, there is still a politics of sex that constitutes certain pleasures, desires, and behaviours as immoral, decadent, and bad. In many respects, this appears to be a domestic thing, something the state concerns itself with only in connection with 'its' people; but as demonstrated in this book, the politics of sex is international. Sex structures foreign policy-making through both homophilic and homophobic internationalist projects, even if in ways that at first appear subtle until one asks 'what's the politics of sex here?'. It is not just Russians who have a stake in the fight against the Russian state's heteronormative project. In part because of its geopolitical mobilisation of a specific homophobic moralising about sex and the example-setting that a successfully executed strategic campaign of domestic politicised homophobia provides, queer people all over the world have a stake in this fight.

The Hidden Flag project can be read as invoking a queer politics: that of community, visibility, joy in not being marked 'normal', and the deliberate confrontation of heteronormative sociality that demonises queerness and disciplines *all* bodies into particular ways of being. Read as such, this returns a queer politics to the rainbow that counters prevailing concerns about the rainbow flag becoming too commercialised and a symbol of an identity-based, assimilationist LGBTI+ rights movement, which has fundamentally different politics than the anti-normativity and anti-sociality of queer (Amin 2017; Bersani 1987; Duggan 2002; Wiegman and Wilson 2015). The politics of the original rainbow flag is thereby reinvigorated and reinstalled through its use in Russia and against Russian politicised homophobia.

Tracing the historicity of the flag in Chapter 4, I showed that there is a radical politics of inclusion, equity, and resistance at the core of its creation. By shifting away from the promotion of vodka or the diluted politics of Pride as it takes place in increasingly commercialised forms, this is exactly what the Hidden Flag is about. Just as Baker's original flag was about establishing the public visibility of the queer community as well as symbolising pride and joy at being 'abnormal', the transformation of six bodies into the different coloured stripes of the queer rainbow flag transforms the human body into a powerful political organism that undermines and antagonises the dominant social order that seeks to render queerness invisible and therefore impossible and unknowable. In this case, that social order is in Russia, but my point also applies elsewhere in other heteronormative spaces.

This form of embodied resistance, while subtle, raises a metaphorical middle finger to the Russian government by publicly and proudly announcing queerness and refusing to submit to the eradication of queerness from society. It also indirectly reiterates the ludicrousness of states' attempts to control the wayward nature of desire by constructing a neat and tidy vision of a heterosexual reproductive citizenry that disciplines every body into particular ways of living and being.

The Hidden Flag therefore transforms the body from something that is worked upon by disciplinary state structures and heteronormative-enforcing apparatuses to something that actively antagonises and resists those structures not just in its very existence but in its transformation into an international icon that represents the very thing sought invisible. It metaphorically reiterates that no matter how much effort and terrorism goes into establishing and policing the boundaries of the 'normal', that erotic desire, sexual behaviour, and bodily pleasures cannot ever be made to fully submit to the state. The Hidden Flag, then, is revelry in being abject and abnormal, flaunting it in the face of the government by making queerness public. In this case, it also shows an inaptitude for dominant sociality and no desire to be made docile. If the queer body antagonises and provokes societies into reinforcing, doubling down on their heteronormative sociality, then those bodies also expose the fragility of the dominant social order, cracking it open to reconfiguration.

An approach to international politics that brings in the body and the visual as additional foci allows for sighting critical spaces that might otherwise be overlooked because of epistemological predilections. It sees acts of resistance taking place across textual, visual, and bodily planes. If the visual 'make[s] us see the world anew, to make us see in a different reality from the one we are used to and the one that is commonly accepted', then interbody visual expressions can 'help us re-view, re-feel, and re-think politics' in ways that 'unmake and remake politics' (Bleiker 2018, 28). As a form of embodied visual protest, the Hidden Flag brings to light the way that a plethora of non-state actors are engaging with the international politics of sex and thereby exposing how the international, the domestic, the personal, the political are inseparable and converge upon the bodies that inhabit the world.

8

The Queer Politics of Play and Gay Clown Putin Memes

Within the burgeoning subfield of visual IR, there has been a focus on the politics of photorealistic genres, though scholars are increasingly asking how more illustrated genres—mostly cartoons and comics—relate to security (e.g., Aradau and Hill 2013; Baspehlivan 2024; Cooper-Cunningham 2019, 2020a; Dittmer 2005; Dodds 2007; Hansen 2011, 2017; Särmä 2018; Shim 2017; Wedderburn 2019). In this chapter, I theorise the implications of memes for IR by exploring how 'Gay Clown Putin' has been used in international activism responding to Russian politicised homophobia. In so doing, I also provide a queer analysis that emphasises the politics of playful delight in abjection, thereby taking queer IR in an important direction that explicitly emphasises the oppositional, anti-normative politics of early queer liberation and AIDS activism.

As outlined in the introduction and Chapter 2, in Russia, queerness and LGBT rights and identities have been constituted as a national security threat emanating from the West. The Gay Clown Putin meme, as part of the international response to that security discourse, has been added to the country's *List of Extremist Materials*. In this context, the meme makes a foreign and security policy intervention, making it of central importance for the study of international politics. Moreover, looking at international responses to state-sponsored phobias around sexuality and gender is also an opportunity to further explore the connections between sexualities and international security (Leigh and Weber 2019; Richter-Montpetit 2014, 2018).

While part of a wave of state-directed politicised homophobia (see Bosia and Weiss 2013b), Russia exhibits a set of phobias that combine fears about gender and sexual expression outside heteropatriarchal structures with a national security discourse. As shown in Chapter 4 to 6, there has been a significant international response to this, starting after the gay propaganda law was passed in 2013 and in the build-up to the Sochi Winter Olympics in 2014. Besides news coverage, foreign government reactions, and NGO

The International Politics of Sex. Dean Cooper-Cunningham, Oxford University Press. © Oxford University Press (2025). DOI: 10.1093/9780197792544.003.0008

reports, a number of oppositional and transnational responses take visual form—the focus here is on memes. Gay Clown Putin, which depicts President Putin in clown-like drag, is one of the most prominent memes to emerge in the last two decades that directly intervenes in international politics. This raises important questions about how to theorise memes for IR. Can we, politically and ontologically, think about memes as critical activist interventions just by being produced? Is it the ways they are used, circulated, and interpreted that make them political? Or, both?

The chapter unfolds as follows. I introduce the Gay Clown Putin meme and the circumstances around its emergence before providing the three building blocks that enable a thorough engagement with the politics they invoke. First, I recount how Russian politicised homophobia is rooted in a national security discourse and how this manifests around the Gay Clown Putin meme. Second, I theorise memes as critical political interventions that can challenge Russian security politics and its heteronormative domestic and internationalist projects. In the empirical analysis, I offer three readings of the meme as: (1) constituting homophobic policies as a threat and challenging normative constructions of gender/sexuality; (2) reproducing homophobic, misogynistic power structures; and (3) drawing on queer theory that has a radical commitment to anti-normativity and delight in deviance, as playful delight in abjection that short-circuits heteronormative power. In the third reading, I suggest that queer is weaponised by activists to resist the Russian state's securitization of non-normative sexual behaviour and erotic desire.

I ultimately argue that memes are important sites of international politics that challenge the Russian state's discourse of queerness as national security threat, while also undermining heteronormative organisations of society and sexuality by embracing queer sex as abject and creating new possibilities for queer subjectivity, thus rearranging power relations. Rather than mere parody or mimicry that reinforces power, Gay Clown Putin is a symbol of the radical potential of anti-assimilationist, anti-normative, oppositional queer (international) politics invested in an endless interrogation of power.

Whereas Nissen's photographs in Chapter 7—which I highlighted might be considered a form of activism and mobilising call—offer different representations of queer life, agency, power, and resistance *in Russia*, the Gay Clown Putin memes are a symbol of a liberatory anti-normative agenda created/shared by many unknown individuals who may be within or outwith Russia. Unlike Nissen's photographs, it is not queer Russians and their complex subjectivities that come into view, but the head figure of the heteronormative internationalist project: Putin. The shift in focus from those targeted (threatened) to the instigator (threat) is politically important; again changing perspective on the issue of politicised homophobia.

The Emergence of the *Gay Clown Putin Meme*

Russian state-sponsored homophobia entered international consciousness when the gay propaganda law was passed in 2013. Domestically, there has been significant queer organising from community engagement and political lobbying to protest and unsanctioned pride events as seen in Chapter 7. Here, however, I focus on the international response and the role images have played. As part of a campaign commissioned by Dutch LGBT rights organisation COC, putinarainbow.com was set up to protest the gay propaganda law. The website invited people to upload images of Putin with rainbows somehow incorporated. Its purpose statement reads: 'The Russian parliament has passed a new law that prohibits "gay propaganda". This includes a ban on the rainbow. We think that the world looks much better with more rainbows, not less. If you agree, upload or share a Putin, and spread the love'.

Since its establishment, international actors have spread hundreds of images on and offline as part of a response to Russian state-sponsored homophobia. All of the images uploaded to putinarainbow.com use photos or drawings of Putin combined with the rainbow. Figure 8.1 shows the *Putin A Rainbow* landing page and a small selection of submitted images.[1] While the *Putin A Rainbow* collection is vast and includes various images that are part of a larger political intervention that has evolved over twelve years, methodologically, I focus on the Gay Clown Putin meme—those images following the visual patterns of Figures 8.2 and 8.3. These have received significant attention online and in international press, they are the most widely circulated, they cross genres, they have provoked a significant response from the Russian government, and they are now symbols of the propaganda law. Unlike other images submitted to putinarainbow.com or most of the images in the previous chapter, the Gay Clown Putin meme is iconic. Studying icons is important because they often come to represent key events in international politics in a shorthand fashion *and* because they are often interventions in international politics (Hansen 2015).

---

[1] See putinarainbow.com and yuriveerman.nl/Putin-a-rainbow to explore the memes and reactions to them.

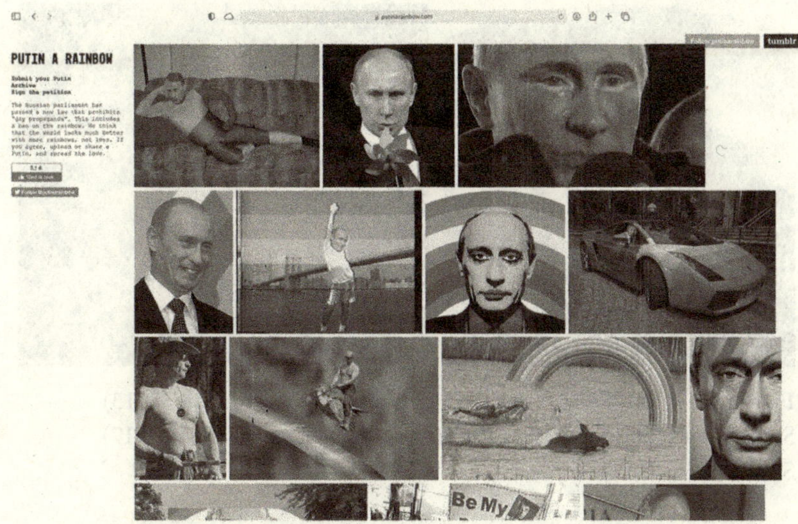

Figure 8.1 Screenshot of putinarainbow.com (16 February 2021).

Gay Clown Putin is a group of linked images that started from Pablo El Terrible's *Warhol* image (Figure 8.2). This image is a photoshopped portrait photograph of Putin, which was shot for TIME magazine in 2007 by the photographer Platon. The memes follow a specific visual pattern, derived and then manipulated from El Terrible's image—as in Figure 8.2. This subset of queered Putins is usually devoid of text, shows the president wearing make-up, and incorporates a rainbow or its colours. After the *Warhol* image was published online (9 April 2013), it became a key visual reference for global political activism on LGBTI+ rights in Russia.

Since its creation in 2013, Gay Clown Putin has been used in protests against the Sochi Winter Olympics, worldwide demonstrations against the propaganda law and the Chechen gay purge, and is salient in news reporting on homophobia across the Russian Federation (e.g., Cresci 2017; Herszenhorn 2013). It has been turned into t-shirts, stickers, and posters. It features at Pride events. The US talk show *The Late Show with Stephen Colbert* did a comedy feature mocking Putin based on the meme.[2] And, testifying to its iconicity, it was featured in the Design Museum London's *Hope to Nope* exhibition (2018), which collected images that played a pivotal role in reacting to major political moments. Recently, after anti-trans and anti-gay posturing, new renditions queering Trump emerged, speaking to a broader

---

[2] See https://youtu.be/Rj_pS8du9R8

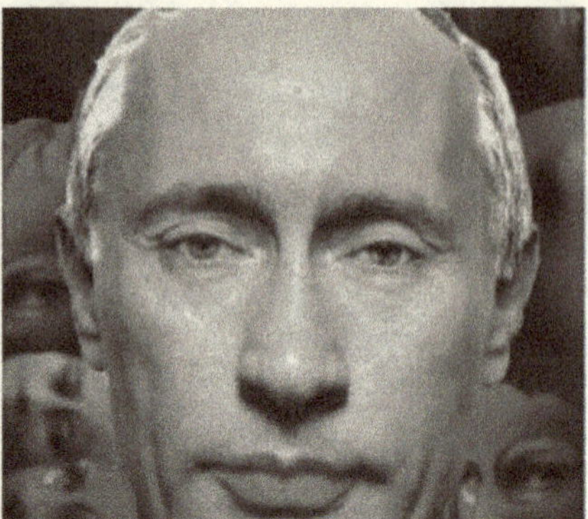

Figure 8.2 Left: 'Drag Putin a la Warhol'—Pablo el Terrible (2013). Source: putinarainbow.com. **Right:** Untitled—TheDavyStar (2017). Source: Reddit.

transnational visual practice in queer activism that uses the rainbow as a visual vehicle to mobilisation and resistance (Figure 8.4). And when Putin launched a full-scale invasion of Ukraine in 2022, David Kvien produced video art titled 'Dicktator' that featured dragged Putin being pounded in the face by multiple yellow and blue dildos in order to raise funds for the United Nation's Ukraine Humanitarian Fund (Figure 8.5). Kvien's image notably has an intervisuality not just with the Gay Clown Putin memes, but the wider collection of images on putinarainbow.com, especially the top right image in Figure 8.1.

Photographs taken at worldwide protests against Russian homophobia since 2013 show how heavily Gay Clown Putin features over the years— mostly the images in Figure 8.2. Searches in two international image databases—Getty Images and AP Images—for 'Russia gay propaganda' show how frequently these memes are used in political activism and how they have been used to protest the ongoing Chechen gay purge. Excluding non-protest images, 11.81% of Getty photographs (66/559) and 12.88% of AP photographs (17/132) included Gay Clown Putin.[3] Given the number of subjects to photograph at protests and that they appear in Asia, Europe, and North America, this is indicative of the meme's saliency.[4] Due to space

---

[3] Search conducted 20 February 2021.
[4] Gay Clown Putin appears at protests in Belgium, Denmark, France, Germany, Hong Kong, Hungary, Italy, Spain, UK, and USA but not in Russia. News outlets where the meme is published include: *The Guardian, Independent, Daily Mail*, ITV News, *Moscow Times, South China Morning Post, New York Times, Washington Post*, CNN, *Boston Globe*, NBC, and *TheJournal.ie*.

Figure 8.3 Left: Untitled—Anton (2013). Source: putinarainbow.com. **Right:** 'The Real Hooligan'—Mandreus (2014). Source: putinarainbow.com.

and the nature of online images, it is impossible to show the full circulation and use of Gay Clown Putin in protests and media coverage about Russian homophobia. That said, what is outlined here is indicative of the saliency of this meme as an activist icon. Like the Muhammad Cartoons that Lene Hansen (2011) studies, there was a strong political reaction to Gay Clown Putin. This included banning the production and circulation of rainbowed and dragged Putin in 2017 by adding the images to the Russian *List of Extremist Materials*, which also includes terrorist beheading videos (Ministry of Justice of the Russian Federation 2021, §4071). This chapter is therefore not only 'gay propaganda' but 'extremist'.

Security, Sexuality, and Russia

The gay propaganda law and Gay Clown Putin memes raise issues of security in a few ways. Classed as extremist and gay propaganda, these images are considered dangerous. This is part of the Russian government's political project of eliminating/invisibilising queerness not just at home but abroad. A project—as outlined in Chapter 2—rooted in the government's construction of 'the West' as 'Gayropa', a space of moral decadence and immorality that existentially threatens Russian state and society

Figure 8.4 Gay Clowns Trump and Putin.
Source: @moceanskipper on Twitter (account now deleted).

founded on 'traditional values'. This is central to what I conceptualised as heteronormative internationalism earlier. These memes also articulate an alternative discourse that constitutes the government's heteronormative, homophobic policies as threatening to queer people by legitimising their persecution.

The propaganda law was justified through a discourse constituting non-heterosexual and non-cisgender—queer—individuals as threats to the 'traditional Christian values' underpinning Russian and 'true European' civilisation (Wilkinson 2014). As European states have increased legal protections for LGBTI+ people and implored Russia to follow suit, Putin has constituted Europe as inferior, sexually deviant, encroaching on Russian sovereignty, and eroding its 'traditional' values. Labelled 'Gayropa', this decadent, meddling queer Europe has been constructed as both a threat and a civilisation in need of saving; a role Russia is happy to play as defender of 'true European values' (Foxall 2019). Queerness, thus, emerges as an internal security threat in the form of queer people and an external ideological/cultural one emanating from 'Gayropa'.

'Security' is a particular type of discursive practice and form of identity construction—that of the Other's radical difference and threat—that is useful in suppressing particular groups of people while establishing the coherence and superiority of the Self (Hansen 2006). Constructing queerness as a national security threat establishes the coherence and superiority of

Figure 8.5 Screenshot of Instagram post by @davidkvien of video artwork 'Dicktator' by David Kvien (25 February 2022). Accessed: 23 January 2025. Image courtesy of the artist.

heterosexuality and ties it to Russianness. Since security discourses legitimate certain actions in the name of the existence of a given entity (Campbell 1992), linking 'normal' sexuality/gender to the survival of Russia and its values legitimates the elimination of queerness. Constructing queerness as a threat to national security and Russian/true European values links queerness with enmity, Otherness, and danger that needs elimination or at least invisibilisation. Sexuality and gender are also tied to the state: 'state-making processes are singularly important for constituting and normalizing binary sex differences and heteropatriarchal "family" relations ... *making states makes sex*' (Peterson 2014b, 390). Sexuality, gender, and nation are entangled, coming together to produce and discipline appropriate bodies that have appropriate sexual desires/behaviours. Here, this is fortified through security discourse.

The production of the 'Russianness' happens by marking non-heterosexual and/or non-cisgender bodies as abject, foreign, Gayropean, pedophilic, bestial, and backward. These bodies, marked as non-Russian because of their divergence from 'traditional', 'normal' sexual practices and gender performances co-constitute what 'Russian' is through normal/abnormal, hetero/homo, Russian/Gayropean dichotomies. In a bid to eliminate the 'queer threat', the propaganda law prohibits the public representation of sexual and gender deviance. This is about invisibilising those who deviate from and call into question the desires and practices prescribed by 'traditional family values'.

Such explicitly homophobic policies are always connected with visuality. They produce competent and failing bodies/citizens and delineate the subject positions available to non-/conforming people. Queer individuals, from the government's perspective, should not be part of 'the people' nor are they to be visible in Russia, which has historically encouraged 'correcting' same-sex desire through surgery that purports to align the gendered body with heteronormative expectations about the object of desire (Essig 1999, 36, 45–6). Domestic policies like the propaganda law and foreign policy discourses constructing a sexually immoral, queer-loving 'Gayropa' establish a national image founded on 'traditional values', heterosexuality, and adherence to gender norms, as well as an internationalist project that has gained significant traction in parts of the Global Far Right (Abrahamsen 2020; Abrahamsen et al. 2024; Ayoub and Stoeckl 2024).

This coalesces into a sexualised (in)security, announced through a series of practices including banning queer visibility, constituting Europe as a queer civilisational Other in need of correction, and classifying Gay Clown Putin as extremist material. These are efforts to regulate which bodies appear in public, how they are seen, and to delineate the boundaries of Russian identity; concomitantly constituting Russia as superior to 'Gayropean' nations and carving Russia's place in the world as the defender of the civilised world from queer peril (Wilkinson 2018). This is a project of making 'appropriate', 'normal' bodies visible and 'inappropriate', 'abnormal' bodies non-existent. Memes challenge this. And they appear to be successful in troubling the government, given its reaction.

Memes as Visual Political Intervention

Like many social concepts, there is no widely agreed conceptualisation of a 'meme', meaning there are no clear boundaries as to what exactly memes are. The many definitions in sociology, cultural studies, and media and communication scholarship include anything from musical notes to catchphrases, hashtags to still images, hand gestures to widely replicated dances (Denisova 2019; Hamilton 2016; Shifman 2014). For the purposes of theorising memes for IR, I start from the social use of the term 'meme'. Most memes emerge on the internet and are images that 'may contain a punchline (aphorism quotes, movie catchphrases, or any witty slogans) or make a statement without added text' (Denisova 2019, 9). Recently, theorising the 'memescape' for IR, Uygar Baspehlivan outlined that memes are 'primarily (but not necessarily) humorous artefacts and often involve a shared sensibility of non-seriousness and playfulness through which everyday social and political conditions and situations can be mocked, criticised, and/or subverted' (2024, 37).

Since most memes are visual and this chapter is about Gay Clown Putin, when referring to memes, I mean *visual memes*, which I define as: *a series of deliberately created, widely circulated, and remixed or imitated images linked by content, composition, and iconological location.*[5] Denisova conceptualises memes as not having additional text. My own experience is that *visual memes* often do have added text that is usually *on/in* the visual element itself (i.e., not separate from or alongside it like a caption would be), thus making that text a part of the image. Given this, like Baspehlivan, who conceptualises memes as a combination of text, image, and sometimes audio, I do not subscribe to Denisova's definition wholesale, even if Gay Clown Putin is one such meme without added text.

What distinguishes memes from other images is that they are appropriated, modified, and widely shared: they are viral images that 'proliferate on mutation and replication' (Denisova 2019, 10). To be a meme an image must be part of a corpus of widely shared, visually linked images 'based on imitation, in which numerous participants create new versions ... preserving and altering various elements in the process' (Gal, Shifman, and Kampf 2016, 1701) (e.g., Figures 8.2 and 8.3). A memetic corpus is characterised by images that follow similar visual patterns. A single image that circulates widely without modification would be a viral, perhaps iconic, image. Identifying memes and studying them therefore involves examining how they are positioned in relation to other images both within and outside the corpus; how they reference older images and the politics that this invokes. The main reference memes usually make is to a founding image: the image that gets remixed and

---

[5] *Iconological location* is the symbolism of the image: what it is understood to argue/show; which ideas are being made visible and how are they framed.

modified by others; the image that kick-started the visual pattern (Figure 8.2 in the case of Gay Clown Putin). There is an intervisuality and internal coherence to the memetic corpus; the images build on and reference each other.

Memes are sometimes compared to iconic images, which have been theorised as interventions into foreign policy discourses (Hansen 2015), but there are some important distinctions. Hariman and Lucaites define iconic images as:

> images appearing in print, electronic, or digital media that are widely recognized and remembered, are understood to be representations of historically significant events, activate strong emotional identification or response, and are reproduced across a range of media, genres, or topics.
>
> (Hariman and Lucaites 2007, 27)

Their strict definition means that not all images meet the criteria of iconicity. While memes are copied, imitated, satirised, and variously appropriated—key indicators of iconicity according to Hariman and Lucaites (37)—the high threshold for iconicity is not one all memes meet. By definition, memes are widely shared and some individual memes or the visual patterns constituting a memetic corpus are highly recognisable. However, memes vary in reproduction across media, genres, or topics; representation of significant historical events; generation of an emotional response; and their longevity.[6]

The distinction between iconic images and memes is important. Some but not all memes are iconic. Some but not all icons are memes. This is even more complicated as some iconic images become memes, which could be argued of the Alan Kurdi images (Adler-Nissen, Andersen, and Hansen 2019; Olesen 2017). Depending on chronology, we might therefore speak of *iconic memes* and *memeified icons* that are 'widely circulated, emotionally responded to, and seen as representing significant historical events ... found across a variety of genres, produced and reproduced by a range of media, and ... frequently appropriated and thus inserted into genres beyond the one in which they originated' (Hansen 2015, 287). *Iconic memes/memeified icons* become important for IR and security studies when they make, or are appropriated to make, interventions in foreign or security policy; as Gay

---

[6] There are some images that could be considered instant or 'fleeting' icons that are highly recognisable and powerful for a shorter period of time. This could also apply to memes when considering iconicity.

Clown Putin was. There is a clear activist politics and resistive intent in the memes exemplified by the website's call to action.

The political status of memes is as much about the images themselves as the texts and practices constituting them as a/political (Adler-Nissen, Andersen, and Hansen 2019; Hansen 2011). While most memes do not circulate offline, Gay Clown Putin is found in a variety of genres across social, print, and textile media: t-shirts, posters, mugs, stickers, for example. It has been discursively linked to, and is thus representative of, a significant event: the passing of the propaganda law, rise of Russian politicised homophobia, and policy discourses about 'Gayropa'. It generated a political and emotional response when it was constituted as a threat and added to the List of Extremist Material, but also in its emergence from emotionally charged experiences of social annihilation and heteronormative oppression much like ACT UP's visual activism discussed in Chapter 5.[7] Thus, Gay Clown Putin can be considered iconic: the Warhol image is iconic in its own right; the other memes have a more generic iconicity that follows its iconic visual pattern.

The queer politics the images themselves invoke; the legal, press, social media texts ascribing them meaning; the repeated use of the images at protests since 2013; their longevity as symbols of queer resistance, even beyond the issue of *Russian* homophobia; and their iconicity combine to constitute Gay Clown Putin as more than entertainment or funny apolitical internet images. They are visual political interventions, albeit playful ones. This is a complexity and politicality not present in all memes.

Reading *Gay Clown Putin*

Ontologically, images do not have their own 'voice' (Barthes 1977). They are multivocal in that audiences determine what they say through their interpretations (Cooper-Cunningham 2019, 389; Hansen Forthcoming). While all images are polysemous, memes are particularly susceptible to competing interpretations. By definition, memes are widely circulated, remixed, and (re)appropriated across boundaries of all kinds. They usually circulate without extra-image textual anchoring such as captions; unlike the press images in Chapter 6. Their continuous reinvention also makes their meaning unstable: do the new renditions of Gay Clown Trump or Gay Clown Orbán that

---

[7] See Gould (2009) on emotion and affect in queer politics; Adler-Nissen et al. (2019) on emotion and images.

have been appearing since both states' homophobic, 'anti-woke' turns alter their meaning? This leaves memes vulnerable to use in social and political projects beyond—even contrary to—those they were envisioned to serve: Pepe the Frog started as an innocent comic book but is now tied to the alt-right.

In part, visual meme's resistive capacity is simultaneously augmented and diminished by the fact that they usually circulate without textual anchoring. Death of the author is intentional and par for the course: the whole point is widespread, remixing, and appropriation. When visual memes become part of an international activist project, their lack of a clear and unambiguous textual anchor both enables them to flow freely across issue areas and borders without hindrance, but it also leaves them wide open to misinterpretation. That said, perhaps this attributes too much power to the text: today, most are fairly visually literate when it comes to memes and their meaning is also constituted from the visual practices surrounding them.

Here, I provide three interpretations of Gay Clown Putin for readers to engage with: (1) as constructing Putin and state homophobia as a threat, and challenging normative sexuality; (2) as homophobic and transphobic; and (3) as a radical commitment to anti-normativity and playful delight in abjection. Each brings out a different possibility for how the meme works politically. This is valuable because it demonstrates the complexity of images and how different interpretations operate. My epistemological approach is not to identify *the* definitive interpretation of Gay Clown Putin but to consider the different politics emerging from different readings of these images; the meme's polytics. Not all interpretations are of equal quality and thus do not merit equal status. The reading of Gay Clown Putin as homophobic and misogynist, advanced by Wiedlack (2020), while possible, relies on an assumption that divergence from cisheterosexuality is undesirable; it adopts a cisheteronormative epistemology. Nor does it attend to their intervisual/intertextual/interbody anchoring in queer activism. That is to say, Wiedlack does not go far enough in terms of their visual analysis and genealogy of visuality in queer activism.

I privilege the third reading, which draws on queer theory and praxis to show how Gay Clown Putin reconfigures queer subjectivities beyond victimhood and oppression towards agentic delight in abjection. This happens in a qualitatively different way than in Nissen's photographs. Drawing on the version of queer outlined in Chapter 2, I move beyond readings of Gay Clown Putin that destabilise the hetero/queer binary or merely show how such a binary is reproduced—as in readings one and two—thereby adding complexity to our theorisations of identity, politicised homophobia, and political activism.

While I disagree with reading two, that the meme is transphobic, such a reading is possible and therefore demands attention; if only to demonstrate the polysemous politics ('polytics') of images. This reading, however, does not preclude the queer(er) reading I offer. Since all co-exist and co-constitute the meme's meaning, they must all be brought into the analysis.

Challenging Homophobia, Flipping the Threat

Gay Clown Putin can be understood as challenging idealised masculinities and heteronormativity through parody and the subversive resignification of gender. The Russian state closely controls Putin's image, which is clear from the Kremlin's website and other carefully curated images of him.[8] The public images of 'macho' Putin are designed to emphasise his embodiment of the *muzhik*, the 'real man' who proves he is not a woman or homosexual but instead sturdy, tough, strong, and 'sexy' (Sperling 2014, 36). As his image is carefully crafted to be the embodiment of national masculinity and that which all Russians ought to emulate and admire (Foxall 2013; Sperling 2014), the contrast between state-crafted images of Putin and the satirical, criminalised Gay Clown Putin images is striking.

By dragging Putin, Gay Clown Putin targets glorified *muzhik* masculinity and parodies the idea of natural, a priori gender that flows from sex assigned at birth and determines erotic desires. Revealing how gender relies on imitation and repetition, how fragile the gender order is, the meme destabilises Putin's position of (moral) authority by causing a dissonance between the curated macho public image and the Gay Clown Putin parody. This puts hegemonic orderings of society into deep water by exposing the fragility of norms around sex/gender/sexuality and their susceptibility to endless resignification. Not only does Gay Clown Putin destabilise notions of fixed and binary gender by showing just how easily they can be transgressed, but also norms around appropriate sexuality and the power Putin derives from embodying the (now unstable) *muzhik* image.

From within the heteropatriarchal matrix, drag Putin reads as abnormal. Operating outside sex/gender norms, questions arise about whether Putin is

---

[8] See Kremlin photobank (en.kremlin.ru/multimedia/photo) and CBS gallery (www.cbsnews.com/pictures/vladimir-putin-doing-manly-things/).

represented as man/woman, gay/straight, and so on. Gay Clown Putin does not 'fit' into these binaries. In an inversion of power, queer activists force Putin to genderfuck—that is, confound expected gender norms. This is closest to what Butler calls 'subversive and parodic redeployment of power' (Butler 1990, 124). Mimicking the way the heterosexual matrix disciplines bodies into performing cisgendered heterosexuality, queering Putin troubles the ontological stability of gender norms using parody and satire. This move scrambles the coherence of the cisheteronormative structure and starts to destabilise entrenched regimes of heteronormative sexuality and patriarchal gender. The destabilisation of normal/abnormal, hetero/homo dichotomies happens through different stylisations of Putin's body that subvert gender norms. Normative constructions around sex, gender, and sexuality become fragile, are cracked open, and thus become susceptible to resignification. The meme, thus, confronts heterosexualised power structures that discipline bodies into appropriate (heteronormative) performances of gender and sexuality.

Besides the rainbow and drag make-up, Putin's lack of a physically strong lower body, from which his muzhik status is secured, is important. The disappearance of his body in the Gay Clown Putin meme provokes the question of the relationship between the body and gender/sex. To remove that which secures his status as the embodiment of virile masculinity, destabilises the link between gender and the body (i.e., genitalia) and highlights how sexuality, gender, and nation are entangled, coming together to produce and discipline bodies into appropriate forms of expression and behaviour. By removing the source of power, his hypermasculine cisheteronormative body, the idea of secure and natural 'masculinity' goes with it. At the very least, the idea of stable and binary gender/sex which attaches to the body is troubled and provokes questions about what 'gender' is and how it works on us to establish what we can/not do.

Read alongside the curation of Putin's hypermasculine image by the Kremlin, Gay Clown Putin undermines and subversively caricatures Putin's authority, his hypermasculinity, and the discipline of heteropatriarchal structures. The government's balking at both Gay Clown Putin images and queerness more generally only reiterates how much terror goes into maintaining compliance and the appearance of a natural, stable gender binary. As the embodiment of Russian masculinity and gender order, the contrast between heteroised state-accepted and queer, satirical, criminalised Gay Clown Putin is vital.

This is not simply the manipulation of Putin's face on a rainbow flag. It represents the inversion of a system that privileges cisgendered heterosexuality and disparages queerness. Thus, giving the meme a clear political dimension that challenges state homophobia, cisheteronormative organisations of society, and establishes queer visibility. Using symbols like the rainbow and thereby invoking a politics that celebrates and takes joy in being abject, these images play a pivotal role in dissenting against legislative moves to make queer bodies conform and invisibilise queerness. They claim public space by combining the media-grabbing tactic of using leaders' faces with queer and feminist symbolism; the rainbow in Figure 8.2 (left) and Pussy Riot-style balaclavas in Figure 8.2 (right).

Since discourses and practices around images attribute meaning to them, adding Gay Clown Putin to the *List of Extremist Material* because it 'promotes' queerness is important to its signification. That it is constituted as promoting non-traditional sexuality imbues it with that status, thereby giving it political power as a challenge to the government's policy position. The images provoked an authoritarian government to strengthen its homophobic politics, to enforce its propaganda law on a set of images. This reaction constitutes the meme as a critical political intervention. Any association of Putin with queerness had to be muted not just because it undermined his hypermasculine image and the propaganda law, but also because it confounded the cisheteronormative discursive foundations upon which Russian identity, security, and foreign policy are built: it triggered an ontological dislocation and ontological insecurity. If, as we know from Hansen (2006), that security is an ontological necessity for the state, then queer(ness) and these memes threaten that by exposing the disciplinary force of state-sanctioned expression of gender.

Gay Clown Putin is politically potent because its content visualises and makes present that which is deemed illegal. Gay Clown Putin images challenge the construction of queerness as anti-Russian and reorder the arrangements of visibility imposed by the propaganda law that sought queer bodies invisible. The meme challenges sovereign power by redrawing the lines that distinguish types of subjectivity and determine individuals' place inside/outside the community, and by articulating an alternate security discourse. One where the threat-threatened relationship is inverted and re-configured: the Russian government and heteropatriarchal hypermasculinised society, which is so deeply tied to so-called 'traditional values', is constituted as *threatening to* queer people not as *threatened by* them.

Homophobic and Transphobic

Another reading of the Gay Clown Putin meme is that it is homophobic, transphobic, and patriarchal; that in seeking to challenge Putin's anti-queer politics, it reproduces the hegemonic heteropatriarchal system by attacking his masculinity and sexuality. In Russia, political opponents frequently challenge each other's masculinity and heterosexuality in a bid to undermine political legitimacy (Sperling 2014). These tactics constitute the opposition as insufficiently or inappropriately masculine, a subordinate form of masculinity, thus reproducing the hegemonic heteropatriarchal gender order and heteronationalist discourse.

Gay Clown Putin is neither the first instance of clowning and dragging the political opposition nor the first (visual) attempt to impugn another politician's masculinity.[9] This is symptomatic of patriarchal structures, which not only differentiate 'men' from 'women' but also between masculinities (Connell 1995). As such, one might interpret Gay Clown Putin as following established heteronormative tactics. While undertaken with professed liberatory intentions, it is undergirded by and reproduces a sociopolitical system that privileges a particular type of virulent heterosexual masculinity, the *muzhik*.

This would make Gay Clown Putin the visual manifestation of nationalism as competing masculinities (Slootmaeckers 2019). Instead of destabilising the heteropatriarchal system and heteronationalism through which sexualised-gendered internal and external enemy Others are produced—as in reading one—Gay Clown Putin supports and reproduces those hierarchies as well as homophobic/transphobic nationalism. When read against the declaration of intent on putinarainbow.com, this suggests that the images backfire and fail to move beyond heteronormativity and bolster Putin's heteronormative geopolitical project by creating a hierarchy of masculinities and denigrating Putin.

Katharina Wiedlack (2020, 67) argues that Gay Clown Putin reproduces phobic discourses by using visual cues of 'feminization and gender transgression' to disparage Putin. Read as such, while these images undermine the hypermasculine, macho image the Kremlin curates, they do so using the very structures sought destabilised (Wiedlack 2020). Wiedlack contends that

---

[9] For example, street murals like 'The Kiss', which features Leonid Brezhnev and Erich Honecker kissing (Berlin Wall), and 'Make Everything Great Again' which features Putin kissing Trump (Vilnius, Lithuania).

these images do not make sense without the tacit knowledge that a particular way of being a 'man' is privileged; that divergence from cisheterosexual masculinity is undesirable. Hence, the joke only works by denigrating queerness as inferior and abnormal.

Through this lens, the meme is not a critical intervention but the reproduction of norms around sex, gender, and sexuality. It fails because the very target of domination that it supposedly resists—heteronormativity—is what makes it offensive, disparaging, and potentially politically powerful. It does not challenge gender norms but reproduces them by delegitimising gender transgression and poking fun at drag, genderfucking and/or trans and/or 'deviant' sexual desire. All of which are abject in a heteronormative structure that constitutes transgression of sex, gender, and sexuality norms as dangerous and deviant. This meme reproduces the powerful and oppressive homosexual/heterosexual hierarchy and glorifies 'normal' performances of gender. Thus, the matrix through which bodies are made to fail and/or succeed, to be constituted part of or excluded from the nation, is not undone but strengthened.

In this second reading, the Gay Clown Putin images might not follow the national security logic of Putin's construction of 'Gayropa' to reinforce Russia's dominant gendered position in a 'masculine hierarchy of nations' (Slootmaeckers 2019 258) but they do disparage feminine masculinities and target queer Putin for punishment. In the context of Russian hyper-masculinity and its historical practices of surgically forcing gender transgressive bodies into their 'correct' sex, the implication that Putin is queer facilitates a reading that his gender failure needs fixing or elimination to save Russia. The product of this reading is strikingly similar to Putin's homophobic project: Gay Clown Putin does not successfully challenge homophobia since it re-inscribes vilified queer subjectivities.

However, this reading overlooks the historicity of queer images of dissent. Gay Clown Putin follows common visual tactics in queer political activism and has an intervisuality with previous images.[10] The way the memes are used at protests harks back to a form of AIDS activism embedded in a radical queer politics of unapologetic delight in abjectness as opposed to

---

[10] See further examples of the manipulation of political figures' faces:
https://digitalcollections.nypl.org/items/510d47e3-53aa-a3d9-e040-e00a18064a99,
https://digitalcollections.nypl.org/items/510d47e3-1cac-a3d9-e040-e00a18064a99,
https://digitalcollections.nypl.org/items/510d47e3-1c9e-a3d9-e040-e00a18064a99,
https://digitalcollections.nypl.org/items/510d47e4-1cf4-a3d9-e040-e00a18064a99.

a homophobic one (Gould 2009). At protests against Russian homophobia and the gay propaganda law in Madrid (23/08/13) several protesters had bloody hands and in London (10/08/13) some used a bloody handprint poster alongside Gay Clown Putin thereby linking Gay Clown Putin to the activist groups ACT UP and Gran Fury and their *The Government Has Blood On Its Hands* campaign. On other occasions the pink triangle is used alongside Gay Clown Putin and ACT UP's famous *Silence = Death* slogan (Madrid, 25/04/17; Hong Kong, 07/02/14).

This is not just a historical but a genealogical point. It puts the historicity of queer activism and past practices into the present, enabling a vitally important reading of these images that shows how they work through a queer logic rooted in AIDS activism and gay liberation that embraces deviance (see Chapter 5). This necessitates a third reading using queer theory about shame, stigma, and abjection, which sat at the core of the queer politics emerging out of AIDS activism and gay and lesbian liberation movements.

Gay Clown Putin as the Productive Embrace of Deviance

Queer, as I gesture towards in the introduction, where I outline an antinormative conceptualisation of queer, can never sever its connection with shame, stigma, and denigration. It always names that which has been considered abject in some way. In this case, queer sexuality and gender performance constituted as an abject threat to Russian state and society. If labelling something 'queer' marks its sexual and gendered impropriety, vulgarity, perversity, and shamefulness then queering can work as a political praxis that embraces abjectness and transforms it into a site of joy, culture, and liberation. Gay Clown Putin queers Putin by marking him with the same shame, stigma, and abjection that queers are subject to. Instead of marking him for correction and extermination, Gay Clown Putin celebrates queerness by taking endless, playful, ridiculing delight in recasting Putin.

The memes are playful and they draw on humour to demean the seriousness of the Russian government's attempts to control the unpredictable, wayward nature of desire by constituting anything outside the heteronormative ordering of sex, gender, sexuality—or 'traditional values'—as a national security threat. They satirise the ridiculous, albeit incredibly powerful, attempts to manage sex, pleasure, and desire. By taking delight in that which is supposed to be abject and celebrating it—a queer epistemology—Gay Clown Putin not only destabilises hierarchies but short-circuits the power derived from constituting something as abject and threatening.

Starting from a queer politics that rejects deviation from cisheteronormativity as undesirable and instead holds it as joyous, desirable even, Gay Clown Putin is part of an oppositional queer politics. One that challenges cisheteronormative hierarchies not by saying 'we are normal' or 'love is love' but by adopting a negative sociality. That negative sociality—contempt for heteronormative society and an unyielding resistance to power and hierarchies—embraces deviation and challenges the political power invested in ordering sex, gender, and sexuality through stigmatisation of the 'abnormal'. Starting from this place, Gay Clown Putin is neither a homophobic nor misogynist attack on an imaginary queer Putin. Rather, Gay Clown Putin is first and foremost a refusal to accept dominant modes of organising the social and political (cisheteronormative patriarchy) that encourage the neutralisation of queerness for its deviation from state-sanctioned practices and desires.

Rather than attacking queerness, Gay Clown Putin embraces the shame, stigma, and abjection attached to queerness and radically alters its relation to power. To queer Putin is not to show contempt for difference and deviation from the norm. It is camp in its contempt of the contemptible and highlights how so few people perfectly align with the socially imposed sex and gender norms governing us all, highlighting how all moralising about sexuality is ultimately arbitrary but infused with power. This underlines the hypocrisy of the propaganda law and politics of sexual shame that work upon bodies to control desires and behaviours by stigmatising 'deviant' desires and acts.

Rejoicing in the very abjectness of queer sexuality, Gay Clown Putin expresses a particular part of queer culture that 'doesn't pretend to be *above* the indignity of sex' but instead teases and abuses until it is clear that sex (and gender) is 'as various as the people that have it' (Warner 2000, 35). This involves an ethical relation to people that starts with the acknowledgment that all sex is indignant, perverted in some sense. Warner (2000, 35) writes that 'Queers can be abusive, insulting, and vile toward one another' but 'abjection is understood to be the shared condition' and so leaning into that abjection and ridiculing Putin by marking him with the same stigmatisation reflected onto queers is a way of re-orienting queers' relation to heteronormative sociality. This pride in sexual deviance weaponises the constitution of queer sex as abject for righteous rebellion against sociopolitical norms.

In its attempt to contain, deny, and suppress queerness as immoral, foreign, and threatening, the government is attempting to contain the uncontainable: sexual desire and the ways people (refuse to) perform gender. By infringing the propaganda law, Gay Clown Putin is a refusal to hide queerness or to acquiesce to state power. Acknowledging the hierarchical constitution of sexual practices and pleasures, Gay Clown Putin challenges heteronormativity and homophobic hierarchies, which are part of state-making and external power projection, by rejoicing in queer aberrance, delighting in it, and claiming dignity in supposedly shameful desires. Ultimately, laying the groundwork for new forms of (queer) subjectivity that challenge what is deemed shameful.

Unlike the politics that emerges from the first reading, in which there is an implicit desire to reconfigure 'Russianness' to include various forms of sexual behaviour and gender expression, the queer politics of the meme expresses no desire to allow queerness to be subsumed as part of 'Russian' identity but entertains a transnational queer alliance of abject and anti-normative individuals. Queering Putin breaks down the distinction between 'normals' and 'queers' and puts Putin into the firing line by subjecting him to perversity as much as anyone else. We are all threatened by the spectre of desire and its uncontrollable and unpredictable workings. By queering Putin, Gay Clown Putin demeans the government's immense efforts to moralise about appropriate 'traditional' sexuality not just on a domestic but international stage. Refusing the invisibility mandated by the propaganda law and plastering Putin with make-up and rainbows, the meme uses deviance to carve out new ways of being that stand in direct opposition to and challenge the 'normal' sexuality delineated in the 'traditional values' project.

Celebrating the queer in Gay Clown Putin moves us away from a heteronormative to a queer epistemology that disrupts phobic logics. A move that mandates the political unacceptability of queerness, its outlaw existence. Queering Putin is, thus, not disparaging in the phobic sense but a radical and productive move that creates new forms of the social and political that repeatedly question hierarchies and relations to power. This short-circuits the power of homophobic, cisheteronormativity by shifting queer from its association as something awful and insidious to something that, even in all its abjectness and antisociality, is joyous, liberating, and revolutionary.

Queerness is about (delight in) violating cisheteronormative social norms of the proper and best way to be and to live. It is a transgression that threatens to disrupt or even destroy the current social order and, consequently, results in punishment, stigma, violence, and even death upon those who dare to transgress. In that sense, this meme is about challenging domination, not about assimilation or seeking out ways to integrate by destabilising normative orders. They do more than destabilise the queer/straight dichotomy, focusing instead on the *power* of heteronormativity to turn every body in society into a battleground upon which gendered, sexualised politics play out.

The creation, circulation, and mobilisation of Gay Clown Putin at protests are acts of dissent not only against the propaganda law and Russia exclusively, but heteronormativity more broadly. The meme explodes homophobic, heteronormative logics by embracing and taking playful joy in those subject positions cast as 'negative' or 'less than'. Consequently, new queer subjectivities emerge from embracing alterity and abjectness in ways that short-circuit the oppressive power structures trying to contain them. The memes deny heteronormativity its *disciplinary* power: by embracing difference rather than disavowing it, queer refuses to secure normativity's identity and privilege thereby undermining its power.

To argue that Gay Clown Putin is homophobic and upholds cisheteronormativity would be to accept that divergence from cisheterosexuality is undesirable; a position that is at odds with queer politics and praxis that celebrate such divergence. The images are embedded in a hegemonic sociopolitical context where divergence from cisheterosexuality is constituted as undesirable but they work through a queer epistemology and arguably move us closer to a vision of queer life rooted in teasing, humour, and antagonism where 'shame is bedrock' and moralism about sex and gender go out the window (Warner 2000, 35–7). To read Gay Clown Putin as homophobic is to inadvertently accept cis-hetero norms where deviance is undesirable and thus secure the dominance of homophobic structures. It assumes they work through a heteronormative logic where deviance is deplorable, rather than a queer one.

As a political refusal to acquiesce to the propaganda law or Russia's heteronormative internationalist project, which attempts to invisibilise queerness, the meme is representative of a broader refusal of queers to be folded into society as some kind of inferior but acceptable citizen. Instead, queer deviance becomes dangerous and extremist. In that sense, queerness *is* a threat to hegemonic cisheteronormative organisations of society that politics reproduces—in and beyond Russia—but not in the way the Russian government targets it for extermination. Rather than a political system built on oppression, domination, and control of every body, queer as a transformational and revolutionary politics is: an alliance of the marginalised that perpetually questions and opposes concentrations of power; that radically reimagines (international) political and social orders; that does not oppose sexual difference or try to hide, justify, or moralise it but instead delights in queer inaptitude for hegemonic social and political arrangements.

In many ways, the memes become a global rejuvenation of the political project envisioned by the *Silence = Death* collective around AIDS by reinvigorating the politics of the anti-normative and taking joyous delight in all the stigmatic abjections attached to queer bodies. They draw societal attention to governments' indifference to phobic violences and their complicity in sanctioning the elimination of sexual and gender dissidents. They are visual political speech that brings attention to the absurd politics of sex and moralising that have not only structured domestic politics, interpersonal relations, and state-making but also international politics and inter-state relations.

Gay Clown Putin is a divestment from hegemonic social and political orders and is, thus, a reimagining of political subjectivity that threatens cisheteronormative power by refusing to submit to it and offering an alternative queer futurity that delights in its deviance from the normative order. Queer as refusal circumvents state power that is so invested in gendered, racialised, heteronormative arrangements of society, and reorients the queer's relation to it. In so doing, the Gay Clown Putin meme provokes fundamental ethical questions about who/what should be constituted as a security referent/threat.

Conclusion

This chapter theorises memes as visual interventions in international politics through the case of the Gay Clown Putin meme. I argue that Gay Clown Putin, which targets Russian politicised homophobia and anti-queer security discourses, is a political intervention that works through a queer epistemology where deviance is celebrated rather than penalised. To enable this reading, I draw on a queer politics that is explicitly anti-normative, delights in sexual difference, revels in abjectness, and embraces the disruptive force of queerness that flouts rigid and punitive norms around sex, gender, and sexual desire (Chapter 2). As the playful embrace of abjection, Gay Clown Putin short-circuits heteronormativity's ordering power and creates new forms of visibility and subjectivities that are distinctly queer and anti-normative.

In Russia, queer gender and sexuality have been constituted as a security threat, evidenced in practices that include banning queer visibility through the gay propaganda law, constituting Europe as its queer civilisational Other in need of correction ('Gayropa'), and classifying Gay Clown Putin as extremist material. The Gay Clown Putin meme has succeeded in troubling the Russian government and its promotion of a heteronormative 'traditional' values system, as exemplified by its securitising reaction to the images. Gay Clown Putin plays a crucial role in representing and contesting state-sponsored homophobia and has generated international attention. Its use across the world as a symbol contesting Russian homophobia is testament to the meme's salience and politicality.

While the Gay Clown Putin images can be read as articulating queer (in)security and resisting demonisation, the way they are received is a more complex story that invokes different types of politics. That memes can be variously interpreted is part of the fraught nature of visual politics. As such, my analysis demonstrates: the polysemic politics ('polytics') and complexity of images; how security is visually enacted and challenged; and how memes intervene in international politics. To bring out the different politics of the images, I offered three readings of the memes as: (1) constituting homophobic policies as a threat and challenging normative constructions of gender/sexuality; (2) reproducing homophobic, misogynistic power structures; and (3) as playful delight in abjection that short-circuits heteronormative power. While not all readings are equal, here all three are political. Thus, pointing to the significance of Gay Clown Putin for international politics broadly and the study of politicised homophobia specifically. This is not something that can be said of all memes.

Ultimately, I argued that Gay Clown Putin playfully delights in abjection and contests the hegemonic heteronormative system that disciplines bodies into a gendered heterosexual/homosexual binary. It takes pride in queerness and its inaptitude for heteronormative society and politics. It weaponises heteronormative ideas about queer sex as abject for righteous rebellion against such powerful sociopolitical norms. As such, it is part of a visual struggle for presence, space, and the ordering of society and politics that provokes questions about which bodies get to be visible and what subjectivities are allowed to exist in Russia. Rather than mere parody or mimicry, Gay Clown Putin is a symbol of the radical potential of anti-assimilationist, anti-normative, oppositional queer (international) politics invested in an endless interrogation of power. That symbol highlights the international politics of sex that is sustained through strategic homophilia and homophobia.

Gay Clown Putin is one of the most iconic memes of the last two decades to directly intervene in international politics. This iconic image has been used globally in protests and has sparked an intense political reaction from the government it targeted. It is not production alone that makes memes political, but their use, circulation, intervisualities, genealogies, and relations to other texts (legal, press, social media) and practices (protests). All of which must be part of our analyses. While not all memes will make a political intervention in the same way as Gay Clown Putin, we must address those that make foreign and security policy interventions as more than mere play. Especially those iconic memes/memeified icons that gain huge attention and political traction internationally. Memes do immensely political work and we must give them due attention if we are to fully understand the dynamics and rhythms of international politics in the age of the (digital) image.

9

Conclusion

This book covers a lot of ground conceptually, theoretically, and empirically. It starts from two observations. First, that sex is doing something in international politics. Second, that images and bodies do something politically, not least in terms of activism against oppressive internationalist projects that, if we follow Judith Butler's (2024) recent work, are characteristically fascist in their ideological contours. On the first point, it focuses on how and when normative, moralising discourses about sex and sexuality are mobilised in service of a foreign policy agenda and international power projection. To draw on Wendy Brown's work (1995, 2006), queerness forces states, elites, and the public to grapple with questions of freedom and what 'type' of (political) community they want to be and what values they want to have. This does not stop at state borders but extends into the international sphere where sex has become an issue of power politics and geopolitical jostling. On the second point, what I have offered here is a theorisation and methodological approach for studying international relations beyond a pure state focus: a whole plethora of actors are affected by and engaged in international politics, particularly those whose bodies are the objects of moralising discourses and disciplining. Taking a tripartite words-images-bodies approach to exploring international politics, I explored how various international actors have represented and contested Russian state homophobia using images and their bodies as means of undermining Russian heteronormative internationalism and challenging the geopolitical ordering project it is engaged in.

▲

I have told a lot of stories throughout this book. That will not change here. In order to illustrate the key arguments I have made here, and building on my argument in Chapter 6 that images can provide theoretical and conceptual inspiration for International Relations scholars, I want to return to a moment from World Pride in 2021, which was hosted in Copenhagen. At the final meeting point of the World Pride march in Fælledparken, I saw a poster that spoke to the core points I make in this book. The poster was very simple, composed

The International Politics of Sex. Dean Cooper-Cunningham, Oxford University Press. © Oxford University Press (2025). DOI: 10.1093/9780197792544.003.0009

solely of graphic text with the words 'sex is sex' on white poster board. Each of the letters was filled in with rainbow stripes, I think coloured in with pen. 'Sex is sex' is a catchy phrase, which at first glance seems rooted in the anti-normative queer politics I introduced at various stages of this book. I initially thought it to be a queer play on the ubiquitous 'love is love' slogan that is so often (and so lazily) deployed in identity-based LGBTI+ activism, which tends to sanitise sexuality—removing sex, abjection, and the antinormative—to the point that queerness becomes emptied of any political power to challenge the heteronormative legal, economic, sexual, racial, and family systems we are governed by (see Cohen 1997, 442–3). I've reflected on that poster for a good deal of time and it captures some of the core themes of this book—at least to a certain degree.

In the first instance, that poster was on display at World Pride, an international gathering of queer people fighting variously for sexual autonomy and liberty, LGBTI+ rights, and freedom from persecution the world over. World Pride, as an international celebration of non-normative sex and gender, calls attention to the politics of sex—even if only in subtle ways. At the very least, World Pride emphasises how queer people are political 'by the very nature of our being because our entire society is constructed to deny our existence' (Unknown in DIVA TV 1989, 00:12:50). Just appearing, making oneself and one's queerness visible, and claiming space is political. As I showed in Chapters 6 and 7, claiming space actively challenges and provokes heteronormative structures by refusing to be invisible.

That poster also captures the power of the visual and the necessity of queer political analysis and a focus on politicised moralising about sex. In terms of the visual, that poster forced me to think deeply about the convergence of queer politics, sex, the body, the state, the international, and activism. In terms of queer politics, it exemplified the problem with 'love is love' as a political commitment in the global LGBTI+ movement. 'Love is love' downplays the politics of sex that sits at the core of homophobia: as a strategy that reinforces heteronormativity, homophobia is fundamentally about the management of sex, intimacy, pleasure, desire, and erotics. This is about power, disciplining, and hierarchy. To say that 'love is love' is to hide the sexual stigma and shame that are part of homophobia—both in its political and social forms. It blinds those who buy into the argument that non-normative sexuality is about a fight for love to the fact that homophobic actors from the state to the church to individuals are not interested in love per se. What they target is the types of sex, intimacy, and pleasure pursued by people who fail or refuse to squeeze their sexual and erotic desires into a heteronormative structure that attempts to control things as wayward and awry as sex, pleasure, and desire. Homophobia is not about love, unless love is a synonym for sex. It is about control and domination of people through sexual oppression. This is political.

That becomes abundantly clear when we look closely at the international politics of sex emerging around the issue of Russian state homophobia, which involves Russia and states from the West strategically shaming and stigmatising the homophobia/homophilia of one another. Western states stigmatise Russia for its homophobia and Russia stigmatises Western states' supposed homophilia in ways that are completely detached from 'love' but everything to do with the types of sex and desire sanctioned by those respective (collections of) states. By transforming 'love is love' into 'sex is sex', I first thought that the poster highlighted the politics of sex, called for less moralising about other people's pleasures, and moved towards an embrace of an antinormative queer politics. It seemed to harness the political power of queer by speaking specifically about sex and alluding to the fact that even the most morally defended sex is perverted because we are all subject to the spectre of desire and its uncontrollable workings; that others' pleasure costs people nothing and so taking any sort of moral position on it is ludicrous (Rubin 2011; Warner 2000). But sex isn't just sex. Sex is deeply political, politicised, and international.

In the case of Russian state homophobia, the stigmatisation of non-normative sex is not only domestic but also underpins a whole internationalist project that is rooted in the spread of 'traditional family values'. As this geopolitical project gains traction among the Global Far Right and other states adopt similar traditional-values-based policies to Russia, queer people everywhere come under threat. There is no clearer illustration at the moment than in Poland, Hungary, the United Kingdom, Italy, or the USA, where the situation is worsening for queer people. Right now, the government of the supposed leader of the free world is signing executive orders that are deeply homophobic and transphobic, mimicking his counterpart in Russia, and there are reports that the US Secretary of State has adopted a 'one flag policy', banning the flying of rainbow flags at US embassies. All of this should serve as an important reminder that the state can withdraw its support, however small that support is, for marginalised groups at any moment should the political need arise.

If we are to heed anything from the queer theorising I draw on here, it should be that while all sex is public and political, queer sex is especially so. The very idea of queer sex—most prominently same-sex sex and desire— has been the subject of much moralising, politicisation, and legislating in states' domestic and foreign policies. Russian state homophobia involves the strategic deployment of homophobia that has distinct domestic and international attributes. Its domestic homophobia, which manifests most profoundly in the gay propaganda law, is underpinned by the idea of a Western queer menace known as 'Gayropa' that threatens Russian national security. In official Russian discourse, the West's increasing tolerance of non-normative sexuality and gender is constituted as immoral, decadent, and regressive. Discoursing about a 'Western gay menace' has become a useful tool in Russian statecraft and it supports what I conceptualised as a heteronormative internationalist project: deploying politicised homophobia as part of foreign policy and an internationalist project to bolster heteronormative sociality abroad through 'traditional family values'. Russia's domestic politicised homophobia and its heteronormative internationalism co-constitute each other; they cannot be disentangled. The stigmatisation and sexual shaming of the non-heteronormative is part of an emergent international politics of sex. That is not to say that sex has not always had an international politics (think of British colonial homophobia, for instance), but that this is a new iteration and a somewhat unique one grounded in a national security discourse.

To say 'sex is sex' is to ignore that sex is public, political, and international. It is to ignore the way that non-normative sex is strategically vilified by states and other important societal actors for political gain that has real impacts on queer people. It is to reduce sex to some activity that just happens between people without any negotiation of politics or reproduction and reification of existent (hetero) norms. Queer bodies are politicised, disciplined, and mobilised in various homophilic and homophobic ways as state and state-adjacent actors moralise about sex and use this as a geopolitical tool that differentiates the 'civilised' from the 'barbaric' and 'deviant'.

Something I gestured towards in the introduction, but want to emphasise more forcefully here is that queer IR should do more to explore antinormative theorising to help us understand and critically engage with the world and the international politics around sexual moralism. Saying 'sex is sex', like that poster did, fundamentally depoliticises queer sex. It strips queer of the political power it gains from the purposive flouting of rigidified, punitive norms around sex, gender, and sexuality. As Leo Bersani wrote: 'the value of sexuality is to demean the seriousness of efforts to redeem it' (1987, 222). So saying that sex is just sex is to buy into the necessity of redeeming non-normative sex and the need to moralise and legitimise the sex and bodily pleasures queers seek out by putting queer and hetero 'normal' sex on the same footing. To revel in the stigma turns queer joy into resistance. To take joy in being constituted as abject is to reject heteronormative society and to mobilise queerness in a potentially revolutionary way that does more than just blur the lines of sexual difference, subvert gender norms, or resignify heteronormative institutions for the queer community (Bersani 1996, 5, 76). When one accepts and celebrates stigmatic abjection, it confounds dominant heteronormative logics and opens up space for new queer subjectivities and new political formations to emerge through a puncturing of (international) social order in its current heteronormative form. Queer sex is not just sex. It is resistance against or, even more radically, inaptitude for heteronormative sociality and all the (international) legal, political, and economic structures it underpins.

The queer activism studied in this book opens space for those queer subjectivities and political formations to emerge using the body and the visual. It opens space for seeing queer counterpublics in which a less oppressive world can be built. Instead of outlining how queer people do not threaten Russian national security and how queers are just 'normal' people trying to find love, the visual and bodily activism studied here does something more radical by showing queerness in all its glory and flouting the rigid norms around sex, gender, and sexuality. These interventions into the international politics of sex—understood as various moves of stigmatising and shaming directed at (collections of) states and rooted in particular moralising about sexual practices and pleasures sought out by individuals—are violations of heteronormative social norms that punish, oppress, and stigmatise those who fail to follow prescribed rules. In this respect, by flaunting queerness and publicly displaying it, the activism I focused on threatens the heteronormativity that underpins Russian foreign and domestic policy by exposing the disciplinary sexual politics that works upon every body to forbid a whole spectrum of pleasures and desires, and by refusing to reify a heteronormative structures where queerness is unfavourable.

Those visual interventions do not try to hide, justify, or moralise queerness but instead delight in queer inaptitude for hegemonic social and political arrangements. They are a divestment from hegemonic social and political orders and thus reimagine political subjectivity in ways that challenge cisheteronormative power by refusing to submit to it and offering an alternative queer vision that delights in deviating from the normative order. In this regard, the visual and bodily international activism against Russia's heteronormative projects holds a potentially radical and transformative politics that harnesses the power of the visual and bodily as political weapons to undermine Russia's attempted management of sex and bodily pleasure on a domestic and international scale.

▼

Our current geopolitical moment features an authoritarian Russian aggressor that has expended significant energy challenging the liberal international order and is painstakingly struggling to forge a new international order. Russian foreign policy is replete with discourse about its security and power emanating from being anti-globalist, anti-liberal democracy, and 'a cultural, axiological, and even civilisational antithesis of the West' (Składanowski 2023, 35). This has included two decades of constituting the West's so-called sexual and gender immorality as a national security threat and more recently using this as part of the justification for its war in Ukraine (Edenborg 2022; Tsaturyan 2024). During this time, Russia's political elite have not only anchored national security policy in ideas about defending Russian culture, traditions, and gender/sexual norms from foreign influence (Gaufman 2017; Wilkinson 2018) but also defending the 'traditional values that have made up the spiritual and moral foundation of civilisation in every nation for thousands of years' internationally (Putin 2013b). Unfortunately, a significant amount of the Russian discourse on traditional values, commitment to a so-called 'anti-woke' politics, and the transformation of queer people into a societal menace and national threat is being echoed in the White House since Donald Trump's re-election in 2024.

This raises a fundamental question about why queer scholarship is often overlooked in studies of international politics. Sex is so often relegated to the bedroom as personal, apolitical, and outside the realm of 'real' or 'high' politics. It is by no means outside the scope of international relations. What I have shown in this book is that sex is definitively political and international: sexual stigmatising/shaming are common state practices through which they advance international political projects rooted in homophilia/homophobia; heteronormative moralising about sex underpins Russia's illiberal internationalist project; and activists from all over the world are contesting Russia's heteronormative projects in ways (visual and bodily) that destabilise which actors and epistemic sites we consider important in IR. The struggle around what types of sex people can have, what types of objects people can desire, and what types of bodily pleasures people can indulge in is foundational to the production of world orders, national identities, transnational ideologies, and, thus, plays a critical role in geopolitics. So much so that even the UN Security Council is discussing sexuality in its work.

While this book focuses quite specifically on the confrontation between the West and Russia, the international politics of sexual shaming and stigmatisation was on full display at the UN Security Council's recent Arria-formula meeting on 'Integrating the Human Rights of LGBTI persons into the Council's Mandate for Maintaining International Peace and Security' (20 March 2023) where competing discourses on non-normative sexuality and gender were particularly pronounced. The UK Mission at the UN, for example, pointed to 'Russia's demonisation of LGBTI+ in Ukraine, the Taliban's policies against them in Afghanistan, and Daesh's persecution of them in Iraq … [as] underpinned by narratives that frame sexual orientation and gender ideology as an attack on national identities and traditional values'—here, calling out politicised homophobia and making stigmatising moves towards those states failing to protect their queer populations. This is not in itself problematic, but the UK Mission then went on to cite a policy report that I co-authored with Jess Gifkins and Protection Approaches as evidence of UK leadership and progressiveness on the queer question (United Nations Security Council 2023, 1:10.00–1:12.00). The UK Mission represented itself *internationally* as backing the inclusion of LGBTI+ people in the work of the Security Council to preserve peace and security internationally all while the Conservative government at home was stridently continuing with its *domestic* hostility towards queer people—particularly trans—during its post-Brexit culture-war-stoking era (Cooper-Cunningham and Kremer 2024; Faye 2022; Gifkins and Cooper-Cunningham 2023). Ironically, the cited report highlights the exact role that the type of politicised homophobia deployed by the UK government domestically plays in creating fertile conditions for mass violence (Gifkins et al. 2022). The UK Mission's comments at the Security Council are an example of states mobilising homophobia and homophilia simultaneously as and when it suits a political agenda.

In this book, I argued that a queer analysis is fundamentally about unpacking the politics of sexual stigma and shame. It centres on the way sex and desire are policed and politicised; how certain forms of sex are permitted and others delegitimised, stigmatised, made abhorrent. The queer political analysis I outlined for the study of international politics not only tunes into the ways that states manipulate and control sex but also how the politics of sexual shame and stigma go international and get implemented in foreign policy projects in ways that have significant ramifications for actual queer people. The international is personal and the personal is international. Attending to this, I theorised an international politics of sexual shame and stigma that involves strategically mobilised politicised homophobia/homophilia and the stigmatisation of other states for the way they treat queer people. Sex, as it becomes part of an international politics replete with shaming and stigmatising practices that affect every individual on the planet, is crucial to the study of IR. Through queer theorising, IR can learn a lot about the international order emerging around (Russian) politicised homophobia and international activism against it, as well as how our bodies, desires, and pleasure-seeking are international. Given this, expanding our sites of analysis can teach us a lot about power politics and the coming intensification of oppressive 'anti-woke' ideological projects that have not only created culture wars and moral panics domestically, but internationally.

The Visual International Politics of Sex

There is a general consensus among queer scholars that state homophobia revolves around the desired invisibility of non-normative sex/gender. In this case, I showed that the visual connects to Russian homophobia in several ways. First, the visual is constitutive of Russian politicised homophobia since invisibility is central to Russia's homophobic oppression and images are used to represent Russian politicised homophobia internationally, thereby shaping how we understand the phenomenon as an international political issue. Second, images are used in international activism, contestation, and condemnation: the visual is frequently deployed to challenge state homophobia, particularly by making queerness visible and showing moments of queer rapture even in all its abject associations. Third, the visual is used to rearrange regimes of queer in/visibility: actors use different forms of visuality from the body to images and the visibility of queerness to (re)claim public space, (re)articulate queer insecurity, and (re)constitute queer subjectivities.

To unpack the politics of visual-bodily responses, I started by conceptualising what exactly was going on with Russian homophobia and the propaganda law. In Chapter 2, I outline what I call Russian heteronormative internationalism and an international politics of sexual stigma and shame. Building on this, I theorised an approach to the study of international politics that considers the visual and embodied components of the international resistance to Russian state homophobia and its heteronormative internationalism. Introducing a new word-image-body approach to the study of visual international politics, I ultimately argued that the visual and the body are important analytical sites because they are means through which marginalised actors participate in international politics—sometimes because those are the only means available.

Political activism, contestation of state policies, and intervention in geopolitics might not always manifest in words—they may happen through the visual or the bodily. Non-state actors, in this case, used the visual and the body as a way of intervening in international politics. From photojournalism and photoessays to meme-making and rainbow-wielding protest, activists are using the visual and body to contest Russian heteronormativity. These are therefore important analytic sites for showing how oppressive power structures (can) get destabilised and overthrown. My tripartite word-image-body approach plays with epistemology and ontology by building on poststructuralist theories of the social and political as constituted in discourse. It provides a theorisation of discourse as encompassing words, the visual, and the body and what that means for the way we study international politics. This is a major reconceptualisation of discourse that opens up new lines of inquiry and brings different actors into IR. It also demonstrates how words, images, and the body interact: visual and bodily practices show and tell stories in conjunction with and/or separately from text/word. In this regard, discourse is multimodal, percolating through societies and maintaining power in complex ways that require expansive methods and epistemologies.

By locating activism not solely at the level of the written/said, my word-image-body approach enabled an engagement with the multiple ways that actors around the world contested Russian state homophobia that would otherwise have been rendered irrelevant or gone unnoticed had I adopted a strict words-based understanding of discourse and what it means to 'do' and intervene in international politics. I bring attention to significant parts of Western representation and the politics of those representative practices that would otherwise have gone unchecked and significant forms of playful resistance that would have gone unseen and untheorised.

The methods we use structure what we see, who we see, and what counts as empirical material worthy of analysis. This means that how we study certain sociopolitical issues has an effect not only on what politics is revealed in the analysis but on who is revealed, how they are revealed, and what possibilities for transformation are made thinkable and therefore possible. A queer politics entails an ethico-political commitment to always interrogating power. That means paying attention to the means those who are being oppressed use to challenge that oppression. Moving forward, those interested in the way non-state actors intervene in international politics can adopt my approach to explore the ways international politics unfolds in spaces often overlooked out of a predilection for studying 'official' actors and in ways that would usually be missed by only looking at words and actions of the 'official' big players.

What a Queer Analysis Offers

At the start of the book, I asked how a queer political analysis helps us understand the use of the visual and the body in international responses to Russian state-directed politicised homophobia. As shown above, queer scholarship emphasises how the politics of sex revolves around arbitrary moralising about sex, erotic desire, and bodily pleasures. This is fundamentally connected to the body: heteronormativity disciplines every body and imposes upon us certain norms and expectations. From birth, a whole set of expectations is imposed on us because of the shape of our body, because of our *visual* appearance. A queer political analysis therefore emphasises the connection of the body and the visual to disciplinary power structures and forces us to think more expansively about our sites of analysis. If disciplining happens to the *body* and because of its *visual* appearance, both the visual and the body can redirect and resist power. Since queer as politics is centred on the ceaseless interrogation of relations to power, a queer political analysis is also focused on the ways that power is contested and resisted—regardless of how. In the case of Russian politicised homophobia and its heteronormative internationalist project, resistance and contestation come in the form of visual and bodily activism.

The queer politics that I bring in here places an emphasis on stigma, shame, and antinormativity. While a fuller exploration of the antinormative thesis within IR will be necessary, this is hopefully the start of that conversation. Taking antinormativity seriously is a significant departure from existing queer theorising in IR, but it will hopefully encourage queer IR scholars to refuse queer as a purely ontological endeavour to destabilise binaries rather than focusing on the politics of sex (see Stoffel and Birkvad 2023). As I theorise it here, queer can never sever its connection with shame, stigma, and denigration. It always names that which has been considered abject in some way. In this case, queer sexuality and gender performance constituted as a threat to Russian state and society. If labelling something 'queer' marks its sexual and gendered impropriety, vulgarity, perversity, and shamefulness then, following my theorisation of queer in Chapter 2, queering becomes a political praxis that embraces abjectness and transforms it into a site of joy, culture, and liberation. Taking delight in that which is supposed to be abject and celebrating it not only destabilises hierarchies but also short-circuits the power derived from constituting something as abject and threatening.

Drawing on queer theory, I showed that the politics of sexual shame is rooted in domination and control of the population. As this goes international, that domination and control extends beyond the state's borders and towards exerting geopolitical influence and control of other populations. The visual and the body are important means of resisting this heteronormative project. Reading those interventions through a queer lens demonstrated the radical political potentiality of those interventions to 'create a space in opposition to dominant norms, a space where political work can begin' (Cohen 1997, 438). That queer lens enabled me to see how the potential of images to remake and remould oppressive political structures (Bleiker 2018, 28) was mobilised by queer activists in a way that embraces abjection and uses queer joy as a mechanism of resistance.

A queer analysis not only directs our attention to the body, the visual, and the way that powerful systems of domination are challenged but also helps us understand the complex (at times, antinormative and antisocial) logics through which these visual and bodily interventions work. Working within a queer epistemology enables us to see the way those visual and bodily interventions not only undermine and resist Russian homophobia but demonstrate an almost revolutionary inaptitude for sociality; how those visual practices reject heteronormative organisations of society and work within a queer praxis that embraces and delights in deviance.

What this does for IR is force us to consider who is acting in the international, to consider what sex is doing in terms of international politics, and to consider new epistemologies that reconstitute how we understand the agency and subjectivities of those people constituted as abject: are persecuted queer people *only* victims? It also encourages a rethinking of the sites we see as worthy of analysis: if the politics of sexual shame and stigma works upon people's bodies and activists are using visual and bodily means to resist heteronormative power structures then we need to properly consider how subjects who are the end points of international power games engage politically regardless of how they do so. Failure to do so only further reifies dominant arrangements of power. In this current moment, where sex and gender are hyper-politicised and securitized in domestic and foreign policies, queer theory offers tools to understand international power politics and resistance to it. As a discipline, we must use it.

Word-Image-Body

Where my contribution to queer IR is a focus on sexual stigma and the start of a conversation on antinormativity in queer thinking on international politics, my contribution to visual IR is introducing a word-image-body approach, visual genealogy as a method, and theorising the political work different genres—from photojournalism to memes to body-based visual protest—do. For visual scholarship, which is anchored in symbolism, metaphor, and context-bound meaning, understanding the historicity and evolution of visual symbols, ways of seeing, or representational practices is crucial and makes for richer political analyses. This is particularly the case in queer activism, which has an established practice of using visuals and the body to resist. Visual genealogy is a critical tool in the visual scholar's methodological arsenal that enables much more thorough and contextualised analyses of the polytical work images and other forms of visuality do. Both the tripartite approach and visual genealogy can be mobilised in future research as methods for unpacking the politics of the visual and the ways that discourse percolates through society in complex and multimodal ways.

Images surround everything we do. We now overwhelmingly gain information and our understanding of the world and international affairs from visual media. Actors of all kinds—though particularly those who are marginalised or sought silent or invisible—use the visual as a way of intervening in international politics in playful and innovative ways that reconfigure the spaces of international relations/International Relations and pose a challenge to entrenched (heteronormative) power structures and ways of researching. Images, especially those that are highly visible, are never mere reflections of reality but profoundly political representations. Images, theorised as representations, produce particular visions of the world and the subjects populating it, which, by establishing the interpretive frameworks within which decisions are made, legitimise state actions and policies that affect people's lives. In short, images have political implications as part of the information space from which we glean knowledge about what is going on at home and in other countries.

The overarching message of this book is therefore that if politics takes place through words, through images, and through bodies, we cannot understand or adequately account for what's going on in the world without investigating each of those sites of politics in our analyses. The tripartite word-image-body approach is crucial for future studies of international politics because it refuses to afford any epistemological privilege to word or visual or bodily interventions in politics and thereby refuses to reify the power structures that come with speaking and being listened to. Sometimes actors do not have the luxury of speaking and being heard: the visual and the bodily thus become important means of entering international political discussions. These require our attention as much, if not more so, than official documents and actions.

My approach does not isolate or privilege visuality above or apart from other discursive planes such as the written/spoken or the bodily. Instead, it acknowledges that the visual and bodily can complement our understandings of the social and political in IR by creating space for new ways of thinking about who and what counts as a subject of international politics as well as how words, bodies, and images combine to make international politics and to make political interventions. The words we take for granted as the bread and butter of foreign policy and geopolitical analysis must be accompanied by an analysis of visual and body politics if we are to fully understand what is going on in the world and how power is maintained and challenged.

In the empirical part of the book, I showed how international political activism takes place across all three terrains, which necessitates analysing all three sites together since they combine and work together in important ways that cannot be studied in isolation without missing some of the politics at stake in the queer international activism. The visual, the body, and words enter in responses to and activism against Russian homophobia in complex and overlapping ways that reveal the necessity of a broadened epistemology for studying international politics—especially with regards to the international politics of sex and international activism.

Political activism, contestation of state policies, and intervention in geopolitics might not always manifest in words—they may happen through the visual or the bodily. To proceed with a focus on language as written and spoken means that other ways of speaking and intervening in international politics, and thereby queer politics in general, get disregarded and left out of our understanding of the international politics of Russian homophobia. What emerges from putting the theoretical chapters and the empirical material into dialogue is an understanding of the ways that the body and the visual structure international politics in complicated ways that confound the epistemological privilege afforded to discourse—and therefore knowledge—as written/spoken.

Beyond the visual, this book contributes to debates about the politics of body. This book picks up and builds on Hansen's (2000b) provocation to think about the ways that the body enunciates security and more broadly the way that bodies are sites of resistance (Bilgiç 2016; Butler 2012, 2020; Cooper-Cunningham 2019; Fierke 2013). Bodies are the battleground upon which geopolitical struggles are fought (Russia versus Gayropa) through control of gender performance, sexual freedoms, and bodily pleasures. The body is not only a site upon which disciplinary power operates. It is a visual site through which political activism takes place. If the queer(ed) body and the pleasures it seeks out antagonise and provoke societies into reinforcing, doubling down on their heteronormative sociality—domestically and internationally—then those bodies expose the fragility of the dominant social order and the potential for its reconfiguration. Bodies 'do' politics. They can provoke dominant orders through various forms of activism. They can disturb hegemonic orders and cause chaos around established norms and dominant forms of sociality by showing their fragility and arbitrary boundary drawing.

Bodies are also sites that upend how we think of spaces and sites of international politics. Their inclusion troubles IR's narrow focus on nations and states. Defiant bodies fail to conform, buck the trend, and in doing so demonstrate the fragility and malleability of discursively constituted power structures. Bodies, then, are not merely objects of discourse, they actively participate in, reconfigure, contest, reify, stabilise, destabilise, and/or undermine discourses. International politics is not just speeches, policy documents, parliamentary debates, and newspaper articles. It is protests, marches, making and sharing images, placing the body in harms way, satirising a politician's face, waving a flag, being a flag, and contesting foreign and domestic policy in a whole manner of ways—any way possible. A whole spectrum of actors engage in international politics through the visual and with their bodies. Sometimes, because they have no other choice; this is the only way to get 'heard'.

Visuals construct truths, produce meanings, and structure how we perceive political problems. If the visual impacts policy by constituting 'interpretive dispositions' that enable and preclude certain actions/policies and ideas, it therefore also plays a role in undermining oppressive political narratives, such as Russian heteronormative internationalism, and reconstituting what is imaginable, thinkable, and doable. The visual is thus an obvious strategy of queer activism that enables the imagining of a more radical, less oppressive world in which sexual autonomy is possible—even if power can never be fully dismantled.

The visual-bodily interventions studied here have at their core the potential to make a more radical and less oppressive society imaginable—not just at the level of the domestic but the transnational. Michael Warner wrote that an ethical vision of queer politics 'recognize[s] the diversity of sexual and intimate relations as worthy of respect and protection' and that it 'cultivate[s] unprecedented kinds of commonality, intimacy, and public life' (1999, 123). The visual and body-based international activism against Russian homophobia both calls attention to queer joy in abjection and emphasise the radical potential of a queer existence that does not effuse moral arguments for non-normative sex in exchange for protection and rights.

In so doing, the forms of visuality that I studied here encourage queer people, groups, and collectives from across the globe to consider how they might coordinate in response to the encroaching transnational threat of the Global Far Right and its adoption of the 'traditional family values' that I have argued sit at the core of Russian heteronormative internationalism. A coordinated, transnational queer counter-move is crucial, but that queer counter-move must respect the diversity of sexual behaviours, erotic desires, and bodily pleasures sought. Words, images, and bodies will be central to this counter-move and the imagining and production of a queerer world.

Looking forward, my recent work with Jess Gifkins, Detmer Kremer, and the team at Protection Approaches has worryingly pointed to the persecution of queer people as a canary in the coal mine for the escalation of violence and the onset of mass atrocities (Cooper-Cunningham and Kremer 2024; Gifkins and Cooper-Cunningham 2023; Gifkins et al. 2022). In a new geopolitical era where sexual norms are part of the game of international power politics, we must extend our research on the patterns of queer persecution and the types of politics underpinning it. For IR scholars of all theoretical and methodological predilections, the question is not does sex matters in IR but rather when, how, and to what extent normative moralising politics around sex/sexuality are instrumentalised in service of power and interest? Addressing this will be the focus of my next tranche of work and I invite others to take up such questions too. This will only become more necessary for understanding our current geopolitical moment as we witness the increasing scapegoating of queer and other marginalised groups across the world.

Bibliography

Abrahamsen, Rita. 2020. 'The Right Family: The Personal is Geopolitical.' *Centre for International Policy Studies*. December 14, 2020. https://www.cips-cepi.ca/2020/12/14/the-right-family-the-personal-is-geopolitical/.

Abrahamsen, Rita, Jean-François Drolet, Karin Narita, Srdjan Vucetic, and Michael Williams. 2020. 'Confronting the International Political Sociology of the New Right.' *International Political Sociology* 14: 94–107.

Abrahamsen, Rita, Jean-François Drolet, Michael Williams, Srdjan Vucetic, Karin Narita, and Alexandra Gheciu. 2024. *World of the Right*. Cambridge University Press.

Ackerly, Brooke, Elisabeth Friedman, Meenakshi Gopinath, and Marysia Zalewski. 2019. 'Visual Global Politics.' *International Feminist Journal of Politics* 21 (3): 353–354.

Adam, Barry. 1987. *The Rise of the Gay and Lesbian Movement*. Boston: Twayne.

Adler-Nissen, Rebecca. 2014. 'Stigma Management in International Relations: Transgressive Identities, Norms, and Order in International Society.' *International Organization* 68 (Winter): 143–176.

Adler-Nissen, Rebecca, Katrine Emilie Andersen, and Lene Hansen. 2019. 'Images, Emotions, and International Politics: The Death of Alan Kurdi.' *Review of International Studies* 46 (1): 75–95.

Adler-Nissen, Rebecca, and Ayse Zarakol. 2021. 'Struggles for Recognition: The Liberal International Order and the Merger of Its Discontents.' *International Organization* 75 (2): 611–634.

Åhäll, Linda. 2018. 'Gender.' In *Visual Global Politics*, edited by Roland Bleiker, 150–156. New York: Routledge.

Ahmed, Sara. 2013. 'Queer Feelings.' In *The Routledge Queer Studies Reader*, edited by Donald Hall and Annamarie Jagose, 422–441. Routledge.

Ahmed, Sara. 2023. 'Queer Use.' In *Queer Then and Now: The David R Kessler Lectures 2002–2020*, edited by Debanuj Dasgupta, Joseph Donica and Margot Weiss, 297–323. New York: Feminist Press.

Alabaster, Olivia. 2018. 'Peter Tatchell Arrested in Moscow After Protest Against Anti-LGBT+ Russia.' *The Independent*, June 15.

Altman, Dennis. 1993. *Homosexual: Oppression and Liberation*. New York: New York University Press.

Altman, Dennis. 1999. 'Globalization, Political Economy, and HIV/AIDS.' *Theory and Society* 28 (4): 559–584.

Altman, Dennis. 2001. *Global Sex*. Chicago: Chicago University Press.

Altman, Dennis, and Jonathan Symons. 2016. *Queer Wars: The New Global Polarization Over Gay Rights*. Cambridge: Polity Press.

Amar, Paul. 2013. *The Security Archipelago*. Duke University Press.

Amin, Kadji. 2017. *Disturbing Attachments: Genet, Modern Pederasty, and Queer History*. Durham: Durham University Press.

Ammaturo, Francesca Romana. 2015. 'The 'Pink Agenda': Questioning and Challenging European Homonationalist Sexual Citizenship.' *Sociology* 49 (6): 1151–1166.

Ammaturo, Francesca Romana, and Koen Slootmaeckers. 2024. 'The Unexpected Politics of ILGA-Europe's Rainbow Maps: (De) Constructing Queer Utopias/Dystopias.' *European Journal of Politics and Gender* 8 (1): 3–25.

Amnesty International. 2013a. Freedom Under Threat: Clampdown on Freedoms of Expression, Assembly and Association in Russia. London: Amnesty International.

Amnesty International. 2013b. 'G20 Leaders Must Reject Russia's Homophobic Law.' Accessed July 29, 2019. https://web.archive.org/web/20130911233809/https://www.amnesty.org/en/news/russia-lgbti-g20-2013-09-04.

Amoore, Louise, and Alexandra Hall. 2013. 'The Clown at the Gates of the Camp: Sovereignty, Resistance and the Figure of the Fool.' *Security Dialogue* 44 (2): 93–110.

Amos, Howard. 2017. 'Kick Out Gays To Purify Us, Says Chechen Leader.' *The Times*, July 18.

Andersen, Rune S., Xavier Guillaume, and Juha A. Vuori. 2016. 'Flags.' In *Making Things International 2: Catalysts and Reactions*, edited by Mark Salter, 137–152. Minneapolis: University of Minnesota Press.

Andersen, Rune S., and Juha A. Vuori (eds). 2018. *Visual Security Studies: Sights and Spectacles of Insecurity and War*. London: Routledge.

Andersen, Rune S., Juha A. Vuori, and Xavier Guillaume. 2015. 'Chromatology of Security: Introducing Colours to Visual Security Studies.' *Security Dialogue* 46 (5): 1–18.

Andersen, Rune S., Juha A. Vuori, and Can E. Mutlu. 2015. 'Visuality.' In *Critical Security Methods: New Frameworks for Analysis*, edited by Claudia Aradau, Jef Huysmans, Andrew Neal and Nadine Voelkner, 85–117. Abingdon: Routledge.

Andersen, Rune S. 2020. 'The security captor, captured. Digital cameras, visual politics and material semiotics.' *Critical Studies on Security* 8 (2): 130–144.

AP. 2013. 'NBC Supporting Gay Workers.' *The New York Times*, August 10.

Applebaum, Anne. 2014. 'Russia's Anti-Western Thinking Takes Hold.' *The Washington Post*, March 30.

Aradau, Claudia, and Andrew Hill. 2013. 'The Politics of Drawing: Children, Evidence, and the Darfur Conflict.' *International Political Sociology* 7 (4): 368–387.

Aradau, Claudia, and Jef Huysmans. 2014. 'Critical Methods in International Relations: The Politics of Techniques, Devices and Acts.' *European Journal of International Relations* 20 (3): 596–619.

Aradau, Claudia, Jef Huysmans, Andrew Neal, and Nadine Voelkner, eds. 2015. *Critical Security Methods: New Frameworks for Analysis*. Abingdon: Routledge.

Ashley, Richard. 1988. 'Untying the Sovereign State: A Double Reading of the Anarchy Problematique.' *Millennium: Journal of International Studies* 17 (2): 227–262.

Atshan, Sa'ed. 2020. *Queer Palestine and the Empire of Critique*. Stanford University Press.

Augstein, Jakob. 2013. 'Tough on Russia, Easy on America.' *Der Spiegel International*, December 9.

Austin, Jack. 2017. 'Fans at Russia 2018 World Cup Will Be Allowed To Fly Rainbow Flags.' *The Independent*, November 30.

Ayoub, Phillip. 2015. 'Contested Norms In New-Adopter States: International Determinants of LGBT Rights Legislation.' *European Journal of International Relations* 21 (2): 293–322.

Ayoub, Phillip. 2016. *When States Come Out: Europe's Sexual Minorities and the Politics of Visibility*. Cambridge: Cambridge University Press.

Ayoub, Phillip, and Kristina Stoeckl. 2024. 'The Global Resistance to LGBTIQ Rights.' *Journal of Democracy* 35 (1): 59–73.

Azoulay, Ariella. 2008. *The Civil Contract of Photography*. New York: Zone Books.

Baker, Gilbert. 2015a. 'Meet The Man Who Created The Rainbow Flag.' 21 June.

Baker, Gilbert. 2015b. 'MoMA Acquires the Rainbow Flag.' 17 June.

Baker, Gilbert. n.d. 'Rainbow Flag: Origin Story.' *Gilbert Baker*.

Baker, Peter. 2013. 'Obama Names Gay Athletes to U.S. Delegation.' *The New York Times*, December 18.

Bakshi, Sandeep, Suhraiya Jivraj, and Silvia Posocco. 2016. *Decolonizing Sexualities*, edited by Sandeep Bakshi, Suhraiya Jivraj and Silvia Posocco. Oxford: Counterpress.

Barabantseva, Elena, and Andy Lawrence. 2015. 'Encountering Vulnerabilities Through 'Filmmaking for Fieldwork'.' *Millennium Journal of International Studies* 43 (3): 911–930.

Barad, Karen. 2003. 'Toward an Understanding of How Matter Comes to Matter.' *Signs: Journal of Women in Culture and Society* 28 (3): 801–831.

Bargu, Banu. 2017. 'The Silent Exception: Hunger Striking and Lip-Sewing.' *Law, Culture and the Humanities* 18 (2): 1–28.

Barthes, Roland. 1977. *Image, Music, Text*. Translated by Stephen Heath. New York: Hill and Wang.

Barthes, Roland. 1981. *Camera Lucida: Reflections on Photography*. New York: Hill and Wang.

Baspehlivan, Uygar. 2024. 'Theorising the Memescape: The Spatial Politics of Internet Memes.' *Review of International Studies* 50 (1): 35–57.

Batchelor, Tom. 2017. 'European Court Rules Russia's 'Gay Propaganda' Law Encourages Homophobia.' *The Independent*, June 20.

Beaumont, Peter, Miriam Elder, Jason Burke, and Afua Hirsch. 2012. 'Gay Rights Campaigners Around The World Hail Obama's Message of Support.' *The Guardian*, May 10.

Berents, Helen. 2019. 'Apprehending the "Telegenic Dead": Considering Images of Dead Children in Global Politics.' *International Political Sociology* 13 (2): 145–160.

Berents, Helen. 2020. 'Politics, Policy-Making and The Presence of Images of Suffering Children.' *International Affairs* 96 (3): 593–608.

Berlant, Lauren. 1997. *The Queen of America Goes to Washington City: Essays on Sex and Citizenship*. Duke University Press.

Berlant, Lauren. 2022. *On the Inconvenience of Other People*. Durham and New York: Duke University Press.

Berlant, Lauren, and Lee Edelman. 2015. 'Reading, Sex, and the Unbearable: A Response to Tim Dean.' *American Literary History* 27 (3): 625–629.

Berlant, Lauren, and Elizabeth Freeman. 1992. 'Queer Nationality.' *Boundary 2* 19 (1): 149–180.

Berlant, Lauren, and Michael Warner. 1995. 'What Does Queer Theory Teach Us About X?' *Publications of the Modern Language Association of America* 110 (3): 343–349.

Berlant, Lauren, and Michael Warner. 1998. 'Sex in Public.' *Critical Inquiry* 24 (2): 547–566.

Bersani, Leo. 1987. 'Is the Rectum a Grave?' *October* 43 (Winter): 197–222.

Bersani, Leo. 1996. *Homos.* Cambridge, MA: Harvard University Press.

Biddolph, Caitlin. 2022. 'Rainbow Jurisdiction at the International Criminal Court: Protection of Sexual and Gender Minorities Under the Rome Statute.' *Melbourne Journal of International Law* 23 (1): 1–7.

Biddolph, Caitlin. 2024. 'Haunting Justice: Queer Bodies, Ghosts, and The International Criminal Tribunal for the Former Yugoslavia.' *International Feminist Journal of Politics* 26 (2): 216–239.

Bilgiç, Ali. 2016. 'World Security: Towards a 'Local' Research Agenda.' In *Ethical Security Studies: A New Research Agenda*, edited by Jonna Nyman and Anthony Burke, 46–59. Abingdon: Routledge.

Bleiker, Roland. 2000. *Popular Dissent, Human Agency and Global Politics.* Cambridge: Cambridge University Press.

Bleiker, Roland. 2009. *Aesthetics and World Politics.* Basingstoke: Palgrave Macmillan.

Bleiker, Roland. 2015. 'Pluralist Methods for Visual Global Politics.' *Millennium Journal of International Studies* 43 (3): 872–890.

Bleiker, Roland. 2017. 'In Search of Thinking Space: Reflections on the Aesthetic Turn in International Political Theory.' *Millennium Journal of International Studies* 45 (2): 258–264.

Bleiker, Roland. 2018. 'Mapping Visual Global Politics.' In *Visual Global Politics*, edited by Roland Bleiker, 1–29. New York: Routledge.

Bleiker, Roland. 2019. 'Visual Autoethnography and International Security: Insights From The Korean DMZ.' *European Journal of International Security* 4 (3): 274–299.

Bleiker, Roland, David Campbell, Emma Hutchison, and Xzarina Nicholson. 2013. 'The Visual Dehumanisation of Refugees.' *Australian Journal of Political Science* 48 (4): 398–416.

Bleiker, Roland, and Amy Kay. 2007. 'Representing HIV/AIDS in Africa: Pluralist Photography and Local Empowerment.' *International Studies Quarterly* 51 (1): 139–163.

Bosia, Michael J. 2014. 'Strange Fruit: Homophobia, the State, and the Politics of LGBT Rights and Capabilities.' *Journal of Human Rights* 13: 256–273.

Bosia, Michael J. 2015. 'To Love or to Loathe: Modernity, homophobia, LGBT rights.' In *Sexualities in World Politics*, edited by Manuela Picq and Markus Thiel, 38–53. London: Routledge.

Bosia, Michael J. 2020a. 'Introduction: Sexual and Gender Diversity Politics 50 Years after Stonewall.' In *The Oxford Handbook of Global LGBT and Sexual Diversity Politics*, edited by Michael Bosia, Sandra McEvoy and Momin Rahman, 1–12. Oxford University Press.

Bosia, Michael J. 2020b. 'Sexual Diversity Politics and the Trouble With LGBT Rights.' In *The Oxford Handbook of Global LGBT and Sexual Diversity Politics*, edited by Michael J. Bosia, Sandra McEvoy and Momin Rahman, 433–449. Oxford University Press.

Bosia, Michael J. 2013a. 'Why States Act: Homophobia and Crisis.' In *Global Homophobia: States, Movements, and the Politics of Oppression*, edited by Meredith L. Weiss and Michael J. Bosia, 30–54. Chicago: University of Illinois Press.

Bosia, Michael J. 2013b. 'Why States Act: Homophobia and Crisis.' In *Global Homophobia: States, Movements, and the Politics of Oppression*, edited by Meredith L. Weiss and Michael J. Bosia, 30–54. Chicago: University of Illinois Press.

Bosia, Michael J. 2018. 'Do Queer Visions Trouble Human Security?' In *Routledge Handbook of Gender and Security*, edited by Caron Gentry, Laura Shepherd and Laura Sjoberg, 94–105. Routledge.

Bosia, Michael J., and Meredith Weiss. 2013a. 'Political Homophobia in Comparative Perspective.' In *Global Homophobia: States, Movements, and the Politics of Oppression*, edited by M.L. Weiss and M.J. Bosia, 1–29. Chicago: University of Illinois Press.

Bosia, Michael J., and Meredith L. Weiss, eds. 2013b. *Global Homophobia: States, Movements, and the Politics of Oppression*. Chicago: University of Illinois Press.

Boyes, Roger. 2014. 'Sochi Will Weaken Putin, Not Elevate him.' *The Times*, February 5.

Boykoff, Jules. 2017. 'Protest, Activism, and the Olympic Games: An Overview of Key Issues and Iconic Moments.' *The International Journal of the History of Sport* 34 (3–4): 162–183.

Bracke, Sarah. 2012. 'From 'saving women' to 'saving gays': Rescue narratives and their dis/continuities.' *European Journal of Women's Studies* 19 (2): 237–252.

Brammer, John. 2018. 'The Hidden Activist Campaign That Spread a Rainbow in Russia.' *them*, July 10. https://www.them.us/story/hidden-russia-rainbow.

Bratek, Rebecca. 2018. 'Activists Create "Hidden" Rainbow Flag to Get Around Russia's LGBTQ Flag Ban.' *CBS*, July 10. https://www.cbsnews.com/news/activists-create-hidden-rainbow-flag-to-get-around-russias-lgbtq-flag-ban/.

Bredekamp, Horst. 2010. *Image Acts: A Systematic Approach to Visual Agency*. Berlin: De Gruyter.

Broadbent, Rick. 2013. 'Nick Symmonds The Lone Dissenter Condemns Russia's Gay Propaganda Law.' *The Times*, August 19.

Broadbent, Rick. 2014. 'Russia Steps Up Attempt To Bring Tainted Games In From The Cold.' *The Times*, January 22.

Broadbent, Rick. 2018. 'Will Gayest Games Be A Turning Point?' *The Times*, February 24.

Bronski, Michael. 2011. *A Queer History of the United States*. Boston: Beacon Press.

Brown, Jonathan. 2013a. 'Clare Balding Urged To Join Campaign To Strip Russia of Winter Olympics in Row Over Homophobic Laws.' *The Independent*, August 10. https://www.independent.co.uk/news/world/europe/clare-balding-urged-to-join-campaign-to-strip-russia-of-winter-olympics-in-row-over-homophobic-laws-8752805.html.

Brown, Jonathan. 2013b. "No Discrimination Against Gay Athletes': Olympic Chief Jacques Rogge Joins Growing Clamour Over Winter Games in Russia.' *The Independent*, August 9.

Brown, Jonathan. 2013c. 'Olympic Chief Challenges Russia Over Gay Rights.' *The Independent*, August 10.

Brown, Wendy. 1995. *States of Injury: Power and Freedom in Late modernity*. Princeton University Press.

Brown, Wendy. 2006. *Regulating Aversion: Tolerance in the Age of Identity and Empire*. Princeton University Press.

Buchan, Lizzy. 2018. 'MPs Fear 'Heightened Risks' for LGBT+ and Ethnic Minority Football Fans in Russia.' *The Independent*, June 8.

Butler, Judith. 1990. *Gender Trouble: Feminism and the Subversion of Identity*. New York: Routledge.

Butler, Judith. 1993a. *Bodies That Matter: On the Discursive Limits of 'Sex.'* New York: Routledge.

Butler, Judith. 1993b. 'Critically Queer.' *GLQ: A Journal of Lesbian and Gay Studies* 1 (1): 17–32.

Butler, Judith. 1997. *Excitable Speech: The Politics of the Performative*. New York: Routledge.

Butler, Judith. 1999. *Gender Trouble: Feminism and the Subversion of Identity*. New York: Routledge.

Butler, Judith. 2004. *Undoing Gender*. New York: Routledge.

Butler, Judith. 2010. *Frames of War: When Life Is Grievable?* London: Verso.

Butler, Judith. 2012. 'Bodies in Alliance and the Politics of the Street.' In *Sensible Politics*, edited by Meg McLagan and Yates McKee, 117–137. New York: Zone Books.

Butler, Judith. 2015. *Notes Toward a Performative Theory of Assembly*. Cambridge, MA: Harvard University Press.

Butler, Judith. 2020. *The Force of Nonviolence: An Ethico-Politial Bind*. Verso.

Butler, Judith. 2024. *Who's Afraid of Gender?* Farrar, Straus and Giroux.

Buzan, Barry, and Lene Hansen. 2009. *The Evolution of International Security Studies*. Cambridge: Cambridge University Press.

BuzzFeed. 2018. 'People Love These Activists Who Secretly Took Rainbow Photos In Russia.' *BuzzFeed News*, July 9.

Callahan, William. 2015. 'The Visual Turn in IR: Documentary Filmmaking as a Critical Method.' *Millennium* 43 (3): 891–910.

Callahan, William. 2020. *Sensible Politics: Visualizing International Relations*. Oxford University Press.

Campbell, David. 1992. *Writing Security: United States Foreign Policy and the Politics of Identity*. Minneapolis: University of Minnesota Press.

Campbell, David. 2002a. 'Atrocity, Memory, Photography: Imaging the Concentration Camps of Bosnia - The Case of ITN Versus Living Marxism, Part 2.' *Journal of Human Rights* 1 (2): 143–172.

Campbell, David. 2002b. 'Atrocity, Memory, Photography: Imaging the Concentration Camps of Bosnia-The Case of ITN Versus Living Marxism, Part 1.' *Journal of Human Rights* 1 (1): 1–33.

Campbell, David. 2004. 'Horrific Blindness: Images of Death in Contemporary Media.' *Journal for Cultural Research* 8 (1): 55–74.

Campbell, David. 2007. 'Geopolitics and Visuality: Sighting the Darfur Conflict.' *Political Geography* 26 (4): 357–382.

Campbell, David, and Michael J. Shapiro. 2007. 'Guest Editors' Introduction.' *Security Dialogue* 38 (2): 131–137.

Carrier, Tom. 1988. 'VEXI-Bits: A Digest of Flag Related Articles.' *North American Vexillological Association* XXI (2): 1–8.

Carroll, Oliver. 2018. 'The Dark Reality Behind Russia's Promise of an LGBT-Friendly World Cup.' *The Independent*, May 22.

Carter, Daniel. 2013a. 'Danish Government Warns Russia Over Anti-Gay Law.' *Pink News*, August 15. https://www.pinknews.co.uk/2013/08/15/danish-government-warns-russia-over-anti-gay-law/.

Carter, Daniel. 2013b. 'German Foreign Minister: Treatment of Gay People in Russia Unacceptable.' *Pink News*, August 12. https://www.pinknews.co.uk/2013/08/12/german-foreign-minister-treatment-of-gay-people-in-russia-unacceptable/.

Chan, Sewell. 2017. 'Russia's 'Gay Propaganda' Laws Are Illegal, European Court Rules.' *The New York Times*, 20 June 2017.

Chan, Stephen. 2018. 'Colonialism.' In *Visual Global Politics*, edited by Roland Bleiker, 68–74. New York: Routledge.

Charlton, Joseph. 2013a. 'G20 Summit: David Cameron to Raise Concerns Over Russian Anti-Gay Policies.' *The Independent*, September 4.

Charlton, Joseph. 2013b. 'Homosexual Delegates to Sochi?' *The Independent*, December 18.

Chen, Angela. 2020. *Ace: What Asexuality Reveals About Desire, Society, and the Meaning of Sex*. Beacon Press.

Christopher Street Liberation Day Committee. 1973. *CSLD '73*. New York.

Christopher Street Liberation Day Committee, 1976, 'Gay Pride Parade.'

Christopher Street Liberation Day Committee, 1983, 'June 26—Thousands of Gay People to Block Afternoon Traffic on Manhattan's West Side.' May 9.

Chute, Hillary. 2016. *Disaster Drawn: Visual Witness, Comics, and Documentary Form*. Cambridge: Belknap Press of Harvard University Press.

Clarey, Christopher. 2013. 'Track Championships Add Layer of Scrutiny to Russia and Doping.' *The New York Times*, August 10.

Clark, Lindsay. 2018. 'Grim Reapers: Ghostly Narratives of Masculinity and Killing in Drone Warfare.' *International Feminist Journal of Politics* 20 (4): 602–623.

Clark-Parsons, Rosemary, and Jessa Lingel. 2020. 'Margins as Methods, Margins as Ethics: A Feminist Framework for Studying Online Alterity.' *Social Media + Society* 6 (1).

ChelseaClinton (@ChelseaClinton). 2018. 'Courageous & beautiful ?.' Twitter.

CLIO Awards. 2019a. 'CLIO Awards: Ben&Jerry's The Unbreakable Rainbow.' Accessed February 4, 2021. https://clios.com/awards/winner/public-relations/ben-jerry-s/the-unbreakable-rainbow-59586.

CLIO Awards. 2019b. 'CLIO Awards: FELGTB The Hidden Flag.' Accessed February 4, 2021. https://clios.com/awards/winner/public-relations/felgtb/the-hidden-flag-73604.

Cohen, Cathy. 1997. 'Punks, Bulldaggers, and Welfare Queens: The Radical Potential of Queer Politics.' *GLQ: A Journal of Lesbian and Gay Studies* 3: 437–465.

Cohen, Cathy. 1999. *The Boundaries of Blackness: AIDS and the Breakdown of Black Politics.* University of Chicago Press.

Cohen, Cathy. 2004. 'Deviance as Resistance: A New Research Agenda for the Study of Black Politics.' *Du Bois Review* 1 (1): 27–45.

Cohen, Cathy. 2023. '#DoBlackLivesMatter? From Michael Brown to CeCe McDonald: On Black Death and LGBTQ Politics.' In *Queer Then and Now: The David R. Kessler Lectures 2002–2020*, edited by Debanuj Dasgupta, Joseph Donica and Margot Weiss, 235–254. New York City: The Feminist Press at the City University of New York.

Connell, Raewyn. 1995. *Masculinities.* Cambridge: Polity.

Conradt, Stacey. 2017. 'How the Rainbow Became Associated with Gay Rights.' *Mental Floss*, 2017, History. http://mentalfloss.com/article/28442/how-rainbow-became-associated-gay-rights.

Cooper, Julian. 2021. *Russia's Updated National Security Strategy.* NATO Defense College. https://www.ndc.nato.int/research/research.php?icode=704.

Cooper-Cunningham, Dean. 2019. 'Seeing (In)Security, Gender and Silencing: Posters in and about the British Women's Suffrage Movement.' *International Feminist Journal of Politics* 21 (3): 383–408.

Cooper-Cunningham, Dean. 2020a. 'Drawing Fear of Difference: Race, Gender, and National Identity in Ms. Marvel Comics.' *Millennium: Journal of International Studies* 48 (2): 165–197.

Cooper-Cunningham, Dean. 2020b. 'Visual Methods and International Security Studies.' *E-International Relations.* https://www.e-ir.info/2020/06/12/visual-methods-and-international-security-studies/.

Cooper-Cunningham, Dean. 2022. 'Security, Sexuality, and the Gay Clown Putin Meme: The Queer Politics of Play in International Responses to Russian State-Directed Homophobia.' *Security Dialogue* 53 (4): 302–323.

Cooper-Cunningham, Dean. 2024. 'The Visual As Queer Method.' In *Queer Conflict Research: New Approaches to the Study of Political Violence*, edited by Jamie Hagen, Samuel Ritholtz and Andrew Delatolla, 83–106. Bristol University Press.

Cooper-Cunningham, Dean. 2025. 'Discourse.' In *Thinking World Politics Otherwise*, edited by Rhys Crilley, Stefanie Fischel, Nivi Manchanda, Laura J. Shepherd and C. Wilkinson, 29–43. Oxford University Press.

Cooper-Cunningham, Dean, and Detmer Kremer. 2024. *Queering Atrocity Prevention: Europe in Focus.* London: Protection Approaches.

Cottet, Caroline, and Manuela Picq, eds. 2019. *Sexuality and Translation in World Politics.* Bristol: E-IR Publishing.

Council of Europe Commissioner for Human Rights. 2021. 'Pride vs. Indignity: Political Manipulation of Homophobia and Transphobia in Europe.' *Council of Europe Commissioner for Human Rights Blog* (blog), *Council of Europe.* October 22, 2024. https://www.coe.int/en/web/commissioner/blog/2021/-/asset_publisher/aa3hyyf8wKBn/content/pride-vs-indignity-political-manipulation-of-homophobia-and-transphobia-in-europe.

Council of the European Union. 2010. Toolkit to promote and protect the enjoyment of all human rights by lesbian, gay, bisexual, and transgender people. Brussels: European Union.

Council of the European Union. 2013. Guidelines to promote and protect the enjoyment of all human rights by lesbian, gay, bisexual, transgender and intersex (LGBTI) Persons. Brussels: European Union.

Council of the European Union. 2014a. Draft EU Annual Report on Human Rights and Democracy in the World in 2014. Brussels: European Union.

Council of the European Union. 2014b. Main aspects and basic choices of the CFSP – Draft Annual report from the High Representative of the European Union for Foreign Affairs and Security Policy to the European Parliament. Brussels: European Union.

Council of the European Union. 2015. Draft Annual report from the High Representative of the European Union for Foreign Affairs and Security Policy to the European Parliament 2014. Brussels.

Crenshaw, Kimberlé. 2019. 'Stonewall 50: Whose Movement Is It Anyway?,' June 28, 2019, in *Intersectionality Matters*, produced by Julia Sharpe Levine, 1:01.27.

Cresci, Elena. 2017. 'Russia Bans Picture of Vladimir Putin in Drag.' The *Guardian*, 2017. https://www.theguardian.com/world/2017/apr/06/russia-bans-picture-of-vladimir-putin-in-drag.

Crocker, Bathsheba Nell. 2022. U.S. letter to the U.N. alleging Russia is planning human rights abuses in Ukraine. US State Department: Washington Post.

Crone, Manni. 2020. 'It's a Man's World: Carnal Spectatorship and Dissonant Masculinities in Islamic State Videos.' *International Affairs* 93 (3): 573–591.

Currier, Ashley. 2019. *Politicizing Sex in Contemporary Africa*. Cambridge: Cambridge University Press.

Daggett, Cara. 2015. 'Drone Disorientations.' *International Feminist Journal of Politics* 17 (3): 361–379.

Dauphinee, Elizabeth. 2007. 'The Politics of the Body in Pain: Reading the Ethics of Imagery.' *Security Dialogue* 38 (2): 139–155.

Dauphinee, Elizabeth. 2018. 'Body.' edited by Roland Bleiker. New York: Routledge.

De Piero, Gloria. 2014. 'Britain Must Make Clear That It Totally Opposes Russia's Treatment of LGBT People.' *The Independent*, January 31.

Dearden, Lizzie. 2017a. 'Reporter Who Exposed Chechen Abuse of Gay Men Goes Into Hiding.' *The Independent*, April 27.

Dearden, Lizzie. 2017b. 'Russia Backs Chechnya Government's Denials Over Killing and Torture of Gay Men.' *The Independent*, April 20.

DeGenaro, William. 2013. Rainbow Flag. In *Encyclopedia of Gay Histories and Cultures*, edited by George Haggerty, 733–734. New York: Routledge.

Delatolla, Andrew. 2020. 'Sexuality as a Standard of Civilization: Historicizing (Homo)Colonial Intersections of Race, Gender, and Class.' *International Studies Quarterly* 64 (1): 148–158.

Denham, Jess. 2013. 'Elton John's Russian Tour at Risk of Cancellation Over Anti-Gay Laws.' *The Independent*, December 3.

Denisova, Anastasia. 2019. *Internet Memes and Society: Social, Cultural, and Political Contexts.* New York: Routledge.

Derrida, Jacques. 2009. *Writing and Difference.* Translated by Alan Bass. London: Routledge.

Derrida, Jacques. 2016. *Of Grammatology.* Translated by Gayatri Chakravorty Spivak. Baltimore: Johns Hopkins University Press. 1967.

Dittmer, Jason. 2005. 'Captain America's Empire: Reflections on Identity, Popular Culture, and Post-9/11 Geopolitics.' *Annals of the Association of American Geographers* 95 (3): 626–643.

DIVA TV. 1989. 'Pride 69 - 89 (VHS #01066).' 00:26:30 New York: DIVA TV. VHS.

Dodds, Klaus. 2007. 'Steve Bell's Eye: Cartoons, Geopolitics and the Visualisation of the 'War on Terror'.' *Security Dialogue* 38 (2): 157–177.

Dorfman, Tommy. 2019. 'Tommy Dorfman on Marching for Those Who Still Cannot, 50 Years After Stonewall.' *Vogue.* https://www.vogue.co.uk/article/queer-liberation-march-stonewall-50-new-york-tommy-dorfman.

Doty, Roxanne Lynn. 1993. 'Foreign Policy as Social Construction: A Post-Positivist Analysis of U.S. Counterinsurgency Policy in the Philippines.' *International Studies Quarterly* 37 (3): 297–320.

Doty, Roxanne Lynn. 1996. *Imperial Encounters: The Politics of Representation in North-South Relations.* Minneapolis: University of Minnesota Press.

Düben, Björn A. 2020. "There is no Ukraine': Fact-Checking the Kremlin's Version of Ukrainian History.' *LSE Blogs* (blog). July 1. https://blogs.lse.ac.uk/lseih/2020/07/01/there-is-no-ukraine-fact-checking-the-kremlins-version-of-ukrainian-history/.

Duggan, Lisa. 2002. 'The New Homonormativity: The Sexual Politics of Neoliberalism.' In *Materializing Democracy: Toward a Revitalized Cultural Politics*, edited by Russ Castronovo and Dana Nelson, 175–194. Durham: Duke University Press.

Duncombe, Constance. 2019. 'The Politics of Twitter: Emotions and the Power of Social Media.' *International Political Sociology* 13 (4): 409–429.

Duncombe, Constance. 2020. 'Social Media and the Visibility of Horrific Violence.' *International Affairs* 96 (3): 609–629.

Duncombe, Constance. 2024. 'See, Touch, Feel: Theorizing Twitter/X Images for Diplomacy.' *Millennium* 53 (1): 191–221.

Dykes Against Racism Everywhere. 1982. 21 May 1982.

Edelman, Lee. 2004. *No Future: Queer Theory and the Death Drive.* Duke University Press.

Edenborg, Emil. 2017. *Politics of Visibility and Belonging: From Russia's 'Homosexual Propaganda' Laws to the Ukraine War. Interventions.* London: Routledge.

Edenborg, Emil. 2019. 'Theorizing Visibility in Global Queer Politics.' In *The Oxford Handbook of Global LGBT and Sexual Diversity Politics*, edited by Michael Bosia, Sandra McEvoy and Momin Rahman, 349–364. Oxford University Press.

Edenborg, Emil. 2020. 'Russia's Spectacle of "Traditional Values": Rethinking the Politics of Visibility.' *International Feminist Journal of Politics* 22 (1): 106–126.

Edenborg, Emil. 2022. 'Putin's Anti-Gay War on Ukraine.' *Boston Review*, March 14.

Eder, Florian. 2021. 'POLITICO Brussels Playbook: Rainbow Wars—Divorce-Aversary—Tough Tusk.' *Politico*, June 23.

Edkins, Jenny. 1999. *Poststructuralism and International Relations*. Boulder: Lynne Rienner.

Edkins, Jenny, and Veronique Pin-Fat. 2005. 'Through the Wire: Relations of Power and Relations of Violence.' *Millennium Journal of International Studies* 34 (1): 1–24.

Eggeling, Kristin A. 2020. *Nation-Branding in Practice: The Politics of Promoting Sports, Cities and Universities in Kazakhstan and Qatar*. Routledge.

Elder, Charles, and Roger Cobb. 1983. *The Political Uses of Symbols*. New York: Longman.

Elliott, Stuart. 2014. 'Activists Try to Hijack Promotions by Sponsors of Sochi Olympics.' *The New York Times*, January 28.

Eng, David L., Judith Halberstam, and Muñoz Esteban. 2005. 'What's Queer About Queer Studies Now?' *Social Text* 23 (3–4): 1–18.

Enloe, Cynthia. 1989. *Bananas, Beaches and Bases: Making Feminist Sense of International Politics*. 1 ed. London: University of California Press.

Epstein, Jennifer. 2013. 'For Sochi: Diversity, Not Diplomacy.' *Politico*, December 17.

Essig, Laurie. 1999. *Queer in Russia*. Durham: Duke University Press.

Essig, Laurie. 2013. 'How Russia's Science of Sex Threatens Gays.' *Washington Post*, August 9. https://www.washingtonpost.com/opinions/how-russias-science-of-sex-threatens-gays/2013/08/09/b1a21128-fedf-11e2-96a8-d3b921c0924a_story.html.

European Court of Human Rights. 2011a. Case of Alekseyev v. Russia. European Court of Human Rights. Strasbourg.

European Court of Human Rights. 2011b. Case of Alekseyev v. Russia. Strasbourg.

European Court of Human Rights. 2018. Case of Alekseyev and Others v. Russia. Strasbourg.

European Court of Human Rights. 2023a. Case of Lapunov v. Russia. Strasbourg.

European Court of Human Rights. 2023b. Case of Romanov and Others v. Russia. Strasbourg.

European Parliament. 2012a. European Parliament plenary meeting of 22 May 2012: Fight against homophobia in Europe.

European Parliament. 2012b. European Parliament resolution of 9 June 2011 on the EU-Russia summit. Brussels: European Union.

European Parliament. 2012c. European Parliament resolution of 18 April 2012 on the Annual Report on Human Rights in the World and the European Union's policy on the matter, including implications for the EU's strategic human rights policy. Brussels: European Union.

European Parliament. 2013a. European Parliament resolution of 13 September 2012 on the political use of justice in Russia (2012/2789(RSP)). Brussels: European Union.

European Parliament. 2013b. European Parliament resolution of 24 October 2013 on the Annual Report from the Council to the European Parliament on the Common Foreign and Security Policy (2013/2081(INI)). Brussels: European Union.

European Parliament. 2013c. Written questions by Members of the European Parliament and their answers given by a European Union institution (C361 E/1). Brussels: European Union.

European Union. 2013. Written questions by Members of the European Parliament and their answers given by a European Union institution. In *OJ C361E*.

Faye, Shon. 2022. *The Transgender Issue: An Argument for Justice*. Penguin Books.

Featherstone, Mike. 2006. 'Archive.' *Theory, Culture & Society* 23 (2–3): 591–596.

Federación Estatal de Lesbianas, Gais, Trans y Bisexuales. 2018. 'The Hidden Flag | 6 Activistas Cuelan La Bandera Arcoíris En Rusia' YouTube. https://youtu.be/M8Or-SfzGJY.

Ferhani, Adam, and Jonna Nyman. 2023. 'What Does Security Look Like? Exploring Interpretive Photography as Method.' *European Journal of International Security* 8 (3): 354–376.

Fierke, Karin M. 2013. *Political Self-sacrifice: Agency, Body and Emotion in International Relations*. Cambridge: Cambridge University Press.

Fierstein, Harvey. 2013. 'Russia's Anti-Gay Crackdown.' *The New York Times*, July 21, Accessed January 31, 2018. https://www.nytimes.com/2013/07/22/opinion/russias-anti-gay-crackdown.html.

Finkelstein, Avram. 2018. *After Silence: A History of AIDS Through Its Images*. California: University of California Press.

Flood, Alison, and Shaun Walker. 2014. 'World Authors Join Protest Against Putin: Anti-Gay and Blasphemy Laws Threaten Freedom, Russia Told On Eve of Games.' *The Guardian*, February 6.

Foucault, Michel. 1972. *The Archaeology of Knowledge and Discourse on Language*. New York: Pantheon Books.

Foucault, Michel. 1977. *Discipline and Punish: The Birth of the Prison*. Translated by Alan Sheridan. New York: Vintage Books.

Foucault, Michel. 1978. *The History of Sexuality, Vol. 1: An Introduction*. Translated by Robert Hurley. New York: Pantheon.

Foucault, Michel. 1980. *Power/Knowledge*. Translated by Colin Gordon, Leo Marshall, John Mepham and Kate Soper, edited by Colin Gordon.

Foucault, Michel. 1984. *The Foucault Reader*, edited by Paul Rabinow. New York: Pantheon Books.

Foxall, Andrew. 2013. 'Photographing Vladimir Putin: Masculinity, Nationalism and Visuality in Russian Political Culture.' *Geopolitics* 18 (1): 132–156.

Foxall, Andrew. 2019. 'From Evropa to Gayropa: A Critical Geopolitics of the European Union as Seen from Russia.' *Geopolitics* 24 (1): 174–193.

France, David. 2012. How to Survive a Plague.

France, David. 2016. *How to Survive a Plague*. London: Picador.

Fraser, Nancy. 1990. 'Rethinking the Public Sphere: A Contribution to the Critique of Actually Existing Democracy.' *Social Text* (25/26): 56–80.

Friis, Simone Molin. 2018. 'Virtual Violence: Militant Imagery, Online Communication, and the Islamic State.' Ph.D. Dissertation, University of Copenhagen.

Fry, Stephen. 2013. 'An Open Letter to David Cameron and the IOC.' Last Modified August 7, 2013. Accessed July 29, 2019. http://www.stephenfry.com/2013/08/an-open-letter-to-david-cameron-and-the-ioc/.

Gal, Noam, Limor Shifman, and Zohar Kampf. 2016. '"It Gets Better": Internet Memes and the Construction of Collective Identity.' *New Media & Society* 18 (8): 1698–1714.

Galtung, Johan. 1969. 'Violence, Peace, and Peace Research.' *Journal of Peace Research* 6 (3): 167–191.

Gaufman, Elizaveta. 2017. *Security Threats and Public Perception*. Cham: Springer.

Gentry, Caron. 2020. *Disordered Violence*. Edinburgh: Edinburgh University Press.

Gentry, Caron, and Laura Sjoberg. 2015 [with Sjoberg]; 2020. *Beyond Mothers, Monsters, Whores: Thinking About Women's Violence in Global Politics*. London: Zed Books.

Gessen, Masha, and Joseph Huff-Hannon. 2014. *Gay Propaganda: Russian Love Stories*, edited by Masha Gessen and Joseph Huff-Hannon. New York: OR Books.

Gibson, Owen. 2013a. 'FIFA Urged to Pressure Russia and Qatar Over Anti-Gay Legislation.' *The Guardian*, September 8.

Gibson, Owen. 2013b. 'Olympic Rules for Protesting Against Russia's Anti-Gay Laws Clarified.' *The Guardian*, December 18. https://www.theguardian.com/sport/2013/dec/18/ioc-sochi-protest-rules-anti-gay-winter-olympics.

Gibson, Owen. 2013c. 'Sochi 2014: The Costliest Olympics Yet But Where Has All the Money Gone?' *The Guardian*, October 9.

Gibson, Owen. 2014. 'Fifty-Two Olympians Urge Russia to Repeal 'Gay Propaganda' Law.' *The Guardian*, January 30.

Gifkins, Jess, and Dean Cooper-Cunningham. 2023. 'Queering the Responsibility to Protect.' *International Affairs* 99 (5): 2057–2078.

Gifkins, Jess, Dean Cooper-Cunningham, Kate Ferguson, Detmer Kremer, and Farida Mostafa. 2022. *Queering Atrocity Prevention*. Protection Approaches (London: Protection Approaches). https://protectionapproaches.org/queeringap.

Glassner, Susan. 2012. 'Letter from the Editor.' *Foreign Policy* 193 (3): 3.

Goldstein, Nancy. 2013a. 'Appointing Billie Jean King to the US Sochi Olympics Delegation Isn't Enough.' *The Guardian*, December 18.

Goldstein, Nancy. 2013b. 'Kudos to the Nobel Peace Prize Winner, But It's Another Snub for LGBT Activists.' *The Guardian*, October 11. https://www.theguardian.com/commentisfree/2013/oct/11/nobel-peace-prize-lgbt-rights.

Goldstein, Nancy. 2013c. 'Shame on the IOC, NBC and Foreign Governments for Turning a Blind Eye on Russia's LGBT Hate Campaign.' *The Guardian*, July 29.

Goldstein, Nancy. 2013d. 'Wentworth Miller's message for the Olympics on Russia's Anti-Gay Law.' *The Guardian*, August 23.

Goode, Erich, and Nachman Ben-Yehuda. 1994. 'Moral Panics: Culture, Politics, and Social Construction.' *Annual Review of Sociology* 20: 149–171.

Gould, Deborah. 2009. *Moving Politics: Emotion and ACT UP's Fight Against AIDS*. Chicago: University of Chicago Press.

Guenter, Scot. 1994. 'A Note From the President... Scot Guenter.' *North American Vexillological Association* XXVII (4): 1–10.

Guillaume, Xavier., Rune S. Andersen, and Juha A. Vuori. 2016. 'Paint It Black: Colours and the Social Meaning of the Battlefield.' *European Journal of International Relations* 22 (1): 49–71.

Gursel, Zeynep Devrim. 2016. *Image Brokers: Visualizing World News in the Age of Digital Circulation*. University of California Press.

Hagen, Jamie. 2016. 'Queering Women, Peace and Security.' *International Affairs* 92 (2): 313–332.

Hagen, Jamie, Samuel Ritholtz, and Andrew Delatolla, eds. 2024. *Queer Conflict Research: New Approaches to the Study of Political Violence*: Bristol University Press.

Hall, Lucy. 2021. 'Logics of Gender, Peace, and Security: Theorizing Gender and Protection at the Intersections of State and Civil Society.' *Global Studies Quarterly* 1 (3): 1–14.

Hall, Stuart. 1982. 'The Rediscovery of 'Ideology': Return of the Repressed in Media Studies.' In *Culture, Society and the Media*, edited by M. Gurevitch, T. Bennett, J. Curran and J. Woollacott, 56–90. London: Routledge.

Halperin, David. 1995. *Saint Foucault: Towards a Gay Hagiography*. Oxford University Press.

Hamilton, Caitlin. 2016. 'The Everyday Artefacts of World Politics: Why Graphic Novels, Textiles and Internet Memes Matter in World Politics.' PhD diss., University of New South Wales.

Hansen, Lene. 2000a. 'Gender, Nation, Rape: Bosnia and the Construction of Security.' *International Feminist Journal of Politics* 3 (1): 55–75.

Hansen, Lene. 2000b. 'The Little Mermaid's Silent Security Dilemma and the Absence of Gender in the Copenhagen School.' *Millennium Journal of International Studies* 29 (2): 285–306.

Hansen, Lene. 2006. *Security as Practice: Discourse Analysis and the Bosnian War*. New York: Routledge.

Hansen, Lene. 2011. 'Theorizing the Image for Security Studies: Visual Securitization and the Muhammad Cartoon Crisis.' *European Journal of International Relations* 17 (1): 51–74.

Hansen, Lene. 2015. 'How Images Make World Politics: International Icons and the Case of Abu Ghraib.' *Review of International Studies* 41 (2): 263–288.

Hansen, Lene. 2017. 'Reading Comics for the Field of International Relations: Theory, Method and the Bosnian War.' *European Journal of International Relations* 3 (23): 581–608.

Hansen, Lene. 2018. 'Reconstructing the Silence-Speech Dichotomy in Feminist Security Studies: Gender, Agency and the Politics of Subjectivity in La Frontière Invisible.' In *Reconsidering Gender, Silence and Agency in Contested Terrains*, edited by Swati Parashar and Jane Parpart, 27–49. London: Routledge.

Hansen, Lene. Forthcoming. *Images and International Security*. Cambridge University Press.

Hansen, Lene, Rebecca Adler-Nissen, and Katrine Emilie Andersen. 2021. 'The Visual International Politics of the European Refugee Crisis: Tragedy, Humanitarianism, Borders.' *Cooperation and Conflict* 56 (4): 367–393.

Hansen, Lene, and Johan Spanner. 2021. 'National and Post-National Performances at the Venice Biennale: Site-Specific Seeing Through the Photo Essay.' *Millennium: Journal of International Studies* 49 (2): 305–336.

Harding, Luke, and Francesca Ebel. 2013. 'Dancing on Thin Ice: How Putin Pulled Off Olympic Masterstroke.' *The Guardian*, December 19.

Hariman, Robert, and John L. Lucaites. 2007. *No Caption Needed: Iconic Photographs, Public Culture, and Liberal Democracy*. Chicago: University of Chicago Press.

Haritaworn, Jin, Tamsila Tauqir, and Esra Erdem. 2008. 'Gay Imperialism Gender and Sexuality Discourse in the 'War on Terror.'' In *Out of Place: Interrogating Silences in Queerness/Raciality*, edited by Adi Kuntsman and Esperanza Miyake, 71–95. Raw Nerve Books.

Harman, Sophie. 2019. *Seeing Politics: Film, Visual Method, and International Relations*. Qeuebec: McGill-Queen's University Press.

Healey, Dan. 2018. *Russian Homophobia from Stalin to Sochi*. 1st ed. New York: Bloomsbury Academic.

Heck, Axel, and Gabi Schlag. 2013. 'Securitizing Images: The Female Body and the War in Afghanistan.' *European Journal of International Relations* 19 (4): 891–913.

Heger, Heinz. 1980. *The Men with the Pink Triangle*. London: Gay Mans Press.

Heimer, Rosa dos Ventos Lopes. 2019. 'Homonationalist/Orientalist Negotiations: The UK Approach to Queer Asylum Claims.' *Sexuality & Culture* 24: 174–196.

Hellman, Gunther, and Benjamin Herborth, eds. 2017. *Uses of 'the West': Security and the Politics of Order*: Cambridge University Press.

Hensher, Philip. 2013. 'Concerned About Gay Rights at the Sochi Winter Olympics? Just Get Boycotting.' *The Independent*, August 11.

Herman, Edward, and Noam Chomsky. 1988. *Manufacturing Consent: The Political Economy of the Mass Media*. New York: Pantheon Books.

Herszenhorn, David. 2013. 'Gays in Russia Find No Haven, Despite Support From the West.' *New York Times*, August 12.

Hidden Flag. 2018. 'Hidden Flag.' Accessed June 28, 2019. http://thehiddenflag.org.

Hoad, Neville. 2000. 'Arrested Development or the Queerness of Savages: Resisting Evolutionary Narratives of Difference.' *Postcolonial Studies* 3 (2): 133–158.

Holm, Minda. 2020. 'What Liberalism? Russia's Conservative Turn and the Liberal Order.' In *Geopolitical Amnesia: The Rise of the Right and the Crisis of Liberal Memory*, edited by Vibeke Schou Tjalve, 82–100. McGill-Queen's University Press.

Holm, Minda, and Vibeke Schou Tjalve. 2018. *Visions of an Illiberal World Order?* NUPI.

Hoyle, Ben. 2013. 'I'm Afraid I Will Meet With Violence, Says Russian Who Staged Solo Gay Protest.' *The Times*, August 14.

Hoyle, Ben. 2014a. 'Bribe-Free and Gay-Friendly: Russian Leader Lays Out His Version of the Sochi Olympics.' *The Guardian*, January 20.

Hoyle, Ben. 2014b. 'I Have Nothing Against Gays - I'd Be Happy to Meet Elton, Says Putin.' *The Times*, January 20.

Hughes, David. 2013. 'David Cameron Rejects Stephen Fry's Call for Russian Winter Olympics Boycott.' *The Telegraph*, August 10. https://www.telegraph.co.uk/news/politics/david-cameron/10235001/David-Cameron-rejects-Stephen-Frys-call-for-Russian-Winter-Olympics-boycott.html.

Human Rights Council, 2019, 'Joint Statement Item 8 General Debate on LGBTI Persons in Chechnya,' March 18, 2019, https://www.gov.uk/government/news/human-rights-council-40-joint-statement-item-8-general-debate-on-lgbti-persons-in-chechnya.

Human Rights Watch. 2014. *License To Harm: Violence and Harassment Against LGBT People and Activists in Russia*. Human Rights Watch (USA).

Human Rights Watch. 2018a. *No Support: Russia's 'Gay Propaganda' Law Imperils LGBT Youth*. Human Rights Watch, December 11, 2018. https://www.hrw.org/report/2018/12/11/no-support/russias-gay-propaganda-law-imperils-lgbt-youth#.

Human Rights Watch. 2018b. *World Report 2018: Rights Trends in Russia*. Human Rights Watch (Geneva). 2018. https://www.hrw.org/world-report/2018/country-chapters/russia.

Human Rights Watch. 2019. *Russia: New Anti-Gay Crackdown in Chechnya*. https://www.hrw.org/news/2019/05/08/russia-new-anti-gay-crackdown-chechnya.

Hunt, Ruth. 2014. 'As the Olympic Flame Is Extinguished in Sochi, Homophobia is Still Burning Bright.' *The Independent*, February 23.

ILGA. 2013. *Annual Review of the Human Rights Situation of Lesbian, Gay, Bisexual, Trans and Intersex People*. ILGA Europe (Belgium).

ILGA. 2016. *State Sponsored Homophobia: A World Survey on Sexual Orientation Laws: Criminalisation, Protection and Recognition*. International Lesbian, Gay, Bisexual, Trans and Intersex Association (ILGA) (Geneva).

ILGA. 2017. *State Sponsored Homophobia: A World Survey on Sexual Orientation Laws: Criminalisation, Protection and Recognition*. International Lesbian, Gay, Bisexual, Trans and Intersex Association (ILGA) (Geneva).

ILGA. 2019. *A New Wave of Persecutions Against LGBT People Reported in Chechnya*. ILGA Europe. January 16, 2019 https://www.ilga-europe.org/resources/news/latest-news/new-wave-persecutions-against-lgbt-people-reported-chechnya.

Ingle, Sean. 2013. 'Winter Olympics' Openly Gay Athlete: I Want Vladimir Putin to Get to Know Me.' *The Guardian*, November 20.

Jackson, Sarah J, and Daniel Kreiss. 2023. 'Recentering Power: Conceptualizing Counterpublics and Defensive Publics.' *Communication Theory* 33 (2–3): 102–111.

Jacobs, Eric Stephen. 1970. Contact sheet 6.

Jagose, Annemarie. 1996. *Queer Theory: An Introduction*. New York: NYU Press.

Jagose, Annamarie, and Donald Hall, eds. 2013. *The Routledge Queer Studies Reader*. London: Routledge.

Jensen, Erik N. 2002. 'The Pink Triangle and Political Consciousness: Gays, Lesbians, and the Memory of Nazi Persecution.' *Journal of the History of Sexuality* 11 (1–2): 319–349.

John, Elton. 2013. 'Elton John: Why I Performed in Russia.' *The Guardian*, December 11.

Kaczorowski, Craig. 2015. 'Paragraph 175.' GLBTQ. Accessed March 12, 2020. http://www.glbtqarchive.com/ssh/paragraph_175_S.pdf.

Karavas, George. 2020. 'How images frame China's role in African development.' *International Affairs* 96 (3): 667–690.

Kangas, Anni, Daria Krivonos, Inna Perheentupa, and Sara Särmä. 2019. 'Smashing Containers, Queering the International Through Collaging.' *International Feminist Journal of Politics* 21 (3): 355–382.

Keeley, James. 1990. 'Toward a Foucauldian Analysis of International Regimes.' *International Organization* 44 (1): 83–105.

Keller, Bill. 2013. 'Russia vs. Europe.' *The New York Times*, December 16.

Kelner, Martha. 2017. 'Gay Fans Warned Holding Hands at Russia World Cup Will Be Dangerous.' *The Guardian*, November 28.

Kennedy, Liam. 2008. 'Securing Vision: Photography and US Foreign Policy.' *Media, Culture & Society* 30 (3): 279–294.

Klein, Alan, and Erika Freiberger, 1994a, 'Giant Mile-Long Rainbow Flag to be Unfurled Along 5th Avenue, Raise Half a Million Dollars for AIDS,' March 28, 1994, http://alankleincommunications.com/media_campaigns/raise_the_rainbow/.

Klein, Alan, and Erika Freiberger, 1994b, 'Record-Breaking Mile-Long Flag for AID S to Lead Stonewall 25 March for Lesbian and Gay Human Rights at Uni ted Nations,' June 24, 1994, http://alankleincommunications.com/media_campaign s/raise_the_rainbow/raise_the_rainbow_media_adv.html.

Kopan, Tal. 2013a. 'Boxer to Putin: Repeal Anti-Gay Laws.' *Politico*, August 23.

Kopan, Tal. 2013b. 'Merkley Bill Targets Russia LGBT Law.' *Politico*, August 2. https://www.politico.com/story/2013/08/jeff-merkley-bill-calls-out-russia-lgbt-laws-095106.

Kramer, Andrew E. 2013. 'Russia Passes Bill Targeting Some Discussions of Homosexuality.' *New York Times*, June 11. https://www.nytimes.com/2013/06/12/world/euro pe/russia-passes-bill-targeting-some-discussions-of-homosexuality.html.

Kramer, Andrew E. 2017a. 'Chechnya's Anti-Gay Pogrom: "They Starve You. They Shock You".' *The New York Times*, April 23.

Kramer, Andrew E. 2017b. 'Gay Men in Chechnya Are Killed, Paper Says.' *The New York Times*, April 2.

Kramer, Andrew E. 2017c. 'Gay Rights Protesters Are Detained in Russia.' *The New York Times*, May 2.

Kramer, Andrew E. 2017d. 'Reporting on Gays Who 'Don't Exist'.' *The New York Times*, April 23.

Kulpa, Robert. 2014. 'Western Leveraged Pedagogy of Central and Eastern Europe: Discourses of Homophobia, Tolerance, and Nationhood.' *Gender, Place & Culture: A Journal of Feminist Geography* 21 (4): 431–448.

Kurowska, Xymena, and Anatoly Reshetnikov. 2021. 'Trickstery: Pluralising Stigma in International Society.' *European Journal of International Relations* 27 (1): 232–257.

KyivPride. 2020. '#Мамазрозумієтапідтримає.' Facebook, June 21.

Laclau, Ernesto, and Chantal Mouffe. 1985. *Hegemony and Socialist Strategy: Towards a Radical Democratic Politics.* London: Verso.

Lally, Kathy. 2013. 'IOC: No Grounds to Challenge Russian Anti-Gay Law as Sochi Olympic Games Approach.' *Washington Post*, September 26. https://www.washington

post.com/world/europe/ioc-backs-off-on-russian-anti-gay-law/2013/09/26/38b392
66-269c-11e3-9372-92606241ae9c_story.html.

Lang, Nico. 2020. 'LGBTQ+ Group Uses Drone to Fly Rainbow Flag Over Ukraine's Statue of Liberty.' *them.*, June 23.

Langlois, Anthony. 2014. 'Human Rights, "Orientation," and ASEAN.' *Journal of Human Rights* 13 (3): 307–321.

Law, John, and John Urry. 2004. 'Enacting the Social.' *Economy and Society* 33 (3): 390–410.

Lazarus, Latoya. 2011. 'Heteronationalism, Human Rights, and the Nation-State.' *Canadian Journal of Latin American and Carribean Studies* 36 (71): 71–108.

Leigh, Darcy. 2017. 'Queer Feminist International Relations: Uneasy Alliances, Productive Tensions.' *Alternatif Politika* 9 (3): 343–360.

Leigh, Darcy, and Cynthia Weber. 2019. 'Gendered and Sexualized Figurations of Security.' In *Routledge Handbook of Gender and Security*, edited by Caron Gentry, Laura Shepherd and Laura Sjoberg, 83–93. Oxon: Routledge.

LGBTI Intergroup (LGBTIintergroup). 2018. '6 Activists Have Found a Creative Way to Bring the Rainbow Flag to Russia.' Twitter, July 9.

Lisle, Debbie. 2007. 'Benevolent Patriotism: Art, Dissent and The American Effect.' *Security Dialogue* 38 (2): 233–250.

Lisle, Debbie, and Heather Johnson. 2019. 'Lost in the Aftermath.' *Security Dialogue* 50 (1): 20–39.

Little Black Book. 2021. 'How Drones and a Rainbow Flag Turned a Communist Statue into a Symbol of Equality.' Accessed August 16, 2021. https://www.lbbonline.com/news/how-drones-and-a-rainbow-flag-turned-a-communist-statue-into-a-symbol-of-equality.

Loken, Meredith. 2021. 'Using Images as Data in Political Violence Research.' *Journal of Human Rights* 20 (3): 373–379.

Longman, Jeré. 2013. 'Outrage Over an Antigay Law Does Not Spread to Olympic Officials.' *The New York Times*, August 6.

MacFarquhar, Neil. 2018. 'Putin Has a Chance to Woo the World. Thank Soccer, and Trump.' *The New York Times*, June 13.

MacFarquhar, Neil, and Alison Smale. 2017. 'Merkel Presses Putin on Treatment of Gays and Jehovah's Witnesses.' *The New York Times*, May 3.

MacKenzie, Megan. 2020. 'Why Do Soldiers Swap Illicit Pictures? How a Visual Discourse Analysis Illuminates Military Band of Brother Culture.' *Security Dialogue* 50 (4): 340–357.

Mälksoo, Maria. 2023. 'The Postcolonial Moment in Russia's War Against Ukraine.' *Journal of Genocide Research* 25 (3–4): 471–481.

Malmvig, Helle. 2016. 'Eyes Wide Shut: Power and Creative Visual Counter- Conducts in the Battle for Syria, 2011–2014.' *Global Society* 30 (2): 258–278.

Marcus, Eric, 2016 '1. Sylvia Rivera Part 2,' in *Making Gay History: LGBTQ Oral Histories from the Archive*, produced by Sara Burningham, 13.00.00.

Marcus, Eric, 2019 'Prelude to a Riot,' in *Making Gay History: LGBTQ Oral Histories from the Archive*, produced by Sara Burningham, 37.00.00.

Martínez, Héctor Llanos. 2018. 'Imaginación Al Poder: Seis Activistas LGTBI+ Cuelan La Bandera Arcoíris Durante El Mundial De Rusia.' *El País*, July 7. https://verne.elpais.com/verne/2018/07/07/articulo/1530983069_031708.html.

Massad, Joseph. 2007. *Desiring Arabs*. Chicago: Chicago University Press.

Mbembe, Achille. 2003. 'Necropolitics.' *Public Culture* 15 (1): 11–40.

McAdam, Doug. 1994. 'Culture and Social Movements.' In *New Social Movements: From Ideology to Identity*, edited by Enrique Laraña, Hank Johnston and Joseph Gusfield, 36–57. Philadelphia: Temple University Press.

McCallum, Shiona. 2018. 'World Cup 2018: Smuggling the Pride Flag Into Russia.' *BBC*, July 10. https://www.bbc.com/news/newsbeat-44765661.

McGarry, Aidan, Itir Erhart, Hande Eslen-Ziya, Olu Jenzen, and Umut Korkut, eds. 2020. *Aesthetics of Global Protest*. Amsterdam: Amsterdam University Press.

McIntosh, Mary. 1968. 'The Homosexual Role.' *Social Problems* 16 (2): 182–192.

Mégret, Frédéric. 2013. 'Practices og Stigmatization.' *Law & Contemporary Problems* 76 (3&4): 287–318.

Meier, Henk Erik, Michael Mutz, Julia Glathe, Malte Jetzke, and Martin Hölzen. 2021. 'Politicization of a Contested Mega Event: The 2018 FIFA World Cup on Twitter.' *Communication & Sport* 9 (5): 785–910.

Michaels, Sean. 2013. 'Elton John Will Perform in Russia Despite Homophobic Protests.' *The Guardian*, Sept 26.

Michaels, Sean. 2014. 'Elton John Condemns Russia's "Vicious" Anti-Gay Legislation.' *The Guardian*, January 23.

Michel, Casey. 2017. 'How Russia Became the Leader of the Global Christian Right.' *Politico*, November 2. https://www.politico.eu/article/how-russia-became-the-leader-of-the-global-christian-right/.

Ministry of Foreign Affairs of the Russian Federation. 2023. The Concept of the Foreign Policy of the Russian Federation.

Ministry of Justice of the Russian Federation. 2021. Экстремистские материалы (Extremist Materials).

Mitchell, William J. T. 1987. *Iconology: Image, Text, Ideology*. Chicago: University of Chicago Press.

Mitchell, William J. T. 1994. *Picture Theory: Essays on Verbal and Visual Representation*. Chicago: University of Chicago Press.

Mitchell, William J. T. 2005. 'There are no visual media.' *Journal of visual culture* 4 (2): 257–266.

Mohn, Tanya. 2017. 'How Gay and Transgender Travelers Can See the World in Safety.' *The New York Times*, January 31.

Møller, Anna Helene Kvist, Rebecca Adler-Nissen, Yevgeniy Golovchenko, and Kristin Anabel Eggeling. 2024. 'The Social Aesthetics of Digital Diplomacy.' *International Political Sociology* 18 (3): 1–26.

Möller, Frank, and David Shim. 2018. 'Visions of Peace in International Relations.' *International Studies Perspectives* 20 (3): 246–264.

Moore, Cerwyn, and Laura Shepherd. 2010. 'Aesthetics and International Relations: Towards a Global Politics.' *Global Society* 24 (3): 299–309.

Moran, Caitlin. 2013. 'Make Sochi the Gayest Olympics Ever.' *The Times*, September 28.

Mouffe, Chantal. 2005. *On the Political*. Abingdon: Routledge.

Mudde, Cas. 2019. *The Far Right Today*. Cambridge: Polity.

Muñoz, José. 1999. *Disidentifications: Queers of Color and the Performative of Politics*. Minneapolis: University of Minnesota Press.

Murphy, Kevin, Daniel Marshall, and Zeb Tortorici. 2014. 'Editors' Introduction: Queering Archives: Historical Unravelings.' *Radical Historical Review* 120: 1–11.

Nagel, Joane. 2003. *Race, Ethnicity, and Sexuality: Intimate Intersections, Forbidden Frontiers*. Oxford University Press.

Nakamura, David. 2013a. 'In Snub to Putin, Obamas and Biden Will Skip Winter Olympics in Russia.' *The Washington Post*, December 18.

Nakamura, David. 2013b. 'Obama Meets With Gay Rights Activists in Russia.' *Washington Post*, September 9. https://www.washingtonpost.com/news/post-politics/wp/2013/09/06/obama-meets-with-gay-rights-activists-in-russia/?utm_term=.6477183f4503.

Nellans, Lily. 2020. 'A Queer(er) Genocide Studies.' *Genocide Studies and Prevention* 14 (3): 48–68.

Neumann, Iver. 2002. 'Returning Practice to the Linguistic Turn: The Case of Diplomacy.' *Millennium: Journal of International Studies* 31 (3): 627–651.

Neumann, Iver. 2017. *Russia and the Idea of Europe*. 2nd ed. New York: Routledge.

Neumann, Iver. 2018. 'Identity.' In *Visual global politics*, edited by Roland Bleiker, 182–188. New York: Routledge.

New York Historical Society, 2019, 'New York Historical Society Commemorates 50th Anniversary of Stonewall,' April 23, 2019, https://www.nyhistory.org/press/releases/new-york-historical-society-commemorates-50th-anniversary-stonewall-uprising-special.

New York Public Library. 2002. AIDS Activist Videotape Collection, 1983–2000.

New York Public Library. 2019. *Love & Resistance: Stonewall 50*. New York: New York Public Library.

Nissen, Mads. 2013/14. LGBT in Russia. Panos Pictures.

Nissen, Mads. 2014. 'Photo Essay: The Dangers of Being Gay in Russia.' *Newsweek*, October 2.

Nunn, Martin, and Martin Foley. 2014. 'Oil and Gas Could Explain Putin's Costly Attempt to Control the Crimea.' *The Independent*, March 14.

Nyman, Jonna. 2021. 'The Everyday Life of Security: Capturing Space, Practice, and Affect.' *International Political Sociology* 15 (3): 313–337.

OHCHR. 2012. 'Best Practice' of Using the Concept of 'Traditional Values' in Russia. Office of the United Nations High Commissioner for Human Rights.

OHCHR. 2013. Threatening the rights of LGBT persons in Eastern Europe. Office of the United Nations High Commissioner for Human Rights.

OHCHR. 2017. End abuse and detention of gay men in Chechnya, UN human rights experts tell Russia. Office of the United Nations High Commissioner for Human Rights.

OHCHR. 2019. Chechnya: UN experts urge action after reports of renewed persecution of lesbian, gay and bisexual people. United Nations Office of the High Commissioner on Human Rights.

OHCHR. 2023. Russia: UN Human Rights Chief deplores Supreme Court's decision to outlaw 'LGBT movement.' Office of the United Nations High Commissioner for Human Rights: United Nations.

Olesen, Thomas. 2017. 'Memetic Protest and the Dramatic Diffusion of Alan Kurdi.' *Media, Culture & Society* 40 (5): 656–672.

Organization for Security Cooperation in Europe. 2018. *OSCE Rapporteur'sReport under the Moscow Mechanism on alleged Human Rights Violations and Impunity in the Chechen Republic of the Russian Federation.* December 13, 2018, OSCE (Warsaw).

Panja, Tariq. 2017. 'Fans Warned About Racism and Homophobia in Russia.' *The New York Times*, November 29.

Panofsky, Erwin. 2009. 'Iconography and Iconology: An Introduction to the Study of Renaissance Art.' In *Art of Art History: A Critical Anthology*, edited by Donald Preziosi, 220–235. Oxford: Oxford University Press.

Parfitt, Tom. 2018. 'Orthodox Leader Attacks Gays in Christmas Speech.' *The Times*, January 8.

Pengelly, Martin. 2013. 'Obama and Fry Have History on Their Side: IOC Should Ban Anti-Gay Russia.' *The Guardian*, August 8.

Peterson, V. Spike. 1999. 'Sexing Political Identities: Nationalism as Heterosexism.' *International Feminist Journal of Politics* 1 (1): 34–65.

Peterson, V. Spike. 2014a. 'Family Matters: How Queering the Intimate Queers the International.' *International Studies Review* 16 (4): 604–608.

Peterson, V. Spike. 2014b. 'Sex Matters: A Queer History of Hierarchies.' *International Feminist Journal of Politics* 16 (3): 389–409.

Peterson, V. Spike. 2021. 'State/nation Histories, Structural Inequalities and Racialised Crises.' *New Political Economy* 26 (2): 291–301.

Peterson, V. Spike, and Anne Sisson Runyan. 2014. *Global Gender Issues in the New Millennium.* Boulder: Westview Press.

Picq, Manuela, and Markus Thiel, eds. 2015. *Sexualities in World Politics.* London: Routledge.

Plant, Richard. 1986. *The Pink Triangle: the Nazi War Against Homosexuals.* New York: H. Holt.

Politico. 2014a. 'Billie Jean King Won't Attend Sochi Opening.' *Politico*, February 5.

Politico. 2014b. 'Game Change.' *Politico*, January 31.

Porter, Catherine. 2017. 'Chechnya's Persecuted Gays Find Refuge in Canada.' *The New York Times*, September 4.

Price, Richard. 1995. 'A Genealogy of the Chemical Weapons Taboo.' *International Organization* 49 (1): 73–103.

Puar, Jasbir. 2007. *Terrorist Assemblages: Homonationalism in Queer Times.* Durham: Duke University Press.

Puar, Jasbir, and Armit Rai. 2002. 'Monster, Terrorist, Fag: The War on Terrorism and the Production of Docile Patriots.' *Social Text* 20 (3): 117–148.

Purnell, Kandida. 2021. *Rethinking the Body in Global Politics*. Abingdon: Routledge.

Purves, Libby. 2014. 'Surprise, Surprise: Dictators Are Also Bigots.' *The Times*, January 20.

Putin, Vladimir. 2013a. 'Meeting of the Valdai International Discussion Club.' Vladimir Putin. September 19, 2013, Speech. Novgorod Region.

Putin, Vladimir, 2013b, 'Presidential Address to the Federal Assembly,' http://en.kreml in.ru/events/president/news/19825.

Putin, Vladimir. 2022. Signing of Treaties on Accession of Donetsk and Lugansk People's Republics and Zaporozhye and Kherson Regions to Russia. Moscow: The Kremlin.

Queer Nation. 1990. *Queers Read This*.

Rahman, Momin. 2010. 'Queer as Intersectionality: Theorizing Gay Muslim Identities.' *Sociology* 44 (5): 944–961.

Rahman, Momin. 2014a. *Homosexualities, Muslim Cultures, and Modernity*. London: Palgrave.

Rahman, Momin. 2014b. 'Queer Rights and the Triangulation of Western Exceptionalism.' *Journal of Human Rights* 13 (3): 274–289.

Rancière, Jacques. 2004. *The Politics of Aesthetics: The Distribution of the Sensible*. Translated by Gabriel Rockhill. London: Continuum.

Rancière, Jacques. 2009. *The Future of the Image*. Verso.

Rao, Rahul. 2014a. 'The Locations of Homophobia.' *London Review of International Law* 2 (2): 169–199.

Rao, Rahul. 2014b. 'Queer Questions.' *International Feminist Journal of Politics* 16 (2): 199–217.

Rao, Rahul. 2020. *Out of Time: The Queer Politics of Postcoloniality*. New York: Oxford University Press.

Rayside, David. 2020. 'Early Advocacy for the Public Recognition of Sexual Diversity.' In *The Oxford Handbook of Global LGBT and Sexual Diversity Politics*, edited by Michael Bosia, Sandra McEvoy and Momin Rahman, 43–62. Oxford University Press.

Remnick, Noah. 2017. 'Fleeing Bias in Russia, Only to Find Brooklyn Isn't Entirely Welcoming.' *The New York Times*, May 23.

Reuters. 2013. 'Council of Europe Head Says Russia Must Protect LGBT Rights.' *Reuters*, 2013. https://www.reuters.com/article/us-russia-europe-lgbt/council-of-eu rope-head-says-russia-must-protect-lgbt-rights-idUSBRE94L0IY20130522.

Reuters. 2018. 'Activists Stage Stealth Rainbow Flag Protest in World Cup Russia.' *Reuters*, July 11. https://www.reuters.com/video/watch/activists-stage-stealth-rainbow-flag-pro-id444051128.

Reuters. 2020. 'Putin Mocks U.S. Embassy for Flying Rainbow Flag.' *Reuters*, July 3. https://www.reuters.com/article/us-russia-putin-rainbow-idUSKBN2442EQ.

Riabov, Oleg, and Tatiana Riabova. 2014. 'The Decline of Gayropa? How Russia Intended to Save the World.' *Eurozine*, Available at: https://www.eurozine.com/the-decline-of-gayropa/.

Riach, James. 2013. 'Amy Williams: Sochi Olympics Boycott Over Anti-Gay Laws Would Not Help.' *The Guardian*, August 22.

Richter-Montpetit, Melanie. 2007. 'Empire, Desire and Violence: A Queer Transnational Feminist Reading of the Prisoner 'Abuse' in Abu Ghraib and the Question of 'Gender Equality'.' *International Feminist Journal of Politics* 9 (1): 38–59.

Richter-Montpetit, Melanie. 2014. 'Beyond the Erotics of Orientalism: Lawfare, Torture and the Racial–Sexual Grammars of Legitimate Suffering.' *Security Dialogue* 45 (1): 43–62.

Richter-Montpetit, Melanie. 2018. 'Everything You Always Wanted to Know About Sex (in IR) But Were Afraid to Ask: The 'Queer Turn' in International Relations.' *Millennium: Journal of International Studies* 46 (2): 220–240.

Riemer, Matthew, and Leighton Brown. 2019. *We Are Everywhere: Protest, Power, and Pride in the History of Queer Liberation*. New York: Ten Speed Press.

Rifkind, Hugo. 2014. 'If Gays Aren't Hugged, Everyone is Stamped On.' *The Times*, July 30.

Ritchie, Jason. 2014. 'Pinkwashing, Homonationalism, and Israel–Palestine: The Conceits of Queer Theory and the Politics of the Ordinary.' *Antipode* 47 (3): 616–634.

Rogstad, Adrian. 2022. 'Stigma Dynamics: Russia and the Crisis of Liberal Ordering.' *Global Studies Quarterly* 2 (3): 1–11.

Rossdale, Chris. 2016. 'Activism, Resistance and Security.' In *Ethical Security Studies: A New Research Agenda*, edited by Jonna Nyman and Anthony Burke, 201–215. Abingdon: Routledge.

Rubin, Alissa J., and Aurelien Breeden. 2017. 'In Their First Meeting, Macron Challenges Putin On Syria and Gay Rights.' *The New York Times*, May 30.

Rubin, Gayle. 2011. 'Thinking Sex: Notes for a Radical Theory of the Politics of Sexuality.' In *Deviations: A Gayle Rubin Reader*, 137–181. London: Duke University Press. Original edition, 1984. https://www.dukeupress.edu/deviations.

Said, Edward. 2003. *Orientalism*. London: Penguin.

Särmä, Sara. 2018. 'Collaging Iranian Missiles: Digital Security Spectacles and Visual Online Parodies.' In *Visual Security Studies: Sights and Spectacles of Insecurity and War*, edited by Juha A. Vuori and Rune S. Andersen, 114–130. London: Routledge.

Savelau, Dmitry. 2017. 'Gay Men in Chechnya Are Some of the Most Disempowered People in the World Today - We Can Do Something About That.' *The Independent*, April 13.

Savelau, Dmitry. 2018. 'It May Seem Like LGBT Rights Aren't Important to Putin – But If You Look Closer, You'll See They're Central to the Russian Election.' *The Independent*, 2018. https://www.independent.co.uk/voices/russia-election-putin-win-anti-lgbt-propaganda-chechnya-persecution-homophobia-a8255186.html.

Sawer, Marian. 2007. 'Wearing Your Politics on Your Sleeve: The Role of Political Colours in Social Movements.' *Social Movement Studies* 6 (1): 39–56.

Scarry, Elaine. 1985. *The Body in Pain: The Making and Unmaking of the World*. New York: Oxford University Press.

Schotten, C Heike. 2018. *Queer Terror: Life, Death, and Desire in the Settler Colony.* Columbia University Press.

Schulman, Sarah. 2021. *Let the Record Show: A Political History of ACT UP, New York, 1987–1993.* Farrar, Straus and Giroux.

Schulz, Carsten-Andreas, and Cameron G Thies. 2024. 'Status Cues and Normative Change: How the Academy Awards Facilitated Chile's Gender Identity Law.' *Review of International Studies* 50 (1): 127–145.

Schwirtz, Michael. 2012. 'A City's Law Against Gay 'Propaganda' Worries Rights Advocates in Russia.' *New York Times*, 2012.

Sedgwick, Eve Kosofsky. 1993. *Tendencies.* Durham: Duke University Press.

Seidman, Steven. 1993. 'Identity and Politics in a 'Postmodern' Gay Culture.' In *Fear of a Queer Planet*, edited by Michael Warner, 105–142. Minneapolis: University of Minnesota Press.

Seidman, Steven. 1998. 'Are we all in the closet? Notes towards a sociological and cultural turn in queer theory.' *European Journal of Cultural Studies* 1 (2): 177–192.

Selby, Jenn. 2014. 'Vladimir Putin Threatened Madonna with Jail for Promoting 'Gay Behaviour' in Russia.' *The Independent*, February 7.

Shapiro, Michael J. 1988. *The Politics of Representation: Writing Practices in Biography, Photography, and Policy Analysis.* Wisconsin: University of Wisconsin Press.

Shepherd, Laura. 2008. *Gender, Violence and Security: Discourse as Practice.* London: Zed Books.

Shepherd, Laura J., and Laura Sjoberg. 2012. 'Trans - Bodies in of War(s): Cisprivilege and Contemporary Security Strategy.' *Feminist Review* 101: 5–23.

Shifman, Limor. 2014. *Memes in Digital Culture.* Cambridge: MIT Press.

Shim, David. 2014. *Visual Politics and North Korea: Seeing Is Believing.* London: Routledge.

Shim, David. 2017. 'Sketching Geopolitics: Comics and the Case of the Cheonan Sinking.' *International Political Sociology* 11 (4): 398–417.

Shim, David, and Dirk Nabers. 2013. 'Imaging North Korea: Exploring Its Visual Representations in International Politics.' *International Studies Perspectives* 14 (3): 289–306.

Sjoberg, Laura. 2012. 'Towards Trans-gendering International Relations.' *International Political Sociology* 6 (4): 337–354.

Sjoberg, Laura. 2014. 'Queering the "Territorial Peace"? Queer Theory Conversing with Mainstream International Relations.' *International Studies Review* 16 (4): 608–612.

Sjoberg, Laura, and Cameron G. Thies. 2023. 'Gender and International Relations.' *Annual Review of Political Science* 26: 451–467.

Składanowski, Marcin. 2023. *Russia's National Security in Aleksandr Dugin's Neo-Eurasianism: a Sacred Fortress.* Lanham: Lexington Books.

Slater, Matt. 2017. 'Four in Five British Fans Would Welcome an Openly Gay Player in Their Team, Poll Reveals.' *The Independent*, December 13.

Slootmaeckers, Koen. 2019. 'Nationalism as Competing Masculinities: Homophobia as a Technology of Othering for Hetero- and Homonationalism.' *Theory and Society* 48: 239–265.

Slootmaeckers, Koen. 2020. 'Constructing European Union Identity Through LGBT Equality Promotion: Crises and Shifting Othering Processes in the European Union Enlargement.' *Political Studies Review* 18 (3): 346–361.

Slootmaeckers, Koen. 2023. *Coming In: Sexual Politics and EU Accession in Serbia.* Manchester: Manchester University Press.

Slootmaeckers, Koen, and Francesca Ammaturo. 2020. 'The Politics of Rainbow Maps.' *Engenderings* (blog), *LSE*. May 28. https://blogs.lse.ac.uk/gender/2020/05/28/the-po litics-of-rainbow-maps/?fbclid=IwAR29xBq9vsBJ5QTOxP4XOQKRFAvX8rYF1V93 93uf0UNZWF_4Bf2qaX1DvE4.

Sobel, Ariel. n.d. 'The Complete Guide to Queer Pride Flags.' *Pride.*

Sokirianskaia, Ekaterina. 2017. 'Chechnya's Anti-Gay Pogrom.' *The New York Times*, May 3.

Sontag, Susan. 1977. *On Photography.* New York: Penguin.

Sontag, Susan. 2003. *Regarding the Pain of Others.* London: Penguin.

Sperling, Valerie. 2014. *Sex, Politics, and Putin: Political Legitimacy in Russia.* Oxford: Oxford University Press.

Staples, Louis. 2018. 'If You're LGBT+ and Travelling to the World Cup, This is What You Need to Know.' *The Independent*, June 14.

Stevens, Christy. 1999. 'Symbols.' In *Encyclopedia of Gay Histories and Cultures*, edited by George Haggerty and Bonnie Zimmerman, 747–748. New York: Routledge.

Stoffel, Alexander, and Ida Roland Birkvad. 2023. 'Abstractions in International Relations: on the Mystification of Trans, Queer, and Subaltern Life in Critical Knowledge Production.' *European Journal of International Relations* 29 (4): 852–876.

Sturken, Marita, and Lisa Cartwright. 2009. *Practices of Looking: An Introduction to Visual Culture.* 2nd ed. New York: Oxford University Press.

Sweeney, John. 2014. 'Winter Olympics 2014: Welcome to Sochi - A City Where "There Are No Gay People".' *The Independent*, January 26.

Sylvester, Christine. 2009. *Art/Museums: International Relations Where We Least Expect It. Media and Power.* Boulder: Paradigm.

Sylvester, Christine. 2013. 'Experiencing the End and Afterlives of International Relations/Theory.' *European Journal of International Relations* 19 (3): 609–626.

Tatchell, Peter. 2018. 'World Cup Fever, Gay Rights Abuses and War Crimes—It's an Ugly Mix.' *The Guardian*, June 13.

The Football Supporters' Federation. 2018. 'LGBT+ Fans and The 2018 World Cup.' The Football Supporters' Association. Accessed April 22, 2021. http://www.fsf.org.uk/ blog/view/lgbt-fans-and-the-2018-world-cup.

The Independent. 2017. 'Chechen Leader Ramzan Kadyrov Denies Massacre of Gay Citizens Saying "Such People Do Not Exist".' *The Independent*, April 10.

The Times. 2013. 'Putin's Games Promise.' *The Times*, October 29.

Tidy, Joanna, and Joe Turner. 2020. 'The Intimate International Relations of Museums: A Method.' *Millennium: Journal of International Studies* 48 (2): 117–142.

Tilly, Charles. 1985. 'War Making and State Making as Organised Crime.' In *Bringing the State Back in*, edited by Peter Evans, Dietrich Rueschemeyer and Theda Skocpol, 169–191. Cambridge: Cambridge University Press.

Tilly, Charles. 2004. *Social Movements, 1768–2004*. London: Paradigm.

Towns, Ann. 2010. *Women and States: Norms and Hierarchies in International Society*. Cambridge University Press.

Trenin, Dmitri. 2021. *Russia's National Security Strategy: A Manifesto for a New Era*. Carnegie Russia Eurasia Center. https://carnegieendowment.org/posts/2021/07/rus sias-national-security-strategy-a-manifesto-for-a-new-era?lang=en.

Tsaturyan, Asya. 2024. 'Visualizing the Emergence of Political Homophobia: Anti-LGBTQ+ and Anti-Ukrainian Sentiment in Russian Public Opinion.' *Socius* 10: 1–10.

UEFA, 22 June 2021, 2021, 'UEFA Proposes Alternative Dates for Rainbow Illumination at Munich Stadium,' https://www.uefa.com/returntoplay/news/026a-129471e04627-8ea0c56c8471-1000—uefa-proposes-alternative-dates-for-rainbow-illumination-at-mun/.

UK Foreign and Commonwealth Office. 2018. 'Be on the Ball: 2018 FIFA World Cup.' Accessed April 22, 2021. https://web.archive.org/web/20180614105815/https://www.gov.uk/guidance/be-on-the-ball-world-cup-2018.

UN Human Rights Committee. 2012. *Communication No. 1932/2010*. UN Human Rights Committee, November 30, 2012, (Geneva: United Nations).

UNICEF. 2014. 'Eliminating Discrimination Against Children and Parents Based on Sexual Orientation and/or Gender Identity.' *Current Issues* 9: 1–6.

United Nations Committee on the Rights of the Child. 2014. Concluding observations on the combined fourth and fifth periodic reports of the Russian Federation. United Nations.

United Nations Independent Expert on protection against violence and discrimination based on sexual orientation and gender identity. 2024. Protection against violence and discrimination based on sexual orientation and gender identity in relation to the human rights to freedom of expression, peaceful assembly and association, A/HRC/56/49. Human Rights Council: United Nations.

United Nations Independent Expert SOGI. 2022. Report of the Independent Expert on protection against violence and discrimination based on sexual orientation and gender identity, Victor Madrigal-Borloz, A/77/235. United Nations.

United Nations Independent Expert SOGI. 2024. Report of the Independent Expert on protection against violence and discrimination based on sexual orientation and gender identity, Graeme Reid, A/HRC/56/49. United Nations.

United Nations Security Council. 2023. United Nations Security Council Arria-formula Meeting: 'Integrating the Human Rights of LGBTI persons into the Council's Mandate for Maintaining International Peace and Security.' New York: United Nations Department of Global Communications.

United Nations Special Rapporteur on extrajudicial, and summary or arbitrary executions. 2024. Report of the Special Rapporteur on extrajudicial, summary or arbitrary executions, Morris Tidball-Binz: Investigating and preventing unlawful deaths of lesbian, gay, bisexual, transgender, gender-diverse and intersex persons, A/79/172. United Nations.

Van Veeren, Elspeth. 2018. 'Invisibility.' In *Visual Global Politics*, edited by Roland Bleiker, 196–200. New York: Routledge.

Vasilyeva, Nataliya, and Alexander Roslyakov. 2017. 'Gay Chechens Report Days of Beatings and Electro-Shock Torture at Hands of Russian Government-Backed Thugs.' *The Independent*, May 2.

Veneti, Anastasia. 2017. 'Aesthetics of Protest: An Examination of the Photojournalistic Approach to Protest Imagery.' *Visual Communication* 16 (3): 279–298.

Venice Convention. 2013. Opinion on the Issue of the Prohibition of the So-Called 'Propaganda of Homosexuality' in the Light of recent Legislation in Some Member States of the Council of Europe. Strasbourg.

Vernon, Patrick. 2022. 'Sexuality, Gender, and the Colonial Violence of Humanitarian Intervention.' *International Studies Review* 24 (3): 1–22.

Visual AIDS. 2019. *What Is 21st Century Liberation*. New York, New York: Visual AIDS. https://visualaids.org/uploads/projects/downloads/FINAL_2019Broadside.pdf.

Vucetic, Srdjan. 2011. 'Genealogy as a Research Tool in International Relations.' *Review of International Studies* 37: 1295–1312.

Vuori, Juha A. 2010. 'A Timely Prophet? The Doomsday Clock as a Visualization of Securitization Moves with a Global Referent Object.' *Security Dialogue* 41 (3): 255–277.

Vuori, Juha A., and Rune S. Andersen. 2018. 'Introduction: Visual Security Studies.' In *Visual Security Studies: Sights and Spectacles of Insecurity and War*, edited by Juha A. Vuori and Rune S. Andersen, 1–19. London: Routledge.

Wæver, Ole. 2002. 'Identity, Communities and Foreign Policy: Discourse Analysis as Foreign Policy Theory.' In *European Integration and National Identity: The Challenge of the Nordic States*, edited by Lene Hansen and Ole Wæver, 20–49. London: Routledge.

Waites, Matthew. 2018. 'Genocide and Global Queer Politics.' *Journal of Genocide Research* 20 (1): 44–67.

Walker, R.B.J. 1992. *Inside/Outside: International Relations as Political Theory*. Vol. 24 *Cambridge Studies in International Relations*. Cambridge: Cambridge University Press.

Walker, Shaun. 2012. 'Gay Rights? That's Europe's Problem.' *The Independent*, March 31.

Walker, Shaun. 2013. 'Elton to Play Moscow Despite Anti-Gay Law.' *The Guardian* December 6.

Walker, Shaun. 2014. 'Sochi Winter Olympics: Who is Going to the Opening Ceremony?' *The Guardian*, February 5.

Walker, Shaun. 2017. 'Journalists Fear Reprisals for Exposing Purge of Gay Men in Chechnya.' *The Guardian*, April 14.

Walker, Shaun. 2018. 'Three Lions Pride Shows Normal Russian Rules Don't Apply During World Cup.' *The Guardian* June 22.

Walker, Shaun, and Owen Gibson. 2014. 'Slip, Slide, Ski, Skate - After the Politics.' *The Guardian*, February 7.

Walker, Shaun, and Martha Kelner. 2018. 'Diversity Fan Zone Blocked From Opening in St Petersburg.' *The Guardian*, June 16.

Ward, Jane. 2015. *Not Gay: Sex Between Straight White Men*. New York: NYU Press.

Warner, Michael, ed. 1993. *Fear of a Queer Planet: Queer Politics and Social Theory*. Minneapolis: University of Minnesota Press.

Warner, Michael, ed. 1999. 'Normal and Normaller: Beyond Gay Marriage.' *GLQ: A Journal of Lesbian and Gay Studies* 5 (2): 119–171.

Warner, Michael, ed. 2000. *The Trouble With Normal: Sex, Politics, and the Ethics of Queer Life*. Cambridge: Harvard University Press.

Warner, Michael, ed. 2002. 'Publics and Counterpublics.' *Public Culture* 14 (1): 49–90.

Washington Post. 2013a. 'Russia's Anti-Gay Law Elicit Criticism From IOC Member.' *The Washington Post*, August 3.

Washington Post. 2013b. 'Russia's War on Gays.' *The Washington Post*, August 9.

Waxman, Olivia. 2018. 'How the Nazi Regime's Pink Triangle Symbol Was Repurposed for LGBTQ Pride.' *TIME*, May 31.

Weber, Cynthia. 1998. 'Performative States.' *Millennium Journal of International Studies* 27 (1): 77–95.

Weber, Cynthia. 1999. *Faking It: U.S. Hegemony in a 'Post-Phallic' Era*. Minneapolis: University of Minnesota Press.

Weber, Cynthia. 2011. *I am an American: Filming the Fear of Difference*. Bristol: Intellect.

Weber, Cynthia. 2014. 'From Queer to Queer IR.' *International Studies Review* 16 (4): 596–601.

Weber, Cynthia. 2015a. 'Queer Intellectual Curiosity as International Relations Method: Developing Queer International Relations Theoretical and Methodological Frameworks.' *International Studies Quarterly* 60 (1): 11–23.

Weber, Cynthia. 2015b. 'Why Is There No Queer International Theory?' *European Journal of International Relations* 21 (1): 27–51.

Weber, Cynthia. 2016. *Queer International Relations: Sovereignty, Sexuality and the Will to Knowledge*. New York: Oxford University Press.

Wedderburn, Alister. 2019. 'Cartooning the Camp: Aesthetic Interruption and the Limits of Political Possibility.' *Millennium: Journal of International Studies* 47 (1): 169–189.

White, Stephen, and Valentina Feklyunina. 2014. *Identities and Foreign Policies in Russia, Ukraine and Belarus: The Other Europes*. New York: Palgrave.

Wiedlack, Katharina. 2020. 'Enemy Number One or Gay Clown? The Russian President, Masculinity and Populism in US Media.' *NORMA: International Journal for Masculinity Studies* 15 (1): 59–75.

Wiegman, Robyn., and Elizabeth A. Wilson. 2015. 'Introduction: Antinormativity's Queer Conventions.' *Differences* 26 (1): 1–25.

Wilcox, Lauren. 2014. 'Queer Theory and the "Proper Objects" of International Relations.' *International Studies Review* 16 (4): 612–615.

Wilcox, Lauren. 2015. *Bodies of Violence*. Oxford: Oxford University Press.

Wilcox, Lauren. 2017a. 'Drones, Swarms and Becoming-Insect: Feminist Utopias and Posthuman Politics.' *Feminist Review* 116 (1): 25–45.

Wilcox, Lauren. 2017b. 'Practising Gender, Queering Theory.' *Review of International Studies* 43 (5): 789–808.

Wilkinson, Cai. 2014. 'Putting "Traditional Values" Into Practice: The Rise and Contestation of Anti-Homopropaganda Laws in Russia.' *Journal of Human Rights* 13 (3): 363–379.

Wilkinson, Cai. 2017a. 'Introduction: Queer/ing In/Security.' *Critical Studies on Security* 5 (1): 106–108.

Wilkinson, Cai. 2017b. '"You're Too Much!": Experiencing the Straightness of Security.' *Critical Studies on Security* 5 (1): 113–116.

Wilkinson, Cai. 2018. 'Mother Russia in Queer Peril.' In *Revisiting Gendered States: Feminist Imaginings of the State in International Relations*, edited by Swati Parashar, Ann Tickner and Jacqui True, 105–120. Oxford: Oxford University Press.

Wilkinson, Cai. 2019. 'LGBT Rights in the Former Soviet Union: The Evolution of Hypervisibility.' In *The Oxford Handbook of Global LGBT and Sexual Diversity Politics*, edited by M Bosia, Sandra McEvoy and Momin Rahman, 233–247. Oxford University Press.

Williams, Michael. 2003. 'Words, Images, Enemies: Securitization and International Politics.' *International Studies Quarterly* 47 (4): 511–531.

Williams, Michael. 2018. 'International Relations in the Age of Images.' *International Studies Quarterly* 62: 880–891.

Wilson, Kalpana. 2018. 'Development.' In *Visual Global Politics*, edited by Roland Bleiker, 94–98. New York: Routledge.

Windfeld, Frederik Carl, Marius Hauge Hvithamar, and Lene Hansen. 2024. 'Gothic Visibilities and International Relations: Uncanny Icons, Critical Comics, and the Politics of Abjection in Aleppo.' *Review of International Studies* 50 (1): 3–34.

Winter, Henry. 2017. 'Backstage at the Kremlin.' *The Times*, December 5.

Wintour, Patrick. 2018. 'England Fans' Safety at Risk in Russia, Say MPs.' *The Guardian*, June 8.

Wright, Oliver, and Alec Luhn. 2014. 'Vladimir Putin's Gay Rights Charm Offensive Ahead of Sochi Winter Olympics is All Lies, Activists Say.' *The Independent*, Jan 20.

Youde, Jeremy. 2020. 'The Global HIV/AIDS and LGBT Movements.' In *The Oxford Handbook of Global LGBT and Sexual Diversity Politics*, edited by Michael Bosia, Sandra McEvoy and Momin Rahman, 301–313. Oxford University Press.

Zanotti, Laura. 2017. 'Reorienting IR: Ontological Entanglement, Agency, and Ethics.' *International Studies Review* 19 (3): 362–380.

Zarakol, Ayşe. 2010. *After Defeat: How the East Learned to Live With the West*. Vol. 118. Cambridge University Press.

Zarakol, Ayşe. 2014. 'What Made the Modern World Hang Together: Socialisation or Stigmatisation?' *International Theory* 6 (2): 311–332.

Zelizer, Barbie. 2010. *About to Die: How News Images Move the Public*. Oxford: Oxford University Press.

Ziegler, Martin. 2017. 'World Cup Warning for Gay Supporters.' *The Times*, November 29.

Index

For the benefit of digital users, indexed terms that span two pages (e.g., 52–53) may, on occasion, appear on only one of those pages.

Tables, figures, and boxes are indicated by an italic *t*, *f*, or *b*.